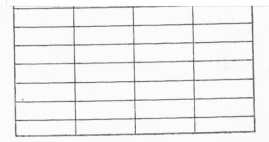

Rebuilding Capitalism

Rebuilding Capitalism
Alternative Roads after Socialism and Dirigisme

edited by
Andrés Solimano, Osvaldo Sunkel, and Mario I. Blejer

Ann Arbor
The University of Michigan Press

Library of Congress Cataloging-in-Publication Data

Rebuilding capitalism :alternative roads after socialism and dirigisme / edited by
 Andrés Solimano, Osvaldo Sunkel, Mario I. Blejer.
     p.   cm.
   Includes bibliographical references and index
   ISBN 0-472-10520-5 (alk. paper)
     1. Economic history—1990- —Congresses. 2. Economic history—1945- —
 Congresses. 3. Economic policy—Congresses. 4. Capitalism—Congresses.
 5. Communism—Congresses. 6. Post-communism—Congresses. 7. Mixed economy—
 Congresses. 8. Industry and state—Congresses. I. Solimano, Andrés.
 II. Sunkel, Osvaldo. III. Blejer, Mario I.
 HC59.15.R42 1994
 338.9—dc20   93-33321
                                                                               CIP

Contents

Contributors

Yilmaz Akyuz
United Nations Conference on Trade and Development (UNCTAD)
Geneva, Switzerland

Alice Amsden
New School for Social Research
New York, N.Y., USA

Nancy Birdsall
Inter-American Development Bank (IDB)
Washington, D.C., USA

Mario I. Blejer
International Monetary Fund
Washington, D.C., USA

Colin I. Bradford, Jr.
Organization for Economic Cooperation and Development (OECD)
Paris, France

Miguel Angel Fernandez Ordoñez
Tribunal de Defensa de la Competencia
Madrid, Spain

Stanley Fischer
Massachusetts Institute of Technology
Cambridge, MA, USA

Alan Gelb
World Bank
Washington, D.C., USA

Manuel Guitián
International Monetary Fund
Washington, D.C., USA

Patricio Meller
Corporación de Investigaciones Económicas para Latino América (CIEPLAN)
Santiago, Chile

Carmelo Mesa-Lago
University of Pittsburgh
Pittsburgh, PA, USA

Dwight Perkins
Harvard University
Cambridge, MA, USA

Luis Servén
World Bank
Washington, D.C., USA

Andrés Solimano
World Bank
Washington, D.C., USA

Osvaldo Sunkel
Corporación de Investigaciones para el Desarrollo (CINDE) and
Economic Commission for Latin America, United Nations (ECLA)
Santiago, Chile

Lance Taylor
New School for Social Research
New York, N.Y., USA

Preface

The main theme of this volume is economic reform in postsocialist and developing countries. The authors examine the topic from several perspectives, contrasting alternative visions of economic reform concerning policy formulation and implementation. They offer a comparative perspective on the practice of reform by looking at a broad cross-section of transition experiences, both postsocialist and "postdirigiste." The volume seeks to combine historical and institutional insights on the origins and development of the current rage of market-based reform in the global economy, with an analysis of the management of different reform components encompassing macroeconomic stabilization, market creation and/or liberalization, privatization, reform of the state, and institution building. Success in macro stabilization, degree of growth response, progress in structural reforms, social costs and the distributive impact of reform, and systemic conformity between economic and political transformation are the main criteria employed to evaluate performance across the different experiences examined.

The chapters were presented at a conference held at El Escorial, Spain, on July 6–8, 1992. This project was made possible by the support of several institutions: The World Bank, the journal *Pensamiento Iberoamericano*, Universidad Complutense of Madrid, UNCTAD, ECLA, and the Spanish Agency for International Cooperation. The logistical and financial collaboration from these institutions is gratefully acknowledged for the realization of this cooperative effort. The kind permission of *Brookings Papers on Economic Activity* to publish chapter 6, "Stabilization and Economic Reform in Russia" by Stanley Fischer, is appreciated. In the preparation of this book, we would like to acknowledge the excellent editorial assistance of Melissa Vaughn, and also the collaboration of Lorrie LeJeune.

CHAPTER 1

Introduction and Synthesis

Andrés Solimano

Stalinist socialism is dead, and state-led development is in retreat. The new engine for growth and prosperity is based on competitive markets, free trade, foreign investment, and a small state. Clearly, a new free-market orthodoxy has replaced the former belief in planning and state-led development (dirigisme) as engines for growth. In the East, the new paradigm of market-oriented reform is shared by Warsaw, Prague, and Moscow-former bastions of Stalinist socialism. In the South, policymakers in Mexico City, Santiago, and Buenos Aires are also fervent enthusiasts of free markets, almost irrespective of their past beliefs. Furthermore, in Asia, Beijing also follows market-oriented economic policies, in spite of Chinese political rhetoric favoring socialism. Certainly, free-market economic reform is a global trend that will extend to the end of this century and shape the economic landscape of the next.

The current rage for the market economy is the historical outcome of the failure of using, on a large scale and for very protracted periods, nonmarket mechanisms—central planning in former socialist countries and state dirigisme in nonsocialist economies—as *dominant* forms of economic organization. Although socialism had its "golden age" in terms of industrialization and rapid growth (the latter probably overstated) from the 1950s to the mid-1970s, it fell in crisis in the 1980s and definitely collapsed toward the end of the decade. Thus socialism proved to be an unfeasible form of economic organization in the long run, as it could not stand the test of time. In contrast, capitalism combines a remarkable capacity to adapt to change, innovate, grow, and improve living standards with a more grim side of instability, a tendency for resource underutilization, and income inequality. Now it is time for reformed capitalism (i.e., relying more on the market and less on the state) to attempt to overcome these flaws.

This volume seeks to understand this global process of economic transformation by looking at five sets of questions: (1) What are the initial macroeconomic and structural conditions in mixed or socialist economies that are entering a process of economic reform? What are the main factors propelling reform? (2) What are the main strategies—shock treatment, gradualism, mixed programs—used in conducting a process of economic reform? (3) What should be the economic role of the state vis-à-vis the market in the transition process? (4) What are the main social costs of reform and the political economy considerations inherent to the process of economic transformation? (5) What have been the main patterns of economic response to the reforms in reforming socialist and nonsocialist economies in terms of indicators such as inflation, growth, fiscal adjustment, external sector sustainability, progress in privatization, real wages, and unemployment.

Initial Conditions and Factors Propelling Reform

A basic question is: What leads a country to adopt a process of economic reform? In general, the propelling factors lie in deteriorated prereform economic conditions, manifested later through the political system in general dissatisfaction with existing economic performance. In turn, that political ferment for change is essential for economic reform to be started.[1]

The standard conditions of an economy in the terminal phase of the socialist experiment include chronic shortages, a severely distorted structure of relative prices, a high degree of vertical integration in industry, slow growth, a sluggish pace of technical change, and other indicators of structural malfunctioning (see table 1.1). At the macro level, money overhang, repressed inflation, and large fiscal and external deficits were not uncommon features of "terminal socialism." Of course the extent of the macro imbalances when the reforms were implemented varied from country to country. A useful distinction is that between *macroeconomic crisis* and *stagnation traps* as initial regimes that propel economic reform. A *macroeconomic crisis* is characterized by high and erratic inflation, unsustainable balance of payments, and/or fiscal imbalances. A *stagnation trap* is characterized by slow growth, a low level of technical progress, and widespread inefficiencies at the microeconomic level. Of course, the two macro regimes may superimpose, as a macroeconomic crisis can be preceded or accompanied by a period of economic stagnation and decline.

Examples of former socialist countries that started from a macro crisis are Poland in 1989, and Russia and most former Soviet republics in 1991–92. In contrast, Hungary and Czechoslovakia started or deepened their reform processes from conditions of slow growth, but without running into open macroeconomic crisis.

China started its reforms in 1978 with moderate macro imbalances, though with considerable micro distortions coupled with overall economic stagnation. China was a rural economy in which agriculture represented a significant share of GDP. Living standards were low, but income distribution was relatively egalitarian.

TABLE 1.1   Structural characteristics of the prereform economic system (crisis phase)

	Eastern Europe	Russia	China	Latin America	Peripheral socialist countries (Angola, Mozambique, Nicaragua)
Repressed inflation/ money overhang	high	high	moderate	low	moderate
Degree of market deepening (goods and factor markets)	low	low	low	moderate	moderate
State ownership of productive assets	over 80%	over 90%	over 90%	25%–30%	50%–60%
Relative size of the industrial sector/ vertical integration	large	large	small	moderate	small
Degree of income inequality	low	low	low	high	high
Levels of education and health per capita	high	high	high	moderate	low
Strength of institutions and the state	low	low	moderate	moderately low	very low

In Latin America, prereform economies were characterized by a considerable degree of repression and/or segmentation in goods and factor markets, relatively closed trade regimes, widespread intervention in the price system, and a very unequal distribution of income and wealth. At the macro level, chronic inflation, fiscal deficits, endemic vulnerability in the external sector, and distributive conflict have been common features of heavily distressed economies. Chile in 1973, Mexico in 1982, Bolivia in 1985, and Argentina in 1991 are Latin American economies starting their adjustment and reform process after a *macroeconomic crisis*.

A group of "peripheral" socialist economies, including Angola, Mozambique, and Nicaragua, have recently initiated partial attempts at reform. These are low-income countries in which—unlike Eastern Europe, the former USSR, or China—socialism was never fully consolidated because of the existence of a weak state and acute (often armed) social and ethnic conflict. In these economies, the goods markets function very imperfectly (with a profusion of parallel or dual markets), capital markets are virtually absent, the basic physical infrastructure is poorly developed, and poverty is rampant. Inflation (open or repressed) and large fiscal and external imbalances (often financed by foreign aid) characterize the macro system in several of these economies.

Finally, an important element propelling reform in most of the countries discussed in this volume is institutional. The crisis of socialism and the exhaustion of state-led development in mixed economies was a *crisis of the state*. In the final stage of the socialist experiment, it became evident that the socialist state could no longer handle the overwhelming number of tasks it was expected to perform at both macro and micro levels, in the areas of stabilization, resource allocation, capital accumulation, distribution, and ownership. In turn, the crisis of dirigisme in developing countries is also the result of a growing inability of the state to undertake the above-mentioned tasks in the same way they had since the 1940s and 1950s, when the dirigiste development model became largely consolidated.

Summarizing, we can list the main factors propelling economic reform as:

- Macroeconomic crisis.
- Stagnation traps.
- Crisis of the state.
- International demonstration effect: imitation of other countries' economic policies.

Alternative Strategies of Economic Reform: Shock Treatment, Gradualism, and Mixed Programs

An important set of issues surrounds to the *intensity* and *sequencing* of the different components of an economic transformation program. Should macroeconomic stabilization, liberalization, and privatization be pursued simultaneously, or is it preferable to advance gradually by trying to reach some targets first (e.g., low inflation) and then move on to the next ones (e.g., liberalized trade and financial markets)? When reforms in different areas are phased in over time in a sort of sequential approach, the reform strategy could be labeled *gradualist*.

An alternative strategy is the "big bang," or *shock treatment*. In this case the strategy would be to stabilize the macro-economy in a drastic fashion, basically through demand contraction, currency devaluation, and one-shot price liberalization, and simultaneously liberalize the economy in several areas (trade, finance, labor markets) to elicit a vigorous supply response, increase economic efficiency, and put the economy on a path of higher growth.

Is it also possible to think in terms of a *mixed* strategy, which would combine shock treatment at the macroeconomic level—to face, say, a hyperinflation or a crisis in the balance of payments—with a more gradualist approach to structural reforms that includes market liberalization and institution

TABLE 1.2 Matrix of reform strategies and initial conditions

Initial conditions	Macroeconomic crisis	Stagnation trap
Reform strategy		
Shock treatment	Poland (1989)	Czechoslovakia (1989)
	Russia (1991)	
	Argentina (1990)	
	Chile (1973)	
	Bolivia (1985)	
Gradualism		China (1978)
		Hungary (1989)

building. Although the "nominal" part of the system (inflation and stabilization) cannot be fully dichotomized from the "real" part (resource allocation and growth), the time dimension of macroeconomic stabilization is often different from the tempo of structural change. Stabilization may take from a few months (transitional inflation) to several years (chronic inflation). In turn, structural reforms hardly consolidate in less than a decade (e.g., the cases of Chile and Mexico). In general, real resources take more time to move from one place to another following changes in the structure of incentives. Moreover, new institutions and habits of behavior cannot be created overnight.

The choice between shock treatment (big bang) and gradualism is shaped by various factors. Table 1.2 illustrates alternative combinations among initial conditions (macro crisis or stagnation trap) and reform strategies (shock treatment or gradualism). The most well observed cases are shock treatments launched in the midst of a macroeconomic crisis (Poland, Russia, Chile, Argentina, and others) and gradualism implemented under traps of stagnation (China, Hungary). However, as the case of Czechoslovakia (shock treatment without macro crisis) illustrates, these are not the only combinations observed in practice.

In general, big-bang policies—at the macro level and on the liberalization front—were adopted when the initial economic conditions before reform were extremely deteriorated, and the political climate existing at the start of the reforms favored radical economic policies. Gradualism, in turn, was applied when there were moderate and manageable macroeconomic imbalances —although the economy was suffering from stagnation and/or other malaises, it was not in a full-blown macroeconomic crisis. In addition, gradualism took place in conditions of tight political control (e.g., China) or where there was a tradition of continuity in reforms (e.g., Hungary). The Latin American reforms (Chile, Mexico, Bolivia) of the 1970s and 1980s in general applied macroeconomic shock treatments. However, the speed of liberalization of

international trade, the development of financial markets, and the implementation of privatization processes was slower than in Eastern Europe and the
former USSR after 1990. Clearly, the programs of economic reform under
way in the 1990s seem to be more radical than those of the 1970s or 1980s.

Besides the magnitude of initial macro disequilibria, other factors influence the choice of reform strategy, including: availability of foreign finance to
smooth the costs of the transition; preference for economic efficiency; concern
for the social costs of adjustment; degree of credibility of government policies; ability of the state versus the market to allocate resources and accumulate
capital; capacity of the government to manage change in complex social and
economic systems; and degree of political and social support for the reformist
government. As the list suggests, there will never exist a preferred (let alone
optimal) strategy valid for all countries at all times. Country-specific conditions will dominate the choice of the reform strategy. Real-life reform is more
a blend of vision, art, and science than an abstract blueprint of policy moves
developed under well-controlled laboratory conditions.

The Role of the State and the Reemergence of Private Owners and Markets

As a consequence of the crisis of the state, a central aim of economic reform is
to redress the balance between the market and the state in favor of the former.
However, a paradox of the postsocialist transitions is that the move to a
market economy involves active state intervention. In Eastern Europe and
Russia, the state is busy stabilizing the economy, restructuring enterprises,
creating laws, and building new institutions. The retreat of the state as the
main producer and owner of productive wealth will demand a new role for the
state as stabilizer, regulator, and redistributor.

This presents the question of what should be the role of the state in
postsocialist transitions. The "Smithian-Hayekian" view envisions the state as
a social guardian in charge of providing macroeconomic stability, public
infrastructure, and law and order. This view, in the context of the collapse of
socialism, points to the fundamental weakness or even corruption of the state
and its inability to play an effective role in the economy. Under these conditions, the market has to take over many functions formerly performed by the
state to avoid further economic collapse.

Another view recognizes the pervasiveness of market failures, incomplete markets, and missing institutions in the postsocialist economies. Goods
markets are still inexperienced, and capital and labor markets are largely
absent or very underdeveloped. In addition, the basic economic institutions of
capitalism such as commercial codes, property laws, and a judiciary system
able to enforce contracts are just starting to appear. Given the "public good"

nature of the institutions to be created and the scope for decentralized market failures in *emerging* market economies, the state is likely to be more than the "night watchman" of a *mature* market economy. Of course, the scope for "government failures" in societies in which the collapse of socialism was, as mentioned, the collapse of the state has to be seriously considered in evaluating the merits of state action. In any case, the "public good" nature of several tasks of the postsocialist reconstruction is still a relevant argument for an interventionist state during the transition period. In addition, historically the state has played an important role in the consolidation of capitalism through the provision of physical infrastructure and credit for industrialization, and the creation of appropriate legal institutions.

In postdirigiste transitions, the reduction in the size of the state is also one of the most important objectives of reform. Of course, the dimension of the problem seems less dramatic than in the postsocialist transitions. The task of redressing the balance between the state and markets could be less complicated in the postdirigiste transitions because market suppression is less severe, there are already entrepreneurial traditions and, in general, the economic institutions of capitalism do not have to be created from scratch. However, progress in the redefinition and restructuring of institutions is still bound to face a host of difficulties, ranging from the lack of human resources to political opposition from entrenched bureaucrats and groups favored by the status quo.

The Social Costs of Adjustment and Political Economy Considerations

An important dimension that affects the feasibility and sustainability of the process of economic reform relates to the social costs of adjustment and the political economy of reform. In Eastern Europe after 1989, (measured) real wages have declined substantially, by 30% or so on average, and unemployment is growing at a rate exceeding 10% in some countries of the region (e.g., Hungary, Poland, Bulgaria) following the implementation of adjustment measures. The rise of unemployment in economies in which full employment was an entitlement brings a sense of economic insecurity and anxiety, which is new for people raised under socialism. In addition, the Darwinian-Schumpeterian process of economic differentiation under capitalism is bound to increase—through fair and unfair mechanisms—the degree of economic inequality in these societies.

Economic reform in Latin America also entailed considerable social costs. Chile had high and persistent open unemployment between 1975 and 1988, and in Mexico the average real wage in 1990 was near 30% below its level of 1980. Unsurprisingly, income distribution worsened in the initial phase (several years) of the adjustment programs in these two economies. Regrettably, comprehensive data on the social costs of adjustment in other regions where reforms have been initiated are less reliable or simply unavailable.

The political economy of reform has several dimensions: one key issue is the *sequencing* of economic and political reforms. In the case of Eastern Europe and Russia in the early 1990s, the sequencing was such that the launching (or acceleration) of market-oriented reforms was made possible by the political collapse of the socialist regime. When both transitions—economic and political—run simultaneously, they become strongly interdependent. Success in economic reform requires political consolidation and social support, or at least tolerance of reforms that very often entail large social costs before yielding an improvement in economic welfare. In turn, the consolidation of political reform (democracy) rests to a large extent on success on the economic front. In fact, multiparty democracies hardly flourish in conditions of economic crises and stagnation. However, economic and political reforms do not always run along parallel courses: in countries like China and Chile under Pinochet, economic reforms were implemented first, delaying the political reform. Nevertheless, in Chile the first democratic government that took office in 1990 ratified the existing economic model first implemented, harshly, by the military. Finally, as mentioned, other levels at which political economy considerations matter is in the choice between shock treatment and gradualism and in the distribution across different groups of the population of the costs (and benefits) of economic reform.

Patterns of Economic Response to Market-Oriented Reform: Main Results

Market-oriented reform involves long-term changes in the economic structure and institutions of the reforming countries (see table 1.3); in consequence, reform efforts cannot be evaluated only from a short-term perspective. The economic performance in the transition period is nonetheless of critical importance both as an indicator of how the reforms are evolving and as a source of lessons for countries yet to embark on reform programs.

The main effects of the last three years (1990–92) of reform in Eastern Europe can be summarized as follows: Initially, there is a protracted and deep recessionary cycle with a cumulative contraction in GDP of over 30 percentage points. The recession is "transformational" in the sense that it entails both a serious contraction of GDP in the state sector along with an expansion in output generated in the new private sector (unfortunately, from a measurement perspective part of that expansion is not fully captured by the official statistics). The liberalization of controlled prices, currency devaluation, and the

TABLE 1.3 Patterns of economic response to market-oriented reform

	Eastern Europe		Latin America (Chile, Mexico, Bolivia)		China		Russia
	Short run	Medium run	Short run	Medium/Long run	Short run	Medium/Long run	Short run
Inflation	accelerates after price decontrol	slow deceleration	accelerates after price decontrol	slow deceleration (except Bolivia)	initial moderate acceleration	moderately low	rapid explosion
Output	declines	declines	declines	slow recovery	increases	increases	declines
Fiscal deficit	improves	worsens	improves	improves	some worsening	moderate deficit	unchanged
Current account of the balance of payments	improves	improves	improves	improves	improves	improves	unchanged
Real wages	declines	declines	declines	slow recovery	increases	increases	declines
Unemployment rate	small increase	persistent increase	increases	slow decline	small increase	declines	small increase
Privatization	rapid progress in retail trade and services	slow progress in industrial sector	slow progress	accelerated progress	no progress	little progress	main progress in retail trade/services
Exports	increases	increases	increases	increases	increases	increases	declines

adjustment of public tariffs tend to produce a large initial outburst of inflation (more severe in Poland, Bulgaria, and Romania); however, price liberalization also allowed a sudden end to shortages, queues, and forced substitution of goods and inputs in most of the countries. After the initial shot of "corrective inflation," the convergence to moderately low inflation—say, to annual rates between 15% and 20%—is a slow process that may take several years. The current account deficits of the balance of payments have been substantially reduced through import compression, export increases, and in some countries (e.g., Poland), debt relief. The fiscal budget, which follows a sort of inverted U-shape during reform, initially improved with the elimination of subsidies and some increase in profit taxes associated with initial price liberalization. Afterward, however, there is a deterioration of the fiscal deficit, which seems to be more permanent, associated with a deep decline in the profits of state-owned enterprises, an increase in safety-net payments, and the fact that the new private sector pays little taxes. A rapid privatization of services, retail trade, and some manufacturing has coexisted with a slow and complex process of privatization of medium- to large-scale state-owned enterprises in industry, public utilities, and state-owned banks. The economic reforms have taken place in a context of considerable political fragmentation and volatile alliances that complicated the process of winning articulate political (parliamentary) and social support for different reform measures.

In Russia, the response of the economy to the economic reforms share several of the features mentioned for Eastern Europe regarding output contraction, deterioration of the fiscal balance, and the pace of privatization. Russia differs with Eastern Europe, however, in at least three main respects. First, inflation has been extremely severe, almost reaching hyperinflation. Second, the politics of the transition have been very complex. This is reflected at two levels: on the one hand, within the Russian government there have been important divisions on the course of economic policy since the reform process began. On the other hand, the parliament elected before the reforms started is dominated by the old *nomenklatura* and former communist *apparatchiks* who display active opposition and hostility to several reforms. Third, the break-up of the former Soviet Union has imposed complex problems of inter-republic trade and payments to Russia (and other former Soviet republics).

China's economic performance after reforms were implemented in the late 1970s has been remarkable: the average rate of growth of GDP per year in the period 1978–92 was 9%, with an annual rate of increase in per capita consumption of around 7% over the same period. Inflation has remained largely under control at low to moderate levels, though punctuated by accelerations in the periods of price decontrol and administrative price adjustments. In addition, fiscal imbalances have been relatively moderate, and exports have grown at a high rate. In spite of this good performance, important problems remain. There is a vast system of dual prices that creates the potential for microeconomic distortions and rent seeking, private property is still very limited, and the state is the dominant owner of most of the productive wealth in the country. The ultimate question regarding China is, of course, whether the country's reforms are oriented to build capitalism or just to create some sort of market socialism.

The main features of the adjustment in reforming Latin American countries (Chile, Mexico, Bolivia) in the 1970s and 1980s in the aftermath of reform are: (1) The transition from high to low inflation has been a slow process (except in Bolivia); in fact, Chile and Mexico took roughly seven years to bring down inflation from three-digit levels to a range below 15%– 20% per year. (2) The resumption of GDP growth after a period of adjustment has been sluggish and punctuated by cycles of stop and go. (3) Public investment (particularly in infrastructure) suffered at the beginning of the adjustment process; in turn, the resumption of private investment was often fragile and delayed. (4) The adjustment in the labor market often involved drastic cuts in real wages and/or increases in open unemployment. (5) There is evidence that income distribution worsened in the initial years of reform in Chile and Mexico.

A summary of the impact of reform in "peripheral" socialist countries of Africa, Latin America, and Asia is complicated, as the reforms have been partial and developed in a context of acute social conflict or war. In socialist Africa, the first steps for economic reform were undertaken in the mid-1980s in Mozambique and in the early 1990s in Angola; both countries, however, had long-lasting civil wars that obviously precluded the implementation of comprehensive economic reforms.

In Latin America, Nicaragua made great progress at the macro level by stopping hyperinflation in 1992; however, the end of the war and the ensuing demobilization of "contra" soldiers and part of the Sandinista army did not bring social harmony, and the country is still divided. In the sphere of economic reform, that has made progress more difficult in some key areas such as privatization. In particular, the impasse on restitution of property confiscated by the former Sandinista government from the Somoza family and those who fled the country after the triumph of the Sandinistas in the late 1970s and the settling of property rights has become a symbol of unresolved social conflicts in the country.

Outline of the Chapters

This book contains twelve chapters and the text of a panel discussion. The chapters are revised versions of papers presented at a conference held at El Escorial, Spain, on July 6–8, 1992.

Chapters 2, 3, and 4 offer alternative views on how to design and implement reform programs in postsocialist countries and in mixed reform economies. In chapter 2, Lance Taylor discusses the postsocialist transitions from the viewpoint of developing countries' experience with stabilization and structural reforms. The author notes that developing countries and postsocialist economies share common features like macroeconomic instability and external vulnerability, backward financial systems, heterogeneous technologies, and a lack of modern and flexible institutions. On the macro side, Taylor emphasizes the possibilities of stagflationary effects of across-the-board price liberalization, monetary tightening, and currency devaluation. These results, once the domain of developing economies, are observed today to different degrees in Eastern Europe and Russia. This, according to Taylor, puts limits on the effectiveness—or heightens the costs—of orthodox macroeconomic management in the context of postsocialist transitions. In other words, shock treatment could be a very costly way to restore macroeconomic balance after socialism. Those costs would show up in terms of slower or negative growth, regressive income distribution, and stubborn inflation. In terms of structural reforms, Taylor discusses trade liberalization and market deregulation, making the point that the evidence does not fully support their alleged beneficial effects on efficiency and growth, which should be kept in mind when evaluating the probable effects of these policies in formerly socialist countries. In addition, Taylor makes the case that the postsocialist transitions will require active state involvement in the economy and "non-OECD forms of economic organization" more suitable to their historical and institutional characteristics.

Chapter 3 by Manuel Guitián offers an alternative perspective on reform and discusses several issues surrounding the design and implementation of market-oriented reforms both in the "East" (former socialist economies) and the "West" (mixed economies). The author takes up rules versus discretion, shock treatment versus gradualism, and the sequencing of reform. Guitián's preference is for rules over discretion and simultaneity on various fronts (e.g., shock treatment) when implementing reform policies. Guitián makes the important distinction between policy decisions, policy actions, and policy outcomes; given the existing lags between policy decisions and policy actions on the one hand, and between policy implementation and policy outcomes on the other, the best strategy would be a simultaneous launching of stabilization policies and liberalization measures at the levels of both institution building and managing policy instruments. These lags would then be a main reason in favor of adopting a sort of big-bang or shock treatment reform strategy. Moreover, the author highlights differences of "essence" and of "degree" between East and West in the design and practice of economic reform. The crucial difference in "essence" between East and West would be that in formerly socialist economies, there is an almost complete lack of market-based institutions and rules. The author points out that building such institutions is the central challenge in the transition toward the market economy. Differences in "degree" would refer to issues of strategy, such as pace and sequencing, as well as lags in the effects of policies that are common to the transitions of both postsocialist and mixed economies. Finally, Guitián argues in favor of generous external assistance to postsocialist countries, although that assistance must be linked to the policy implementation of reforms.

Chapter 4 by Alice Amsden adopts a microeconomic and sectoral perspective on economic reform and focuses in the role of industrial policy and other forms of state intervention in reforming Eastern Europe. The discussion is conducted based on the experience of Korea, Taiwan, and other East Asian cases in terms of industrial policy, technological innovation, and rapid trade expansion. The author argues that comparative advantages based only on highly competitive labor costs (e.g., depressed product wages in dollars terms) will not be enough for productive modernization, sustainable industrial growth, and export expansion in postsocialist economies. The author presents conceptual arguments and some evidence drawn from the East Asian experience in favor of employing industrial policy in Eastern Europe as a preferred alternative to laissez-faire.

Chapters 5–8 deal with experiences of economic reform in socialist economies. Chapter 5 by Alan Gelb discusses the postsocialist transitions in Eastern Europe compared to other transitions of former socialist countries in Africa, Asia, and Latin America. The chapter offers several criteria for evaluating systemic reform in former socialist countries: macroeconomic stabilization and adjustment; market creation; change in ownership and privatization; and reform of the state. The chapter shows that reforms in former socialist economies have made more progress in eliminating shortages and repressing inflation, triggering the emergence of a dynamic private presence in the services sectors, stimulating export response, and in the initial setting of a legal and institutional framework supportive of the new market economy. In contrast, the record of reform has not been so good in large-scale privatization, in reforming the state apparatus, and in avoiding the social costs of adjustment. Moreover, Gelb highlights differences in the specific modalities of reform and its outcomes within the postsocialist transitions in Eastern Europe, Africa, Asia, and Latin America.

Chapter 6 by Stanley Fischer examines the still short experience with market-based reform in Russia. The author first documents the main macroeconomic and structural features of the Russian economy. Then he discusses previous attempts at reform in Russia such as the Shatalin 500-Day plan. Then he turns to the program of 1992 in the areas of macroeconomic stabilization, incomes policy, exchange rate and current account convertibility, and enterprise reform and privatization. Then the chapter examines the problems of inter-republic trade and payments mechanisms in the establishing of new independent states in the former Soviet Union. Finally, the author provides a postscript on recent developments in Russia between 1992 and mid-1993 on the inflation and stabilization fronts and concerning the political economy of reform.

Dwight Perkins analyzes the economic reform process in China after 1978 in chapter 7. The author discusses the gradualist and selective approach followed by China in the last decade or so. He analyzes the conditions at the beginning of the reform process, noting that, unlike Eastern Europe, there was no breakdown of foreign trade at the time of reform, because, among other things, China was a (large) closed economy. Moreover, macroeconomic imbalances in China were apparently of small magnitude when reforms were initiated in the late 1970s. The chapter highlights the role of agriculture and foreign trade as the two areas on which reforms focused initially, followed by reform of industry and the services sector. The chapter documents that in spite of invigorated private sector activity, the reform process involved little privatization. Finally, Perkins analyzes the outstanding performance of China in terms of accelerated GDP growth, improvement in living standards, and expansion of manufacturing exports after the implementation of the reforms.

In chapter 8, Carmelo Mesa-Lago examines one of the last examples of existing socialism, Cuba. This is a case of a small island, very close geographically to the United States, that is surviving the effects of the collapse of socialism in Eastern Europe and the former USSR, with the ensuing drying up of financial transfers, commercial ties, and political support to the island. Mesa-Lago documents the efforts of Cuba in the late 1980s to reverse the tendency toward economic decline through highly orthodox socialist policies of economic recentralization and the elimination of the scarce market mechanism operating in some segments of the economy (*Programa de Rectificación Económica*). Clearly, these policies are in stark opposition to those followed in Eastern Europe and Russia in the 1980s. Cuba's economic situation has further worsened since the early 1990s, with the complete elimination of subsidized trade and direct transfers from the former Soviet Union. The author discusses the limits and costs of extreme domestic austerity and the tightening of rationing as a way to cope with adverse external shocks and systemic disintegration.

Chapters 9–10 deal with the postdirigiste transition process in Latin America and Spain. Patricio Meller turns to economic reform in Latin America in chapter 9. Market-oriented economic reform started in the 1970s in Chile and in the 1980s in Mexico and Bolivia, with a similar trend arising in Argentina and Venezuela in the early 1990s. Meller focuses on three dimensions of the economic reform process: stabilization policies and fiscal reform, trade reform, and privatization. The author's main conclusion is that the implementation of structural reforms is a slow processes measured over several years. For example, the reduction of inflation took half a decade or so in Mexico and Chile, in spite of stiff stabilization measures. In addition, the completion of fiscal and trade reforms also took several years in the reforming economies of Latin America. Moreover, as in chapter 12, the author finds that the recovery of capital formation and growth in the aftermath of stabilization and adjustment was a slow process in the reforming economies of Latin America.

Chapter 10 by Miguel Angel Fernandez-Ordoñez and Luis Servén discusses the process of economic reform in Spain in the last fifteen years following the end of the authoritarian regime of General Francisco Franco. The chapter analyzes the transition to full democracy, the integration of Spain into the European Community, and the effort at modernization and the building of a market economy. In these respects, the Spanish experience is highly relevant for Eastern Europe, which faces some of these problems today, particularly as regards the transition from authoritarian rule and from a protectionist and overregulated economic system to a more liberal one. In turn, the authors analyze the Spanish experience with regional integration—an important issue on the agenda in the medium run once the basis of a market economy is established and consolidated. Pending problems like currency appreciation, the growing deficit in the current account, and persistent high unemployment are highlighted as current problems of the Spanish model.

Chapters 11–12 provide a retrospective and integration of economic reform after socialism and dirigisme. In chapter 11, Osvaldo Sunkel provides a historical overview of the evolution of the concept of economic reform, with special emphasis on the changing role of the state through most of the twentieth century. The author shows the evolving perceptions of the role of the state over time. In the 1930s, in developing as well as developed countries, the state was seen as a central part of the solution to the economic problems of that period; in the 1970s and 1980s, the state has been regarded more often as part of the problem. This change in the perception of the role of the state is an important feature of the quest for market-oriented economic reform. Moreover, Sunkel discusses the performance of developing countries over a period of "state-led growth" after World War II, trying to elucidate the contribution of the state to both the good postwar growth performance of developing countries as well as their economic decline in the 1980s (particularly in Latin America).

In chapter 12, I look at the experiences of market-based economic reform in both former socialist countries and mixed economies from a comparative perspective. The chapter discusses the analytical underpinnings of the choice between shock treatment and gradualism and the relative importance of macroeconomic versus liberalization components in the design of reform programs. The strategies of shock treatment in Eastern Europe are compared with the more gradualist and evolutionary approach followed in China in terms of three indicators of economic performance: ability to stabilize the economy, impact on investment and growth, and distributive impact. The analysis shows that programs of shock treatment in Eastern Europe came along with output contraction, high initial inflation, and large drops in real wages. In contrast, economic reform in China produced rapid output and consumption growth, while avoiding macroeconomic dislocation. The relative contributions of the policies implemented, the initial conditions, and the external shocks are assessed in generating these outcomes.

Country experiences with economic reform in mixed developing economies in Latin America and East Asia (Korea) are examined in terms of the policies applied and the performance indicators just mentioned. The analysis concludes with lessons on the sequencing and intensity of programs of economic transformation and the interactions between economic and political reform.

The book concludes with the comments of a panel composed of Yilmaz Akyuz, Nancy Birdsall, Colin Bradford, Jr., and Lance Taylor, summarizing the main topics discussed at the El Escorial conference.

What Have We Learned?

Let us highlight some of the main lessons and findings of this volume:

1. The postsocialist and postdirigiste transitions have to be seen as historical processes. Stalinist socialism and economic dirigisme in developing countries went through different phases of transition, maturity, decline, crisis, and eventual collapse. The causes of the endogenous disintegration of socialism and the exhaustion of state-led development in nonsocialist countries are very complex and remain a fascinating subject for further research. An important lesson from these historical experiences is the large-scale failure of the attempt at suppression (or repression) of the market as the dominant mechanism of economic coordination in complex societies.

2. The macroeconomics of the postsocialist transitions of Eastern Europe and the former Soviet Union is characterized by large initial price blips after price reform, a deep and protracted collapse in aggregate output, a worsening in the fiscal budget, and external sector vulnerability. Interestingly, several of these qualitative features of macro response have been common to both shock and gradualist programs, whether the countries entered the reform process from

open macroeconomic crisis or from traps of stagnation. Of course, the intensity of the macro effects is affected by these dimensions.

On the positive side, macro adjustment led to the virtual elimination of shortages, an increase in the level and variety of consumption opportunities and, in several cases, an expansion in exports. The strong macro and growth performance of China after the reforms makes this a special case, very different from Eastern Europe and the former Soviet Union.

3. The microeconomic and sectoral dimension of the transition after socialism is characterized by a change in the relative output mix between the state and nonstate sectors. In fact, a substantial decline in output in the state sector has coexisted with a very dynamic expansion of private sector production, particularly in services, small-scale agriculture, and manufacturing. An important change brought by the reforms is the introduction of a price system that reflects relative scarcities in the economy in place of a cumbersome planning system. The private sector response to the reforms, on the supply side, have ranged from Schumpeterian entrepreneurship devoted to real production and innovation to rent seeking and other socially unproductive activities involving large redistributions of income and wealth.

4. Transition experiences suggest the existence of "easy" and "hard" areas of structural and institutional reform. Privatization in retail trade, services, and shops is relatively "easy" when compared to the privatization of medium- to large-scale public enterprises in industry, public utilities, and state-owned banks. Another "hard" area of reform is the creation of a new tax system tailored for a market economy. Moreover, making the emergent private sector pay taxes has not been easy. In general, the reform of the state and the redefinition of its economic role is one of the most complicated of systemic reforms.

5. The sustainability of the reforms is a complex issue. The initial euphoria with the end of communism has given way to social concern with the hardship of transitions that entail cuts in real wages, higher unemployment, and reduced social benefits. In addition, the fragmentation of the political system emerging after communism has made it harder to articulate stable political support for the reforms at the parliamentary level.

6. The postdirigiste reforms in Latin America show that the phase of macroeconomic stabilization and adjustment might be longer than expected in economies characterized by chronic inflation, external vulnerability, and distributive conflicts. In that context, the transition from high to low inflation and the resumption of investment and growth is a long-term process often measured in

18   Andrés Solimano

decades rather than a few years. Latin America's reforms clearly show that the macro dimension of the transition may be as complicated as the implementation of structural reforms, even in economies that start from more favorable conditions in terms of market deepening, private sector entrepreneurship, and institutional development than the former socialist countries.

7. Economic reform in small, agrarian socialist economies like Nicaragua, Angola, Mozambique, and Vietnam highlights the importance of basic social consensus and the need for working institutions to support reform. In fact, social and armed strife, widespread poverty, and extremely weak economic and social institutions make the management of complex economic reform virtually impossible. The basic lesson of these small postsocialist countries is that a *minimum core* of stability and governance is required to launch and sustain economic reform.

8. Finally, the different country experiences analyzed in this volume show the enormous variety in the possible routes to a reformed market economy, both across and within the group of former socialist and nonsocialist countries. Universally valid blueprints showing how to conduct reform hardly exist. However, other countries' experiences—of both success and failure—provide important information and analysis for those embarking on reform. Systemic transformation in real life ultimately requires informed judgment, political vision, and good luck.

Note

The comments by Alice Amsden, Mario I. Blejer, Ricardo A. Lagos, Raimundo Soto, and Lance Taylor on a first draft of this chapter are appreciated.
1. Another factor behind the adoption of a reform program is a sort of "bandwagon effect" or "leader-follower effect": the fact that many countries have embarked on market-based reform encourages others to follow the lead. This is by no means a minor factor instigating economic reform.

Part I
Strategies of Reform:
Alternative Views

CHAPTER 2

The Postsocialist Transition from a Development Economics Point of View

Lance Taylor

The road to the free market was opened and kept open by an enormous increase in continuous, centrally organized, and controlled interventionism.

Karl Polanyi (1944)

The ongoing transitions of Leninist centrally planned (or "socialist") economic systems toward the market are of enormous social significance; more prosaically, they are the latest academic rage. Hundreds of papers address the topic already; the only justification for adding another is that the ones from Western(ized) economists largely say the same thing. Most authors start from a common base—the economic institutions of advanced market economies as reified in current neoclassical theory—and extol stabilization, price liberalization, privatization, and restructuring along Western lines.[1] The observations offered here begin from an alternative perspective: the difficult changes that developing economies have been going through for the past ten or twenty years. Their message is that transition will not be easy, that it will largely have to be mediated by the state, and that non-OECD forms of economic organization should be explored.[2]

There are profound historical and institutional differences between postsocialist and "market-oriented" developing countries, and these should not be ignored. Moreover, conditions vary within the postsocialist camp; for example, after only a generation of collectivization, the return to peasant agriculture in China and Vietnam was far less painful than it will be in Russia and the Ukraine. But the gulf between postsocialism and underdevelopment is surely no wider than the one dividing it from the Western economies from which advice so copiously flows. Common sense suggests that the people riding the transition tiger would be better off communicating with Indians or Brazilians instead of the Japanese about how to run a semimodern industrial sector with big public- and foreign-controlled segments, or with Chileans rather than Americans about how to rebuild a simple financial system under duress. Similarities in economic structure are invoked in both these examples;

21

the goal of this chapter is to spell out their implications as illustrated by recent history.

The emphasis is on traps to be avoided and options that might prove interesting to explore. In a general presentation, the historical specificity of each economy precludes any more pointed thoughts, nor does the author have the knowledge required to provide them. Developing countries' experience suggests that all aspects of economic change are interconnected: short-run "stabilization" of internal or external macroeconomic shocks is interlinked with medium term "adjustment" in the process of "reform." However, for exposi-tional purposes it is hard to avoid an analytical breakdown.

Macroeconomic Adjustment

Developing-country experience with stabilization shows that aggregate de-mand can fall well short of potential supply for a long time (Taylor 1988). Prolonged recession is a well-known means to run a trade surplus and (with luck) contain a serious inflation. On the other hand, national demand cannot continue to exceed supply unless unlimited foreign exchange for imports to cover the shortfall is at hand. Along lines laid out by Kalecki (1971) and elaborated in Taylor (1991), one can distinguish three means by which excess aggregate demand can be erased:

1. Quantity adjustment via reductions in demand "injections" or autono-mous components of spending, such as investment and public outlays. Alternatively, regressive income redistribution will restrain consump-tion but stimulate exports via lower production costs and investment by raising the share of profits in GDP. If the first effect is stronger—as is true in most developing economies and likely in the postsocialist world—aggregate demand will fall. Progressive redistribution, sim-ply modeled as a real wage increase, will make demand rise in a "wage-led" expansion with complications to be taken up shortly.
2. Inflation-induced reductions in spending. A familiar channel is "forced saving" or a shift in the income distribution from low- to high-saving groups, for example, from workers whose money wages are not fully indexed to price increases toward profit recipients and/or the state. Another route is via the "inflation tax" whereby price increases erode real money balances and induce people to save more. Both income and wealth redistributions can hold down demand, but at high social cost. In the 1980s, developing countries had to reduce absorp-tion to meet supply contraction caused by scarce foreign exchange. African and Latin American economies ended up with inflations at double- or triple-digit annual rates and real wage reductions of 50% or more.[3]

3. Administrative means to limit demand to available supply. The traditional socialist procedures led to a "shortage economy" with "soft budget constraints" (Kornai 1981) or "repressed inflation" in a mainstream phrase (Malinvaud 1977).[4]

Taking into account these three modes of adjustment plus inflationary implications to be developed as we go along, we can say something about stabilization problems that postsocialist economies face. Figure 2.1 illustrates the implications of relaxing the administrative system, with the real wage and the rate of capacity utilization (actual divided by potential output) as the variables that adjust.

The "potential supply" curve shows the maximum amount that can be produced at a given real wage. Supply does not go up very much as the wage declines, in a shorthand description of how lack of an entrepreneurial tradition and entrenched monopoly positions make potential output unresponsive to price changes in the postsocialist world.[5]

The economy is assumed to be wage led, but the "aggregate demand" schedule also is steep, that is, demand reductions require substantial price increases and wage cuts in forced saving/inflation tax regimes. The curve is dashed to show its "virtual" nature to the right of the potential supply schedule. At the real wage, ω_0, for example, unrestricted demand would be at point B, but the observed level is held down to A by one of the mechanisms discussed above.

The relevant assumption is that initially many sectors in the economy are in shortage, or repressed inflation is in force. If constraints in all markets are suddenly lifted in a "global shock," demand will surge from A toward B.

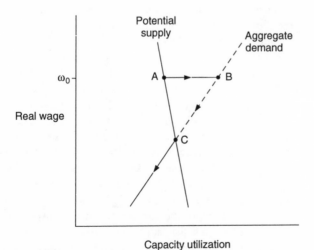

Figure 2.1 Macroeconomic adjustment to a global shock

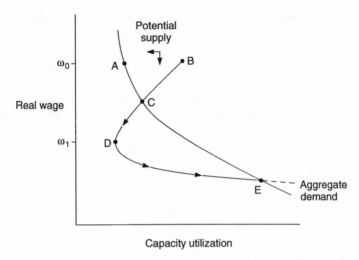

Capacity utilization

Figure 2.2   Hypothetical long-term response to a global shock

Some new limiting mechanism must appear, and with producers in monopoly positions, price increases are the likely outcome (e.g., the 500% to 600% inflation in Poland in 1990 and the many-fold price jumps in Russia after decontrol in January 1992). The inflation tax and forced saving kick in, driving the economy toward C. As demand falls, inflationary pressure will abate, but there is no reason for real wage reductions to stop at full capacity use. Especially under contractionary macro policy, the economy will follow the arrows down the observable (solid) aggregate demand schedule below C.[6]

Figure 2.2 illustrates the sort of global adjustment that shock therapists may have in mind. For low levels of the real wage, the potential supply curve is assumed to become less steep as its elasticity rises. Also at the wage level ω_1, the demand curve changes slope, presumably as "our" exports become cheap enough to make them competitive in world trade. Further wage cuts stimulate sales abroad as the economy becomes "profit led." It can converge through D to a new low wage/high output equilibrium at point E.

There is no obvious institutional reason why dynamics like those in figure 2.2 should apply. There could, for example, be cycling or chaotic fluctuations in the "Bermuda triangle" defined by the administered equilibrium point C, stagnation at D, and the market solution E (Kuznetsov 1991). Even if the system converges toward E, no time scale can be inferred from the diagram. Developing-country experience suggests that one has to think in terms of decades for transitions of the sort illustrated to transpire. Edwards (1990), for example, underscores the similarities between the Chilean post-1973 and Polish post-1989 economic packages, and observes that even with unstinting support from official aid donors, the former took a dozen years to lead to sustained economic growth. After almost a decade of orthodox treatment and a recent swing of 1.5% of GDP toward a deficit on current account, in 1991 Mexico may just have turned the corner to slow growth of per capita output.

With hindsight, from a mainstream perspective, the Chilean transition could have been shorter, had policymakers seen through veils of ignorance and misunderstanding in real time. It is hard to imagine that postsocialist authorities will be any less maladroit than the Chileans with their ample advice from the University of Chicago, World Bank, and International Monetary Fund. A more relevant observation is that Chilean, Turkish, Korean, and other successful developing-country adjustments were not led by the invisible hand—substantial state intervention over decades sowed the seeds of sustained output growth. The role of the state in directing developing-economy capitalism has not been widely discussed in the literature on postsocialist transitions, and is taken up below.

In closing this section, two lines of thought are worth sketching out. First, the obvious way to avoid the overshooting of figure 2.1 is *not* to undertake a global shock. As Zhukov and Vorobyov (1991) point out, a messy "multifaceted price system" (or MPS) with diverse values and rationing for the "same" commodity in different markets may be a necessary crutch for the transition from an administered toward a market regime, as monopoly structures are gradually broken down and entrepreneurship is nurtured. The Polish MPS of the 1980s has been roundly condemned, but its homely virtues are perhaps becoming more evident in light of the crash of 1990–91.[7]

The second observation is that designing policy for stabilization and growth is trickier in wage-led than profit-led systems, for several reasons. Both the real wage and inflation usually respond positively to output, for example. But then a wage reduction will cut demand, reducing wage growth further still as inflation slows down. This is one mechanism behind overshooting below point *C* in figure 2.1.

Overkill can also result from currency depreciation, which in wage-led systems is likely to create both inflation and output contraction in the short run. Devaluation drives up prices from the side of intermediate import costs. If money wages are not fully indexed to rising prices, real wages will fall and output contract. This effect is reinforced if there is an initial trade deficit, for then devaluation raises exporters' incomes less than importers' costs, again reducing local spending power.

Among other implications, if devaluation is contractionary, it should be combined with fiscal expansion in a package aimed at improving the balance of payments while maintaining steady output growth. The more commonly applied fiscal restriction is only appropriate when devaluation leads to output expansion in the short run. Despite substantial export growth, contractionary devaluation mixed with fiscal restraint deepened East Germany's and Poland's output depressions.

Finally, a positive wage/output linkage complicates adjustment to increases in labor productivity. If unemployed labor is present, a productivity gain (or a fall in the labor/output ratio) is not likely to be accompanied by a higher real wage. At the initial level of output, total wage payments will decline, reducing consumption demand and ultimately investment and potential output growth via the accelerator. On the other hand, if exports are sensitive to local production costs, they may jump enough to raise total output in profit-led fashion. The price elasticity of "our" exports becomes a crucial parameter, key to absorbing productivity growth as well as the pleasant outcome of figure 2.2. Unfortunately, market mechanisms alone are not likely to make export demand responsiveness rise. A national agency or a transnational corporation (TNC) has to go out and look for buyers and pressure local producers into making goods and services that sell.

Money and Inflation Conundrums

The supply and demand inelasticities just discussed are one of two major macroeconomic problems confronting postsocialist economies. Muddling through with imperfect allocation systems like an MPS may be the only means of dealing with these rigidities until they are softened by institutional change. A go-slow strategy also makes sense in dealing with the other big macro imbalance: the monetary/financial disequilibrium that transition provokes.

Much ink has spilled over the postsocialist "monetary overhang." It came from instant thawing of frozen enterprise countertrade accounts in the banking system and expansionary fiscal policy financed by money creation, especially in the former Soviet Union.[8] Calculations based on the equation of exchange suggest that substantial price jumps (from 50% to doubling or more) would be required to eliminate excess money supply.

Such arithmetic is amusing so far as it goes, and it does emphasize that confiscating or refreezing balances—probably some household holdings as well as all those of enterprises, which had no true financial meaning under central planning in any case—makes sense as part of a stabilization package. But the quantity theory elides other factors behind inflation under postsocialism. It also diverts attention from financial fragilities that have provoked crises of very diverse nature in developing countries over the years, as discussed in the following section.

With regard to inflation, several potentially destabilizing linkages stand out:

1. As figure 2.1 emphasizes, postsocialist systems are prone to static excess demand. A frozen or unfrozen monetary overhang is the financial counterpart, via Walras's law in a rudimentary system with money as the dominant nonreal domestic asset. This fundamental disequilibrium traces back to inelastic supply, which in turn is due to institutional rigidities that will only weaken with directed policy and time.

2. However, excess demand is not the only problem. The long, sad experience of Latin America emphasizes that price excursions have causes on both the cost and demand sides. When inflation settles in, it becomes increasingly "inertial" as all actors learn to index (tacitly or explicitly) the prices that affect them to the ongoing spiral. The state will also get into the act, for example, indexing the nominal exchange rate to the domestic inflation rate in a "crawling peg" to avoid currency overvaluation (most Eastern European countries opted for this sensible policy in 1991).

Postsocialist institutions—firms with monopoly positions and newly aggressive labor unions with an eye toward raising enterprise wage funds—tilt the system toward indexation. The implication is that deep, long-lasting recession may be required to break a serious inflation. For example, two bouts of heavy contraction were required to overcome inertia in Chile between 1973 and 1985; in the latter year per capita GNP had fallen 13% from its 1970 level, and the unemployment rate was well over 20%. Wage indexation was not liquidated until the 1980s. Despite Poland's massive output contraction in 1990–91, inflation still runs at annual rates in the upper double digits.

The alternative to pure contraction is a "heterodox shock" combining a price and wage freeze (under a "social compact") with demand restraint, relative price adjustments such as real wage reductions or exchange appreciation, and foreign exchange inflows or reserve losses to bring in imports to cut excess demand. The record of such packages is mixed, with Mexico and Israel succeeding on the basis of strong institutions for social control (especially of wages) and Argentina and Brazil failing in repeated attempts (Taylor 1991).[9] Whether a postsocialist government could manage a heterodox package, especially in the face of widespread public mistrust of price controls, is a tricky question.

3. Specific items of cost may be crucial. Imported intermediates have already been mentioned in connection with the inflationary effects of devaluation. Interest costs of financing working capital have proven to be stagflationary in developing-country circumstances.[10] They may become important for postsocialist enterprises as they turn from subsidized official credits to quasi-private sources to borrow for working balances at high rates. Enterprise

monopoly power makes it easy to pass along curb-market interest rate hikes into jumping prices, which can feed into inflation via indexation.

4. Despite money's dominance as a financial asset, the amount that firms and households wish to hold can shift in response to favorable or unfavorable events. Money does compete in portfolios, at least with real assets, informal financial placements, and hard currency. A slowdown in inflation may lead to a switch from foreign holdings toward local currency, adding reserves to the banking system. Unless the inflow is sterilized (difficult in a monetary system lacking open market operations), available bank credit will grow and the informal interest rate will decline. On the other hand, if speculators or curb-market lenders switch toward money instead of providing credit to firms, the cost of financing working capital could easily go up.[11]

5. Aggregate demand will respond negatively to more rapid price increases as the inflation tax and forced saving begin to bite and increasing uncertainty makes investors curtail new capital projects.

6. Potential output also may decline in response both to higher interest rates in the informal market and credit restriction from official sources. On both counts, repressed and visible inflation will become more acute as the potential supply schedule shifts left from point A in figure 2.1. Even IMF economists such as Calvo and Coricelli (1992) argue that high real interest rates and a credit squeeze contributed à la Cavallo (1977) to Polish stagflation in 1990–91.

These linkages will vary in importance over space and time. In any given setting, their potential magnitudes make it difficult to pinpoint elementary schedules like IS and LM. Figure 2.3 illustrates some possibilities in the interest rate/inflation rate plane.[12] The IS curve has been given a positive slope presupposing strong interest rate cost-push. In the upper diagram, the LM curve has the "standard" positive slope; it has to be less steep than IS for macroeconomic stability. The lower diagram illustrates the "important curb-market" case in which slower inflation pulls speculators toward holding money and informal lending rates rise.

The dashed lines show potential effects of a standard contractionary monetary policy, implicitly preceding price liberalization at a point of full capacity use like A in figure 2.1. In the upper diagram, tighter credit restrictions on firms drive them toward curb markets, shifting LM up as interest rates rise. Output contraction due to tighter credit overall adds to repressed inflation spilling over into explicit price increases as IS shifts to the right. The out-

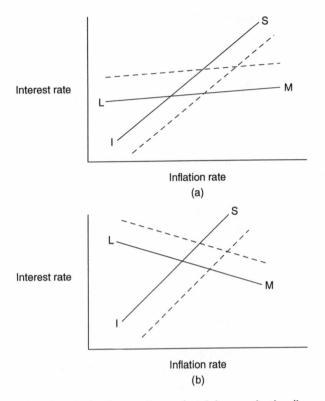

Inflation rate
(a)

Inflation rate
(b)

Figure 2.3   Stagflation (upper diagram) and demonetization (lower diagram) after a monetary contraction

comes are higher interest costs, more rapidly rising prices, and lower output —monetarist stagflation.

The interest rate jump and (possibly) the output loss are ameliorated in the lower diagram, as rising inflation leads the financially alert to switch portfolios away from currency and deposits toward curb-market lending. On the other hand, the banking system loses significance in financial intermediation.

The thought experiments of this section suggest that both rapid price liberalization and monetary contraction are dangerous maneuvers under postsocialist institutions: specific perils include inertial inflation, stagflation, and demonetization of the local currency. All are unpleasant, but may prove difficult to avoid during postsocialist transitions.

Financial Irrelevance and Fragility

The possibility of demonetization just discussed illustrates the uncertain role of finance under postsocialism. For practical purposes, the old financial system boiled down to money and banks, because credit instruments historically did not exist. Money itself "served as a means of exchange and store of wealth at best in consumption. In exchanges between enterprises, it was only an auxiliary planning instrument used to reduce physical flows to the same denominator. Imbalances resulting from resource allocation by the center were corrected in physical terms by barter transactions among enterprises and flows through the black market, and in financial terms by frozen accounts in the banking system" (Zhukov and Vorobyov 1991).

This system is now vanishing, leaving obvious questions about what sort of financial structure besides the monetary overhang of unfrozen enterprise balances plus monetized fiscal deficits will emerge in its place. A straightforward answer is impossible, but developing-country experience suggests four unpleasant scenarios that might play out:

1. The banking system can mainly finance public enterprises, which as argued below are unlikely to disappear in any brief period of time. Its balance sheet would feature deposits from the public as liabilities and credits to enterprises as assets. If parastatals do not reform effectively, the loans would be nonperforming. On a flow basis the banks would emit monetary liabilities to capture savings via the inflation tax; the proceeds would be fed to white elephants.

Transactions of this "quasi-fiscal" sort characterize bank finance of state enterprises throughout the developing world. In a familiar variant, provincial political leaders in control of regional development banks borrow from them for not necessarily productive investment projects, confident (if they ponder the question at all) that the national central bank will have to rediscount the provincial banks' paper. Local potentates emerging from the ex-*nomenklatura* would be subject to obvious temptations along these lines.

Such waste can be controlled only if banks consciously enter (or are pushed) into the arena of productive finance. In postsocialist circumstances, such credits may now be flowing among enterprises, or from speculators or curb marketeers. In both cases, the banks will face competitors from which they have a lot to learn. Alternatively, the state may be able to use the banking system to direct credit to targeted (private and public) enterprises, enforcing strict performance criteria as in 1970s South Korea (Amsden 1989). Whether postsocialist bureaucracies will be up to such a demanding task is a crucial industrial strategy question.

2. As observed above (note 4), consumers may abstain from buying if goods are simply not available; national savings rates rise as a consequence. In Zimbabwe (an industrially and financially sophisticated developing country as far as the upper income strata are concerned), import controls keep many consumer items off the market. The household savings flows resulting from this involuntary abstinence are placed with insurance companies and pension funds. The government borrows from these intermediaries to finance its chronic deficits of around 15% of GDP in nonmonetary fashion.

This system has functioned far more than a decade, but is fragile. A reduction in import compression could reduce savings rates overnight. Without fiscal reform, the state would have to resort to massive monetary emission, presumably with inflation following in its wake. This possibility is relevant to postsocialism on two counts:

First, rapid import liberalization can release a flood of novel goods into the market, reducing national savings rates as well as using foreign exchange. Dealing with the macroeconomic implications of "incentive consumption" can be a tricky task.

Second, if nonbank financial intermediaries are created, they run the risk of being captured by the state. Ex-British colonies besides Zimbabwe (India, Jamaica, etc.) have well-developed intermediaries that the treasury habitually taps for resources in exchange for its own liabilities. The issue is how to keep such "statutory borrowing" under reasonable check. Fiscal discipline, as argued below, will be essential to a successful transition.

3. Argentina's disastrous experience with capital flows moving in and out of local banks has already been discussed (see note 11). This is a classic example of financial instability of the sort analyzed by Minsky (1986), whereby swings in wealth-holders' confidence in different assets lead to destabilizing portfolio shifts. In the particular case of foreign capital movements, maintaining exchange controls can save an economy without a solidly established currency a lot of grief. Conversely, eliminating controls can provoke a perfectly avoidable capital flight, as occurred in Chile in the early 1980s in one of that country's numerous misadventures along the trail to the free market.

4. Finally, in Chile, Kuwait, Turkey, and elsewhere (not to mention the savings and loan crisis in the United States), lax financial regulation has been associated with destabilizing speculation. The Chilean scenario involved high interest rates from monetary contraction, ample savings flows from abroad and the local upper classes as the income distribution became increasingly concentrated under Pinochet, and stagnant investment demand. Under such

circumstances, high potential saving cannot be realized in the form of capital formation, and moves toward speculative ends.

The Chilean boom was based on shares of companies controlled by financial "groups" to which the state had sold assets nationalized under the Allende regime.[13] These conglomerates started borrowing from banks under their control to bid up their own shares' prices. Total financial holdings ballooned, in a characteristic signal of financial fragility, as Minsky points out. After the inevitable crash, a quarter of the assets of the banking system were nonperforming and the two biggest banks (each central to a conglomerate) lost more than five times their capital.

A clear implication of this history is that as private wealth builds up under postsocialism, a combination of strict regulation and productive investment outlets will be needed to prevent its financially unsophisticated owners from replicating Chile's excellent adventure.

In sum, postsocialist economies start from extreme financial backwardness. The first challenge they face is establishing the national currency *as* money. The possibilities of destabilizing capital flows and exchange misalignment quoted above suggest that relaxing capital controls is precisely the wrong way to go about this task. At the same time, internal portfolio shifts among money, informal loans to firms, and destabilizing speculation have to be monitored and perhaps countered by adjustments to interest rates and other incentives.

Second, the extensive discussion about creating a "two-tier" central/ commercial bank structure under postsocialism does not directly address the question about how the entities in the commercial tier are to be encouraged to *act* like banks. Effective state-owned banks in India versus ineffective private ones in Argentina provide an interesting contrast in this regard: the moral may be that there has to be effective pressure toward competition exerted from the top.

Third, commercial banks are not necessarily the dominant channel for investment finance in much of the Third World (and in many industrialized economies as well). As noted above, non-bank intermediaries may be essential in finance, whether they are "informal" in the sense of the South Korean curb market or "public" in the form of directed credits from the treasury (Korea) or development banks (Brazil). As we will see, conglomerate "groups" in which banks support productive enterprises in an intimate, long-term relationship can also play an important role. Keeping relevant credit channels open for productive lending while not going overboard for capital-market frills (say stock exchanges) are essential tasks.

Finally, any reform process creates financial traps that can be tripped, in the form of big quasi-fiscal deficits, fiscal imbalances as in Zimbabwe, speculation as in Chile, capital flight as in Argentina and Mexico, or a novel game still to be invented (such as the recent joint creation of junk bonds and lax S & L regulation in the United States). Ardent free marketeers are especially prone to running financial regulatory risks.[14]

Saving, Investment, and Trade Relationships

Recent patterns of financial intermediation and public saving and capital formation in developing economies have characteristic features, illustrated in table 2.1.[15] Five points stand out:

1. The public sector plays an important role in capital formation in all the countries, from free-market bastions like Chile and Malaysia to statist India, Turkey, and Zimbabwe. Beyond traditional public investment in infrastructure, additional considerations are involved. One is that collaboration and division of sectoral control among the state, foreign enterprise, and local private capital have for decades been standard practice throughout the devel-

TABLE 2.1 Developing-country trade, investment, and savings flows (percentages of GDP)

		Investment					Saving		
	Intermed. imps.	Imp. cap. goods	Dom. cap. goods	Pub. sector	Priv. sector	Total	Pub. sector	Priv. sector	Trade def.
Argentina (1988)	6.0	1.8	12.6	7.6	6.8	14.4	0.8	15.6	−2.0
Brazil (1987)	3.8	2.1	17.9	6.2	13.8	20.0	6.2	18.3	−4.5
Chile (1988)	14.9	6.8	11.6	7.9	10.5	18.4	5.7	15.6	−2.9
Colombia (1988)	5.4	3.5	14.6	7.1	11.0	18.1	4.0	16.7	−2.6
India (1987–88)	4.5	2.4	20.8	12.7	10.5	23.2	2.4	18.9	1.9
S. Korea (1987)	24.7	15.7	13.9	6.2	23.4	29.6	11.1	28.5	−10.0
Malaysia (1988)	22.1	11.5	11.7	9.3	13.9	23.2	5.9	27.5	−10.2
Mexico (1988)	7.9	2.5	18.1	6.4	14.2	20.6	4.2	20.1	−3.7
Nicaragua (1989)	17.5	12.1	12.1	2.1	22.1	24.2	−2.0	9.5	16.7
Nigeria (1986)	1.7	3.8	8.1	7.6	4.3	11.9	3.1	8.9	−0.1
Philippines (1988)	11.4	4.4	13.8	3.0	15.2	18.2	0.0	19.2	−1.0
Sri Lanka (1987)	11.5	6.5	19.9	14.9	11.5	26.4	4.4	18.0	4.0
Tanzania (1986)	5.7	11.9	15.0	8.3	18.6	26.9	5.6	11.8	9.5
Thailand (1987)	9.8	8.6	15.0	6.7	16.9	23.6	5.4	19.7	−1.5
Turkey (1987)	13.5	1.0	24.4	13.3	12.1	25.4	8.2	19.5	−2.3
Uganda (1987)	5.6	8.6	8.4	3.9	13.1	17.0	−5.6	16.0	6.6
Zambia (1987)	30.7	8.0	2.7	7.7	3.0	10.7	−16.7	32.5	−5.1
Zimbabwe (1986)	11.1	7.1	15.4	11.9	10.6	22.5	−5.1	30.9	−3.3

Source: Taylor (1993).

34   Lance Taylor

TABLE 2.2   Ownership of capital stock (percentages)

	Ownership class					
India (1989)	Public	Foreign	Closed private	Open private	Finance	Total
Agriculture	6.7	0.0	7.8	0.8	0.9	16.2
Mining	3.6	0.0	0.0	0.1	0.2	3.8
Manufacturing	7.7	0.6	0.3	9.4	3.9	21.9
Electric, gas, and water	9.3	0.0	0.0	0.1	0.4	9.8
Communication	1.2	0.0	0.0	0.0	0.0	1.2
Transport	4.7	0.0	1.7	0.3	0.2	6.9
Finance	1.4	0.1	2.0	3.3	12.5	19.2
Other	11.2	0.4	3.1	3.1	3.1	20.9
Total	45.7	1.1	14.9	17.0	21.3	100.0

Souces: *Monthly Abstract of Statistics*, December 1988; *National Accounts Statistics*, June 1991; *Shape of Things to Come* (Bombay: Centre for Monitoring the Indian Economy, September 1990).

	Ownership class		
Brazil (all sectors)	Domestic private firms	Foreign firms	State firms
1969	45	27	28
1975	44	24	32
1974	43	18	39
1984	41	9	50

Sources: Andrea S. Calabi *et al. Geração de Poupanças e Estrutura de Capital das Emprasas no Brasil* (São Paulo: Instituto de Pesquisas Economicas, Universidade de São Paulo), 1981; *Visão*, various issues from 1975 to 1985.

oping world. Table 2.2 illustrates with data from India and Brazil how mixed public, private, and (in the latter country) foreign ownership of the capital stock is a pervasive institutional factor in semi-industrialized economies.

The division of labor among the public, private, and foreign sectors has not always been harmonious: the private sector feared public takeover in Brazil in the late 1970s, and public enterprises dread privatization today. However, universal multiple ownership reflects the fact that effective, large-scale capitalist enterprises do not exist automatically and without assistance.

This observation has both macroeconomic and firm-level implications. Between broad sectors, in one of the few growth models addressing the transition, Dutt and Gibson (1990) argue that state and private enterprises can coexist in a steady state if there "is a high responsiveness of the state and the private sector to acquire and privatize capital in response to changes in private profitability . . . In the absence of such a social agreement, [postsocialist] economies will be inexorably led to becoming either predominately capitalist or back to . . . socialist."

Well prior to steady states, if there is any developing-economy rule, it is that state and/or foreign support are needed to get new industrial activities under way. Production facilities in technically advanced branches may be publicly owned (the model in Turkey, India, Brazil, etc.) or just publicly supported (as were the *chaebol* in South Korea), but historically have not been the product of private initiative itself. When new capacity creation relies on inputs from transnational corporations, the state has to be active as well, in regulating and bargaining with the TNCs. Otherwise, it has to help local producers search aggressively for new technology along Japanese and Korean lines (Amsden 1989; Katz 1991). In a poor country, private entities lack the economic sophistication and clout to undertake these tasks alone.

In Eastern Europe, initial conditions differ to a degree from the developing world in that (even after widespread scrapping) industrial capital stocks and expertise exist. However, producers will be no more experienced with capitalist markets and in many cases less technically adept than their counterparts in São Paulo, Bombay, and Seoul. The fact that intimate public/private collaboration persists in these industrial capitals suggests that Dutt-Gibson conditions will be arranged in such a way as to let it flourish under postsocialism as well.

An important aspect of this complementarity is that public capital formation facilitates or "crowds in" private investment. This linkage was found in most of the country studies underlying table 2.1 (Taylor 1993), and appears to be the rule in industrial countries as well. For macro programming, public capital formation may be the only vehicle for stimulating investment after transitional shocks. Unless an export boom bootstraps up investment in a cumulative process along Korean lines (certainly an outlying case among developing economies), it is hard to see how private capital formation will flourish in and of itself.

2. Table 2.1 also illustrates that the public sector is typically a strong net saver. The only exceptions are macroeconomically distressed Nicaragua, Uganda, and Zambia, along with Zimbabwe with its financial imbalances, which have already been described. High saving by the public sector reflects its activity in capital formation, as well as the unique ability of the state to gather resources. This developing-country pattern resembles the one in some industrialized nations, which historically have arrived at diverse institutional means for generating savings (Kosonen 1991). For example, household savings shares of GDP range from around 20% in Japan and Italy to 5% in Finland, Norway, and Sweden.

The low Nordic household rates complement the data in table 2.1 in suggesting that the government can be pivotal in the accumulation process; its saving in these economies has traditionally been in the range of 5%–10% of GDP (although declining in Sweden since the mid-1970s). Postsocialist systems may be pushed in this direction insofar as weak financial intermediation and tempting incentive imports hold household saving down. With slow privatization of industrial firms (the most likely outcome, as argued below), enterprise savings flows will be nominally "public." But if the state is to play a role in industrial activity like the one prevailing under "social corporatism" in small, rich industrial economies as well as most of the developing world, it will have to generate fiscal savings flows as well.

The obvious question is whether the extra saving should come from cutting current expenditure or raising revenues. In some ways, the choice in Eastern Europe is inevitable, because the state will be faced with decrepit national capital stocks, big regulatory responsibilities, and the need to provide social benefits approaching the Western European standard. Although "tax and spend" policies are now viewed dubiously even by social democrats, they will be hard to avoid in the East—the tricks will be to keep current spending below tax receipts and restrain state capital formation enough to hold the public sector borrowing requirement (PSBR) to less than (say) 5% of GDP. Immediate public revenue sources are likely to be privatization, price increases for products from state enterprises, and a broadened scope of chargeable public services. Establishment of simple, broadly based tax structures will be an essential move (Kornai 1990).

3. Private savings flows in table 2.1 are also large, and their intermediation into capital formation and/or loans to the state to cover the PSBR poses both financial questions of the sort discussed above and problems for privatization and structuring of new financial intermediaries, as described later.

4. Most economies in table 2.1 have negative trade deficits, that is, surpluses. In many cases, these reflect foreign shocks suffered in the 1980s. Latin American and other debtor nations had to run positive trade balances to make foreign interest payments. At the same time, their governments sought to avoid internal financial collapse by nationalizing foreign debts; hence they needed fiscal surpluses (apart from interest payments) to meet external obligations. Such a "double transfer" problem is likely to arise for nations with big foreign liabilities such as Poland and Russia under postsocialism. If these debts are not massively forgiven, the latter country may be less pressed than the former because its fiscal authorities will presumably have access to natural resource rents (as did governments in Mexico and Venezuela in the 1980s, as opposed to less successful adjustors such as Argentina and Brazil).

Other countries listed in table 2.1 enjoy surpluses due to strong exports (e.g., South Korea and Malaysia). The latter's position may erode as its timber and oil are depleted, while Korea's results from decades of export-led growth beginning at a point like E in figure 2.1. As argued above, it is not obvious that postsocialist economies will soon find their way to such a jumping-off position.

Another danger is that countries reliant on primary exports will face falling terms of trade and declining export volumes, as have Uganda, Tanzania, Sri Lanka, etc., as shown in table 2.1. These nations run trade deficits because they have become highly dependent on foreign donors to offset their external bad luck; such support robs governments of much of their sovereignty and is not sustainable in the long run. Nor would it be an option for a big economy: a few hundred million dollars will cover a trade deficit amounting to 10%–20% of GDP in Tanzania or Estonia but not Nigeria or the Commonwealth of Independent States.

5. The final point to be noted in connection with table 2.1 is the extreme import dependence of developing economies: when the negative effect of a nation's size on its trade shares is taken into account, the proportions of both intermediate and capital goods imports in GDP are large, especially in East Asian economies such as Korea, Malaysia, and even the Philippines.

Given that postsocialist economies will be redirecting their technologies along Western lines, they seem destined toward East Asian import ratios. Old questions about import substitution, export promotion, and appropriate directions for industrial strategy are bound to arise (Shapiro and Taylor 1990). The answers are likely to vary from place to place—one can easily imagine Hungary opting for a small open economy strategy, while Russia or the Commonwealth pursues import substitution in a reaction to the old Soviet Union's substantial opening to trade after the mid-1970s, when it contracted oil-export-induced Dutch disease (Zhukov and Vorobyov 1991).

Industrial Structure

The central industrial policy question is whether new firm managers and owners will adopt a business mentality, and how they can be encouraged to do so. Once again, a Chilean angle is relevant. According to the late Paul Rosenstein-Rodan, a shrewd observer, Chile always had a "bourgeoisie of the aperitif." Only *after* the trauma of the post-Allende transition are those families' sons (as yet not many daughters) plus a few newcomers seriously addicted to making money. Meanwhile, older forms of gentility as well as worker exploitation have fallen by the wayside.

Two distinctions that arise in development economics may prove useful in thinking about such changes. Following Hjalmarsson (1991) and UNCTAD (1991) with reference to industrial and financial strategies respectively, the first is between "allocative efficiency" and "productive efficiency." Improving allocation is the Holy Grail of agencies like the World Bank (1991). They aim to remove all wedges separating prices, especially between international and national valuations of potentially tradable goods. If this goal of eliminating "distortions" is attained, then the theorems of neoclassical economics are supposed to guarantee that the economy will perform as well as it can. Subtler variants suggest that in a stable situation, reasonably competitive capital markets will encourage productive efficiency within the firm. However, even this contingent guarantee breaks down during the transition (Tirole 1991), while Murrell (1991b) points to both theoretical and empirical evidence suggesting that socialist economies may not have been productively inefficient after all.

Developing-country experience also shows that reality is more complex: Rather distorted economies such as South Korea's and Brazil's have historically grown fast;[16] unavoidably open Portugal's and Jamaica's growth performances for decades were poor. More fundamentally, one cannot assess economic development outside a nation's historical context. That is where policies aimed at promoting efficiency in production enter in.

One interesting possibility under postsocialism may lie with the Nordic/Korean (or NK) model of accumulation, which emphasizes the advantages of workers' productivity growth when they are employed by firms big enough to benefit from best-practice technology and economies of scale. Such enterprises were consciously sanctioned by Nordic and Korean authorities as monopolies or oligopolistic participants in international trade. After relatively short learning periods, governments sought allocative efficiency by supporting their local champions in competition with counterparts abroad. They learned to meet world prices of commodities and services with elastic export demands, so that labor productivity increases could be absorbed into foreign sales, permitting profit-led growth as at point E in figure 2.2.

Pressures toward productive efficiency came not from capital markets, but from Scandinavian trade unions and the South Korean state. The Nordic workers promoted higher productivity on the understanding that it would be translated rapidly into real wages; without underwriting wage growth, the South Korean economic bureaucracy followed their Japanese mentors in adopting a pro-productivity line. Given the tightly held nature of (say) the Swedish Wallenberg "group" of companies or the *chaebol*, stock market discipline scarcely figured in production or investment decisions. Industrial subsidies and targeted, cheap credit in restricted national capital markets certainly did (Kosonen 1991; Amsden 1989).[17]

The Nordic tradition in industrial policy dates to Heckscher (1918). He

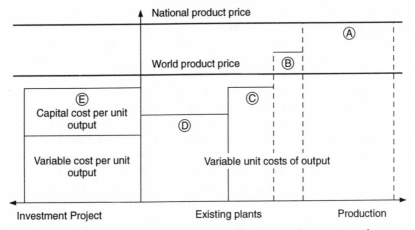

Figure 2.4 Scrapping and investment decisions under a putty–clay technology with economies of scale

reasoned in terms of a diagram like figure 2.4, also relevant to postsocialist sectoral investment choice. The industry in question has a putty-clay or vintage technology. In *typical* circumstances, due "to economies of scale at the investment stage, modern plants are larger than older plants. The small, older plants survive as long as they cover their operating costs. When operating costs increase, or the product price level decreases, some plants are no longer able to cover their operating costs and are closed down. New capacity enters the industry gradually, and transforms its structure" (Hjalmarsson 1991).

The problem is that productive structures under postsocialism are anything but typical. Plant A in the diagram used to be the Lenin Shipyard, Steel Works, or Heavy Chemical Factory—huge, hopelessly costly, and surely noncompetitive at world prices. Plant B is a small, leaner counterpart, while C and D continue the standard size/cost pattern. Economic logic suggests that investment project E should be undertaken while plants A and B go out of business.

Obvious questions arise. Will it be socially and politically feasible to close A and B? (Thousands of workers would lose their jobs.) Can a big enough devaluation at least allow them to export at variable unit cost? (No one would be willing to import an East German Trebant automobile at any price.) Should potentially profitable factories C and D be privatized, thereby depriving the government of a potential income flow? Will there be enough resources on hand to undertake the interesting project E?

The answers will depend on social pressure and politics as much as economics in practice, and cannot be provided ex ante. An NK response would be to close the losers, build the winner, and retrain the workers for employment there or elsewhere. Cooperation among the state and classes would be essential to these tasks, as well as investable resources.

Whether such coordinated changes can be orchestrated under postsocialism is at this stage not clear. As Kuznetsov (1991) emphasizes, inherited market and production structures are more complicated than those illustrated in figure 2.4, involving fixed versus flexible prices, "lazy" versus aggressive monopolists (Hirschman 1970), and diverse forms of environmental degradation in different branches. One proposed resolution of this complexity is via "evolutionary" change, whereby essentially capitalist firms may emerge from a socialist hull (Murrell 1991a). More likely, perhaps, is a tension-ridden trajectory involving uneven advance of different sectors, disproportionalities and disequilibria, with inflationary and balance-of-payments problems arising at different points. If a postsocialist economy breaks out of Kuznetsov's "Bermuda triangle" in figure 2.2, it will almost certainly go through an extended phase of hard-to-predict, unbalanced growth à la Hirschman (1958) and Streeten (1959).

The Effects of Country Size

A second distinction often drawn in development economics is between growth patterns in small and large countries (Syrquin and Chenery 1989). Population size sets an analytical boundary between the two types, in the range of 20 million to 50 million. On this criterion, Russia, China, and Vietnam are large; Hungary, Czechoslovakia, and Cuba small; and Poland and the Ukraine somewhere in between.

Katzenstein (1985) and Pekkarinen et al (1991) suggest that economically successful small countries prospered along NK lines, with close state/capitalist/labor collaboration in supporting "thrust" sectors under an open trade (although not necessarily capital market) regime. With extensions toward government deals with TNCs and more or less explicit labor repression, this rule is not destructively tested by experience in small, growing raw material exporters like Malaysia and Chile. It is also fair to ask how long the former country can successfully court potentially footloose TNC assembly operations without a coherent national industrial structure,[18] or the latter can defer distributional strife[19] (Taylor 1993).

While small countries necessarily concentrate on a limited number of export industries in the search for profitable niches, large ones usually follow a more uniform pattern of industrial change. They enter earlier into import substitution and have higher manufacturing shares of GDP than do small nations at the same per capita income level; they pursue import substitution further into intermediate and capital goods and producers' services. The statistically "typical" large country's import and export shares of GDP are likely to be around 10% (with a standard deviation of about the same size; e.g., South Korea with import and export shares in the 30% range is far more open than the norm), whereas a small country's shares may be more than one-half.

The basic premise of large-economy strategies is that protected markets at home can permit economies of scale and scope. At the same time, they allow the luxury of allocative inefficiency for extended periods of time—high-cost production is a static loss, but need not represent a binding restriction on inward-oriented growth. In a favorable context, a statically inefficient industrial sector may become the base for breaking into world trade with import-substituted products, as suggested by Turkey's example during the 1980s.[20]

The implication of large-country growth experience for postsocialism is that an attempt at instant merging of (say) the Russian, Chinese, or Commonwealth economy with the world market would prove counterproductive. Big countries have an internal economic space that it is socially efficient to explore, even if there are "welfare" losses in the form of distortions from world prices and limited access to a variety of goods. In the long run, confrontation with external competition makes sense (as the Turkish experience demonstrates), but large countries have the freedom to pick a place and time. In the medium term, intelligent use of multitiered pricing systems and targeted incentives along Indian lines can help transform an industry with an unbalanced capital stock like the one illustrated in figure 2.4 into something closer to a potential world competitor.[21]

Liberalization

The question posed earlier—by what processes will a profit-seeking mentality emerge under postsocialism?—is still being (and in part will continue to be) begged. Liberal rhetoric and recommended policy steps in support of market liberalization and privatization of state enterprise are presumably directed toward this end, and are discussed in this and the following sections.

We begin with a narrower query: Will interventions aimed at "leveling the playing field" for diverse sectors and firms lead to faster output growth? Theoretical models in diverse contexts suggest that no clear answer exists (Taylor 1991). Nor is empirical evidence conclusive. Among the countries discussed in the WIDER project (Taylor 1993), for example, trade liberalization perhaps aided Chile's growth since the mid-1980s (at least psychologically), but after a mid-decade devaluation, faster-growing Thailand raised tariffs for revenue purposes. Turkey's export boom was accompanied by real depreciation and export subsidies of up to one-third of sales value, combined with replacement of a baroque system of import quotas with bureaucratically manipulated levies; in the absence of productivity growth, exports faltered when steady exchange depreciation was reversed late in the decade. Throughout the 1980s, Mexico liberalized conscientiously and grew slowly. Among the relatively poor performers, Argentina and Zambia dabbled with liberalization, while until recently Brazil, Nicaragua, and Senegal did not.

Country experience thus provides no clear reading on the effects of liberalization. A few observations can be made, but they scarcely constitute a complete tool kit for policy choice:

1. As has been stressed repeatedly, examples like Turkey's and Chile's suggest that the basis for a growth spurt can be state/capitalist collaboration appropriate to a given set of circumstances, while the more enduring success of small European economies implies that labor has to brought into a social contract as well. If South Korea unravels politically, it will do so on the latter grounds.

2. Unless trade liberalization is begun with a weak exchange rate and ample foreign support, it can easily misfire. Moreover, effective protection rates have to be tuned to the local industrial structure. Colombia has recently been successful along these lines (with good "minor" export growth from industries previously nurtured via policies aimed at import substitution and recently propelled by numerous stimulative measures), while failed external liberalization attempts in Zambia and Argentina suffered from these problems.

3. Rapid capital market liberalization can be an extremely risky enterprise, as the examples discussed above attest. With any degree of inertial inflation, liberalization plus a fixed exchange rate peg are precisely the wrong way to go about establishing a "hard" currency. Closed capital markets plus a crawling peg (the latter adopted in Eastern Europe in 1991) will at least keep the local currency in international play.

4. While getting important prices "right" can be a major element in supporting growth—as for example with devaluations in Chile, Colombia, Malaysia, Thailand, and Turkey in the 1980s—revising the price system is at best a *necessary* policy move. As the history of each country demonstrates, other structural conditions were essential for growth. In addition, potential short-term adverse effects of liberalizing moves—contraction from devaluation, deindustrialization from reduced import protection—have to be factored into policy choice.

5. There are plenty of cases where liberalizing moves were irrelevant or counterproductive: Uganda's and Zambia's foreign exchange auctions fed into

luxury goods imports and capital flight; Mexico's frantic privatizations and deregulations throughout the 1980s underwrote slow growth (although the hope is that they will stimulate local animal spirits enough to reverse capital flight and stoke investment during the present decade);[22] Kenya, Tanzania, and Zambia tried hard to promote agriculture with price and other liberal policies with scant success, due to diverse causes such as poor weather and lack of transportation infrastructure.

6. Fast growth with widespread illiberal public intervention is historically common—South Korea between the 1950s and 1990s, Brazil between the 1930s and 1980s, and Turkey between the 1930s and 1970s and again in the 1980s are just three examples.[23]

7. Finally, there is a new and growing literature on "sequencing" of reform (Fischer and Gelb 1991; Nuti 1991). At best, not much is offered beyond neoclassical common sense, which outside its own institutional context can easily mislead. Chile—again—is an obvious counterexample to the usual recommendation to stabilize macroeconomically before attempting medium-term reforms. Pinochet's successive economic teams doggedly pursued trade liberalization and wage repression for years, while stumbling through one stabilization debacle after another. As with Bunyan's Pilgrim, endless tribulations may have strengthened the local bourgeoisie in their capitalist faith, a form of transition that fans of Hirschman (1958) can relish.

The sequencing discussion *does* raise one interesting question: whether reform should be pursued gradually or with a "big-bang" shock. The arguments already presented against such radical moves reflect the bias of people familiar with developing countries: shocks such as Argentina's in the late 1970s, Bolivia's in 1985, and Poland's in 1990 severely disoriented those economies without compensatory positive results in any reasonable period of time. From a longer-run, industrial policy perspective, big shocks are not likely to be helpful to either evolutionary or unbalanced processes of change.

The bottom line, perhaps, is that trying to stay mounted during the macroeconomic tiger ride (offsetting to the extent possible the potential lurches) while attempting context-relevant trade and industrial interventions make far more sense than lunging for liberalization *tout court*. Rodrik (1992) summarizes the current state of knowledge about freeing trade as follows: "if truth-in-advertising were to apply to policy advice, each prescription for trade liberalization would be accompanied with a disclaimer: 'Warning! Trade liberalization cannot be shown to enhance technical efficiency; nor has it been empirically demonstrated to do so.'" This summary applies to other forms of liberalization as well.

Privatization and Finance

Insofar as inherited industries are maintained in the face of the difficulties illustrated by figure 2.4, the transfer of ownership from the state to the private sector will animate arias at policy's center stage. To an extent, the singing will be beside the point because the outcomes are fairly easy to foretell: closely held national conglomerate groups will emerge, or else whole branches will be taken over by TNCs. The modalities are best controlled by nationals with a long view and concern for workers' health care and pension funds. Schemes suggested by academic outsiders are likely to be sources of journal articles at best. Foreign deal makers, on the other hand, could help blow away academics' and politicians' gauzy abstractions about how markets are made.

We can begin to address these issues by observing that the private savings flows recorded in table 2.1 are not easy to break out into household and corporate components. In practice, the two blend together. Throughout the developing world, productive enterprises are closely held—company-*cum*-bank "groups" steer industrial activity under every flag.[24] These multifirm conglomerates usually invest and produce in diverse commodity lines. They may draw savings from sources beyond retained earnings, often through associated banks or relationships within particular ethnic or religious communities.

Insofar as such ownership structures are congenial to low- and middle-income capitalism, they may be expected to appear in postsocialist settings. Indeed, this may already be happening under reform in Vietnam (Ljunggren 1991). If capitalist control of enterprise really sets in, it will probably involve close holding of companies by small, homogeneous sets of people, kinship or confessionally based. They will maneuver within whatever formal privatization mechanisms are put into place. Especially in Eastern Europe, as ancient animosities suppressed under socialism for forty years are beginning to reemerge, the tendency toward formation of community-anchored economic "groups" is bound to be an issue of social and political concern.

A second question regarding privatization is how exactly it is to be financed. Fanelli, Frenkel, and Rozenwurcel (1990) observe that local private sectors can pay for acquisitions of public firms in just four ways:

1. An increase in private saving;
2. A fall in private investment;
3. A decrease in private sector flow demand for financial assets; and
4. An increase in private sector flow demand for credit.

Alternative (1) could be helpful for growth if accompanied by a jump in investment. The public sector would probably have to be the motor, taking into account the crowding-in effects discussed in connection with table 2.1. In other words, privatizing governments should reinvest the proceeds instead of cutting the current fiscal deficit. This observation becomes double relevant if the private sector reduces its own capital formation to take over public firms.

Alternative (3) is more likely than (4), especially in postsocialist economies with primitive financial markets. But then the government will find it difficult to place its own liabilities, provoking it to emit money or bear higher interest burdens or both. There will be strong pressures to use the proceeds of privatization just to cover the current PSBR with no spillover to capital formation.

Finally, if public firms are sold to foreigners, is their direct foreign investment (or DFI) "additional" to what would have arrived, in any case? What about remittance obligations in the future? It *is* true that TNCs that are doing more than simple sourcing do not readily leave a country once they have entered and built up sunk capital, and that they can serve as vehicles for technology acquisition. But can the same be said of debt-swapping banks? Even in terms of current financial flows, privatization need not produce great benefits.[25]

Apart from privatization per se, there is also a question of what forms of financial markets should be nurtured, while avoiding the fragility risks described earlier. How to attain productive as opposed to mere allocative efficiency is again a crucial issue.

UNCTAD (1991) points out that two broad forms of organization present themselves. One amounts to a financially sophisticated version of company "groups." Since the last century, banks in Germany and Scandinavia have been closely associated with productive firms, owning stock and holding seats on boards of directors. With insider knowledge and their own incomes in mind, bankers can impose discipline on managers while providing credit (often rolling over short-term loans) cheaply. Similar market structures have also emerged in Japan. Insider speculation along Chilean lines is a risk with this form of market organization, but it can be avoided with adequate regulation and a financial ideology of prudence.

In an alternative Anglo-American model, firms pay for investment by borrowing from banks (or, more recently, by entering the money market), and then refinance short-term debt from internal saving and by issuing long-term liabilities in the capital market. One implication is that the final cost of funds tends to be higher in the United States, as German and Japanese shareholder banks can internalize information flows and exploit scale economies in credit provision. The American cost disadvantage widened in the 1980s as financial deregulation removed nominal anchors on interest rates. A broad, liberalized capital market may help equalize returns to different sorts of holdings, but it can also be productively inefficient, creating high costs of finance and short-ening economic horizons.

The implication is that postsocialist economies might consider German bank-type institutions to provide long-term finance, instead of trying to under-write capital markets. Indeed, credit provision by the state—either directly or through development banks—has functioned successfully on all three poor continents.

Adopting the development bank institution with due care to avoid rent seeking and inflationary finance for the benefit of chronically derelict parasta-tals is at least as appealing an option as the high interest rates, stagflation, deregulation, and financial crashes that orthodox financial reforms have pro-vided. Because development banks can tap public savings flows (especially after fiscal restructuring), they fit naturally with the public/private patterns of saving and capital formation set out in table 2.1.

For the reasons just presented, privatization and financial restructuring cannot be taken casually. To the contrary, private firms will have to be care-fully nurtured from the bottom up in environments such as Russia's, which will not be very friendly. From the top down, there are obvious risks from buccaneers and speculators along Chilean lines, but if money is to be made it will flow into the hands of flesh-and-blood people and profit-taking busi-nesses, not the abstract "agencies" operating somewhere between big pri-vatized firms and small shareholders that much of the literature propounds.[26]

Because buyers will be hard to find (recall figure 2.4), privatization of big firms is bound to be a time-consuming, messy process. Despite his nos-talgia for a von Mises/von Hayek form of capitalism—which scarcely existed outside of those authors' imaginations—Kornai (1990) is right on target in recognizing this fact.[27] Once again, the fundamental issue is how the means of collaboration among the state, emergent conglomerate groups or capitalist-minded managers of public enterprises, and farm and labor organizations will be built up. Developing-country models are diverse, but many are effective. Face-to-face discussion between postsocialist authorities and the people who designed and run these schemes, not mediated by organizations like the World Bank, would make practical sense. The scholarly studies cited here can also provide guidance along these lines.

For all that happens in industry, entrepreneurship may well sprout first in smaller-scale operations in services and agriculture. Unfortunately, shrewdly dealing grain merchants and storekeepers are likely to be swamped by super-markets and eighteen-wheeler trucks in Eastern Europe (after the state up-grades the highways), but this area of capitalist learning will be open in the European part of the Commonwealth and Asia.

Farms, then, may have to provide the seedbed for capitalist mentalities. Contrary to the general bias expressed here for gradualism, all the "roads" toward commercial agriculture that Lenin (1964) distrusted should be opened as fast as they can be. "Farmers" or (better) "peasants" rather than "Junkers" ought to dominate the outcome, but even some of the latter may be essential in an Eastern Europe where only large, efficient agrobusinesspeople will have a ghost of a chance of selling their products over the barriers created by the European Community's Common Agricultural Policy.

Market management issues already raised figure strongly in agriculture (Rao and Caballero 1990). As with any commodity market with low demand and supply elasticities and long investment and production lags, the state will have a stabilization and regulation role cut out for it:

1. Land and other inputs have to be made available to new agriculturalists. Depending on local circumstances, privatization via reform of state or collective farm lands in favor of people (not necessarily the descendents of ancient owners) who will actually cultivate them may make sense. Another option is to pursue land-grant schemes as used in the nineteenth-century United States, if speculators can be controlled.

2. Progressive income redistribution may help support demand (and thereby farm prices) as labor productivity and yields rise; at the same time foreign vents for surplus products have to be aggressively pursued à la Malaysia and Chile.

3. Creating and disseminating new agricultural technology lies traditionally within the province of the state, but supply enterprises can also be encouraged to act in these areas. Crowding-in effects of public investment (e.g., irrigation projects) on private farmers' own capital formation are likely to be strong.

4. Price incentives matter in agriculture, but largely by affecting resource allocation among different crops and input packages. Overall land and labor productivity increases typically require capital formation, new technologies, and nonprice incentives such as access to valued consumer goods and improved rural quality of life. Private markets alone cannot be relied on to provide these stimuli—even rural capitalists need public help.

Politics and Society

Issues of short-term credibility and commitment arise with regard to all aspects of postsocialist reform; at the same time, it has to lay the base for sustained growth under the exotic institutions of mixed capitalism. In closing, we take up these challenges in turn.

The main message from the foregoing discussion is that economic transition—if it does occur—will be a lurching, unpredictable process. A whole zoo of potentially destabilizing or stagnationist macro "effects" combined with a necessarily unbalanced accumulation process will make any detailed projections about economic developments virtually meaningless. Applying common sense to policy design is immensely difficult under such circumstances; selling economic snake oil (with a fashionably liberal taste) becomes a correspondingly profitable occupation.

In an interesting political extrapolation of Latin American reform experience to Eastern Europe, Przeworski (1991) assumes that economists more or less know what they are talking about when they quantify tradeoffs between short-term output losses versus future welfare gains, likely distributional changes from alternative policies, and so on. He argues that initially democratic systems may indeed opt for shock treatments, with the citizenry likely to press for short-term amelioration as time goes on.

The trouble with this view is that it leaves out policy Bermuda triangles and chaotic or bifurcating trajectories of growth. As emphasized repeatedly in this chapter, transition has been a protracted and poorly understood process in the developing world, and will be no more transparent under postsocialism. This lack of clarity coupled with the fact that sensible policy will often run counter to the liberal recommendations proffered by Western consultants and institutions will put a severe strain on the political process.

One recalls how Western professors (now senior colleagues of the current crop of advisors) went out to Japan and Korea during their rapid growth spurts, telling policymakers that they could expand ever so much faster if they would just liberalize their systems. They were politely received—and their suggestions ignored. Will the leadership in possibly stagnating postsocialist systems have the courage to follow similar nonliberal convictions?

Latter-day mainstream/neoclassical economic missionaries will probably be no more prescient than their predecessors in East Asia. Their presence will become more and more embarrassing as their repeatedly upbeat projections continue to fail. Chile's Pinochet and Mexico's famously authoritarian Institutionalized Revolutionary Party were able to maintain social control during economic transitions whose duration and severity were systematically understated for years. The same may not be true of new democracies in the postsocialist world.

Such doubts carry over to institutional development in the long run: We come full circle to Polanyi's (1944) view of the nineteenth century, an historical experience that postsocialist political leaders seem hellbent to repeat. Contrary to liberal mythology, Polanyi argued that there was a "double movement" toward creation of markets for commodities, labor, land, and money, combined in natural social course with their regulation:

"There was nothing natural about *laissez-faire;* free markets could never have come into being by allowing things to take their course, . . . *laissez-faire* was enforced by the state." But soon after, the "legislative spearhead of the countermovement against a self-regulating market as it developed in the half century following 1860 turned out to be spontaneous, undirected by opinion, and actuated by a purely pragmatic spirit."

The first wave of development economists wrote in Polanyi's time, and in effect amplified the state's required role: beyond creating and then regulating markets to keep them functioning as well as for social ends, it had to push the private sector into acquisition of physical capital and modern techniques, or purchase and manage them on its own. Gerschenkron's (1962) "relative backwardness" was the compelling metaphor: its relevance has been reflected by a proactive public role in all development "success" cases since the Second World War.

The challenge faced by postsocialist societies now is to combine required public interventions in the market with the renewal of civil liberties with stable political systems—under uncertainty about the future in Keynes's sense of a fundamental human inability to model and put probability distributions or unprecedented future events. The von Hayek/von Mises premise of the economic advice that they are currently receiving—that fully liberalized markets are a prerequisite for political freedom—is both untrue and unhelpful toward this end.

Generation, regulation, and control of markets is not some sort of plot on the part of socialists, monopolists, farmers, and trade unions intent on destroying a perfectly self-regulating liberal system; it just turns out to be necessary to achieve social goals (from the prohibition of child labor, through bringing national firms up to best-practice technology, to staving off environmental catastrophe in the decades to come) when the capitalist system, with all its flexibility and ability to absorb technical change, is used to produce and distribute most of a nation's goods. Tensions arise, sometimes overwhelmingly as in the 1930s and 1940s, as a consequence of the "double movement," but in nations in the process of modern economic growth, they are impossible to avoid completely.

Gradual, spreading appreciation of how to structure public economic intervention in a state of imperfect knowledge about its effects but in full collaboration with financial institutions, national and foreign capital, and the popular classes in the wake of central planning will be the key to postsocialist recovery. Until newly formed governments learn to play their essential role in creating and steering markets and facilitating productive efficiency, economic stagnation will be inevitable. The longer the state is economically inactive, the greater is the risk of decades more of political degradation.

50   Lance Taylor

Notes

Research assistance from Rabindram Abraham and Heather White, help from G. S. Guha and Helen Shapiro, and support from the World Institute for Development Economics Research are gratefully acknowledged.

1. The list comes from the chapter headings in the sensible mainstream pamphlet by Blanchard et al. (1991).
2. According to the usual criteria, postsocialist economies *are* developing or semi-industrialized, albeit with unusual initial conditions. Their per capita GDP ranges roughly from $200 (Laos, Vietnam) to $3,000 (Eastern Europe); they all have a high degree of state control, a mixture of antiquated and brand new technologies, unsophisticated financial systems, lack of an entrepreneurial tradition, and so on.
3. Forced saving may have especially weak effects on demand in postsocialist systems where the boundary between enterprise wage and surplus funds is vague. The base for the inflation tax may rapidly erode as people flee from local currencies with minimal credibility. These considerations suggest that inflations and income and wealth redistributions large even by developing-country standards may be needed to curb excess aggregate demand, especially during rapid transitions away from administered allocation systems.
4. There can also be reductions in consumption if many goods simply are not available; lower spending may be involuntary under explicit rationing or perhaps by choice. Blanchard et al. (1991) call this sort of noninflationary abstinence "forced saving," in an unconventional usage of the term. It may presage financial fragility, as discussed below.
5. For a convincing institutional argument, see Zhukov and Vorobyov (1991). Their analysis underlies figure 2.1 and other ideas in this chapter.
6. Overshooting or "overkill" of output adjustment is a familiar feature of recessions induced by price increases or policies shifting the demand curve to the left in developing economies. It was certainly present in the radical Polish program of 1990—the first such experiment by a nation-state in the postsocialist world.
7. Over the past decade or two, Indian industrial planners have made a virtue of necessity by developing effective multitiered pricing systems for their nationalized industrial firms and even in agriculture (Alagh 1991). Also, transitional regimes may prove less trying in more agricultural economies. The switch from state- to privately held property has gone fairly smoothly—with a few fortunes no doubt being created along the way—in Vietnam (Ljung-gren 1991). Haste can also make waste—Murrell (1991a) aptly compares East Germany's "largest economic disaster in Europe in the post-war period" after a global shock to the far more gradual and successful transition in China.
8. Between 1979 and 1990, the Soviet money supply (M1) rose by 170% while real GNP only increased 40%.
9. The widely publicized Bolivian program of 1985 was orthodox, combining fiscal and monetary austerity with massive wage cuts for government workers and dismemberment of the tin miners' union (Pastor 1991). These indelicacies were perhaps politically inevitable, but relied on the fact that the economy had not arrived at sophisticated forms of indexation. Inflation stabilization was followed by overvaluation and export stagnation when the nominal exchange rate was frozen as an anti-inflationary move as in Argentina and Chile in the late 1970s. Since 1985, recorded Bolivian output growth per capita has been essentially zero, and would probably have been negative if coca production had not provided rural income support.
10. This "effect" has a long intellectual history (Taylor 1991), but Latins lately ascribe it to an influential Ph.D. thesis by Cavallo (1977). He later found it politic to discard the possibility

of inflation due to interest rate cost-push as he rose via the central bank toward his present position of finance minister in Argentina.

11. Both stories have developing-country precedents. An orthodox inflation stabilization attempt in Argentina in the late 1970s led to capital inflow, interest rate reductions, and an output boom with renewed inflation. The nominal exchange rate had been frozen as part of the stabilization package and overvaluation ensued. An export collapse and massive capital flight followed; the economy is still struggling to recover from them (Frenkel 1983; Taylor 1991). The importance of the curb market in financing working capital in South Korea in the 1970s was emphasized in econometrics by van Wijnbergen (1983). Informal financial structures have been equally important elsewhere.

12. The underlying model comes from Zhukov and Vorobyov (1991) after van Wijnbergen (1983) and Taylor (1983). If q stands for potential output, i for the interest rate in informal credit markets, $\hat{P}$ for the inflation rate, M^d for money demand and M^s for money supply, it can be written in three equations. The first is an aggregate supply function, $q = f(i, \hat{P}, M^s)$, with the first two partial derivatives negative. The derivative $\partial f / \partial M^s$ will be positive, as supply responds directly to money creation under credit rationing. The second equation is for inflation, $\hat{P} = g(q, i)$ with $\partial g / \partial i > 0$ from the Cavallo effect. The partial $\partial g / \partial q$ can take either sign—positive if higher output pushes up inflation via Phillips curve linkages and negative if lower production leads to excess commodity demand. The third equation is a demand-supply balance for money, $M^d(q, i, \hat{P}) - M^s(\hat{P}) = 0$, where money demand rises with q and declines with i, while the overall effect of $\hat{P}$ can go either way for reasons discussed in the text. Figure 2.3 follows as an illustration of potential forms of adjustment at initial full capacity use, after substituting the first equation into the other two.

13. The financial roles of private sector "groups" and associated banks in developing economies are discussed later. Elsewhere during the early 1980s, booms and crashes involved real estate and shares of firms incorporated "elsewhere in the Gulf" in Kuwait, and informal financial activities outside an oligopolistic banking system in Turkey.

14. Alternatively, while praising its invisible analog, a putative regulator may have his or her own hand in the till. Losses in Polish check-kiting and official debt buyback swindles may total well over $1 billion (*Washington Post*, January 2, 1992). One can confidently expect similar episodes elsewhere under postsocialism.

15. The numbers were put together in connection with country studies on the political economy of reform in a project sponsored by the World Institute for Development Economics Research (WIDER). They are published as Taylor (1993).

16. Not to mention the United States, which aggressively pursued the large economy industrialization strategy discussed in the next section. The United States was highly protectionist until after World War II, as well as generous to targeted sectors via devices such as the Land Grant Act, incredible subsidies to the Western railroads, and more recently defense contracts along with import quotas on textiles, cars, and other lower technology goods.

17. Chang (1990) observes that the conglomerate nature of the *chaebol* led to a "bundling of issues" that eased bargaining among themselves and with the state. Their size and ability to move into any line of business generated competitive pressures and held down start-up costs. High profitability from their rapid productivity growth (*not* fully offset by real wage growth in Korea) supplemented the ample subsidies they received.

18. Besides being favored by its raw material endowments, Malaysia has aggressively pursued manufacturing assembly operations via "free trade zones" and "licensed manufacturing warehouses." Depending on the skill level of the labor force, transport linkages, and local political conditions, this option is open under postsocialism: Slovenia would outcompete Bulgaria in assembly, and ultimately Laos could (sub-) subcontract for Thailand or export zones in Vietnam could give Malaysia a run for its footloose money. The real questions for

national policy are whether assembly plants generate local intermediate and capital goods linkages, promote local technical and management skills, and so on. In many instances, such benefits do not materialize. Dominican workers for years have used high technology to make ready-to-wear garments for the U.S. market and remain abysmally poor; Mexico's state-of-the-art auto plants are managed directly from Detroit, and control of garment production runs a grave risk of being denationalized as well (Hanson 1991).

19. Chile's trade shares have risen rapidly, buoyed by favorable copper prices and expansion of fishery, fruit, and forestry exports from $191 million to $2,134 million between 1972 and 1988. Under distinct political regimes, the national development corporation, or CORFO, created the base for the noncopper export push by afforestation programs and promotion of pulp and paper production; solving problems of transport, cold storage, quality control, and marketing for fruits; and setting up a mixed public/private fishmeal industry, rationalizing production from several preexisting plants. There were also subsidies for pine plantations, soft credits for fruit growers, significant devaluation (real wage reduction in other language), elimination of export red tape, relaxation of labor legislation, ownership guarantees, etc. With these initiatives designed to support private sector activity, Chile's "miracle" was very much a state/bourgeoisie joint affair (ECLAC 1990). Since 1973, however, workers have borne most adjustment costs.

20. Turkey entered early into state-led development under Ataturk in 1931. Waves of industrialization followed on ten-year cycles, through the "easy" to "difficult" stages of import substitution. Inefficiency as measured by the standard methods ran rampant; indeed, Turkey was the launching pad for Krueger's (1974) early generalizations about economically destructive rent seeking. Then in 1980, following a relatively mild but regressive IMF-style stabilization with ample capital inflows, Turkey launched into state-sponsored export growth in *il*liberal fashion. Boratav (1988) shows that the export miracle rested upon the preexisting industrial base, regressive redistribution and other policies leading to contraction of domestic demand for manufactures, export subsidies and import quota/levy manipulations, and rapid growth in demand for products like cement and steel on the part of culturally compatible buyers in the region (the Gulf and the Iran-Iraq War). Had any of these factors been missing, the boom could well not have happened.

21. The case for phased restructuring becomes stronger when it is recognized that much of the capital stock in postsocialist economies is nearly obsolete. Zhukov and Vorobyov (1991) present evidence for the former Soviet Union.

22. If Mexican growth does take off in the wake of a free trade agreement with the United States, it will do so in part because bilateral dispute-resolution procedures will be put into place, for example, for the now-integrated automobile sector. Formalized free trade in the U.S.-Mexican case boils down to blessing a fait accompli that as yet is far from consummated between postsocialist economies and the rest of the world.

23. Hong Kong—the most widely cited opposing case—benefited from the migration of the Shanghai textile industry (the fruit of import-substituting industrialization), and its government is active in land-use policy and other areas. In any case, Hong Kong and (highly interventionist) Singapore exemplify an ancient form of city-state prosperity that is simply not available to most poor economies in the world.

24. Leff (1979) gives the classic description. The ubiquitous nature of "groups" has not been widely discussed in the development economics literature, possibly because most workers in the field take their existence for granted.

25. In the developing world, Mexico's bid via privatization and opening to trade for capital repatriation and American or Japanese DFI to turn the country into a low-wage export platform illustrates the hopes and dangers. If the gamble fails, capital will not flow in, interest rates will be high, and the economy will relapse into the financial fragility and

stagnation that characterized it during the 1980s. If opening and privatization succeed, Mexico's geographical position almost dooms it to become a *gran* Puerto Rico—with expatriate control of much of its productive capacity but without the island's access to the flimsy American social safety net. The Mexican case is extreme, but it does underline the riskiness of the privatization option.

26. That is, the "privatization agencies" (Blanchard et al. 1991) and "mutual funds" (Sachs 1991) that Western academic consultants propose for Eastern Europe are likely to be beside the point. Creation of stock markets—another widely discussed ploy—will be wholly tangential to the privatization process. For the most part in developing economies, bourses are fancy playgrounds where ruling generals and politicians juggle the prices of public enterprise shares. As noted in the text, equity of productive private firms in middle-income economies (even if they are incorporated) tends to be very closely held.

27. In the German test case, in over a year the Treuhand privatization agency succeeded in transferring one-half of 20,000 small service outlets (bars, shops, etc.) but only 100 of a total of 8,000 large firms (*Financial Times,* April 9, 1991). Despite massive publicity hype, the Mexican privatization program in the first two years of the Salinas administration (1989–90) sold off large firms to the tune of about $4 billion—one % of the value of the nation's fixed capital stock.

References

Alagh, Yoginder K. 1991. *Indian Development Planning and Policy.* New Delhi: Vikas.

Amsden, Alice. 1989. *Asia's Next Giant: South Korea and Late Industrialization.* New York: Oxford University Press.

Blanchard, Olivier, Rudiger Dornbusch, Paul Krugman, Richard Layard, and Lawrence Summers. 1991. *Reforming Eastern Europe.* Cambridge, MA: MIT Press.

Boratav, Korkut. 1988. "Turkey." Helsinki: WIDER Stabilization and Adjustment Policies and Programmes Country Study No. 5.

Calvo, Guillermo, and Fabrizio Coricelli. 1992. "Stagflationary Effects of Stabilization Programs in Reforming Socialist Countries: Enterprise-Side and Household-Side Factors." *World Bank Economic Review* 6: 71–90.

Cavallo, Domingo. 1977. *Stagflationary Effects of Monetarist Stabilization Policies.* Cambridge, MA: Department of Economics, Harvard University (unpublished Ph.D. dissertation).

Chang, Ha-Joon. 1990. "Interpreting the Korean Experience—Heaven or Hell?" Cambridge: Faculty of Economics and Politics Research Paper No. 42.

Dutt, Amitava Krishna, and Bill Gibson. 1990. "Accumulation Patterns in a Mixed Economy: A Model for Eastern Europe." Notre Dame, IN: Department of Economics, University of Notre Dame.

ECLAC (Economic Commission for Latin America and the Caribbean). 1990. *Changing Production Patterns with Social Equity.* Santiago: United Nations.

Edwards, Sebastian. 1990. "Stabilization and Liberalization Policies in Eastern Europe: Lessons from Latin America." Los Angeles: Department of Economics, UCLA.

Fanelli, Jose Maria, Roberto Frenkel, and Guillermo Rozenwurcel. 1990. "Growth and Structural Reform in Latin America: Where We Stand." Buenos Aires: CEDES.

Fischer, Stanley, and Alan Gelb. 1991. "The Process of Socialist Economic Transformation." *Journal of Economic Perspectives* 5 (no. 4): 91–106. Cambridge, MA: Working Paper No. 567. Department of Economics, MIT.

Frenkel, Roberto. 1983. "Mercado Financiero, Expectativas Cambiarias, y Movimientos de Capital." *El Trimestre Economico* 50: 2041–2076.

Gerschenkron, Alexander. 1962. *Economic Backwardness in Historical Perspective.* Cambridge, MA: Harvard University Press.

Hanson, Gordon H. 1991. "U.S.-Mexico Free Trade and the Mexican Garment Industry." Cambridge, MA: Department of Economics, Massachusetts Institute of Technology.

Heckscher, Eli F. 1918. *Svenska Produktionsproblem.* Stockholm: Bonniers.

Hirschman, Albert O. 1958. *The Strategy of Economic Development.* New Haven, CT: Yale University Press.

Hirschman, Albert O. 1970. *Exit, Voice, and Loyalty: Responses to Decline in Firms, Organizations, and States.* Cambridge, MA: Harvard University Press.

Hjalmarsson, Lennart. 1991. "The Scandinavian Model of Industrial Policy." In Magnus Blomström and Patricio Meller, eds., *Diverging Paths: Comparing a Century of Scandinavian and Latin American Economic Development.* Washington, DC: Johns Hopkins University Press.

Kalecki, Michal. 1971. *Selected Essays on the Dynamics of the Capitalist Economy.* Cambridge: Cambridge University Press.

Katz, S. Stanley. 1991. "East Europe Should Learn from Asia." *Financial Times,* April 24.

Katzenstein, Peter. 1985. *Small States in World Markets: Industrial Policy in Europe.* Ithaca, NY: Cornell University Press.

Kornai, Janos. 1981. *Growth, Shortage, and Efficiency: A Macrodynamic Model of the Socialist Economy.* Oxford: Basil Blackwell.

Kornai, Janos. 1990. *The Road to a Free Economy.* New York: W. W. Norton.

Kosonen, Katri. 1991. "Saving and Economic Growth in a Nordic Perspective." In Jukka Pekkarinen, Matti Pohjola, and Bob Rowthorn, eds., *Social Corporatism—A Superior Economic System?* Helsinki: WIDER.

Krueger, Anne O. 1974. "The Political Economy of the Rent-Seeking Society." *American Economic Review* 64: 291–303.

Kuznetsov, Yevgeny. 1991. "Transition or Development Strategy? Structuralist Considerations in Elaboration of the Russian Federation's Strategy of Market Transformation." Ithaca, NY: Peace Studies Program, Cornell University.

Leff, Nathaniel H. 1979. "'Monopoly Capitalism' and Public Policy in Developing Countries." *Kyklos* 32: 718–737.

Lenin, Vladimir I. 1964. *The Development of Capitalism in Russia.* Moscow: Progress Publishers.

Ljunggren, Borje. 1991. "Market Economies under Communist Regimes: Reform in Vietnam, Laos, and Cambodia beyond Socialist Renovation." Cambridge, MA: Harvard Institute for International Development.

Malinvaud, Edmond. 1977. *The Theory of Unemployment Reconsidered.* New York: Halstead Press.

Minsky, Hyman. 1986. *Stabilizing an Unstable Economy.* New Haven, CT: Yale University Press.

Murrell, Peter. 1991a. "Evolutionary and Radical Approaches to Economic Reform." Washington, DC: Woodrow Wilson International Center for Scholars.

Murrell, Peter. 1991b. "Can Neoclassical Economics Underpin the Reform of Centrally Planned Economies?" *Journal of Economic Perspectives* 5 (no. 4): 59–76.

Nuti, Domenico Mario. 1991. "Comment: Sequencing and Credibility of Economic Reform." In Anthony B. Atkinson and Renato Brunette, eds., *Economics for the New Europe.* London: Macmillan.

Pastor, Manuel Jr. 1991. "Bolivia: Hyperinflation, Stabilization, and Beyond." *Journal of Development Studies* 27: 211–237.

Pekkarinen, Jukka, Matti Pohjola, and Bob Rowthorn, eds. 1991. *Social Corporatism—A Superior Economic System?* Helsinki: WIDER.

Polanyi, Karl. 1944 (1957). *The Great Transformation: The Political and Economic Origins of Our Time.* New York: Rinehart (1957 reprint, Boston: Beacon Press).

Przeworski, Adam. 1991. *Democracy and the Market.* Cambridge: Cambridge University Press.

Rao, J. Mohan, and Jose Maria Caballero. 1990. "Agricultural Performance and Development Strategy: Retrospect and Prospect." *World Development* 19: 899–913.

Rodrik, Dani. 1992. "Closing the Productivity Gap: Does Trade Liberalization Really Help?" In G. K. Helleiner, ed., *Trade Policy, Liberalization, and Development.* Oxford: Clarendon Press.

Sachs, Jeffrey D. 1991. "Accelerating Privatization in Eastern Europe." Paper presented to the World Bank Annual Conference on Development Economics.

Shapiro, Helen, and Lance Taylor. 1990. "The State and Industrial Strategy." *World Development* 18: 861–878.

Streeten, Paul. 1959. "Unbalanced Growth." *Oxford Economic Papers* 11: 167–190.

Syrquin, Moshe, and Hollis B. Chenery. 1989. "Patterns of Development: 1950 to 1983." Washington, DC: World Bank Discussion Paper No. 41.

Taylor, Lance. 1983. *Structuralist Macroeconomics.* New York: Basic Books.

Taylor, Lance. 1988. *Varieties of Stabilization Experience.* Oxford: Clarendon Press.

Taylor, Lance. 1991. *Income Distribution, Inflation, and Growth.* Cambridge, MA: MIT Press.

Taylor, Lance, ed. 1993. *The Rocky Road to Reform.* Cambridge, MA: MIT Press.

Tirole, Jean. 1991. "Privatization in Eastern Europe: Incentives and the Economics of Transition." Cambridge, MA: Department of Economics, MIT.

UNCTAD (United Nations Conference on Trade and Development). 1991. *Trade and Development Report 1991.* New York: United Nations.

van Wijnbergen, Sweder. 1983. "Credit Policy, Inflation, and Growth in a Financially Repressed Economy." *Journal of Development Economics* 13: 45–65.

World Bank. 1991. *World Development Report.* New York: Oxford University Press.

Zhukov, Stanislav V., and Alexander Yu. Vorobyov. 1991. "Reforming the Soviet Union: Lessons from Structural Experience." Moscow: Institute of World Economy and International Relations, Soviet Academy of Sciences.

CHAPTER 3

The Process of Adjustment and Economic Reform: Real and Apparent Differences between East and West

Manuel Guitián

Nothing so needs reforming as other people's habits.

Mark Twain

Some years ago, few if any observers would have predicted the historic events under way in Central and Eastern Europe as well as in the former Soviet Union, either in scope or in speed. It is clear that those events are changing the shape of the Old Continent-and of the world at large, for that matter. The period in which we live offers a unique opportunity to build an orderly international system of a truly universal character, free of the tensions that influenced so strongly the order that was established and the environment that prevailed after World War II.

The dimensions of the tasks ahead for the whole region are daunting and go well beyond the realm of economics; but even within the limitations of the economic domain, the challenges that confront the Central and Eastern European nations and the former Soviet republics—as well as the major countries in the world economy, if they are to help the reforming countries along— are unprecedented. Meeting the challenges and completing the tasks will require not only persistence of intent and firmness of purpose in the economies in Eastern Europe, but also vision in the rest of the world to prevent the numerous risks that lie ahead from obscuring the immeasurable returns that can be derived from a truly harmonious international environment.

On the economic front, these countries have decided to move their systems of economic organization from central planning toward market-based regimes.[1] This endeavor, at first perceived with a good deal of optimism, is by now increasingly seen as an arduous process, fraught with risks and calling for a large dose of determination and persistence in the reforming societies. As for the rest of Europe and the world at large, the fundamental aim clearly must be to help the reforms along actively, so that these economies can be integrated into the world economic system with a minimum of disruption.

Paradoxical in this context is the diversity of trends under way in Europe. In Western (and Southern) Europe, the economics of integration are proceeding ahead of the politics of integration; indeed, politics may prove the thorniest obstacle to economics. In Eastern (and Central) Europe (including the former USSR), in contrast, the politics of reform are moving faster than the economics of reform; in fact, the divergence between the two may well turn out to be the toughest hurdle to overcome in the reforming economies.

Desirable though the aims of reform and integration are, there can hardly be any doubt of their complexity. Indeed, a strong argument can be made that the transition to a market economy will prove harder that its opposite, the process of collectivization. As in most areas of human endeavor, it is easier to destroy than to build, and markets are no exception.[2] There is of course a good deal of accumulated knowledge about the starting and ending points of the journey-that is, the workings of centrally planned systems and the operation of market-based regimes. Unfortunately, the former is rapidly becoming obsolete (except from a historical perspective) and the latter has yet to become applicable. Little is known, however, about the transition between the two points, as illustrated by the frequent invocation of its similarity to the proverbial voyage on "uncharted waters."

Care should be taken, however, to avoid exaggerating the width of the knowledge gap. This is the main theme of this chapter, which will seek to identify and discuss the real and apparent differences between East and West in the specific context of the process of economic adjustment and reform.

General Setting

Interplay of Economic and Political Factors

Recent events in Central and Eastern Europe as well as in the former Soviet Union (with the emergence of the Commonwealth of Independent States) provide a good illustration of the interaction of political and economic factors over time.[3] A fundamental force behind the rapid political change and reform that have taken place in those regions must have been the accumulation of evidence of subpar economic performance under central planning, evidence that became clearer as advances in communications technology and growing world economic interdependence rendered the iron curtain increasingly porous. In turn, the rapid pace of political transformation has contributed to raising expectations and creating demands for economic reform at commensurate speed. Encouraging though these events are, sight should not be lost of the difficulties likely to arise in fulfilling the expectations of a rapid completion of economic reform.

Common Themes

A number of common themes can be gleaned from the experience of the various countries in the area. The first and most dramatic message is the widespread recognition that central planning has not worked well as a principle for efficient economic organization. Although there have been sporadic glimpses of this acknowledgment in individual countries at different times, it is only at present that there is general acceptance of the inadequacy of central planning, as demonstrated by the preference revealed by the concrete actions taken to dismantle it.

In contrast with most past reform efforts, there is also broad recognition that attempts made to improve the central planning system without discarding the fundamental tenets of a command economy will fail. There is an essential difference between current events in Central and Eastern Europe and in the CIS republics on the one side, and reform attempts undertaken earlier by individual countries on the other. In general, early attempts were based on the premise that reform within the central planning regime was feasible and would work. Accordingly, partial efforts were made to improve elements of central planning without seeking to change the regime as a whole; those efforts included, for example, actions to improve the operations of the state enterprises, or to provide for a measure of decentralization in decisionmaking, or to allow a somewhat larger role for private activities.[4] At present, in contrast, the aim no longer entails an improvement of selected parts within the whole centrally planned system. The objective instead is a wholesale change in regime, a radical reform in the principles of economic organization. Another critical aspect of the evolving situation is that such a comprehensive economic transformation will likely take time and call for persistence in the reform effort.

Elements of an Effective Strategy

The interaction of the rhythm of political evolution with the likely pace of economic reform, given the intent of bringing about a complete transformation of economic regime, underscores some of the most difficult challenges faced by these reforming countries. The first factor fuels expectations of a speedy reform; the second factor raises the specter of the impossibility of fulfilling those expectations.

The solution of this potential conflict created by expectations overrunning reality will require a large measure of transparency in the process of reform. A few basic principles can help enhance clarity of both policy actions and policy results, and as such they may contribute to building the cohesion and resilience in the social and political fabric required for radical transformation to be carried through effectively.

Basic Principles

It is no longer a novelty to say that the transition from a command economy regime to a market-based system will not only be protracted, but will also be complex. And there are neither categorical answers nor unambiguous blueprints to guide the process of reform. But in the abstract an argument can be made that a few strategic principles can help reform, at least in the macroeconomic policy sphere. These principles are: simplicity, reliance on policy rules, and provision of unequivocal signals that irrevocable changes in economic policy are under way, so that economic agents can adapt their expectations once and for all.

Simplicity in the design of a policy strategy will ease not only its implementation but also its acceptance. Reliance on policy rules will help contain inertia and reflexive reactions in the economy based on past behavior (a strategy providing significant scope for policy discretion, in contrast, would tend to perpetuate such inertia, adding to the obstacles to change). A strong announcement effect for the introduction of the new policies will be required to elicit and encourage the attitudinal changes without which no reform can succeed.

Typical among the features of centrally planned economies are the prevalence of global and sectoral shortages as well as relative price distortions. These two characteristics are behind certain well-known and necessary ingredients of a strategy of transition toward the market: the introduction of domestic financial discipline (to eliminate global shortages or excess demand), and the implementation of domestic price liberalization together with the opening of the economy (to ease sectoral shortages, introduce a rational relative price structure, and let competitive forces operate). But for these policy initiatives to yield results, action must have been undertaken from the outset to establish the rules of the game to steer economic behavior in the new environment.[5] Such rules are necessary for the operation of a market economy, and they include: the establishment of clear ownership and property rights; the dismembering of the state's role in the economy; and the consequent buildup of legal, fiscal, and social security institutions that provide the framework for a constructive and sustained interaction of the government with the private economy. The list of actions required for the transition is long, and it has given rise to issues and questions concerning the pace and sequence of reform.

Issues of Pace and Sequence of Reform

With respect to the pace of reform, views continue to differ about the relative merits of a fast ("shock") versus a slow ("gradual") approach. I think the balance of opinion and, most important, the revealed preference in the countries undertaking economic reforms has been for rapid action. Two different though not mutually exclusive reasons account for this preference. One is the conviction that speed in policy implementation will likely increase the effectiveness of the reform process. Another is the recognition that fast action is often made inevitable by lack of resources; on this reasoning, speed of implementation is more a matter of necessity than of choice. I also believe that the preferable course of action is rapid policy decision and implementation, and this applies particularly to those areas in which measures are likely to take a long time to yield results. I would temper this view by acknowledging that the challenge confronting the policymaker will be to select a path fast enough to provide clear signals, thus eliciting supporting responses in the economy, but not so abrupt as to prove counterproductive or unfeasible.

Much has been written on the subject of the appropriate sequence of reform. Views also differ widely on this issue, but perhaps because of my own inclination, I perceive the kernel of an agreement in the body of opinion. In the abstract, coherent arguments can be made about the desirability of staggering or phasing reform measures over time, if only because there is a limit to how much can be done at once. But a strong case can also be made for a comprehensive approach to reform, that is, for simultaneous rather than sequential action.[6] It is true that only so much can be done at the same time, but it is no less true that partial actions rarely add up to a complete result.[7] Simultaneous action may foster synergy, not only by averting the potentially adverse effects of isolated or partial measures, but also by contributing to steering expectations in favor of the reform process. Here again, this view must be tempered by acknowledging the inherent difficulty in reform implementation. The list of actions required for effective reform is typically nothing less than staggering: fiscal discipline, monetary stabilization, price liberalization, opening to international trade and capital flows, enterprise sector restructuring, privatization, etc. Each step seems necessary, and yet no single item nor any subset of those actions appears sufficient as conditions for effective reform. This leaves the policymaker with the difficult choice of where, if anywhere, to draw the line.

Stabilization, Adjustment, and Growth

It may be possible to clarify the subject of the pace and sequence of reform by distinguishing among three stages in policy decisionmaking: decisions, actions, and results. The time profiles of these three categories do not coincide, yet they represent nevertheless conceptually separable phases in what is essentially a continuous process.[8]

Speed and simultaneity apply particularly to the policy decisions that need to be taken in a variety of areas: economic, institutional, legal, and social. Some of those decisions call for translation into immediate policy actions, while others require follow-up in the form of measures to be undertaken later in the process. Thus, although policy decisions are best taken together at the outset of the reform effort, their conversion into concrete policy actions need not be simultaneous and may in effect have to be staggered over time. The speed and timing of policy results are most difficult to predict. Some results can be obtained very rapidly indeed, while others often prove protracted. The reality that policy actions take time to yield results is not unique to the centrally planned economies in transition, but applies to all sorts of economies. Experience on this front indicates that the attainment of results, in both timing and degree, depends critically on the appropriateness—also with respect to timing and scope—of the required policy actions. Indeed, given the interaction between expectations in the economy and the timeliness and credibility of policies, it can be argued that opportune, determined, and credible policy actions will elicit synergetic reactions, thereby hastening the attainment of results.

Issues of Stabilization and Adjustment

It was pointed out earlier that one of the characteristic features of centrally planned economies was the existence of shortages and relative price distortions. The elimination of chronic global shortages can be seen as one of the major aims of the macroeconomics of reform, a central aspect of which revolves around the introduction and maintenance of domestic financial discipline in the reforming economy. But for financial discipline to yield the desired results, it must be accompanied, inter alia, by the elimination of relative price distortions. Actions to establish an economically sound relative price structure are essential for the effectiveness of macroeconomic management. But they also provide the link with the microeconomics of reform, which by correcting relative price distortions contribute to allocating resources efficiently and thus easing sectoral shortages.

The establishment of domestic financial discipline will require the correction of global stock (accumulated) and flow (current) imbalances. These imbalances, which are the counterpart of past and present global shortages in the economy, have monetary and fiscal aspects, and therefore policy actions in both of these domains will be called for.

Stock Imbalances
A stock imbalance in centrally planned economies typically surfaces in the monetary sphere in the form of a liquidity overhang, that is, an excess supply of money or, more broadly, of bank liabilities. But there is another, less often

mentioned, stock imbalance that affects bank assets and is closely connected with accumulated public sector deficits. This is the amount of essentially unrecoverable assets in bank portfolios, which typically are claims on nonviable state enterprises.[9] The correction of these stock imbalances involves monetary and fiscal measures. In the monetary sphere, some of the liquidity overhang will be absorbed through price-level increases associated with the process of correction of relative prices. But its full elimination may require additional action, such as the implementation of a monetary reform or its equivalent.[10] In the fiscal domain, action will be required to strengthen the asset portfolio of banks. This will call for the generation of resources in the public sector to rehabilitate and capitalize the banks, and therefore will influence the design of fiscal policy.

Flow Imbalances
A flow imbalance is the reflection of current global shortages in the economy, and its elimination will also depend on fiscal and monetary action. From the standpoint of monetary management, the solution will entail keeping the rate of change in the stock of money in line with the evolution of the demand for money. As experience in market economies indicates, keeping the balance between the supply of and demand for money is no mean endeavor. This is an area in which the principles outlined in the previous section can help, particularly in the context of centrally planned economies, where estimates and forecasts of money demands are likely to be especially hazardous. The simplest rule for monetary management in these cases is that given by the adoption of a currency board principle. This principle provides scope for domestic monetary expansion only to the extent that it is purchased with foreign exchange. As such, it represents a clear rule and a sharp departure from the accommodating monetary management typical of a centrally planned economy; if held to, this principle can have a strong demonstration effect and consequent impact on expectations. Apart from its clarity and simplicity, the attractiveness of the currency board approach lies in the presumption that any domestic monetary expansion to which it gives rise is demand determined, as it can occur only on account of voluntary sales of foreign exchange.

Of course, less stringent monetary rules can be devised to permit monetary growth to reflect factors other than the accumulation of international reserves. It would be also possible to allow increases in the money stock to reflect purchases of domestic assets, or in other words, domestic credit expansion. The lesser stringency of such an alternative rule, however, will exact a price in terms of credibility. This is because the rule will exhibit less clarity with regard to the nature of the monetary expansion—that is, whether it is demand or supply determined—and less simplicity because, rather than a single source, it embodies two sources of monetary expansion.

From the standpoint of fiscal management, the typical (possibly minimum) aim will be the attainment of budget balance in the accounts of the government or the public sector at large. As pointed out earlier, however, in the presence of weak bank portfolios, fiscal management must encompass among its objectives the requirements of bank capitalization. This will call for the generation of budget surpluses on a scale at least sufficient to service the government paper issued to the banks in lieu of their unrecoverable assets.

The Question of Anchors

Domestic financial policy rules such as those just described typically call for underpinning through the establishment of nominal anchors, in particular, to help in the attainment and maintenance of price stability. An anchor that has been increasingly used has been the exchange rate. The exchange rate exhibits a specific advantage in the case of command economies. As noted earlier, these economies traditionally suffer from distorted relative prices, and an exchange rate anchor immediately translates the world relative price structure into domestic currency terms. Accordingly, the establishment of the exchange rate as an anchor rapidly helps ascertain the extent of prevailing domestic relative price distortions that will need to be corrected by price liberalization.

For the anchor and the price liberalization to be effective, however, not only will domestic financial discipline be required, but income (specifically wage) moderation will have to prevail, particularly when a process of inflation is already under way. Indeed in such circumstances, a wage anchor will most likely have to provide supplementary support to the exchange rate, at least in the initial period of reform. A wage anchor may also be necessary, even when inflation is not a particular problem, to prevent wage costs from constraining domestic output and reducing exports.[11]

Complexities in Policy Design and Implementation

A dilemma often arises when the exchange rate serves as an anchor to help bring about price stability in an inflationary setting. Domestic financial and wage discipline rarely arrest inflation immediately, and price increases are bound to continue (albeit, at declining rates) for some time in a setting where the nominal exchange rate remains unchanged. During this period, the presence of the exchange rate anchor contributes to keeping down the pressure on the price level, but this may be at the expense of impaired competitiveness. Thus even when domestic financial and wage moderation are put in place, there are risks for the viability of the exchange rate anchor. Those risks of course are increased when discipline on the financial domain or on the incomes front falters.

In principle, a useful perspective when confronting this dilemma would be to ascertain the relative priority to be attached to price and balance-of-payments objectives. When control of inflation is uppermost, the role of the exchange rate anchor may be so essential that it may justify the consequent risks to competitiveness. The argument would be that the actual and potential impairment of competitiveness is precisely the incentive that will provide the stimulus to attain and maintain domestic financial and wage discipline. The danger associated with this line of reasoning is that if such discipline is not restored promptly and inflation does not fall sufficiently fast, the damage to competitiveness may be so large as to bring the balance-of-payments constraint to the forefront, thus rendering the credibility of the exchange rate suspect and its anchor role unsustainable.

When priority is attached to balance-of-payments objectives, protection of competitiveness is of the essence and the risks attached to the use of the exchange rate as an anchor are not worth running. An exchange rate management is called for that envisages the exchange rate as a policy instrument for balance-of-payments purposes rather than as an anchor for price stability. Such management will need the support of financial and income moderation just as much as the anchor strategy did. This is because in the absence of such moderation, although adjustments in the exchange rate will (temporarily at least) protect competitiveness and the balance of payments, they will also contribute to domestic price increases. Inflation may thus reach levels that make the control of such increases a critical policy objective.[12]

In practice, however, the dilemma is often resolved by the characteristics of the economic imbalance at stake. In circumstances of no access to international capital markets and limited international reserve availability, exchange rate policy must be geared to balance-of-payments objectives. On the other hand, in situations characterized by relatively strong international reserve positions and price increases as an important policy concern, setting the exchange rate as an anchor for price stability is the appropriate course of action. This also often requires international financial support to supplement international reserve use and enhance the credibility of the strategy.

Difficulties also arise in the closely related area of monetary management. In cases in which the exchange rate is to be used as an anchor, a most relevant but difficult question is the level at which the anchor is to be set. In effect, the choice of an appropriate level can be critical for the resolution of the price stability versus competitiveness dilemma. But apart from the level of the exchange rate, other complex issues confront the design of monetary policy in reforming economies. These include the estimation of the monetary overhang, particularly in light of the uncertainty surrounding the size of the upward price level adjustment likely to be induced by price and trade liberalization. These difficulties compound the complexity of designing the path of monetary expansion. Errors in the measurement of the overhang and the price-level change can render a given rate of monetary expansion either too tight or too expansionary.[13]

Apart from these issues of policy design, implementation of monetary management in reforming economies is complicated by the rudimentary state, or even lack, of financial markets and by general structural weaknesses in the financial system. Some reforming economies exhibit the already discussed problem of vulnerable bank balance sheets, but also face lack of competition, segmentation of credit markets, and inadequate accounting practices.

Fiscal policy implementation is also fraught with difficulties. As in the case of other policies, this not only reflects the large scale of uncertainty that surrounds the operation of reforming economies in transition, but also deep-seated resistance to essential aspects of fiscal adjustment and reform. The issue of curtailment of subsidies acquires particular importance here, as does the subject of state enterprise restructuring.[14] Subsidies are difficult to eliminate, and hard budget constraints are not easy to establish in any type of economic system, but even more so in centrally planned economies where subsidies and soft budget constraints have long been a central feature. In addition, the disruptions associated with the reform process call for public social expenditures, such as the provision of income support to those becoming unemployed, which stretch even more the effort required to attain fiscal balance, let alone a fiscal surplus.[15]

Incomes policy is another area where close vigilance is warranted. Typically, nominal wage guidelines will be an important component of macroeconomic management. Such guidelines can be critical to bringing demand developments in line with the evolution of supply and, where the exchange rate performs as an anchor, to providing a most useful safeguard for competitiveness. Incomes policy serves as a means to control costs; as such, it can help focus enterprise attention on the importance of the control of costs as a means of helping diminish the recurrence of soft budget constraints.

Interaction with Structural Reform

We come now to the subject of the microeconomics of reform, as well as the institutional aspects. Although for expository purposes these are often separated from macroeconomic management, in practice these dimensions of the reform process must be intimately linked for the transition to a market system to be effective.

Design and Implementation Issues

The microeconomics of reform include the liberalization of domestic prices; the opening of the economy to international trade in goods, services, and capital; and the dismantling of exchange controls.[16] Though in principle reforms such as these would appear to be fairly straightforward, in practice they involve numerous difficult choices, and to carry their effects through, they require support from other areas of reform. Questions such as the scope and speed of liberalization must be addressed in this context. And liberalization must be accompanied by the development of competitive market structures if it is to yield results. The process of liberalization and opening up of the economy will have a bearing on state enterprises, some of which are likely to prove nonviable in the new environment. An immediate corollary of this reality will be the desirability of closing those enterprises. In turn, this will require the establishment of bankruptcy laws and procedures. As experience gathers in the process of reform, it appears that in many previously centrally planned economies, restructuring may not be sufficient and revamping of many industries may be required to set economic activity and growth on a sound and sustained path.[17]

In effect, what is at stake is the viability of a capital stock built over a period of several decades on the basis of persistently distorted relative prices. An important proportion of such a capital stock is unlikely to prove capable of competing in a market environment, and the question is whether to devote scarce resources to try and salvage it or to channel them instead to building an altogether new capital stock base. It can be strongly argued that the best strategy to further the reform process would be to address first the sectors in which decisions to start anew are required, because those are likely to be the most difficult to make. Determination in undertaking difficult measures may prove the best route for establishing the credibility of reform and eliciting the required behavioral changes. An unfortunate but inevitable corollary of these harsh realities is that output declines will likely be among the characteristics of the reform process; to the extent that they reflect decisions that, by discontinuing nonviable activities, release resources for productive endeavors, temporary falls in output are part of the solution rather than representing a problem.

Institution-Building Efforts
Just as the macroeconomics of reform can hardly be separated in practice from its microeconomic aspects, both are closely dependent on the prompt buildup of market-supporting institutions and rules. In essence this amounts to the development of an institutional infrastructure to buttress the functioning of a market system.[18] Such infrastructure includes: a legal system that guides the conduct of economic transactions and helps enforce market-determined accountability; an accounting and auditing system that contributes to economic decisionmaking and serves to measure accountability; a fiscal system that fosters efficiency and is in line with social preferences; a social insurance system that contains the hardships of market solutions and provides for intergenerational transfers; and sectoral reforms that encompass areas such as the labor market, the state enterprise sector, the external sector, and the banking system, as well as the pricing regime. Perhaps the most fundamental priority

in this broad institutional area is the establishment of clear ownership and property rights. Without clarification of those rights, many of the necessary ingredients of reform—investment, changes in attitude toward work and production, progress in the process of privatization—are unlikely to materialize. A clear system of ownership therefore is an urgent priority, and means must be found to ensure its feasibility; otherwise other aspects of reform—for which the establishment of ownership rights is a necessary condition and which will necessarily take time to be completed, such as restructuring—cannot be launched, thus impairing the effectiveness of the reform effort.[19]

Balance in the Policy Mix

The requirement of balance in the mix of policies surfaces in most if not all areas of reform: the macroeconomic sphere, the microeconomic area, the structural domain, and the realm of institutions. With regard to macroeconomic management, balance is essential on at least two levels: the mix must ensure consistency of domestic financial policies with the nominal anchors (if those are part of the policy package) or with income guidelines and exchange rate management (if anchors are not relied on). Balance must also prevail among fiscal, monetary, and incomes policies to avoid burdening any one set of policies with the shortcomings of the others. A typical example of an unbalanced policy mix is one in which monetary policy carries the full burden of inflation control—that is, without the support of the other two policy areas. In general, experience shows that under those circumstances, strict implementation of monetary policy can help to contain inflationary pressure, but it is unlikely to lower it for long without impairing other aspects of economic performance. In essence, a balanced domestic macroeconomic policy mix is but a reflection of the need to attain and maintain an appropriate level as well as an appropriate composition of aggregate demand. And the composition of demand has to be balanced in three key dimensions: its public and private components (hence the importance of fiscal policy); its consumption and investment components (hence the importance of monetary—e.g., interest rate—policy); and its domestic and foreign components (hence the importance of competitiveness, i.e., consistency between exchange and incomes policy with the domestic financial stance).

Balance is also required on the microeconomic front to ensure the generation of supply responses in the economy. Domestic price liberalization without the support of steps to open the economy to foreign competition and of action to improve the distribution system will not be sufficient as a guide for efficient resource allocation.

But a successful transition toward the market, in addition to needing balance at the macroeconomic and microeconomic levels, will require balance between the two aspects on their own and with respect to actions to restructure the economy and build up its institutions. Only in the presence of such (admittedly complex) balance can the interplay of demand (macroeconomic) and supply (microeconomic) conditions in a sound market (structural and institutional) setting be expected to yield optimal results.

In sum, it is clear that fundamental issues are involved in the search for balance in the global policy mix, such as the role of government, state enterprise reform, and privatization. Transparency in these domains can go a long way toward eliciting the change in economic behavior without which the process of transition cannot ultimately succeed. This will require the development of a strategy that encompasses all aspects of reform—macroeconomic, microeconomic, structural, and institutional—in the manner similar to that of a musical score that includes all parts of a complete symphony.[20]

Differences in Essence or in Degree?

There can be no doubt that differences between centrally planned and market-based economies abound. Accordingly, there are risks in seeking to transfer the experience of market economies to the environment of command economies.[21] On the other hand, it would also be inadvisable to start from the presumption that little if anything can be derived from the experience with stabilization, adjustment, and growth recorded in developed and developing market economies that can be used in the transition from central planning.

Differences in Essence

The essential difference between the starting point of Central and Eastern European economies as well as the former Soviet republics and their final destination is the absence of market-supporting institutions and rules. And the creation of those institutions and the establishment of such rules will be the hardest challenge to meet—not least because most economic literature on adjustment and growth in market-based economies takes for granted the existence of a market-supporting institutional infrastructure. But there can hardly be any doubt that a necessary condition for an effective transition to a market regime will be the building up of such an infrastructure.

It is beyond the scope of this chapter to analyze this subject in detail; major areas of difference in essence have already been pointed out. They include: the absence of a legal and regulatory framework to provide order and assign responsibilities in the conduct of economic activity; the lack of an accounting and auditing system to help guide economic decisions and measure economic performance; the absence of a fiscal system that fosters the market and reflects real social preferences; and the lack of a social insurance framework geared to a market system to soften the impact of economic fluctuations and permit intergenerational transfers.

A critical element required to underpin this market-supporting institutional framework is the existence and observance of a code of conduct, a set of rules of the game that is typically absent in centrally planned economies. Such a code of conduct includes principles like willingness to make individual economic decisions, to assume risks, and to accept accountability for the consequences of those decisions and risks. Only through overcoming these essential differences will the transition work. And establishing the institutional framework and the corresponding code of conduct are time-consuming endeavors. But it is only in the context of these systemic changes that attitudes in reforming societies will adapt to the change in economic setting and circumstances.

Differences in Degree

The differences in degree between market and centrally planned economies are numerous and straddle most economic policy spheres. In terms of strategy, it has been pointed out already that the issues of pace and sequence of adjustment and reform as well as related topics such as the lags in the effect of economic policies are of a general nature and analytically equivalent in the two types of systems. Even such central questions (though not necessarily the answers) as the role of government are common to market and command regimes.

In terms of specific economic policy areas, most of the differences are more apparent than real, that is, they are more a matter of degree than of intrinsic nature. On the macroeconomic front, it is clear that the complexity of coping with fiscal issues such as soft budget constraints, subsidies, budget deficits, and state enterprise management do not belong exclusively to centrally planned economies. And the same is true with regard to monetary issues, such as the liquidity overhang (a specific instance of an excess stock supply of liquid assets), or the difficulty of forecasting the path of the demand for money. On the exchange rate front, the dilemma between the attainment of price-level stability and the maintenance of competitiveness and the difficulty of determining the appropriate level of the exchange rate when it is to be used as an anchor are also applicable both to market and planned economies.

In the microeconomic and structural domains, similarities also abound. Relative price distortions are not typical of centrally planned economies alone; issues connected with state enterprise reform and control are also widespread. And the problems of vulnerability of banking and financial institutions that confront a number of reforming economies have also arisen in the context of market-based systems.

Differences of degree also characterize the issues of policy mix. Indeed, the need for balance between monetary and fiscal policy and for consistency of these and incomes policy with exchange rate management has been made explicit in market-economy settings. In turn, the importance of keeping progress in the macroeconomic and microeconomic areas commensurate is by no means a new revelation. It has been repeatedly underscored in the context of the linkages between the adjustment, development, and growth processes. The need for proper balance between macroeconomic management and system reform poses equivalent analytical challenges.

Concluding Remarks

It is abundantly clear that the tasks confronting countries in Central and Eastern Europe and the former Soviet area in their voyage toward market environments are daunting. But the benefits that they and the world economy at large can derive from a successful transition are immeasurable. It appears therefore imperative to ensure that efforts are made from all quarters to maximize the effectiveness of the reform efforts under way.

As far as the reforming countries are concerned, an urgent order of business will be to eliminate promptly the differences in essence discussed above. Decisions must be taken at the outset with regard to the establishment of market-supporting institutions. In parallel with this, it will be important to draw lessons from the experiences of the developed and developing market economies in those areas where only differences in degree were identified. In the process, critical questions, such as the role of government, will have to be addressed and priority given to fundamental issues such as the establishment of clear ownership and property rights. Activity on these various fronts will help induce the supply responses that can ease the reform path.

Reaching the final destination, however, will require persistence in policy implementation, even in the face of adversity, if the proper signals are to be given and credibility ensured. It will also be important to exhibit transparency in the strategy, instruments, and objectives of reform to gather the necessary consensus. Building such a consensus will likely call for prompt acknowledgment of the unlikelihood of fulfilling overly optimistic expectations concerning the speed of the reform process. But these are areas in which support from the rest of the world economy can help.

The role of the market economies in easing the process of reform in Central and Eastern Europe and Eurasia can be critical on a variety of fronts. Given the importance of setting market-supporting rules of the game in the countries in the region, a first responsibility of market economies is to abide themselves by those rules. This implies openness of markets, respect of budget constraints, and support for the integration of national economies into the world system. Policy advice in the areas of institutional infrastructure building and macroeconomic and structural management also will contribute to smoothing the reform process.

Thus assistance at one level consists of preaching by example and drawing lessons from past mistakes. On another level, it consists of making resources available to support and smooth the adjustment effort required for reform. But in making resources available, two considerations must be borne in mind: one, that their amount and terms be compatible with the adjustment effort and the prospects in the reforming economies; and two, that their disbursement be clearly linked to performance under the reform process. These two considerations are related in a particularly complex way in that they exhibit elements of both substitutability and complementarity. It can be argued that if policy conditionality (the linkage of resource availability to performance in policy implementation) is well defined and indicative of a substantial adjustment effort, there is a case for providing ample amounts of resources on favorable terms or on terms that do not produce undue risks. But then if performance is strong, the likelihood is that less rather than more financing on soft terms will be required.

Given the importance of fostering reform efforts, I contend that generous support (in both scale and terms) is a reasonable price to pay for determination and breadth in policy implementation. In other words, an appropriate trade-off may be established between the degree of concessionality and the degree of conditionality attached to external assistance. Such a trade-off seems particularly well suited to the reforming economies in Eastern Europe, where emphasis must be placed on setting conditions for the prompt establishment of a market-based system. Given the externalities that can be expected from a successful transition in the region, the question of the terms of repayment of the assistance, though admittedly important, may not be the only or even the main consideration. This is because the effectiveness of the effort to create a market will depend critically on the determination, persistence, and strength of policy implementation rather than on the particular time pattern of policy results, on which repayment is contingent. Policy implementation is at the very center of the broad subject of conditionality, so it is conceivable that, by stressing it more than the financial terms of external assistance, it may be possible to increase the likelihood of success of the reforms under way. A cautionary note must be sounded at this point, however; this approach, like many others of a similar nature,[22] carries a risk of moral hazard. To minimize this risk, it will be critical to design and measure policy conditionality in a manner sufficiently clear and precise that the related access to concessional assistance and aid will help, not hinder or delay, the reform process. This is an important and delicate problem, but it is not new and it is amenable to reasonable solutions, though they may point to the need to extend conditionality to areas in which it had not ventured in the past.[23]

A trade-off between concessionality and conditionality can also be a means to resolve potential conflicts between political and purely economic objectives. But apart from that, it can be argued that it may give rise to an important measure of synergy. Generous financial support will permit the establishment of protective mechanisms on a variety of fronts: it will provide time for policy safeguards designed to correct slippages or to adapt to unexpected deviations to yield results; it will also make it possible to establish financial safeguards to cover unanticipated needs or shocks that do not require policy adjustment (e.g., transitory and reversible events); and it will also allow social safeguards to be set up to soften the burdens of change and thus help widen the acceptance of reform.

By way of conclusion, I would note that an approach like the one just outlined also conforms to comparative advantages developed in the international economy for nearly five decades. On the side of international institutions, the International Monetary Fund is well poised to provide the broad framework of conditionality and to develop, as appropriate, new criteria to measure policy performance in areas not normally covered by the traditional scope of a conditionality framework. Though it would continue to provide its own assistance, the central focus of participation and the contribution of the IMF would be the monitoring, follow-up, and adaptation of policy implementation. The financial terms and scale of access to IMF resources would continue to be dictated by the cooperative and monetary nature of the institution. As necessary, IMF conditionality could be supplemented by work undertaken elsewhere, such as by the OECD in the structural area and by the World Bank in the project and sectoral domains.[24] Other multilateral institutions (e.g., the World Bank, the newly established European Bank of Reconstruction and Development), together with other official sources of bilateral flows, would provide the bulk of the financial assistance to support the reforms on terms very much tailored to the economy's capacity to adapt its production patterns and structure to market signals, thus laying the ground for a resumption of sustained activity and growth. Whenever it is clear at the outset that such prospective capacity to recover falls short of what would be required to sustain the servicing of external assistance on market terms, the trade-off between conditionality and concessionality would provide a logical means to help reforms along without wasting scarce resources. And although the basis for such a trade-off is well established, it should be clear that the essential requirements for transforming central planning into a market-based regime are policy determination and persistence on the part of the government. Such policy resolve and durability are fundamental aims of conditionality. There-

74   Manuel Guitián

fore, the trade-off suggested here is one whereby concessional resources are used to promote firm and sustained policy action. Only in this manner will reform be effective. And reform is critical for the preservation and orderly development of the societies to Eastern Europe and Eurasia. After all, as Macaulay once said, "Reform, that you may preserve."

Notes

The views expressed here are my own and they should not be attributed to the International Monetary Fund. I am grateful to Peter B. Kenen and William H. Branson for their comments. An earlier version of this chapter was presented at a Seminar on International Economics, International Finance Section, Princeton University, April 1991. Subsequently it was delivered at a Finnish-Soviet Banking Seminar held in Helsinki in September 1991. In a slightly revised form, the chapter was published as section IV in Guitián (1992a).
1. The scope of the reforms is of course much broader and encompasses actions to establish democracy and pluralism in Central and Eastern European societies, as well as in those of the republics of the former Soviet Union. Viewed from this broad perspective, the transition toward a market economy is only one specific aspect of a widespread process of transformation. For a lucid discussion of economic opening in the region, see Williamson (1991a) and Havrylishyn and Williamson (1991).
2. This seems to be the case if only because processes like nationalization are easier to accomplish than those of restitution or privatization. The fact that gradualism has hardly characterized the process of collectivization also points in this direction; as my colleague Massimo Russo notes, the shock approach was typical of the introduction of central planning. It should also be pointed out that the intrinsically complex reforms under way in Central and Eastern Europe have been rendered even more difficult by the dismantling of the trading and payments arrangements under the Council for Mutual Economic Assistance (CMEA) at the end of 1990. For a timely analysis of transitional arrangements for the CMEA countries, see Kenen (1991); see also Schrenk (1990). For an early view on the reform steps taken in Russia, see Williamson (1992).
3. These events are not the only illustration of such interaction. Another recent example of the intertemporal interplay—this time mainly among economic factors—is given by developments with regard to international indebtedness; for a recent discussion, see Guitián (1992a, section III, and 1992b).
4. There is an ample literature dealing with these partial reform efforts. See, for example, Kornai (1990a and 1990b); in the latter article, Kornai discusses at length the issue of transformation without reform and the weaknesses of "third form" or hybrid solutions. See also the collection of papers on Hungary and Poland in Commission of the European Communities (1990), as well as Hinds (1990), Institute for International Finance (1990), Prust et al. (1990), and Wolf (1990a and 1990b).
5. The importance of transparent rules of the game can hardly be overstressed in circumstances where behavioral changes are to be effected; for a discussion of this subject in the general context of international economic relations, see Dam (1982) and Guitián (1992a, section II).
6. For further elaboration on the strategy discussed in this section, see Guitián (1991a); the subject of the scope of reform and policy priorities as well as of sequence of actions have been discussed recently by Dornbusch (1991) and Williamson (1991b); see also Portes, "Introduction," in Commission of the European Communities (1990), Genberg (1991), Fischer and Gelb (1991), Calvo and Frenkel (1991a), and Ronald McKinnon (1991).

7. For a lucid and forceful set of arguments in favor of simultaneous policy action, see Kornai (1990c).

8. Recent discussions of the adjustment process can be found in Bergsten (1991) and Krugman (1991). Evidence on these issues can already be found in the relatively short period since reform in Central and Eastern Europe took off. For example, a shock approach was taken in Poland to effect stabilization and liberalization and in Yugoslavia to prompt stabilization. In Hungary, where the initial domestic imbalance was more limited, a more gradual approach was pursued; see Lipton and Sachs (1990a), Coricelli and Rocha (1991), Kornai (1990a and 1990c), Commission of the European Communities (1990), and "Stabilization Efforts in Poland and Yugoslavia—Early Lessons" in World Bank (1991).

9. Issues connected with financial reform in centrally planned economies have been recently discussed by Brainard (1991), Blejer and Sagari (1991), Sundararajan (1991), and Calvo and Frenkel (1991a). An excellent discussion of financial imbalances in East Germany can be found in Lipschitz and McDonald (1990). An examination of events in the former Soviet Union has been provided by Havrylishyn and Williamson (1991).

10. A timely and useful analysis of historical experience with issues of liquidity overhang and monetary reform will be found in Dornbusch and Wolf (1991); see also Calvo and Frenkel (1991a and 1991b).

11. I am indebted to Peter Kenen for having brought this wage-cost argument to my attention. Bruno (1990) provides an extensive examination of nominal anchors in open economies, including the possible need for a multiplicity of them. On the issue of system overdetermination, Bruno acknowledges the "prima facie contradiction in an argument that calls for the fixing of more than one nominal variable at a time," but he points out that the argument "rests on the assumption of full certainty." He goes on to argue that in conditions of uncertainty, the issue "must be redefined in an expectational sense. Given the potential benefits of success and the high risks of failure of a sharp disinflation, tying one's boat to several anchors rather than one would seem to be a prudent policy as is the portfolio diversification of risk in the optimal menu of risky assets" (p. 26). I believe Peter Kenen's point concerning the supply effects of wage costs is important in this context. After all, though Bruno's reasoning is appealing, "more" instruments need not be equivalent to a "less uncertain" environment. Actually, it can be argued that uncertainty calls less for additional tools than for a relatively predictable use of those that are available.

12. Here again, evidence can be found in the experience of Hungary, Poland, and Yugoslavia. The predominant aim in the case of Hungary was strengthening the balance-of-payments position and correspondingly, nominal adjustments in the exchange rate were effected to ensure competitiveness. In the cases of Poland and Yugoslavia, on the other hand, inflation was paramount, and therefore the exchange rate was anchored at a fixed level vis-à-vis the U.S. dollar in the former country and vis-à-vis the deutsche mark in the latter. Examples of the difficulties involved in either policy choice—but also of their potential effectiveness— are well illustrated by these country experiences: Hungary witnessed an increase in inflation and Yugoslavia, confronting a severe balance-of-payments constraint, had to adjust the exchange rate; in Poland, on the other hand, price performance has improved as has the external position, so the exchange rate anchor has not yet exhibited strains: see "Stabilization Efforts in Poland and Yugoslavia—Early Lessons," in World Bank (1991). These statements are of course time contingent, and they apply to the period in which the chapter was written.

13. For further discussion of these issues in the case of Poland, see Calvo and Coricelli (1991), Coricelli and Rocha (1991), and Lipton and Sachs (1990a). See also Calvo and Frenkel (1991a) for an extensive examination of the demand, supply, and portfolio effects of credit policies.

14. For a more extensive discussion of fiscal issues in the process of transition to market-based regimes, see Holzmann (1991), Tanzi (1991a, 1991b, and 1992), and Kopits (1991).

15. Yugoslavia provides a good illustration of some of the problems discussed in the text; see World Bank (1991). A brief examination of the social aspects of the transition in reforming economies can be found in Schweitzer (1990).

16. The chapter will not enter into the issue of the scope of external liberalization, that is, whether it should be complete (with regard to both the current and capital accounts) or partial and staggered (current account first and capital flows later on). This same issue arises in reforming centrally planned economies in connection with currency convertibility, the scope of which can also be complete or partial; for an extensive discussion of the subject of convertibility in these economies in transition, see Polak (1991) and Williamson (1991a); issues of capital flows are examined in Guitián (1991b) and in International Monetary Fund (1991).

17. In addition to the issues discussed in the text, the microeconomics of reform encompass also a variety of sectoral questions that are not addressed in this chapter; they include areas like distribution systems, energy, environment, housing, agriculture, and manufacturing. As for the need for wholesale revamping of sectors in the economy, in the case of East Germany, Gros (1991) notes that the "disastrous state of the environment, obsolete industry and outdated public infrastructure require that almost the entire stock of private and public capital be rebuilt."

18. General and insightful discussion of the importance of the institutional aspects of reform will be found in Dornbusch (1991) and Williamson (1991b).

19. An insightful discussion of the dilemmas posed by the interconnection and different time horizons of privatization and restructuring can be found in Blanchard et al. (1991). For a specific country example, Lipton and Sachs (1990b) have examined in extenso the issue of privatization in Eastern Europe, with particular focus on the case of Poland.

20. Blanchard et al. (1991) go in depth into the intricacies of bringing together the major building blocks of reform, grouped into the following categories: stabilization, liberalization, privatization, and restructuring.

21. The need for caution in the extrapolation of developed market-economy experiences to regimes based on central planning is the main subject of discussion in Marer (1991). In the context of this essay, which argues that real differences between East and West should not be exaggerated, Marer's message is that neither should apparent differences or similarities be overstressed. Once again, an issue of balance is at stake here.

22. Such issues of moral hazard are part and parcel of the exercise of conditionality in general, so the risk mentioned in the text is not new, though it may give rise to relatively complex questions in the context of reforming economies. A specific example of an area where moral hazard risks clearly arise is the international debt strategy; see Guitián (1992a, section III, and 1992b) for an extensive discussion.

23. This expansion is what may give rise to complex questions in the sense that to be effective, conditionality may have to extend beyond its traditional macroeconomic sphere and purely economic efficiency criteria. Admittedly delicate issues are involved here, but I would argue that they are definitely not insoluble.

24. The argument in this concluding paragraph deals only with the economies in transition in the East of Europe and addresses basically the question of how to foster reform. But it can also apply to the reform efforts of other countries, such as the CIS republics. The effectiveness of reform requires completion, so the trade-off between conditionality and financial terms of assistance is, in this sense, a once-and-for-all event. But the general argument for such a trade-off can be extended beyond the issue of reform to areas like development; in this context, the idea would be to keep the terms of assistance commensurate with the economy's

capacity to develop and examine the possibility of a trade-off when the latter falls short of the former.

References

Bergsten, C. Fred, ed. 1991. *International Adjustment and Financing: The Lessons of 1985-1991*. Washington, D.C.: Institute for International Economics.

Blanchard, Olivier, Rudiger Dornbusch, Paul Krugman, Richard Layard, and Lawrence Summers. 1991. *Reform in Eastern Europe*. Cambridge, MA: MIT Press.

Blejer, Mario I., and Silvia B. Sagari. 1991. "Hungary: Financial Reform in a Socialist Economy." World Bank, PRE Working Paper Series, WPS 595 (February).

Brainard, Lawrence J. 1991. "Reform in Eastern Europe: Creating a Capital Market." *Federal Reserve Bank of Kansas City Economic Review* 76 (January/February).

Bruno, Michael. 1991. "High Inflation and the Nominal Anchors of an Open Economy." NBER Working Paper Series No. 3518 (November).

Calvo, Guillermo, and Fabrizio Coricelli. 1991. "Stagflationary Effects of Stabilization Programs in Reforming Socialist Countries: Enterprise-Side vs. Household-Side Factors." Unpublished manuscript (February).

Calvo, Guillermo, and Jacob Frenkel. 1991a. "From Centrally Planned to Market Economies: The Road from CPE to PCPE." *Staff Papers*, Vol. 38, International Monetary Fund (June).

Calvo, Guillermo, and Jacob Frenkel. 1991b. "Monetary Overhang, Non-Performing Loans and Fiscal Pressures." In Paul Marer and Salvatore Zecchini, eds., *The Transition to a Market Economy*.

Commission of the European Communities. 1990. "Economic Transformation in Hungary and Poland." *European Economy* 43 (March).

Coricelli, Fabrizio, and Roberto de Rezende Rocha. 1991. "A Comparative Analysis of the Polish and Yugoslav Programs." In Paul Marer and Salvatore Zecchini, eds. *The Transition to a Market Economy*.

Dam, Kenneth W. 1982. *The Rules of the Game: Reform and Evolution in the International Monetary System*. Chicago: University of Chicago Press.

Dornbusch, Rudiger. 1991. "Strategy and Priorities for Reform." In Paul Marer and Salvatore Zecchini, eds. *The Transition to a Market Economy*.

Dornbusch, Rudiger, and Holger Wolf. 1991. "Monetary Overhang and Reforms in the 1940s." Unpublished manuscript (January).

Downes, Patrick, and Reza Vaez-Zadeh, eds. 1991. *The Evolving Role of Central Banks*.Washington, D.C.: International Monetary Fund.

Fischer, Stanley, and Alan Gelb. 1991. "Issues in Socialist Economy Reform." In Paul Marer and Salvatore Zecchini, eds., *The Transition to a Market Economy*.

Frenkel, Jacob A., and Morris Goldstein, eds. 1991. *International Financial Policy-Essays in Honor of Jacques J. Polak*. Washington, D.C.: International Monetary Fund and De Nederlandsche Bank.

Genberg, Hans. 1991. "On the Sequencing of Economic Reforms in Eastern Europe." *IMF Working Papers*, WP/91/13 (February).

Gros, Daniel. 1991. "The New Germany: An Emerging Deficit Economy." *International Economic Insights* (March/April).

Guitián, Manuel. 1991a. "The Role of International Organizations: International Monetary Fund." In Paul Marer and Salvatore Zecchini, eds., *The Transition to a Market Economy*.

Guitián, Manuel. 1991b. "Economic Integration and Capital Flows." Paper presented at an International Symposium on *Turkey's Experience in Developing a Market Economy and its Relevance for the Reforming Countries of Central and Eastern Europe*. Antalya, Turkey, April 1–3, 1991.

Guitián, Manuel. 1992a. *Rules and Discretion in International Economic Policy*. Occasional Paper No. 97. Washington, D.C.: International Monetary Fund, June.

Guitián, Manuel. 1992b. "Remarks on the Debt Crisis." In Paul Volcker and Toyoo Gyohten, *Changing Fortunes: The World's Money and the Threat to American Leadership*.

Hinds, Manuel. 1990. "Issues in the Introduction of Market Forces in Eastern European Socialist Economies." World Bank Report No. IDP-0057 (April).

Holzmann, Robert. 1991. "Budgetary Subsidies in Centrally Planned Economies in Transition." *IMF Working Papers*, WP/91/11 (January).

Institute for International Finance. 1990. *Building Free Market Economies in Central and Eastern Europe: Challenges and Realities*. Washington, D.C., April.

International Monetary Fund. 1991. *Determinants and Systemic Consequences of International Capital Flows: A Study by the Research Department of the International Monetary Fund*. Occasional Paper No. 77. Washington, D.C.: International Monetary Fund, March.

Kenen, Peter B. 1991. "Transitional Arrangements for Trade and Payments Among the CMEA Countries." *Staff Papers*, Vol. 38, International Monetary Fund (June).

Kopits, George. 1991. "Fiscal Reform in European Economies in Transition." In Paul Marer and Salvatore Zecchini, eds., *The Transition to a Market Economy*.

Kornai, János. 1990a. *Vision and Reality, Market and State*. New York: Routledge.

Kornai, János. 1990b. "The Affinity Between Ownership Forms and Coordination Mechanisms: The Common Experience of Reform in Socialist Countries." *Journal of Economic Perspectives*. 4, No. 3 (Summer).

Kornai, János. 1990c.*The Road to a Free Economy-Shifting from a Socialist System: The Example of Hungary*. New York: W. W. Norton.

Krugman, Paul R. 1991. *Has the Adjustment Process Worked?* Policy Analyses in International Economics No. 34, Institute for International Economics, Washington, D.C., October.

Lipschitz, Leslie, and Donogh McDonald, eds. 1990. *German Unification: Economic Issues*. Occasional Paper No. 75. Washington, D.C.: International Monetary Fund, December.

Lipton, David, and Jeffrey Sachs. 1990a. "Creating a Market Economy in Eastern Europe: The Case of Poland." *Brookings Papers in Economic Activity* 1.

Lipton, David, and Jeffrey Sachs. 1990b. "Privatization in Eastern Europe: The Case of Poland." *Brookings Papers in Economic Activity* 2.

Marer, Paul. 1991. "Pitfalls in Transferring Market-Economy Experiences to the European Economies in Transition." In Paul Marer and Salvatore Zecchini, eds., *The Transition to a Market Economy*.

Marer, Paul, and Salvatore Zecchini, eds. 1991. *The Transition to a Market Economy*. Paris: Organization for Economic Cooperation and Development; 2 volumes.

McKinnon, Ronald I. 1991. *The Order of Economic Liberalization: Financial Control in the Transition to a Market Economy*. Baltimore: Johns Hopkins University Press.

Polak, Jacques J. 1991. "Convertibility: An Indispensable Element in the Transition Process in Eastern Europe." In John Williamson, ed., *Currency Convertibility in Eastern Europe* Washington, D.C., Institute for International Economics.

Prust, Jim, and IMF Staff Team. 1990. *The Czech and Slovak Federal Republic: An Economy in Transition*. Occasional Paper No. 72. Washington, D.C.: International Monetary Fund, October 1990.

Schrenk, Martin. 1990. "Whither Comecon?" *Finance and Development* 27, No. 4 (December).

Sundararajan, V. 1991. "Financial Sector Reform and Central Banking in Centrally Planned Economies." In Patrick Downes and Reza Vaez-Zadeh, eds.,*The Evolving Role of Central Banks*.

Tanzi, Vito. 1991a. "Tax Reform in Economies in Transition: A Brief Introduction to the Main Issues." *IMF Working Papers*, WP/91/23 (March).

Tanzi, Vito. 1991b. "Mobilization of Savings in Eastern Europe: The Role of the State." *IMF Working Papers*, WP/91/4 (January).

Tanzi, Vito, ed. 1992. *Fiscal Policies in Economies in Transition*. Washington, D.C.: International Monetary Fund.

Volcker, Paul, and Toyoo Gyohten. 1992. *Changing Fortunes: The World's Money and the Threat to American Leadership*. New York: Times Books.

Williamson, John. 1991a. "The Economic Opening of Eastern Europe." In John Williamson, ed., *Currency Convertibility in Eastern Europe*. Washington, D.C.: Institute for International Economics.

Williamson, John. 1991b. "Current Issues in Transition Economics." In Jacob A. Frenkel and Morris Goldstein, eds., *International Financial Policy-Essays in Honor of Jacques J. Polak.*.

Williamson, John. 1992. "The Prospects for Russian Reform."*International Economic Insight* (January/February).

Wolf, Thomas A. 1990a. "Reform, Inflation and Adjustment in Planned Economies."*Finance and Development 27*, No. 1 (March).

Wolf, Thomas A. 1990b. "Market-Oriented Reform of Foreign Trade in Planned Economies."*IMF Working Papers*, WP/90/28 (April).

World Bank. 1991. *Transition: The Newsletter About Reforming Economies* 2, No. 1 (January).

CHAPTER 4

Can Eastern Europe Compete by "Getting the Prices Right"? Contrast with East Asian Structural Reforms

Alice Amsden

The Arrow-Debreu general equilibrium theory is a beautiful system in which competitive markets can operate in amazingly efficient ways. . . . Yet understanding the real economy and considering policy objectives require a completely different way of thinking from that of the Arrow-Debreu model . . . American economists tend to incorporate a fictitious assumption that the real economy does unconditionally operate along the same lines as perfectly competitive markets. . . . Japanese economists in charge of the reconstruction of postwar Japan never made such an unintelligent [orokana] mistake.

Kotaro Tsujimura, founder, Japan Econometric Society
(1984, pp. 145–151)

Competitive Theory versus Competitiveness

A major challenge facing postsocialist Eastern Europe is placing its industry on a competitive footing. As a first step in this direction, most East European countries have "shocked" their enterprises by opening domestic markets to foreign competition and introducing other policies to "get prices right." This chapter contrasts the East Asian and East European experience with liberal structural reforms. It suggests that East Asia's past economic reforms (South Korea's and Taiwan's are mainly examined) deviated from free-market principles, and that Eastern Europe's current free-market policies (the focus is on Poland) are generally inadequate to render potentially promising manufacturing enterprises competitive in world markets. The source of evidence for the latter is a study I helped prepare for the OECD (1992a) on Polish industry, and follow-up investigations I made of fifteen Polish state-owned enterprises.[1]

The nominal anchor of this conference volume is Andrés Solimano's observation that a new economic reform paradigm based on free-market principles is sweeping the land. Yet East Asia's stellar growth performance, in conjunction with its ambiguous liberalization record and extensive use of industrial policy, concretely challenges free-market reform as a structural development strategy. It is this aspect of reform, rather than macroeconomic stabilization, that is analyzed below.[2]

Why did the governments of Japan, South Korea, and Taiwan intervene so actively in economic development? Wouldn't it have been simpler for them to rely on market forces rather than provide business with so much support? These questions are intriguing particularly in light of the competitive assets Korea and Taiwan enjoyed relative to other late industrializers: ultra-low wages and good physical and human infrastructure (owing to foreign aid), which should have made it relatively easier for them to compete internationally on the basis of market-determined production costs.

As discussed briefly in the next section, South Korea and Taiwan deviated from the free-market model not out of theoretical conviction, but rather from practical necessity. They succeeded partly because they created the institutions required for government intervention to work well: they fed rather than starved their state bureaucracy, and adopted a principle of subsidy allocation that tied incentives to transparent, monitorable performance standards, including export targets. In all late-industrializing countries the government has disciplined labor, but in East Asia the government has also disciplined capital (Amsden 1992a).

The East Asian experience, therefore, sharply poses the question for Eastern Europe of how practical it is for them to rely on free-market reforms to reindustrialize. In what follows, the term "free-market reform" is used specifically to mean "getting the prices right" and pursuing comparative advantage to gain international competitiveness. The international angle is emphasized because of its importance in East Asian development, and increasingly, in postsocialist recovery.[3] Imports in total domestic use in Poland rose from 14.6% in 1989 to 17.1% in 1990 and to 24.9% in 1991. Simultaneously, exports in total sales rose from 16.4% to 24.2% (OECD 1992a). Given that most postsocialist debt-ridden countries cannot easily borrow further abroad, and given that the foreign aid they have received has generally been tied to privatization rather than restructuring, it follows that financing reindustrialization is heavily dependent on export earnings. Moreover, the clearest conception held by shock therapists of what is supposed to happen to their patient after treatment centers on the international division of labor: it is hoped that Eastern Europe will be integrated into the world economy, absorbing foreign investments and exporting the products that have been made competitive due to relative price changes (a decline in real wages, a rise in real interest rates, an increase in energy costs, a devaluation of the exchange rate, and free trade).

An international focus should not be interpreted to mean that the only cause of Eastern Europe's sharp decline in output in 1990–1991 was exogenous (overseas competition and the loss of the COMECON market). In reality, a domestic credit crunch and decline in demand were also critical and interacted with foreign competition to drive Eastern Europe's economies into deep depression.

East Asia's Inability to Compete on the Basis of Market-Determined Production Costs

South Korea and Taiwan were unable to rely on the free-market model to industrialize because they could not compete on the basis of market-determined production costs against Japan.[3] In the 1960s they needed to be protected from Japanese competition in their leading sector, cotton spinning and weaving. Wages were higher in Japan than in either Korea or Taiwan (although Japan's segmented labor markets meant below-average wages in labor-intensive industries), but Japan's productivity advantage was proportionately greater. In the 1970s, Japanese competition made it necessary for the Korean and Taiwanese governments to support basic industry, and in the 1980s and beyond, support was required for entry into high-technology sectors (Amsden 1989).

In standard market theory, low-wage countries with the right prices are guaranteed comparative advantage in labor-intensive industries by two assumptions, neither of which operated well enough to dispense with government intervention in Korea or Taiwan. First, standard price theory implausibly assumes that firms in the same industry in all countries operate with the same production function, so that productivity and quality in the same industry are identical everywhere (by definition, therefore, low-wage countries have the advantage in labor-intensive products). In practice, Korea and Taiwan imported large quantities of foreign technology and capital goods, and invested heavily in education, but because no technology is ever completely codified, it took a long time for some of their industries to reach world standards before exporting could commence (for the example of automobiles, see Amsden 1989, ch. 7; for advanced consumer electronics, see Amsden 1992b).

Second, Ricardian trade theory assumes that productivity does differ between countries in the same industry, but further assumes that exchange rates can always be devalued enough to give low-wage countries the edge in labor-intensive goods. Korea and Taiwan did devalue their real exchange rates in the mid-1960s to appease American aid administrators, but there was a practical limit to real devaluation in the form of inflation, because of the heavy incidence in export goods of imported inputs (in cotton textiles and wood processing, for instance), not to mention the disruption to investment of low worker morale as imported food costs rose.

84   Alice Amsden

An historical footnote is helpful to understand the problem of "backward" countries being unable to compete in labor-intensive industries on the basis of market-determined production costs. This problem was largely unknown in the First and Second Industrial Revolutions because international competitiveness at that time was driven by innovation in new products and processes, rather than simply by low wages. In contrast, "late" industrialization has been characterized by an absence of pioneering technology even in leading enterprises (the definition of lateness), and this has made the need for government intervention to subsidize industry decisively greater than in the past (Amsden 1989). Moreover, in the dynamic industries that are close to the world technological frontier in which the advanced countries operate, the basic rules of international competition changed in the twentieth century, as global enterprises arose with "organizational capabilities" based on a core technology (Chandler 1990). The institutionalization of R & D in such enterprises allowed them to erect entry barriers around their proprietary technology family. Because of this historical condition, the idea of Alexander Gerschenkron (1962)—of backward countries leapfrogging to the world technological frontier in the most dynamic sectors—could no longer work. In contrast, when British firms in the nineteenth century failed to establish equally impenetrable international entry barriers, leading American and German enterprises could and did follow a Gerschenkron-like strategy. They leapfrogged ahead of England with only minimalist government support (Hikino and Amsden forthcoming).

To stimulate industrial development starting in the mid-1960s, the governments of Korea and Taiwan introduced a set of incentives that nullified or neutralized some of the liberal reforms they were pressured to introduce by aid donors.[4] In South Korea, advisors encouraged the government to set a positive real interest rate on certain deposit accounts, but the state-owned financial system continued to provide targeted firms in targeted industries with loans carrying low or even negative real interest rates, and deposit rates stayed high for only seven years. Tax reforms to encourage fiscal prudence were also introduced, but considering all consolidated accounts, the public sector budget between 1963 and 1982 was in deficit in all years except 1964–1966 (after which time foreign aid was withdrawn and the influence of aid advisors ceased).[5] From the 1960s through the 1990s, the real effective exchange rate showed a remarkable degree of stability, as well as a consistent anti-export bias (Kim 1991, forthcoming). Nevertheless, exports grew at 41.7% in 1962–69 and 38.1% in 1970–79 owing to an export targeting system (Rhee, Ross-Larson, and Pursell 1984). Although the imported inputs required by exporters were liberalized, Korean industry remained highly protected (Presidential Commission 1988; Kim 1990, 1988, 1987). Thus "inward"- and "outward"-oriented development were not mutually exclusive and proceeded pari passu.

Taiwan's reputation is one of less government intervention than Korea's, but Taiwanese industry was in fact more heavily subsidized than Korean industry in the late 1960s (according to estimates of Balassa et al. 1982). In the early 1990s, subsidization in Taiwan probably again became relatively greater because the government accounted for 80% of R & D in Taiwan, compared with only 20% in Korea (OECD 1990, 1991).

Allegedly both Korea and Taiwan finally got serious about liberalizing their trade and financial regimes in the 1980s. Nevertheless, the financial systems of both countries remained fundamentally repressed (Amsden and Euh 1993). Trade barriers also continued to impede high-technology imports (Presidential Commission 1988). Professor Yung Chul Park, a former Korean government advisor, noted that in spite of the liberal goals set by both Korea and Taiwan in the 1980s, "the two economies have hardly followed classical liberal principles of laissez-faire." He continues:

> Policymakers have been by and large passive and conservative in liberalizing the Korea and Taiwan economies, in that they have implemented reforms mostly when they were forced to do so by internal and external developments. Even when they were compelled to liberalize, they were reluctant to make policy changes unless disruptions to the economy could be minimized. (Park 1991: 152)

Getting the Prices Right and East European Restructuring

> An opening of free trade with Western Europe should increase the demand for Poland's skilled workers who are now earning (at around $1) about one-tenth to one-fifteenth of what comparable skilled workers earn just 500 miles to the West. (Jeffrey Sachs and David Lipton 1990)

> The policy of opening the Polish market to all imports (i.e., not subject to quota, etc.) without having time to train and educate local industry as to how to react and the necessary quality requirements has been a high risk strategy and has put the domestic industrial base in great difficulty. (IDI Report on the Uniontex Textile Company, Lodz, August 1991)

Static "Comparative Advantage" and "Cash Cows": Industry-Level Analysis

To ascertain whether or not Eastern Europe—and in particular, Poland—is able to compete internationally after having been shocked to its senses with the "right" relative prices, one must first inquire how its industries with comparative advantage are faring, because these are the industries one would expect to be most competitive in world markets. For the moment, we may follow the OECD (1992a) and define a country's static comparative advantage in terms of industries in which the country specializes relative to those of its major trading partners. This is not necessarily the best definition of comparative advantage, but it is somewhat intuitive and easy to measure. Later the question is raised of whether the concept of comparative advantage is relevant to postsocialism at all.

According to this definition, Poland's static comparative advantage lies in industries that occupy a larger share of its employment than the same industries occupy in the employment of OECD countries.[6] That is:

$$N_i^p \Big/ \sum_{i=1}^{n} N_i^p > N_i^0 \Big/ \sum_{i=1}^{n} N_i^0,$$

where N refers to employment in the ith industry, and superscripts p and o refer to Poland and the OECD respectively. Setting the OECD's ratios to 100, table 4.1 indicates the Polish industries with comparative advantage (ratios greater than 100) vis-à-vis the OECD's. Given the OECD's superiority over Poland in terms of technological capability, it is not surprising that, with the exception of shipbuilding, Poland's static comparative advantage lies in light, labor-intensive goods (textiles, clothing, and leather products), and in certain processed raw materials (food, wood, iron and steel, and nonferrous metals). Given the emphasis on real wage reduction of transition economic policy, this is also the set of industries it favored.

A variant on the above definition of comparative advantage compares the structure (distributive shares) of the OECD's exports to the world with that of Poland's exports to the OECD. As table 4.1 indicates, the two measures of comparative advantage provide roughly similar results. In both cases, exports of ships and labor-intensive and raw-material-based products are found to be Poland's strength in OECD markets.

Poland's comparative advantage bundle contains almost no high-technology products and, with the exception of ships, few mid-tech ones, although mid-tech is what one would expect a semi-industrialized country like Poland to emphasize in its reindustrialization strategy. Instead, it comprises products that are based on resources that in the course of economic development are either nonexpandable (land) or nonreproducible (cheap labor and depletable natural resources). Therefore Poland's specializations will have to change over time if its income is to rise dynamically. Nevertheless, the immediate question is whether or not in the short run Poland's comparative advantage bundle contains enough "cash cows" to generate sufficient income and employment to finance an eventual move up the ladder of comparative advantage.

**TABLE 4.1   Poland's "comparative advantage"
with respect to the OECD (specialization in terms
of OECD employment and OECD exports)**

Industry	Index of specialization	
	Employment[a]	Trade[b]
Food products	138	265
Textiles	152	79
Clothing	144	311
Footwear	188	207
Wood products	148	338
Paper	46	43
Printing, publishing	31	7
Industrial chemicals	92	74
Other chemicals	68	—
Pharmaceuticals	44	—
Rubber products	55	54
Plastic products	48	30
Pottery, china	60	99
Glass products	121	212
Non-metal products	86	67
Iron and steel	143	107
Non-ferrous metals	156	264
Metal products	68	179
Mechanical engineering	95	36
Electrical engineering	62	29
Transport equipment	119	26
Shipbuilding		378
Professional goods	128	16
Other industries	252	—
All industries	100	100

Source: OECD (1992a).

a. Ratio of an industry's share in Poland's total industrial employment
relative to its share in the OECD's total industrial employment, with the
latter's share equal to 100.

b. Ratio of an industry's share in Poland's exports to the OECD relative to
its share in the OECD's industrial exports from the world, with the latter's
share equal to 100.

The higher each ratio, the greater Poland's "comparative advantage."

To answer this question we examine mainly Poland's non-COMECON
exports, because these have grown the fastest and by 1991 accounted for
about 85% of total exports (see table 4.2). The period in question (1989
through the first eight months of 1991) is too short to draw any firm conclusions about Poland's postsocialist export patterns. The data should merely be
taken as preliminary and their reliability not considered absolute. (Rodrick

TABLE 4.2   Growth rates of Poland's industrial exports, and the non-COMECON share of each industry, 1989–1991 (percent)

Industry	1989	1990	1991[a]
Food industry			
Total	2.5	18.7	−5.9
Non-COMECON	5.1	20.2	−11.1
N-C share	91.3	94.4	85.7
Light industry			
Total	−18.9	2.6	−6.9
Non-COMECON	−16.0	15.0	−2.2
N-C share	76.4	81.2	89.2
Wood and paper			
Total	−11.0	16.4	37.6
Non-COMECON	−8.3	—	37.6
N-C share	88.9	97.6	99.9
Ferrous and non-ferrous metals			
Total	−1.3	44.2	31.8
Non-COMECON	−0.2	52.7	35.0
N-C share	85.4	91.7	93.5
Mineral products and miscellaneous			
Total	−7.9	29.5	22.5
Non-COMECON	−5.9	—	23.9
N-C share	87.9	92.3	93.5
Fuel and energy			
Total	−2.2	7.1	−8.2
Non-COMECON	0.4	3.9	6.7
N-C share	64.9	90.0	87.4
Engineering products			
Total	1.7	−1.2	−22.2
Non-COMECON	—	8.7	−9.9
N-C share	45.0	55.4	70.0
Chemicals			
Total	1.1	41.0	−10.8
Non-COMECON	−0.6	42.9	−1.7
N-C share	67.2	81.6	83.9
ALL INDUSTRIES			
Total	−1.2	12.3	−3.3
Non-COMECON	1.1	3.9	6.7
N-C share	63.7	77.7	85.5

Source: Ministry of Industry.
a. First eight months.

TABLE 4.3   Distribution of Poland's non-COMECON industrial exports, by industry, 1988–1991 (percent)

	1988	1989	1990	1991[a]
Food products	14.2	15.4	12.6	9.9
Light industry	8.7	7.4	7.8	6.4
Textiles	4.3	3.5	2.8	2.0
Clothing	2.7	2.5	2.9	2.8
Leather products	1.6	1.3	2.0	1.6
Wood products	4.4	3.7	3.8	4.4
Glass products	1.1	1.0	1.2	1.7
Metallurgy				
Iron and steel	5.6	6.9	9.7	12.2
Non-ferrous metals	10.6	9.2	10.0	10.7
Metal products	3.4	4.0	4.3	4.6
Shipbuilding	2.3	3.2	1.8	3.5
Total "comparative advantage" products (see table 4.1)	50.2	50.7	51.1	53.4
Coal products	10.8	9.4	8.5	8.8
Engineering products (including metal products)	27.0	28.4	25.8	22.5
Chemicals	13.1	12.6	13.9	15.4

Source and notes: See table 4.2.

[1992] has argued that Eastern Europe's exports in the early transition tended to be somewhat understated, although not nearly as much as its imports.)

It is clear from the data that Poland does not have a leading sector comparable to the one that Japan, Korea, and Taiwan enjoyed in cotton spinning and weaving. Poland's exports are more widely dispersed across industries than East Asia's were, as indicated in table 4.3. Cotton textiles accounted for almost half of Korea's and Taiwan's exports in the 1960s. They represented a similar percentage of Japan's exports in 1950 and as much as 37% of Japan's total exports as late as 1955 (in which year steel accounted for another 24%) (Nakamura 1981, pp. 60–61). No one industry among Poland's exports to non-COMECON countries in 1988–1991 accounted for more than 13% of the total. East Asia's export concentration provided an important shock absorber by creating both jobs and easy entry conditions for small entrepreneurs in industries with labor-intensive production techniques. The learning period required to enter world markets was also short. The wider dispersion of Poland's exports across industries has the advantage of risk-diffusion. All of Poland's comparative advantage industries, as defined above, also accounted for almost half of Poland's total employment (see table 4.4). Nevertheless, as

TABLE 4.4 Sales growth rate of Poland's "comparative advantage" products, ranked by employment shares

Industry	Share of industrial employment, 1990	Growth rates sales[a]
Food products	12.3	−10.3
Textiles	8.9	−17.0
Metal products	6.9	−9.8
Clothing	6.0	−8.1
Iron and steel	4.2	−14.4
Footwear	2.7	—
Wood products	2.6	−4.4
Non-ferrous metals	1.8	−13.6
Glass products	1.4	−8.0
Shipbuilding	1.1	—
Total "comparative advantage" products (see table 4.1)	47.9	
Coal	11.3	
Engineering products (including metal products)	35.2	
Chemicals	5.1	
ALL INDUSTRY	100.0[b]	−12.1

Source: Ministry of Industry.
a. 1989–1991 (I–VIII).
b. May not add to 100 due to rounding.

yet Poland has no single export item with as big—or as unproblematic—a capacity to generate employment, entrepreneurial opportunities, and income for reinvestment as East Asia once enjoyed. Its reindustrialization problem, therefore, is that much more difficult.

Metallurgy

Poland's single most important export category by 1991 was metallurgy, which included the processing of ferrous (iron and steel) and nonferrous (say, copper and aluminum) metals. Metallurgy accounted for almost one-fourth of total exports. The share of the iron and steel industry in non-COMECON exports doubled in about three years, reaching a share of 12.2% of total exports in 1991 (about half the share of what steel exports represented in Japan in 1955). The export growth rate of ferrous and nonferrous metals far exceeded the growth rate for other manufacturing sectors, as indicated in table 4.2. Total exports grew by 12.3% in 1990 and −3.3% in 1991 (first eight months), while metallurgical exports grew by 44.2% and 31.8% in the same period. The employment share of the metallurgical sector in 1990, however, was only 6%.

Whatever its employment impact, the problems of Poland's metallurgical sector make it an unlikely candidate to spearhead laissez-faire export growth in the immediate future. First, metallurgy is generally energy inefficient and polluting. For example, one index indicated that Poland's steel industry used 4.3 times as much energy as the world average (OECD 1992a). As energy costs have risen in Poland with the abolition of government energy subsidies, costs have risen. Poland's metallurgical sector requires major investments to meet the environmental standards of the OECD and now Poland itself. It is unlikely that the private sector—foreign or local—will be willing or able at market-determined production costs to undertake the necessary clean-up operations, especially as domestic real interest rates have become extremely high (OECD 1992b). Therefore, if the metallurgical sector is to become an export leader, it initially requires some government intervention to clear its path.

Second, "getting the prices right" in the form of devaluation may, in theory, boost the metallurgical sector's international competitiveness. In 1992, for example, Poland was not fully using the quota the U.S. government gave it for steel sales to the American market, partly because demand for all imported steels in the United States was soft and partly because the Polish steel industry was not able to compete in terms of price against either mini-mills or integrated steel companies from abroad. Export success in 1990 and 1991 may have depended on below-marginal-cost pricing. According to managers at the Huta Katowice Steel Company, one of Poland's largest and possibly efficient mills, the European Community has threatened to take it to court for dumping. Further devaluations could conceivably improve the Polish steel industry's cost position. But in practice, even if it were possible to engineer further real devaluations to lower costs, the metallurgical sector suffers from problems other than environmental pollution that devaluation cannot solve.

One problem concerns the need for restructuring. Observers of the steel industry note that there are twenty-six steel mills in Poland (competing against one another), which need to be consolidated. Some mills need to be shut down and others expanded. Investment, financing, and marketing need to be integrated. Some steel managers argue that before it is possible to attract foreign investors, it is necessary to know the overall target capacity of Poland's steel industry, and which plants are likely to survive and which to fail. Given all the externalities involved in this restructuring, a government role is inevitable.

A related problem concerns necessary investments to sustain exports once excess domestic capacity is exhausted. As in virtually every industry in Poland, the metallurgical sector's exports reflect a diversion of capacity from the severely depressed home market to the export market (see Rodrik 1992). This reorientation is not altogether without its price. Huta Katowice managers, for example, note that their mill was designed to export only about 30%–35% of its output, which it was doing before 1989, not 70%, which it began to do thereafter. Huta Katowice mostly produces by-products that ought to be further processed by other Polish steel mills to add maximum value, rather than exported directly. Table 4.5 indicates that the share of exports in total sales of the iron and steel industry rose from 13.2% in 1988 to 22.9% only two years later. (Comparable figures for nonferrous metals were 26.5% and 34.7%.) Exports in total sales for all industries showed a similar trend, rising from 18.8% in 1988 to 24.2% in 1990.

TABLE 4.5   Share of exports in an industry's total sales, Poland, 1988, 1989, 1990 (percent)

	1988	1989	1990
Food products			
COMECON	0.8	0.5	0.4
Non-COMECON	9.0	9.5	14.1
Total	9.8	10.0	14.5
Textiles			
COMECON	2.3	1.7	1.4
Non-COMECON	7.7	6.8	14.4
Total	10.0	8.5	15.8
Clothing			
COMECON	4.7	2.4	1.2
Non-COMECON	12.0	12.9	41.1
Total	16.7	15.3	42.3
Footwear			
COMECON	7.6	3.3	1.0
Non-COMECON	8.6	7.3	30.6
Total	16.2	10.6	31.6
Wood products			
COMECON	1.6	0.9	0.5
Non-COMECON	14.2	12.9	22.8
Total	15.8	13.8	23.3
Glass products			
COMECON	3.2	1.7	1.5
Non-COMECON	16.8	16.5	32.1
Total	20.0	18.2	33.6
Iron and steel			
COMECON	3.2	2.6	0.9
Non-COMECON	10.0	12.9	22.0
Total	13.2	15.5	22.9

(continued)

Table 4.5   *(Continued)*

	1988	1989	1990
Non-ferrous metals			
COMECON	1.1	0.9	0.1
Non-COMECON	25.4	26.0	34.6
Total	26.5	26.9	34.7
Metal products			
COMECON	6.3	5.8	3.4
Non-COMECON	8.4	11.2	19.4
Total	14.7	17.0	22.8
Shipbuilding			
COMECON	38.6	41.7	32.5
Non-COMECON	29.4	49.3	54.7
Total	68.0	90.0	87.2
Fuel and energy			
COMECON	4.2	3.6	1.9
Non-COMECON	9.3	14.5	14.3
Total	13.5	18.1	16.2
Engineering products			
COMECON	21.4	26.4	13.3
Non-COMECON	12.8	15.8	24.0
Total	34.2	42.2	37.3
Chemicals			
COMECON	7.7	6.9	4.8
Non-COMECON	14.4	16.8	27.8
Total	22.1	23.7	32.6
All Industries			
COMECON	7.5	6.6	4.0
Non-COMECON	11.3	13.0	20.2
Total	18.8	19.6	24.2

Source: Ministry of Industry.

The danger of an abrupt shift toward exports is that if and when the domestic market recovers, capacity may suddenly be shifted back to home sales. Exports will then decline at a time when rising domestic income sustains high import demand. To give stability to export promotion requires investments in export capacity, but as table 4.6 and common sense suggest, investment activity in Poland has crashed. Although investments in the iron and steel industry (and in chemicals) were positive in 1990, this reflected earlier investments that were in the pipeline rather than new ventures. Given high domestic interest rates and the fact that lumpy investments in metallurgy in virtually every country require government guarantees, some role for the government in the metallurgical sector appears indispensable.

**TABLE 4.6   Fixed investment in industry,
1988–1990 (percentage change)**

Industry.	1988	1989	1990
Food products	19.0	38.5	−9.5
Textiles	26.7	25.2	−42.5
Clothing	15.5	24.6	−37.5
Leather products	32.9	−7.1	−50.0
Wood products	28.1	30.9	−11.0
Glass products	−3.0	46.3	0.0
Iron and steel	−4.8	25.0	70.0
Non-ferrous metals	7.7	16.1	−5.5
Metal products	14.7	0.8	−24.0
Fuel and energy	−6.2	−17.2	−11.0
Engineering products	4.1	−3.8	−11.5
Chemicals	12.4	19.1	6.5
ALL INDUSTRIES	4.4	3.8	−18.0

Source: OECD (1992a).
Investment values are in constant prices.

Food Processing

Food processing is one of Poland's most promising export industries. It can use Poland's potentially rich agricultural resources to raise farmers' incomes, create manufacturing employment, and earn foreign exchange. It accounted for about 10% of total exports in 1991 (down from about 15% earlier) and about 12% of total employment. It still has a long way to go, however, before it can become a leading export sector. In 1990, the share of exports in the food processing industry's total sales was only about 15%, which was below the all-industry average of 24.2% (see table 4.5). Food processing exports to the OECD also showed a negative trend in the first eight months of 1991 (table 4.2).

One problem is that many foodstuffs are inefficiently processed given current production methods. Along with coal mining, food processing was one of Poland's most subsidized industries before the transition (Schaffer 1992). According to some unpublished estimates of postsocialist Poland's domestic resource costs undertaken for the OECD by Paul Hare, only some food processing branches are competitive at world prices. Others, despite Poland's rich agricultural resources, cannot compete against the world's leading food industry oligopolies. Foreign investment in the food processing industry may resolve some of these inefficiencies, but it is unlikely that enough foreign investors will arrive in the near future to transform the entire sector.

A more serious problem is that Eastern Europe may be "getting the prices right," but Western Europe's trade barriers remain highest for processed foods. Poland's association agreement with the European Community is more restrictive for agricultural and food products than for other potential export leaders—coal, steel, and textiles—but even for these possibilities the outlook is unfavorable due to protectionism. Poland may be lucky to have an export bundle that is not concentrated in one or two products, but the bulk of its exports tend to be concentrated precisely in those industries in which most advanced countries erect the highest trade impediments. The EC has not granted Poland favorable asymmetry in the timetable for reciprocal market access liberalization.

Food processing is likely to become more important over time in Poland's exports, but given different global trading conditions in the 1990s compared to the 1960s, it is unlikely to attain the same stature of leading sector as cotton textiles assumed in East Asia. To expand, Poland's processed food industry requires market access overseas, which, in turn, at minimum requires investments in a competent team of government bureaucrats to negotiate Poland's case.[7]

Light Industry

According to a foreign consulting firm's international labor cost comparison of the spinning and weaving industry in 1989–1990, Poland's textile workers earned $0.45–$0.50 per hour (IDI 1991). This compared favorably (for Poland's competitiveness) with hourly rates of $0.72 in India and $0.67 in the Philippines, but unfavorably with $0.39 in Pakistan and $0.37 in China. Workers in Poland in 1989–1990 undoubtedly had a higher living standard than workers in all these developing countries because a large share of their income took the form of social services rather than wages (one reason unemployment has not appeared more "open" in Eastern Europe). Nevertheless, Poland's postsocialist wage rates are undeniably low by world standards. This notwithstanding, its "light," labor-intensive industry has enjoyed anything but stellar growth. As table 4.2 indicates, in 1989 and 1991, the export growth rate of light industry was negative. In 1990 it was only 2.6%. The share of light industry in total exports declined after 1988 (see table 4.3).

There are significant variations among light industries in economic performance. Cotton spinning and weaving ("textiles") has fared the worst, as indicated both by its decreasing share of total exports (table 4.3) and sharp decline in sales (table 4.4). The major reason why the textile industry has done so badly is poor product quality (since the late nineteenth century it has catered to the Russian and East European market), which neither further wage declines nor devaluations can cure.

Apparel manufacturing has done better and is believed to be seriously underrepresented in official statistics of exports and output. This underestimation is inferred from the absence of many of the typical signs of open unemployment in Poland. Given the absence of these signs, it is assumed that workers dismissed from state-owned enterprises create a livelihood for themselves in an informal economy, which supposedly includes such activities as apparel making. Nevertheless, the absence of visible suffering on the part of the unemployed (estimated in early 1992 to number over 12% of the workforce) may be due in Poland and other postsocialist economies to the high incidence of subsidized social services in labor income, most of which (housing, fuel, transportation) have not yet been cut, rather than to official underreporting of economic activity. Even if an informal sector is thriving, moreover, it need not necessarily include much manufacturing activity. Certainly the officially recorded private sector that has mushroomed in the transition includes little manufacturing activity (OECD 1992a).

In support of the hypothesis that a large informal clothing manufacturing sector does not exist in Poland (greater than, say, twice what official statistics suggest), is the difficulty of physically locating and identifying it; like unemployment, it too is invisible. For example, in Lodz, Poland's former textile center, there is tangible evidence of some small apparel-making shops emerging, but not on a massive scale. For what the official statistics are worth, they indicate that by early 1991 the apparel industry accounted for a mere 2.8% of total exports (table 4.3).

Given Poland's proximity to Western Europe and the country's supply of cheap labor, the apparel industry may flourish in the immediate future on the basis of the "right" prices, if not in the form of capitalist production, then in the form of the "putting out" system: West Europeans will supply Polish labor with more and more cloth to cut, trim, and sew for export. This may increase employment, but the low value-added involved may do little to finance Poland's greater reindustrialization needs. One reason East Asia's textile industries contributed so much to economic development was their vertical integration, embracing first cotton spinning and weaving and later the production of synthetic fibers (which the government was responsible for encouraging) and apparel.

By way of concluding this section, the answer to the question of whether or not Poland's comparative advantage industries can compete on the basis of market-determined production costs, without East Asian-style government support, is mixed. On the one hand, the very fact that a wide range of industries, most of them still state-owned, is scrambling to export suggests that enterprises in these industries are responding to some market signals. They do not all deserve the epithet of inert communist relics that must be swept away in a wave of crash privatization if Poland is to proceed. On the other hand, the mere expansion of exports to OECD countries should not be taken as prima facie evidence that Poland's comparative advantage industries can compete at world prices. Under conditions of extreme domestic recession, firms everywhere tend to sell overseas below marginal costs, as evidence for the Huta Katowice steel mill indicates. Reliable data on profitability in the transition are difficult to find. For what it's worth, a careful enterprise-level study undertaken by the World Bank Resident Mission in Warsaw (Pinto, Belka, and Krajewski 1992) found that by the fourth quarter of 1990, five out of ten metallurgical firms and one out of twelve chemical firms were making losses on exports. Twelve months later, these figures had shot up to a "staggering" eight out of ten and five out of twelve firms respectively. Rodrik (1992) also found a strong negative correlation between profitability and exports throughout Eastern Europe.

With the exceptions of the clothing and wood processing industries (Poland has been exporting hand-decorated wooden boxes), Poland's major exports show the same signs of not being able to expand at market prices without some form of government assistance as those of Korea and Taiwan exhibited in the 1960s. Poland's metallurgical sector requires government support to restructure and raise the capital necessary to meet environmental standards. The textile industry needs a period of protection from foreign competition in order to improve its product quality, and so forth.[8] Further emphasis on getting the prices "right," moreover, will not solve these structural problems.

Enterprise-Level Bottlenecks

Thus far, the ability of Eastern Europe to compete in world markets has been analyzed in terms of the comparative advantage of industries, but the concept of comparative advantage itself is arguably not very relevant to postsocialism. The "law" of comparative advantage, which calls for a country to specialize in industries whose factor proportions harmonize with its own factor endowments, is applicable, if ever, mostly to countries that are just starting to industrialize, as was the case of Korea and Taiwan in the 1960s. The law makes little sense once a country has commenced industrializing and already has in existence a diverse endowment of skills (some backward, others highly advanced), as well as a mixture of industries of different factor proportions. Such a blend of capabilities and industries exists in postsocialist Eastern Europe and also existed in postwar Japan, which is one reason why Japan deliberately flouted comparative advantage theory, and instead made it a policy to promote only those existing industries with potentially high productivity and market growth, whatever their factor proportions (see, for example, Okita 1967). Given the limitations of applying comparative advantage policy prescriptions to postsocialism, the issue of competitiveness should be examined at the enterprise level.

The wisdom of this focus is suggested by the diversity of industries already engaged in exporting in Poland (and in Hungary and the Czech and Slovak Federal Republic). Many industries other than those the OECD classified as possessing "comparative advantage" have had considerable export success. Poland's engineering industry, for example, accounted for almost one-quarter of non-COMECON exports, and its chemical sector accounted for another 15% (see table 4.3).

Making the enterprise rather than the industry the unit of analysis in assessing competitiveness under postsocialism recommends itself because in almost every industry, some good firms coexist with bad ones. This coexistence became evident from the firm-level research I carried out in conjunction with the OECD's project on Polish industry (1992a). Consultant's enterprise reports, contracted to further the privatization effort by international lenders, also tell a mixed story. While data on profitability (for 1990) are far from reliable, they do show fairly unambiguously a wide dispersion in profit rates across firms within the same industry (see OECD 1992a).

With respect to the "good" firms, the meaning of "good" requires clarification. Many firms in Poland that appear to be inherently viable and hold potential as world competitors were not profitable when we studied them in late 1991 or the first half of 1992. Although economists understandably equate a good firm with a profitable one, "good" did not always mean profitable amid the profound disequilibria characteristic of postsocialist Poland (where, for instance, even relatively efficient firms were being made insolvent by an interfirm credit market). Instead of using a profitability criterion, we somewhat arbitrarily classified a firm as potentially "good" based on eclectic considerations (supplemented, where available, by information in consultants' reports): its history (whether or not it had been able to export to the West before the transition, for example); whether it had a potentially salable product; and, perhaps most important, the capabilities of its managers and workers. The information we collected to arrive at a judgment on a firm's potential was sometimes supplemented by in-depth reports on the same firm undertaken by management consultants financed by the international organizations interested in promoting privatization (e.g., the World Bank).

What we noticed even about "good" firms was that all suffered generally from managerial weaknesses, especially with respect to marketing and cost control. In addition, each suffered from one or another type of bottleneck. These would have to be relieved if such enterprises were to prosper. Here we merely provide brief examples of four generic types of bottlenecks that "good" enterprises suffered from (some from more than one): (1) market access; (2) technology; (3) product; and (4) equipment. More detailed analysis of each bottleneck (and the conditions necessary for their alleviation) will appear in Amsden, Kochanowicz, and Taylor (forthcoming). The question at issue in examining enterprise-level bottlenecks is whether market forces alone can overcome them.

Market Access Bottleneck

Aside from some managerial weaknesses (about which no more will be said), some firms in Poland suffered from almost no bottleneck other than one associated with the market imperfections existing in other countries. Increasingly, Eastern Europe operates on an uneven playing field, with its own markets much more free than those of its neighbors or competitors (see OECD 1992b for Poland's revised tariff structure). An example of a market-access-constrained enterprise was a copper processing company that had ultramodern equipment, good technology (including skills), and excellent people (energetic managers, conscientious workers, good labor relations). What was holding this company back was simply a European cartel that controlled copper exports in the region. As noted earlier, many promising Polish food processing companies suffered from a similar market access constraint (as well as other bottlenecks).

Another company confronting a different type of market access barrier was the old Lenin Shipyard (LS for short) where the Solidarity union got its start. Despite this shipyard's bad press as a competitive entity, it had succeeded in transforming itself into a joint stock company and operated with two years of orders on its books. It was thinking of expanding, provided it could find capable workers who were willing to work as hard as a job in shipbuilding demands. Ironically, the LS's relatively bright future contrasts with that of a more modern Polish shipyard that was threatened with bankruptcy because it assumed (incorrectly) that it would be bought by foreign buyers after the transition and, therefore, did not aggressively seek new orders. The type of market access barrier the LS was suffering from was a shortage of supplier credits. Shipyards the world over offer potential clients attractive financial packages, which typically require credit guarantees from their own government. The LS was having trouble getting the Polish government to give it such credit guarantees (because conditionality on a World Bank loan prevented the newly formed "development bank" from arranging such guarantees) (see Amsden, Kochanowicz, and Taylor, forthcoming). This type of access barrier exists in a world of imperfect markets, which are proving to be more of a binding constraint for East European firms in the 1990s than for East Asian firms in the 1960s, if only because the production structures of East and West European firms in the 1990s are more similar to one another than the production structures of East Asia and its major trading partner, the United States, were in the 1960s.

Technology Bottleneck

Many postsocialist companies, particularly in the engineering sector, suffer from inferior technology-cum-skills (relative to that of their competitors). For example, two companies—one Hungarian and another Polish—happen to produce a roughly similar product, which in the past was supplied to the COMECON market: instruments for control systems in continuous process industries (sugar refining and petrochemicals). Both companies are multi-product. The Polish firm has managed to keep itself alive by exporting more to the West of one minor "cash cow" product line (amounting to only 12% of sales). Although the quality (measured in terms of conformance to specification) of both firms' control instruments is generally regarded as good, it is also slightly below international standards in terms of performance design. To upgrade, the Polish company needs foreign technology, either in the form of a foreign license or a joint venture, but as yet has been unable to find a foreign partner.

Premier firms in Korea and Taiwan invested in their own technology development rather than become too heavily dependent on foreign technology transfers. In Poland, in-house investments in technology will also be necessary if foreign technology is to be imported more successfully. But it is unlikely that postsocialist firms can rely as much on "reverse engineering" and in-house technology development as East Asian firms were able to do in the 1970s. Generally the product lines of postsocialist engineering firms are already too advanced to enable this strategy to work, and it is a strategy that takes time—and tariff protection—to master.

Product Bottleneck

Analogous to a technology bottleneck is a product bottleneck: many firms in Poland do not offer products that are as appealing to consumers as those foreign competitors offer, either because the products they supply are not attractive or because their performance is poor. These firms do not lack advanced technology so much as a knowledge of consumer markets, and the organizational capabilities (ranging from product design to quality engineering, to marketing) necessary to capture them. Some companies in the textile industry are good examples of promising enterprises that now find themselves confronting a product bottleneck.

Equipment Bottleneck

An equipment bottleneck refers to a fetter on a firm's competitiveness due to a capital good constraint. Some Polish firms with adequate skills, products, and market access suffered from high costs or low quality due to old equipment that did not embody the latest technology. The Huta Katowice Steel Company is a good example of such a firm. Its future competitiveness depends both on the restructuring of the Polish steel industry, to weed out excess capacity, and its own acquisition of continuous casting equipment. The company found a Swiss investment bank interested in financing this large equipment purchase, but with the proviso that Huta Katowice be given a credit guarantee by the Polish government.

We may conclude this section by briefly examining whether or not firms suffering from one or more bottleneck are likely to be able to overcome them under a political regime of laissez-faire. It is worth recalling that in standard price theory, if a country follows its comparative advantage and "gets the prices right," then the competitiveness of its industries is ensured by two assumptions: in neoclassical trade theory, firms are assumed to operate with the same production function as efficient firms in other countries; in Ricardian trade theory, technology can vary across firms in the same industry, but competitiveness along comparative advantage lines is guaranteed by currency devaluation. What do these assumptions imply for Eastern Europe?

Identical Production Functions/Foreign Investment

If, of course, firms in Eastern Europe operated with the same production functions as their foreign competitors, they would not be facing any of the bottlenecks outlined above (with the possible exception of the market access constraint). The corollary of the assumption of identical production functions is the assumption that Eastern Europe's bottlenecks will vanish with the arrival of foreign investors, with state-of-the art technology, attractive products, modern capital equipment (i.e., world standard production functions), and possibly even the power to batter down foreign trade barriers.

Suffice it to say here that East Asia's experience with foreign investment suggests that this alternative assumption is naive. In East Asia, foreign investment tended to lag rather than lead industrial development; it arrived only after a semblance of political stability had been achieved and industrialization had started, and only then did it accelerate growth (Herman 1991). Foreign investment inflows also never amounted to a very high share of the region's total capital formation, as indicated in table 4.7.

Devaluation

Even ignoring the inflationary effects of further devaluations, this method of creating competitiveness is unlikely to work miracles in Eastern Europe—although a case could be made that some East European currencies are overvalued, and that certain industries would benefit from a more competitive exchange rate (a case in point being Poland's pollution-intensive metallurgical sector).

Nevertheless, case studies of Polish firms suggest that the competitive

TABLE 4.7   Inward direct foreign investment (IDFI) in gross investment, selected countries, 1967–86

	IDFI	
	Amount (million $)	Share (%)
Republic of Korea		
1967–75	51.0	1.7
1976–80	61.0	0.4
1981–86	168.0	0.7
Taiwan		
1967–75	47.0	2.0
1976–80	106.0	1.2
1981–86	212.0	1.7
Indonesia		
1967–75	99.0	4.4
1976–80	253.0	2.4
1981–86	230.0	0.9
Malaysia		
1967–75	173.0	13.7
1976–80	559.0	11.6
1981–86	991.0	10.5
Thailand		
1967–75	66.0	2.9
1976–80	98.0	1.5
1981–86	276.0	3.1
United States		
1967–75	1,750.0	0.8
1976–80	8,947.0	2.0
1981–86	20,077.0	3.0

Source: UNESCAP (1990).

problems of postsocialism are not related so much to costs as to noncost factors or "quality" (including pollution). Although free-market reformers stress the importance of lowering labor costs, labor costs as a share of total costs in Eastern Europe tend to be extremely low—around 15% in Hungary (both before and after the transition) and about the same percentage in Poland (depending on how costs are measured) (World Bank 1984; MIT 1991; Pinto, Belka, and Krajewski 1992; Amsden, Kochanowicz, and Taylor, forthcoming). Instead of high costs, the bottlenecks impeding Polish industry are largely qualitative in nature and relate to market access, product design, and technology. A policy of devaluation cannot cure these noncost hindrances, and may make matters worse if devaluation increases the costs of imported machinery and technology.

Barring divine intervention, therefore, and for want of a better alternative, the solution to these bottlenecks lies with government intervention, much as it did in East Asia. This is not to say that all promising postsocialist firms need government assistance, or that all can use it. In the case of firms suffering from a technology constraint, for example, it is hard to see how any reasonable amount of government support could supplant the need for foreign technical assistance; the two must work in concert. It is simply to say that the market mechanism, operating alone, is unlikely to be able to transform Eastern Europe's potentially productive enterprises into international competitors without some form, however temporary, of government coordination and support.

Conclusion: Stop the Infantilization!

Orthodox transition economics regards enterprise restructuring as either the purview of privatization or free-market forces. It denies an activist role for the state. But because privatization has in fact proceeded very slowly—and in any event is not a panacea—enterprise restructuring policy has been reduced to "getting the prices right."

In theory, this liberal restructuring strategy may be suitable for the least industrialized countries (although East Asian experience in the 1960s suggests otherwise), but it is altogether unsuitable for the semi-industrialized countries of Eastern Europe.[9]

Price liberalization in Eastern Europe has meant increasing the production costs of energy and capital and decreasing labor costs, thereby favoring the growth of relatively labor-intensive industries. "Getting the prices right" has effectively anointed sectors with high labor content as Eastern Europe's "comparative advantage," and has left low wages as its major competitive asset. In terms of international trade, Eastern Europe is supposed to find it easy to export low-end products to neighboring high-wage industrialized countries.

This policy, however, infantilizes Eastern Europe, which already has in existence a wide array of industries with differing skill levels. Specialization according to narrowly defined factor proportions is impractical. Almost all of Eastern Europe's industries have at least one or two promising state-owned enterprises which, if seriously restructured, could almost certainly compete in world markets. Getting the prices right by slashing wages, however, does not address these enterprises' problems, which are principally related to poor product quality and outdated technology—not to too high costs. Wage cutting is injurious to constructive labor relations and beside the point, especially since wages in Eastern Europe are such a small fraction of enterprise production costs.

Moreover, export-led growth for semi-industrialized countries, based on static comparative advantage, is an even trickier proposition politically than it is for developing countries, because semi-industrializers possess a set of industries that substantially overlaps that of high-wage countries (with many heavy industries in common). The expectation of open markets is particularly naive for Eastern Europe because for geographical reasons, Eastern Europe's natural resource-based exports are more similar to those of its highly industrialized neighbors than are the resource-based exports of poor, far-off tropical countries.

The East Asian experience indicates that neither developing nor semi-industrialized countries has grown by "getting the prices right." Instead, growth has been a matter of systematic, disciplined state intervention, at all development stages, to help selected industries and firms overcome their low quality and productivity problems. State intervention has been less a matter of ideological conviction than practical necessity, given that late industrializers have had to navigate world markets without the competitive advantage that drove earlier industrializers: technologically new products and processes.

Selective support of state-owned enterprises in the immediate future will be crucial in Eastern Europe if only because the one bright economic spot in the transition, a rise in exports, has largely been undertaken by state-owned firms, on the basis of excess capacity that cannot last forever. In Poland, it was estimated that in 1991 state-owned enterprises accounted for 79.1% of total exports and only 51.1% of total imports (see OECD 1992a, table 11). In Hungary, the largest fifty enterprises, most of them almost certainly state-owned (or technically owned by the state property agency and awaiting private suitors), accounted for 86% of total exports in the first part of 1990 (Gacs 1991). Unless these state-owned enterprises are restructured, export activity in manufactured products will decline and the foreign trade balance will register serious deficits.

Thus, seeing the East European dilemma through the eyes of the East Asian experience suggests that if economic development is to continue, dirigisme cannot die. Life after dirigisme must involve systematic, performance-based state intervention, away from the extremes of central planning and neoliberalism, toward some variant of the modern capitalist model of the most successful late-industrializers. "Getting the prices right" *tout court* never accounted for industrialization in East Asia and does not appear to be capable of the reindustrialization of Eastern Europe.

Notes

I am thankful to Jean Guinet and Daniel Malkin of the OECD for helpful suggestions and material support. A summary of an earlier version of this paper was published in *Transition* 4,4 (May 1993), and I benefited from discussions with its editor, Richard Hirschler.

1. More than fifteen state-owned enterprises were studied, in industries that included steel, shipbuilding, textiles, food processing, and metalworking, but only fifteen held much promise of attaining profitability if restructured.
2. Attention is focused on structural reform, particularly of state-owned enterprises, rather than price stabilization, because inflation was not a central issue in East Asia starting after the Korean War, so comparing East Asia and Eastern Europe along this dimension is not particularly helpful.
3. Murrell (1990) effectively uses trade as a barometer to study the socialist economies before the transition.
4. Cole and Lyman (1971) present an account of the role of aid donors that is sympathetic, but also indicative of the enormous power aid donors wielded over Korean economic policy. Amsden (1989) summarizes the reforms. See also the overview of Mason et al. (1980).
5. The reality of persistent budget deficits in Korea contrasts with the argument of Sachs (1989), to the effect that East Asia fared better than Latin America in the 1980s debt crisis because of its balanced budgets.
6. This analysis was prepared for the OECD study by Jean Guinet.
7. Trade negotiators in the Austrian ministry of industry in Vienna affirmed that in discussions between the Austrian government and East European trading partners, the Hungarian delegation was usually much better prepared than the Polish delegation.
8. Rather than protection, a better policy might be to give garment makers incentives to buy locally made fabrics (Amsden, Kochanowicz, Taylor, forthcoming).
9. The application of neoclassical theory to understand the East European predicament is skeptically analyzed by Murrell (1990). Richard Portes (1992), the eminent director of the Center for European Policy Research, has begun to argue that after two years of disappointing results, the reform policies in Eastern Europe need to be significantly changed.

References

Amsden, Alice H. 1992a. "A Theory of Government Intervention in Late Industrialization." In Louis Putterman and Dietrich Rueschemeyer, ed., *The State and Market: Rivalry or ?* Boulder, CO: Lynne Rienner.

Amsden, Alice H. 1992b. "The Spectre of Anglo-Saxonization is Haunting South Korea." In Lee-Jay Cho, ed., *Korea's Political Economy: Past, Present, and Future*. East-West Population Institute, East West Center, University of Hawaii, Honolulu.

Amsden, Alice H. 1989. *Asia's Next Giant: South Korea and Late Industrialization*. New York and Oxford: Oxford University Press.

Amsden, Alice H., and Yoon-Dae Euh. 1993. "South Korea's 1980s' Financial Reforms: Good-bye Financial Repression (Maybe), Hello New Institutional Restraints." *World Development* 21, 3 (March): 379–390.

Amsden, Alice H., Jacek Kochanowicz, and Lance Taylor. Forthcoming. *The Market Meets Its Match: Re-Industrializing Eastern Europe*.

Balassa, Bela, et al. 1982. *Development Strategies in Semi-Industrial Economies*. Baltimore: Johns Hopkins University Press.

Boston Consulting Group, Ltd. 1991. *Polish Textile and Clothing Industry Restructuring Program*. London: Boston Consulting Group.

Chandler, Alfred D., Jr. 1990. *Scale and Scope: The Dynamics of Industrial Capitalism*. Cambridge, MA: Harvard University Press.

Cole, David C., and P. N. Lyman. 1971. *Korean Development: The Interplay of Politics and Economics*. Cambridge, MA: Harvard University Press.

Gacs, Janos. 1991. "Foreign Trade Liberalization (1968–1990)." In Andras Koves and Paul Marer, eds., *Foreign Economic Liberalization: Transformations in Socialist and Market Economies*. Boulder, CO: Westview Press.

Gerschenkron, Alexander. 1962. *Economic Backwardness in Historical Perspective*. Cambridge, MA: Harvard University Press.

Herman, Barry. 1991. "International Finance of Developing Asia and the Pacific in the 1990s." Mimeo. Department of International Economic and Social Affairs, United Nations, New York.

Hikino, Takashi, and Alice H. Amsden. Forthcoming. "Staying Behind, Stumbling Back, Sneaking Up, Soaring Ahead: Late Industrialization in Historical Perspective." In W. Baumol, R. Nelson, and E. Wolff, eds., *Convergence in Productivity*. New York and Oxford: Oxford University Press.

IDI (International Development Ireland, Ltd.). 1991. *Final Report on Uniontex*. Warsaw: IDI.

Kim, Kwang-Suk. Forthcoming. "Industrial Policy and Trade Regimes in Korea: Past, Present, and Future." In Lee-Jay Cho and Yoon-Hyung Kim, eds., *Korea's Political Economy: Past, Present, and Future*. East West Center, Hawaii.

Kim, Kwang-Suk. 1991. "Trade and Industrialization Policies in Korea: An Overview." World Institute for Development Economics Research, Helsinki.

Kim, Kwang-Suk. 1990. "Import Liberalization and Its Impact in Korea." In Jene K. Kwon, ed., *Korean Economic Development*. New York: Greenwood Press.

Kim, Kwang-Suk. 1988. *Economic Impact of Import Liberalization and Industrial Adjustment Policy in Korea* (in Korean). Seoul: Korea Development Institute Press.

Kim, Kwang-Suk. 1987. "The Nature of Trade Protection by Special Laws in Korea." Discussion Paper No. 87-01, Graduate School of Business Administration, Kyung Hee University, Seoul.

Mason, E. S., et al. 1980. *The Economic and Social Modernization of the Republic of Korea*. Cambridge, MA: Harvard University Press for the Council on East Asian Studies, Harvard University.

MIT (Ministry of Industry and Trade, Hungary). 1991. *Hungarian Industry and Trade, 1980–1990*. Budapest: MIT.

Murrell, Peter. 1990. *The Nature of Socialism: Lessons from East European Foreign Trade*. Princeton: Princeton University Press.

Nakamura, Takafusa. 1981. *The Postwar Japanese Economy: Its Development and Structure*. Tokyo, University of Tokyo Press.

OECD (Organization for Economic Co-operation and Development). 1992a. *Industry Review of Poland: Structural Adjustment Issues and Policy Options*. Paris: OECD.

OECD. 1992b. *OECD Economic Surveys, Poland 1992*. Paris: OECD.

OECD. 1990; 1991. *Industrial Policy in OECD Countries, Annual Review*. Paris: OECD.

Okita, Saburo. 1967. *Causes and Problems of Rapid Growth in Postwar Japan and Their Implications for Newly Developing Economies*. Center Paper No. 6, Tokyo, Japan Economic Research Center.

Park, Yung Chul. 1991. "Liberalization in Korea and Taiwan." In Andras Koves and Paul Marer, eds., *Foreign Economic Liberalization: Transformations in Socialist and Market Economies*. Boulder and Oxford: Westview Press.

Pinto, Brian, Marek Belka, and Stefan Krajewski. 1992. "Microeconomics of Transition in Poland: A Survey of State Enterprise Responses." Country Economics Department, The World Bank, September, WPS 982, Washington, D.C.

Presidential Commission on Economic Restructuring (Korea). 1988. *Realigning Korea's National Priorities for Economic Advance: Presidential Commission Report on Economic Restructuring*, Seoul.

Rhee, Yung-Whee, Bruce Ross-Larson, and Garry Pursell. 1984. *Korea's Competitive Edge: Managing the Entry into World Markets*. Baltimore: Johns Hopkins University Press.

Rodrik, Dani. 1992. "Foreign Trade in Eastern Europe's Transition: Early Results." Working Paper No. 4064, National Bureau of Economic Research, Cambridge, MA.

Sachs, Jeffrey. 1989. *Developing Country Debt and the World Economy*. Chicago: University of Chicago Press.

Sachs, Jeffrey, and David Lipton. 1990. "Creating a Market Economy in Eastern Europe: The Case of Poland." *Brookings Papers on Economic Activity* 1.

Schaffer, Mark E. 1990. "State-Owned Enterprises in Poland: Taxation, Subsidization, and Competition Policies." *European Economy* 43 (March).

Tsujimura, Kotaro. 1984. *Nippon no Keizaigakushatachi (Japanese Economists)*. Tokyo: Nihon Hyoronsha.

United Nations Economic and Social Council for Asia and the Pacific. 1990. *Restructuring the Developing Economies of Asia and the Pacific in the 1990s*. New York: United Nations.

World Bank. 1984. *Hungary: Economic Developments and Reforms*. Washington, D.C.: World Bank.

Part II
The Postsocialist Transitions

CHAPTER 5

Socialist Transformations: An Overview of Eastern Europe and Some Comparators

Alan Gelb

Following the breakup of the USSR and the fragmentation of Yugoslavia, there are now some forty-two countries that are reforming away from a communist or strongly socialist past, while only two countries remain staunchly and traditionally communist.[1] About twenty-eight of the above forty-four countries (equal in number to one-fourth of current UN membership) are deeply and directly affected by the breakup of the CMEA trading system and the fragmentation of the Soviet Union. Some of the others are affected by cuts in Soviet economic and military aid, as are a number of countries, many with heavily intervened economies, which are not considered here as "socialist."[2] Because of its autarkic economy, the direct economic effects of Soviet collapse are relatively small for most countries outside the CMEA. However, countries not in the group of twenty-eight have been undergoing an ideological reorientation accelerated by the collapse, which promises to be its most lasting legacy.

This is not to say that laissez-faire economic philosophy will dominate—indeed, with the fading of ideological confrontation there are signs to the contrary. Rather, government interventions in the reforming countries are increasingly being analyzed in terms of market-based concepts such as externalities, market failures (including in the area of information), risk bearing, and distributional effects of market processes.

Political Transition and Economics

Socialist transformations are deep political and social processes, rather than simply economic events. This has given rise to an extensive debate on the interaction between political and economic reforms. One central issue is the extent to which comprehensive economic reform requires a political transformation toward some type of pluralistic system. This argument has been made most forcefully in the context of Eastern Europe. The counterargument—that partial economic reforms may be initiated prior to political reforms, and that

111

they may cumulate to the point that the political system sheds or modifies its ideology and itself evolves toward democracy—is usually put forward in the East Asian context.[3]

This chapter focuses on the current state of socialist reforms and does not pursue this broad political debate. Certain aspects of the interaction between politics and economics should, however, be borne in mind as directly affecting economic reform programs. The political transitions toward pluralism have been remarkably peaceful, most located somewhere along the spectrum of evolution–revolution rather than at one of the poles. Where a country stands on this continuum has two important implications for the economic transition:

1. The faster and more revolutionary the political transition, the stronger the impulse toward a "big-bang" economic transition, as opposed to an "evolutionary" or managed approach. This is partly because the political transition leaves a power vacuum in the economic sphere, as the new government cannot rely on the existing bureaucratic structures of control.

2. Revolutions or abrupt transitions open windows of opportunity for rapid economic reforms, but leave the state poorly equipped to manage certain critical parts of the reform process that cannot easily be left to the market. On the other hand, economic reforms carried out under a more gradual political evolution will need to include mechanisms for the transformation of the elite, and this will especially affect the process of ownership reform.

Reforms in Eastern Europe after 1990

A Framework for Analysis

Socialist transitions follow country-specific patterns depending on the economic and political features of each country. Nevertheless, there is now quite a wide consensus on the essential components of reform.[4] These are set out in figure 5.1, which groups them into four categories:

1. Taking measures to regain macroeconomic equilibrium and maintain it through the reform period.

2. Introducing broad and competitive markets for goods, factors of production, and foreign exchange.

3. Reforming ownership arrangements, developing private sector activities, and restructuring productive capacity toward market-based needs.

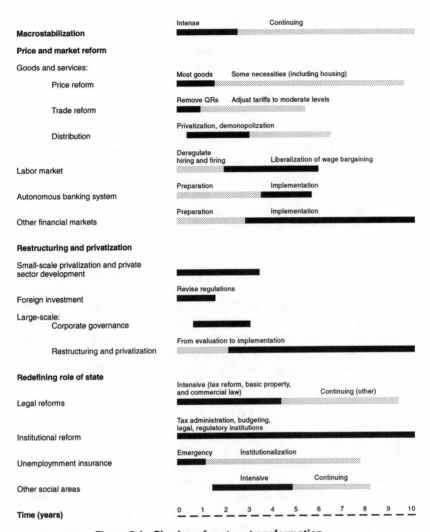

Figure 5.1   Phasing of system transformation

4. Making the essential changes in the role of the state that must initiate or accompany these reforms. In particular, government must enact legislation to provide the legal basis for the functioning of the market system and must reshape the social safety net, in particular to cope with the new phenomenon of open unemployment. More broadly, government will need to change its role of a dominant participant in the economy toward one of supporting the activities of decentralized agents.

Figure 5.1 also offers a stylized time phasing of these measures, derived from a mixture of theory and experience. Its main implications are as follows: severe macroeconomic imbalances require fast actions up front; goods markets can "work" faster than factor markets; and the process of asset and ownership restructuring is likely to be relatively slow. Without repeating details discussed elsewhere, two points may be noted:

1. Because so many measures are complementary, the phasing of reforms in figure 5.1 is not linear. Reforms proceed on a broad front, with some elements taking far longer than others. Political economy arguments are also sometimes advanced for an initial broad package of measures to enhance the credibility of reform.
2. Some reforms proceed in the absence of desirable preconditions. How serious such tensions are depends on the speed of reforms and on the initial conditions of the country concerned.

There is less agreement on the appropriate sequencing of reforms than on their main elements, and some proposals have offered different sequences. One example is the Shatalin 500-Day Plan, which stressed speedy privatization to help absorb part of the monetary overhang prior to extensive price liberalization. China's reforms also appear to be very different because of the country's different initial conditions, but as discussed below, there is now an interesting parallel between the stage of its reforms and those of Eastern Europe.

Initial Conditions for Europe's Reforms

The reforms in Eastern Europe have been driven by several objectives: marketization, privatization, and in particular, integration with Western Europe, especially the EC. The countries shared many common features of Soviet-type economies. For example, all had highly monopolized, overdeveloped, and autarkic industrial sectors, heavily integrated with each other and with Soviet industry through the CMEA system. There were few small firms, service sectors were underdeveloped, open unemployment was negligible, and incomes were rather equally distributed. Welfare was underpinned by an extensive system of social transfers. However, by the start of 1990 the countries differed in some important respects.[5]

The first is the extent to which they were still planned economies. In addition to the former GDR, Czechoslovakia and Bulgaria were the most tightly planned, whereas Hungary (after 1968) and Poland (after 1981) had moved to substitute markets for formal plans in their phases of reform socialism. Reform socialism has been criticized as giving enterprises autonomy without introducing market discipline, and in the process weakening macroeconomic controls and further muddying ownership rights—besides the case of Yugoslavia, by 1990 about 70% of Hungarian and Polish firms were self-managed. Nevertheless, at least in Hungary these changes set the stage for further reforms and introduced an important element of behavioral and institutional adaptation to market conditions.[6] More generally, the partial reforms contributed to a process of reengagement with world markets that somewhat counterbalanced the autarkic tendencies of the CMEA system. The more reform socialist countries—Hungary, Yugoslavia, and Poland—had higher trade shares with non-CMEA countries than did Bulgaria and Czechoslovakia, where market reforms were far less pronounced.[7]

A second difference was the extent of macroeconomic imbalance. Czechoslovakia stands out as having the most favorable macroeconomic balance, with little external debt, low inflation, and no obvious monetary overhang. Romania had repaid its external debt over the past decade, but faced serious internal political and social problems. All of the other countries confronted serious macroeconomic imbalances. External debt was high for Poland, Bulgaria, and Hungary, and the first two countries also faced domestic imbalances in the form of excessive monetary accumulation or monetary overhang. The overhang of Poland was virtually eliminated by the partial price liberalization that left the reform of 1990 confronting hyperinflation.[8] To some extent, macroeconomic imbalances were encouraged by partial reforms that gave enterprises autonomy without imposing full accountability through market mechanisms.

Despite these differences, the Soviet trade shock introduced a large element of macroeconomic imbalance to all countries especially after 1990, somewhat evening out the situation. And except for Hungary, the debt legacy has perhaps been a less important difference than might have been expected. Poland and Bulgaria failed to service their debt, its absence of debt offered Romania little access to external resources, and Czechoslovakia's tight macroeconomic policies left little room for a large debt buildup after reform.

Key Reform Measures

The Polish program initiated in January 1990 involved a combination of macroeconomic and structural reform measures. Its cornerstones were:

- an almost complete price liberalization;
- an open trade regime with low tariffs and virtual elimination of licensing and QRs,[9]

- sharp devaluation of the official exchange rate and exchange rate unification at a new peg 50% lower than the previous official rate, steps that rendered the currency widely convertible on current account;
- tight fiscal policy, including the substantial elimination of price subsidies, sharp nominal interest rate hikes, and the establishment of strict monetary targets; and
- a tax-based policy to limit increases in wage bills to below the rate of inflation.

About one year later Czechoslovakia, Bulgaria, and Romania adopted essentially similar programs. Czechoslovakia, like Poland, pegged its exchange rate to provide a third nominal anchor;[10] in an innovative move, wage earners were provided lump-sum compensation for price increases due to the removal of product subsidies prior to price liberalization. Lacking foreign exchange reserves or special stabilization funds,[11] Bulgaria and Romania floated their exchange rates, which depreciated by some 70% from past official levels.[12]

Hungary's reform represented a deepening of previous measures rather than a decisive break. The exchange rate was devalued more modestly (only by 15%), and price liberalization was extended to cover 90% of the consumer basket by 1991, a progressive rise from 50% in the mid-1980s. Hungary's program also included restrictive monetary, fiscal, and incomes policies, sharp cuts in subsidies, and a progressive move to trade liberalization and current account convertibility.

Together with their macroeconomic reforms, all of the countries undertook intensive measures to establish the foundation for the new market economy. Legislation was intensively drafted to lay the framework for a market system. Systems of unemployment insurance were created. Arrangements began to facilitate rapid privatization. All countries initiated programs of financial sector reform. Negotiations intensified to widen access to EC and other markets.

The Progress of Reforms

The Successes. . . .
Two years is a short period in which to judge the success of such programs, but in some areas reforms can already be considered to have been relatively successful.

1. Inflation has been contained in most countries, although at higher levels than desirable. The "shock therapy" reforms resulted in an initial price shock that was substantially larger than expected.

Monthly inflation peaked at 80% in Poland,[13] 110% in Bulgaria, and 35% in Czechoslovakia, and averaged 13% in the first four months of Romania's program. Only in Hungary, which avoided shock therapy, was initial monthly inflation moderate. Nevertheless, by the end of 1991, monthly inflation had declined to under 2% in Czechoslovakia and Hungary and 3% in Poland. It showed more persistence in Bulgaria and Romania, probably because of these countries' more difficult starting conditions.

There has been much debate on whether the initial devaluations were excessive, in particular for Poland, and whether it would have been preferable to maintain some temporary price controls to blunt the initial increases. There is probably no definitive answer to these questions, except to note that a concern that the reform programs should appear credible for their nominal anchors to be sustained was an important factor in their formulation.

2. Shortages vanished quickly. Price liberalization and the opening of trade dramatically increased the availability and variety of goods. The quantitative impact on welfare is hard to measure and has also been debated strongly, but some positive effect must be set against the adverse macro effects discussed below.

3. Exports to the market economies responded more strongly than anticipated. In 1990–91 the dollar value of such exports rose by 50% for Poland and by 33% for Hungary; data for Czechoslovakia are less clear because of unregistered private trade, but according to OECD statistics its exports have also registered a sizable increase.[14] Combined with the remarkable collapse in the volumes of intra-CMEA trade, mostly because of the situation within the Soviet Union,[15] this signifies an impressive trade reorientation in the direction of plausible longer-run market-based patterns,[16] which did not simply arise from the redirection of exports from the East.

4. Relative to expectations, current account outcomes have been reasonably good. This is especially noteworthy in view of the unexpectedly large Soviet trade shock. For the East European countries as a whole (but excluding, of course, East Germany), the noninterest current account in 1991–92 is roughly in balance. This means that they face the formidable task of stabilization and economic restructuring with very little transfer of real resources.

5. Foreign direct investment into the region has grown steadily. It is still far lower than some had enthusiastically projected at the start of the reforms, but at some $3 billion annually, it is now double initial World Bank projections, with Hungary accounting for over half of the total. Foreign investment into Hungary has been closely connected with the

process of privatization. Of the thirteen largest sales of state companies in 1991, foreign strategic investors acquired majority control in
twelve cases.[17]

6. All of the countries have accomplished a great deal in the area of legal
and regulatory reform, although there are still uncertainties and problems, particularly in areas such as property rights and bankruptcy.[18] In
drafting new legislation, they have drawn on their own precommunist
legal traditions (which in some cases had not been formally repealed),
as well as on the current legal frameworks of industrial countries. In
certain areas, particularly competition policy, reforms are somewhat
less advanced in Romania and Bulgaria than in the three northern
countries.

Success in legal reform is qualified by the need of all the countries to develop the institutions of effective legal administration. In
Czechoslovakia, for example, the number of legal disputes is rising
rapidly (over 121,000 in 1991 alone). This will skyrocket as cases
related to bankruptcy, restitution, and privatization enter the courts.
The number of bankruptcy petitions in Hungary has soared, from 384
in 1989 to 630 in 1990 and more than 1,000 in 1991, and this trend
can only accelerate as restructuring gets under way.

7. Private commercial activity has responded well to reforms, particularly in small-scale trade and distribution and to a modest extent in
production. Hungary has seen explosive growth in the number of
firms, from 8,000 in 1985 to 11,000 in 1988, then to 52,000 by the
end of 1991, mostly new starts but also split-offs from larger enterprises. This number does not include sole proprietorships. Meanwhile, the number of state enterprises has remained steady at some
2,200.[19] The number of economic units in Poland has also soared.
Between 1989 and 1991 the number of partnerships rose from 17,000
to 54,000, and that of sole proprietorships rose from 800,000 to 1.4
million, while the number of state enterprises increased only from
7,300 to 8,200.[20] Starting from a far smaller base, the number of
private ventures in Czechoslovakia has also soared. Since the start of
small-scale privatization in February 1991, almost 20,000 state business units, or half of the total number, have been sold and there are
over a million registered sole proprietors. As of October 1991, there
were some 150,000 registered private businesses in Romania. Numer-
ically at least, the public enterprises are being engulfed in a sea of
private firms, but the vast majority of these are still very small.[21]
Private trade and distribution firms have been instrumental in widening markets and making these more competitive. Only perhaps in
Hungary have private producers begun to introduce a serious element
of competition for the state enterprises.

. . . and the Failures

In other areas, the results from reform have been less satisfactory. This threatens their longer-run political and economic sustainability and has also raised a number of questions concerning the approach to reform.

1. All countries in the region have experienced sharp declines in measured output, which have averaged over 20% in 1990–91 for the better performers in the region.[22] Led by falling industrial output, the declines have been far sharper than anticipated in the reform programs. The recovery to 1989 levels of income per capita is projected to take a number of years, particularly in the Southern tier, as shown in figure 5.2.[23]
2. There have been sharp declines in the statistical real wage, that is, the wage deflated by the consumer price index.
3. Governments are facing serious fiscal difficulties. Tax receipts from traditional sources, in particular the profits of state enterprises, have declined sharply.[24] Meanwhile, administrative capacity is inadequate to tax the emerging private sector. Privatization revenues have been smaller than expected, and to judge by the results of East Germany, they may turn out to be negative in net terms.[25] On the expenditure side, governments face calls to support declining sectors, and recapitalize their banking creditors, many of which are technically insolvent.[26] There may be a direct relationship between the speed of structural and ownership transformation on the one hand and concurrent fiscal imbalances on the other.

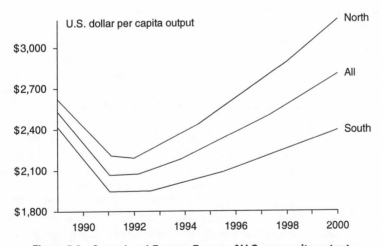

Figure 5.2   Central and Eastern Europe, $U.S. per capita output

4. Governments must also cover insurance for the rapidly rising number of unemployed. Despite slow restructuring of the productive sectors, the number of those filing for unemployment benefits has risen steadily in all countries, to around 12% of the labor force in Poland and Bulgaria, for example. The experience of East Germany, where 30% of the labor force is unemployed, and where only half of the employees are often retained when firms are restructured, suggests that unemployment will be a very serious long-term problem.
5. Large-scale privatization has proceeded slowly, and the level of economic restructuring activity is far too low to support a speedy transition.
6. Except for introducing unemployment insurance, there has also been little restructuring of social safety nets in the direction of improved targeting of benefits to the poorest.

A Reform Puzzle—And a Dilemma

The Puzzle of Falling Output
A shift from an allegedly inefficient planned system toward market organization might be expected to increase efficiency and output, yet the reverse appears to have occurred in Eastern Europe. Does socialist transformation necessarily involve a J-curve, a period of lower output prior to the reemergence of growth?[27] Is the contraction a *cost* of reform, or is it part of the *solution* to the problem of improving efficiency? These questions are important, not only for understanding Eastern Europe, but for other countries undertaking reforms.

Five explanations have been advanced to account for the sharpness and ubiquity of the output declines.

1. *Measurement errors*. For several reasons, official data may overstate both the decline in output and the impact on welfare of falls in deflated wages. Some have argued that they are seriously misleading, and that living standards have not in fact declined much if at all.[28] A more consensual view is that output and real incomes have indeed fallen, though probably by somewhat less than indicated by official statistics.
2. *The Soviet shock*. Developments in the Soviet Union, Eastern Europe's most important trading partner (and also the union of East with West Germany) resulted in a dramatic contraction of trade within the CMEA area, by 80%–90% between Eastern Europe and the former USSR, as well as a terms of trade loss of perhaps 5% of GDP for Eastern Europe.[29] Falling exports within the CMEA zone may have directly accounted for slightly less than half of the output declines: see

Causes of output fall

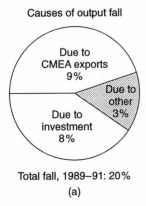

Total fall, 1989–91: 20%

(a)

CMEA exports and output losses 1989–91

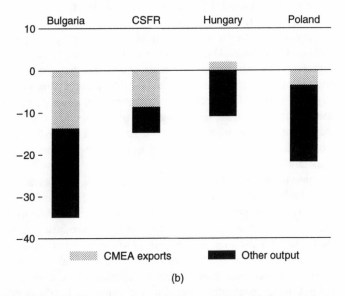

(b)

Figure 5.3   Causes of CMEA output fall and extent of export and output losses

figure 5.3. Using a multiplier of 2, Rodrik (1992) estimates that the shock may have been responsible for 35%, 139%, and 80% of the output losses for Poland, Hungary, and Czechoslovakia respectively. One possible comparator is Finland, where GDP fell by 6% while losing Soviet markets equivalent to 2.5% of GDP, but other factors were also involved.

There is wide agreement on the importance of the trade shock in explaining output decline in Eastern Europe and on the Soviet shock as its main cause, but some debate on whether it could, or should, have been alleviated.[30]

3. *Import competition.* Except in the case of East Germany, competition from imports does not seem to have been the main initial factor depressing output, despite the speed with which trade was opened. This was probably due to the depth of the initial devaluations, which provided a period of respite to domestic producers. As initial sharp real devaluations have been eroded by inflation, import competition has become a serious problem for some producers. Poland, for example, raised tariffs (from very low levels) in mid-1991 for revenue purposes and to increase protection for increasingly embattled firms— including private manufacturers.[31] An increased role for import competition is consistent with the shift from the first, macroeconomic, phase of reform toward the second stage of structural reform shaped by competitive market pressure.

4. *An excessive credit crunch.* The initial effect of tight credit policies in Poland, Czechoslovakia, and other countries may have been more contractionary than expected because of a higher than projected initial price jump.[32] One indication of the possibly undue tightness of monetary and fiscal policies has been the better-than-expected current account outcomes of the reforming countries. Together with sharp increases in energy prices, sharply higher nominal credit costs also represented a sizable supply shock to enterprise sectors, as well as constraining demand.

5. *The microfoundations for reforms.* The depth of the contractions and their likely duration may partly have been caused by unexpected microeconomic responses that slow the reallocation of factors toward more productive uses. Uncertainty over the future business environment caused many enterprise managers to cut output at the start of the reforms with a view to safeguarding their financial balances, and some enterprises even paid lower wages than permitted by wage norms. In Poland, firms repatriated foreign assets to pay off costly zloty debts, and even many weaker firms therefore entered the reform period with a healthy balance sheet. Many managers in Czechoslovakia and probably in other countries have waited for the outcome of privatization proposals rather than responding speedily to reforms.

Compounding "sit-tight" behavior, weak factor market institutions reduced the transmission of macroeconomic signals to the micro level. Despite the strength of worker organizations, labor markets are beginning to adjust;

while industrial output declined by 35%–40% in the period 1989–91 in Poland, Hungary, and Czechoslovakia, their industrial labor forces fell by about 25%. Capital market adjustment has been far weaker, however. Despite indications that at least 30% of firms may not be viable, only a handful have been liquidated. There are also some signs that credit market response may have been perverse, with an increasing proportion of banking and interenterprise credits being taken by weaker firms, so that arrears have continued to accumulate.[33] The combination of tight credit ceilings and mounting arrears necessarily squeezes the margin of finance available for growing firms even more sharply.

The Dilemma of Privatization and Restructuring

Privatization and economic restructuring have moved ahead far more slowly than initially anticipated. Perhaps 800 medium and large firms have been privatized in Eastern Europe so far, mainly in Hungary (about 300) and Poland. Only a handful of firms have been liquidated. This excludes of course East Germany, where some 4,000 medium- and large-scale firms have been privatized.

Privatization
The immediate concern in transitional socialist countries is to establish ownership rights clearly and to assign them to appropriate economic agents. As an essential component of this process, privatization's role is somewhat different from that in market economies, where it involves transferring well-established ownership rights to private agents. Slow privatization reflects the difficult macroeconomic environment, the small size of private domestic savings relative to public assets, still-unformed legal institutions, and shortages of expertise and information in key areas. Conflicting views on the appropriate methods of privatization and politicization of the process have also slowed progress.

The methods of privatization used in Eastern Europe may be considered in four categories. Each has advantages and drawbacks, shown in table 5.1.

1. Spontaneous privatization involves the sale of the firm or parts thereof to "insiders," normally managers with superior information. Waves of spontaneous privatization took place in Hungary, Poland, and other countries in the initial stages of reform. Following a reaction against abuses, only Hungary now plans to rely intensively on this process, supervised against abuse by its privatization agency, although management buyouts are now possible in the other countries.
2. All countries have relied to some extent on sales to "outside" buyers,

TABLE 5.1   Privatization

Method	Strengths	Weaknesses
Spontaneous Hungary, former USSR, Slovenia	Fast. Pragmatic. Decentralized. "Real" owner.	"Unfair." Possible political reaction. Valuation difficult.
Other sales Germany, all other countries to some extent	"Real" owners. Fiscal revenues. Attracts foreign investment.	Slow. Administratively demanding. Valuation difficult.
Free distribution CSFR, Poland, Mongolia	Fast. "Equitable." Avoids valuation problem.	Still untested. No revenues. "Token" owners. Can be complex and politically contentious.
Reprivatization Especially for smaller assets. Germany, CSFR, Poland, Bulgaria, Romania, Hungary (properties)	Recreates middle class. "Fair."	Severe legal congestion. Risks, delays. Loses revenues. Possibly arbitrary asset distributions.

mostly other firms in related lines of business. This has been the dominant method used in Germany, except for the smaller firms where management buyouts have been common.

3. Free distribution to the population via a voucher system has begun in Czechoslovakia with the auction of some 1,700 firms in the first round in 1992. Attempts to approve a voucher program for Poland have foundered in legislative debate for two years. The Czechoslovak and Polish proposals differ in important respects. In particular, the latter aims to distribute shares in twenty management companies controlling 400 firms rather than in the firms themselves, because of a concern that large numbers of small shareholders will not form an effective locus to promote the interests of the owners. Free distribution is an untested system, with some advantages, including that of minimizing the problem of valuation that is especially intractable for transforming economies. But there are also many concerns, including the possibility that debates over the details of a general program can slow all privatization and so lengthen the period of uncertain ownership, with adverse results for industrial restructuring in the interim.[34]

4. Reprivatization to past owners has been endorsed to some extent in all countries, normally for smaller assets and for land and real estate. Its main drawbacks are the arbitrary nature of the resulting distribution and the potential for legal congestion, delays, and a consequently extended period of uncertainty.[35]

Much of the privatization debate has centered on large enterprise assets, but these are by no means the largest, even for industrialized market economies. For example, total fixed assets represented 311% of West German GDP in 1988. Housing comprised 132% of GDP, services (mostly commercial buildings) 72%, infrastructural capital 63%, and industrial capital only 34%. The value of land represented a further 115% of GDP, mostly in urban areas (92% of GDP).[36] This suggests that the financial gain to the state from privatization of industrial assets will depend more on the indirect effects—in terms of raising efficiency and output and enhancing the value of other components of the public asset stock—than on the sales value of industrial assets themselves.[37] Indeed, provided that ownership rights are tradable, their exact initial distribution may be less important for long-term efficiency relative to the need to establish them quickly.

Enterprise and Bank Restructuring
Restructuring naturally confronts political pressures to sustain nonviable enterprises, but there are other factors that slow the process:

1. *Weak creditors.* Despite the enactment of bankruptcy laws, the incentives for commercial banks do not encourage them to initiate actions against delinquent clients. Interfirm arrears have provided another cushion for weak firms, rising sharply as bank credit has been curtailed. In Romania, for example, interfirm debts mushroomed to the equivalent of 90% of GDP.
2. *Inactive owners.* Government has not taken the lead in restructuring assets, and managers have had little incentive to do so other than through the vehicle of spontaneous privatization.
3. *Temporary buffers.* Enterprises in Eastern Europe have realized temporary profits from stock revaluation. Although some of these profits were taxed away, the remainder provided a temporary buffer to the firms. In some countries, inflation had eroded the real debt burden of firms, and governments had assumed exchange rate losses, so that many enterprises were in a relatively strong financial position at the start of reforms.
4. *Strategic uncertainty.* It is not always clear which firms to close and which to restructure and assist to survive. This is partly due to the volatility of markets (will Soviet demand revive?) and partly because

the potential of some Eastern European firms (which are more like factories than firms in the market sense) is hard to assess.

5. *Inadequate legal frameworks.* Legal systems are not capable of handling a flood of bankruptcies.

The contrast between the speed of macroeconomic reforms and the slowness of microeconomic restructuring points to a possible conflict between the credibility requirements for policy at these two levels. Macroeconomic credibility may require decisive measures, but initiatives that imply across-the-board shutdowns of a large part of the existing economy confront the "too big to fail" problem and are not likely to be credible.[38]

The interaction between enterprise and bank restructuring is therefore now the most problematic area in East Europe's transformation process. While the first financial sector priority must be to develop the payments system to support a market economy, the second is solvency. Without clean portfolios and adequate capital, banks do not face the appropriate incentives to operate prudently in competitive financial markets, and cannot be privatized. On the other hand, a lack of effective financial markets and institutions while state enterprises are being restructured will impede the potentially faster emergence of private business. Financial sector reform must therefore follow the "two-track" progress of the real economy, where a growing small business sector coexists for some time with a shrinking state sector in which losses are progressively concentrated.

Various approaches to this problem have been advocated. Most involve a partitioning of the banking system's portfolio, between loans to problem enterprises and loans to sound enterprises and the private sector.[39] This would permit the creation of a class of clean, adequately capitalized financial intermediaries to serve the emerging business sector. There would then need to be some process for containing and shrinking the bad debt of the problem enterprises, for sorting out those enterprises to be rehabilitated and those to be closed, and for writing down debts as needed to permit suitable enterprises to be privatized. No country has yet formulated a comprehensive plan to address these problems.[40,41] Who should own the banks themselves is another question not yet resolved in Eastern Europe.

Restructuring the Social Safety Net

The problem facing the Eastern European countries in rebuilding their safety nets is summarized in figure 5.4. Relative levels of social transfers are comparable with those of the far richer Western European countries, but they are less well targeted on the poor. In fact, transfers in Eastern Europe are received on a uniform basis without regard for levels of income, so that in absolute terms

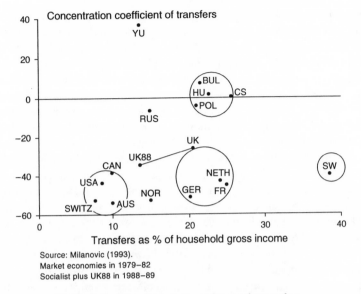

Source: Milanovic (1993).
Market economies in 1979–82
Socialist plus UK88 in 1988–89

Figure 5.4   Size of social transfers and targeting

there is no net redistributive effect at all. Developing the capacity to target transfers better will be a vital component of efforts to limit the growth of poverty while under severe fiscal constraints and facing mounting unemployment. This is probably the most important longer-run problem facing the reforming countries.

A Comparative Review of Some Other Socialist Reforms

Reforming developing socialist countries such as Nicaragua, Tanzania, Mozambique, Vietnam, Laos, and China are clearly different from each other and are also very different from Eastern Europe. Their socialist systems are of more recent vintage and generally less comprehensive, they are less industrialized and, except for Vietnam, they were not part of the CMEA system. Some, such as Tanzania, maintained their presocialist legal systems and a formal private sector that operated within prescribed limits. Of the above countries, only Nicaragua has seen a political transition (through the ballot box), although both Tanzania and Mozambique are moving toward multiparty systems.

The reforms initiated by *Nicaragua's* new government in February 1991 had many parallels with the "big bangs" of Eastern Europe.[42] The currency was devalued to 20% of its previous level against the U.S. dollar and then pegged; trade was liberalized and government trade monopolies were abolished. Monetary and credit policies were tightened. Inflation declined sharply from very high levels; in the first four months of 1992, monthly inflation averaged only 0.4%. However, the initial price jump virtually offset the devaluation, so that the real exchange rate showed only minor fluctuations about a constant trend. Although Nicaragua may not have experienced the sharp contractions of Eastern Europe, its economy remains depressed because of the impact of foreign competition on manufacturing and a 30% fall in the world prices of coffee and cotton.

Nicaragua's reforms go beyond those of Eastern Europe, however, in the speed of privatization. At the beginning of 1990, 351 enterprises producing 31% of GDP and including 28% of total landholdings were under state control. By May 1992, half of these enterprises and most of the state landholdings had been privatized. About 30% of the assets had been returned to former owners, a further 35% was distributed to peasants and workers, and most of the remainder was allocated to demobilized *contras* and army personnel. This pattern of asset distribution sought to widen the basis of ownership to consolidate social stability. The long-run effect on efficiency and income distribution remains to be seen.

African socialist countries include the four poorest nations in the world.[43] During *Tanzania's* socialist period, tightened import licensing, foreign exchange allocation, and price controls in the face of more stringent resource constraints reduced levels of capacity use; this produced an acute shortage of goods, particularly in rural markets, and growth of the parallel economy.[44] Official figures show that per capita income fell by 3%–4% in 1975–83, but some estimates suggest larger declines in living standards. After 1983 the Tanzanian Economic Recovery Plan (TERP) has seen gradual liberalization and a return to modest growth. Following an estimated decline of 30% in GDP in 1982-85, *Mozambique's* Economic Rehabilitation Program (MERP) succeeded in restoring growth to 5% in 1987–89, despite a still-unresolved security situation.

The cornerstone of the TERP and MERP has been price and market reform, although this is less complete than in Eastern Europe. Sharp devaluations caused real exchange rates to depreciate sharply, as shown in figure 5.5, and the ratio of parallel to official rates to decline. Convertibility is less advanced than in Europe despite the introduction in Tanzania of foreign exchange bureaus and in Mozambique of the system for nonadministrative allocation for foreign exchange (SNAAD). An insufficient part of foreign exchange has been channeled through the market, and although administrative allocation systems (such as the Open General License window in Tanzania) have been broadened, the prevalence of tied donor aid in the supply of foreign exchange is an obstacle to further liberalization. The government also retains

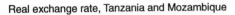

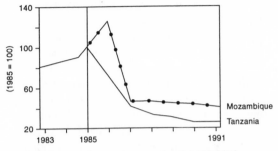

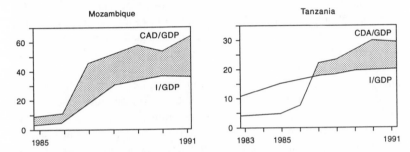

Figure 5.5   Real exchange rate, and investment and current account deficit/GDP, Tanzania and Mozambique

a key role in the marketing of some major export crops, despite the progressive "deconfinement" of activities to private entry.

In both countries, market reforms aimed to increase the availability and variety of goods and raise incentives to farmers. The share of budget revenues raised through export taxation fell in Tanzania from 62% in 1980 to 24% by 1990, and the scope of controlled prices was greatly reduced.[45] Controlled producer prices were freed or replaced by price minima adjusted toward border levels in Mozambique, while fixed prices for manufactures were replaced by price reviews. The overall share of products with fixed prices fell from 69% in 1986 to 17% by 1991.

Tanzania and Mozambique have seen the initial impact of reform in their rural and small-scale sectors. Indeed, the most notable source of growth in Tanzania has been agriculture, whose output rose by 40% in 1983–90, primarily in foodgrains and nontraditional exports. Reform also appears to have induced an explosion of small-scale nonagricultural production and trade activities. In Mozambique, recovery mostly reflected a substantial rise in marketed agricultural transactions and a pickup in light industry.

Tanzania has taken measures to tighten the budget constraints on state enterprises, and there may have been some improvement in their efficiency. However, continued heavy government intervention in the banking system and the government's failure to collect aid counterpart funds have provided a cushion, so that despite several years of reform enterprises are only slowly being pushed toward liquidation. There is still no broad consensus on the merits of widespread privatization.[46] Mozambique has moved forward with enterprise reform and privatization more rapidly. Budgetary subsidies to enterprises are being cut sharply (although banking and counterpart fund subsidies remain). About 120 smaller and medium-sized firms have been privatized, many apparently in a spontaneous manner. The next phase is to include the largest state enterprises. Other methods of improving management, including joint ventures and management contracts, are being developed. Since 1987 the number of state farms has been cut from 130 to 80, and the area under their control has been halved in favor of private smallholders, although the new constitution keeps technical landownership in state hands. Both countries are moving ahead with a number of common reform areas, including the banking system, an area more advanced in Tanzania.

One notable similarity between Tanzania and Mozambique, and a difference between them and most of the other reforming countries, is the level of their external assistance. Encouraged by reform, and seeking to help adjustment take place without a large contraction in consumption, aid inflows have risen rapidly for Tanzania and Mozambique, financing growing current account deficits and causing foreign savings to outstrip domestic investment levels in both countries, as shown in figure 5.5. The only other reform program supported to a similar extent is that of East Germany, where inflows from West Germany represent some 76% of GDP and cover twice the level of investment (34% of GDP). The noninterest current account of Eastern Europe, excluding Germany, is in approximate balance, so that these countries must reform with no extra real resources from abroad. Vietnam's reforms are proceeding with virtually no aid at all, following the phaseout of Soviet assistance.[47] Aid can contribute to reform in many ways, covering fiscal gaps, financing debt write-downs, and facilitating the extensive programs of technical assistance required by all of the reforming countries. However, care must be taken, especially for tied commodity aid, to ensure that it does not covertly subsidize public enterprises or fragment product and foreign exchange markets.

Vietnam's reforms, which began with experimental agricultural decollectivization in 1979, accelerated in 1989 with a wide-ranging price and market liberalization, devaluation, a sharp increase in interest rates to encourage the holding of dong-denominated assets, and tightened fiscal policies. These reforms were spurred by a macroeconomic crisis in 1988 plus the phasing out of massive Soviet aid flows.[48]They resulted in some impressive initial gains. Inflation fell sharply as the economy remonetized, output growth jumped to 7% in 1989, and the country switched from being a rice importer to a sizable rice exporter as rice trading and exporting were liberalized. Exports rose from 3.9% of GDP in 1980 to over 15% by 1992. State sector employment fell by 12% between 1988 and 1990, but this was offset by a sharp rise in private activity; the nonstate sector now accounts for over half of industrial output, and it provides considerable competition for the state sector.[49]

With the ending of Soviet assistance and unsupported by Western aid, Vietnam's growth slumped to 3% by 1991, and stabilization and developmental investments were threatened by an acute shortage of fiscal revenues. The poor performance of the state enterprises, which are struggling to survive in increasingly competitive markets, remained a serious problem; although they have been severely squeezed by the ending of Soviet commodity aid and by the elimination of direct budget subsidies, a large volume of credit remains outstanding to the enterprise sector, constraining interest rate policy and raising the prospect of costly loan losses.

Laos's reforms have many parallels with those of Vietnam, including the initial emphasis on agricultural decollectivization. More wide-ranging initiatives have been put in place in the area of enterprise reform, however, involving privatization, leasing (including to foreign companies), and closures. Laos has also moved to put in place the legal infrastructure for a private market economy.

In one decade, 1978–88, *China's* income and living space per capita doubled, and possession of typical consumer goods rose by factors of 3, 4, or more. China is usually advanced as the counterexample to the two propositions that reforms have to be fast, costly, and across-the-board to succeed, and that comprehensive change is impossible in the absence of political transformation. Reforms in 1978 began with agriculture; following pressure from local and provincial governments, and taking into account their successful experimentation with family farming, this was restored, and land tenure was revised toward long-term leaseholding. Agricultural prices were raised and progressively liberalized. The result was a burst of agricultural productivity that peaked in 1983–84; productivity and output both grew at 6% in the decade 1978–88.

The next stage of reform involved combining the labor released from agriculture with growing rural savings to manufacture goods increasingly demanded due to rising rural incomes. The result was an explosion of rural industrial growth, and the creation of township and village enterprises (TVEs), which accounted for one-third of the growth of China's material product in 1980–88. In that period, labor productivity rose at a rate of 12%, and total factor productivity growth also greatly exceeded that in the state enterprises.[50] By the end of the 1980s, the TVEs produced a quarter of China's exports and had absorbed 70 million workers.

In contrast, the reform of China's large state enterprises only began on a wide scale in 1984. It emphasized a progressive reduction of plan targets and planned input allocations, and greater enterprise autonomy through a multi-year contract responsibility system subject to targets for profits, remittances, and taxes. Government continued to play an active industrial policy role, but enterprises were permitted greater discretion in their use of funds. Government revenue extracted from state enterprises fell from over 30% of GNP to under 20% of GNP in the period 1978–87.

Studies of the comparative performance of state and nonstate enterprises suggest that state enterprises allocated a larger part of their resources to social expenditures than the nonstate sectors. Even allowing for this, output and total factor productivity growth rates were far more dynamic in the nonstate sector.[51] By the start of the 1990s, there were clear indications of the need for substantial restructuring and downsizing of the state sector. Exposed to market competition, some 40% of the firms were reportedly making losses.[52] The share of the nonstate sector in industrial output across provinces correlates strongly with total factor productivity. The nonstate sector has also been a strong source of competition for state enterprises, and competitive pressures have tended to equalize marginal factor returns, thus raising efficiency.[53]

Through this process, domestic markets were progressively liberalized to reduce the scope of plan allocations, rather than freed abruptly.[54] China also did not immediately try to integrate the domestic price system with world prices by moving to free trade, but combined import protection with measures to encourage exports. With the progressive opening to foreign trade and investment, exports rose from 5% of GDP in 1978 to 18% in 1990, and foreign investment grew from almost nothing to $3.4 billion a year, mostly from Hong Kong and Macao.

The incentives and governance structures involved in the growing nonstate sector—as well as in agriculture—are clearly central in explaining China's economic performance. Private property rights were not legally enshrined in China and there was no great burst of privatization, although "private" firms have developed in some regions. But the rural reforms devolved substantial de facto ownership rights to agricultural households in the form of long-term land leases, and to rural communities whose local governments became owners of local enterprises. Industrial profits formed a major part of the revenue bases for local governments. This resulted in an aggressive and competitive "local corporatist" approach toward industrial development, especially in the more advanced regions. Naturally the incentive to industrialize efficiently could not have been sustained with extensive redistribution between communities, and the mechanisms for such redistribution were in fact relatively weak outside the state sector.[55] One consequence of this component of the reforms was therefore widening regional disparity, mostly depending on the success of regional industrial efforts. Against this is, of course, the general improvement in income distribution that resulted from the enrichment of the rural population relative to their wealthier urban peers.[56]

Conclusion: Some Lessons of Experience

The outcome to date of reforms in Eastern Europe reflects far more the effects of CMEA trade and payments collapse and stabilization programs than structural transformations. The latter phase of reform is still in its early stages, except in East Germany where markets have been opened to competition from Western producers without the protection of a macroeconomic constraint.[57] If the various explanations for output decline are considered together, the paradox becomes less puzzling. Embarking on a process of socialist reform in a country with less highly developed large-scale industry, in reasonable macroeconomic balance, and not facing severe disruption of trade and payments links is unlikely to produce a catastrophic contraction.

Big Bang or Evolution?

The verdict is still out on the question of whether a big-bang approach is preferable to more phased reform. However, the choice is usually constrained, for a given country, by macroeconomic stresses and the nature of political conditions. Macroeconomic stabilization forces an immediate choice between stronger controls and market liberalization. A new government committed to reform may have neither the desire nor the capacity to retain an active role in the economy, let alone to implement tight price controls and commodity allocations. Cross-country experience suggests that having a clear "model" for the reformed economy encourages transformation (Eastern Europe looks to Western Europe and China to the Pacific-rim "tigers"). The rejection of the previous system as imposed by others and a clear appreciation of its failure also encourages rapid change.

However, posing the question as a dichotomy between big bang and evolution is misleading. Only the price liberalization and macro stabilization components of reform can be carried out quickly. At the level of the real economy, successful reform is likely to follow an evolutionary two-track economy, with a growing, smaller-scale private sector coexisting with, and hopefully outgrowing, a shrinking state sector placed under increasing stress by having to operate in competitive markets. This phase of adjustment is starting in Eastern Europe and has been seen in many of the other countries. It is well advanced in East Asia, especially if China's nonstate sector is accepted as a surrogate private sector—or as the surrogate for open trade in the far smaller East European economies. The core of the structural reform problem is therefore substantially the same across countries.

The two-track vision of reform has a number of implications, especially for financial sector and fiscal policies. To release financial and budgetary resources for new enterprises, it is vital that the losses of the state sector be curtailed, even if there are reasons to avoid wholesale shutdowns. Because there are no ready market mechanisms to handle this process on a large scale, it probably calls for a degree of government involvement even if the intention is to ultimately eliminate any active role for government in the economy. There may be a conflict between the macro and micro aspects of policy credibility. A credible response to severe macroeconomic imbalance requires somewhat of a big-bang approach.[58] But instantaneous bankruptcy of much of the economy is neither a credible nor an administratively feasible strategy.

Within such an outcome, there are still many unresolved issues in the areas of privatization, banking, and enterprise reform. Insufficient attention has been given to the problem of how to raise the efficiency of enterprises not yet privatized. Because the value of industrial capital is only a small part of total national asset value, efficiency rather than immediate revenues probably ought to be the main criterion for privatization. While elimination of quantitative import restrictions is important to encourage competition, there are probably good fiscal and temporary protection reasons to maintain tariffs for some time.

Even under favorable conditions, the changing structure of the economy will result in fiscal stress, as the undeveloped tax system struggles to compensate for the losses of profit remittances from the state enterprises.[59] Macroeconomic stability can also be compromised by inadequate financial sector institutions and regulations, coupled with failure to address the property rights issue clearly. The weakness of measures to restructure larger enterprises on the part of the nominal owner (the government) is mirrored in a buildup of bad debt in the banking system, and this inevitably ends up as a government liability. The expansion of credit to cover losses, possibly under pressure from local governments, further undermines macroeconomic controls.

Fiscal pressure coupled with rising unemployment and a probable increase in income inequality will place severe stress on the systems of social protection that have been developed by many socialist countries. This presents a long-term threat to their most favorable performance characteristic, their high social indicators relative to their income levels.

Notes

The views expressed in this paper are those of the author and do not necessarily represent those of the World Bank and its associated organizations.
1. The dividing line between "socialist" and other countries is necessarily somewhat arbitrary.

This number comprises: fifteen ex-Soviet states, Afghanistan, ten East European countries (considering former Yugoslavia as four countries), Cuba, North Korea and Mongolia, China, Laos, Vietnam, Kampuchea, Burma, Algeria, Nicaragua, and eight Sub-Saharan African countries.

2. Countries like Egypt, India, and Zambia have large state sectors and heavy state intervention but are not considered "socialist" for present purposes. For a review of Soviet military and economic assistance resource transfers, see Ofer and Peltzman (1991).

3. Laos and Vietnam, for example, have significantly changed their ideologies to formally recognize the role of private business, despite still being communist monostates; for discussion, see Ljunggren (1992).

4. The discussion here draws on Gelb and Gray (1991) and Fischer and Gelb (1991).

5. The common features were less applicable to Yugoslavia, which was not a CMEA member, had a considerably less equal distribution of income because of its federal structure, and had some experience of open unemployment because of the self-managed nature of its firms. For more discussion, see Gelb and Gray (1991).

6. By 1982 it was estimated that half of Hungary's consumer goods' prices were free (see Bruno 1992). Marrese (1991) provides an assessment of reform socialism in Hungary from the perspective of facilitating adaptation to full reform.

7. In addition, in Poland and Yugoslavia 70% of agriculture was in private hands.

8. The former USSR went through an essentially similar phase in 1991–92.

9. At the start of 1992, tariffs averaged about 13%–14% in Poland (which raised them again in August, partly for fiscal reasons) and Hungary, and 5% in Czechoslovakia. For a review of trade policies in the transition, see Rodrik (1992).

10. The Polish and Czechoslovak programs relied on three nominal anchors: the exchange rate, monetary ceilings, and wage controls. At least until mid-1992, of these three anchors the former USSR targeted only credit.

11. Poland's effective reserves were bolstered by a $1 billion stabilization fund.

12. Romania moved toward exchange rate unification somewhat less abruptly, partly because of serious problems in its petroleum-based industry.

13. Initial inflation was anticipated to be only 45%; for the whole of 1990, inflation was expected to be below 100%, but it was actually about 250%. For more discussion, see Bruno (1992).

14. For discussion and data, see Rodrik (1992).

15. It is difficult to measure the size of CMEA-area trade before 1991 because of uncertainties over pricing and conversion of the transferable ruble. By 1991, however, former CMEA markets received less than one-fifth of Polish and Hungarian exports, and one-third of Czechoslovakia's. The share of the EC meanwhile had risen to over 40%; see Rodrik (1992).

16. For discussions of such "normal long-run" patterns based on gravity models and on the patterns of comparator countries, see Brada (1992) and Havrylyshyn and Pritchett (1991). Brada concludes that still further reorientation away from CMEA markets can be expected, in some contrast to the earlier work that found that the realized reorientations of Poland and Hungary already surpassed projections of normal patterns. With recovery of the CMEA area and a working payments system, a possible temporary period of reengagement with the Soviet states could be expected, because of hysteresis effects from long-standing trade, service, and communications patterns.

17. Marrese (1992a).

18. For reviews of legal developments in Poland and Romania, see Gray et al. (1992a,b).

19. Marrese (1992). The number of new joint ventures also rose sharply—4,000 in 1990 and almost 6,000 in 1991.

20. Webster (1992).

21. Data on the numbers of private firms and their average size and composition may be

misleading in some cases, because of underreporting, failure to register exits, and taxes that bias the form of response. In Czechoslovakia, for example, many of those working for private companies probably are hired as self-employed to avoid payment of wage taxes equivalent to 50% of the wage bill.

22. The most spectacular output declines—by over 50%—have been due to special factors. Albania's collapse mirrored the end of its unusually closed and repressive regime rather than any market-oriented reform program. Output fell sharply in most of the former Yugoslavia, due to civil war. The sharp contraction of East Germany's economy, including the loss of 70% of industrial production following unification, resulted from the absence of a macroeconomic constraint that would otherwise have provided a measure of natural protection through the exchange rate as the economy opened abruptly to the West.

23. The estimates in figure 5.2 included Yugoslavia and do not allow for the sharp decline in output due to civil war.

24. Tax receipts were temporarily sustained in Poland and Czechoslovakia in their first year of reform by faulty accounting and taxing the capital gains on inventories due to inflation. See Estrin, Schaffer, and Singh (1992).

25. The activities of the Treuhandanstalt have been estimated to involve a net loss, possibly on the order of DM 40 billion.

26. Bruno (1992) offers a concise summary of fiscal difficulties following reform.

27. Brada and King (1992) discuss the concept of the socialist J-curve.

28. Statistical systems are not able to capture adequately the growing contribution of private activities. They may not allow properly for quality and variety improvements as enterprises move away from mass standardization, with the result that price increases are overstated and real output is understated. Greater availability of high-quality foreign goods and increased purchasing power of wages converted at official exchange rates, rather than the previous parallel rates, may also be a factor; for example, ownership of important consumer durables rose in Poland in 1990 even while food consumption fell. Berg (1992) suggests that estimates from the demand side and from the supply side place the 1990 decline in Poland's GDP at 4.9% and 8.7% respectively, rather than the recorded fall of 12%. See also Milanovic (1992).

29. See Gelb and Gray (1991) for OECD estimates of terms of trade losses, Brada (1992) and Rodrik (1992) for discussion of the trade shock, and Anderson (1992) for data on the re-orientation of Russia's trade.

30. Anderson (1992) notes that Russian trade held up well with developed market economies, and offers several reasons for the sharp reorientation of trade away from Eastern Europe. Progressive liberalization of CIS trade, as well as the failure to develop an effective foreign exchange market (probably for reasons related to problems in the payments and financial system) resulted in compartmentalization of foreign trade, with exporters spending foreign exchange on pent-up demand for Western consumer goods and importers relying substantially on Western export credits. Much CMEA trade was also in areas such as investment goods and defense, where Russian demand has fallen sharply.

31. Webster (1992) found that by mid-1991 private Polish manufacturers faced severe import competition unless in niche markets.

32. For discussion of the credit crunch hypothesis, see Calvo and Coricelli (1992).

33. Dabrowski, Federowitz, and Levitas (1991) find that interfirm debts were typically accumulated by the less profitable firms.

34. One particular concern in Czechoslovakia is the concentration of shares in the hands of unregulated investment funds offering high guaranteed returns to voucher depositors.

35. More than a million claims, sometimes with up to fifteen claimants to the same asset, foreshadow years of sorting out the restitution problem in Germany; see Dornbusch and Wolf (1992).

36. Pohl (1992), Table 3.

37. Indeed, taking into account debt relief and various concessions to buyers, it seems that the privatization activities of the Treuhandanstalt (THA) have yielded negative revenues, but the THA appears to have retained a considerable portfolio of real estate. The main concerns of the THA have, however, been that purchasers commit to future investments and employment generation rather than that they pay the highest price for assets.

38. Commander and Coricelli (1992) suggest that this may not be as severe in Hungary as in Poland, because of the less abrupt reforms of the former country.

39. Partitioning could involve dividing the portfolio of existing banks, as suggested by Gelb and Gray (1991), or privatizing a few commercial banks with clean portfolios to service new clients and turning the rest into investment banks, charged with working out their problem clients (Thorne 1992).

40. Czechoslovakia is perhaps the most advanced in addressing the bad debt problem. Low-yielding loans have been removed from the banks' balance sheets, and the banks have been provided with some resources to facilitate provisioning for loan losses. Hungary and Poland have been less able to recapitalize their banks (see Marresse 1992b). Hungary, however, possesses the most advanced financial sector, which includes a number of foreign banks. A concentration of bad debt in the hands of the large state banks, whose relative loan portfolio size is shrinking, would produce a "good and bad bank" solution along the lines advocated by Thorne (1992) for Bulgaria.

41. More radical suggestions are to effect an across-the-board write-off of all debts. Interenterprise debt would be netted out, and the residual transferred to the banks. Government bonds would replace commercial loans in the banks' balance sheets. This approach has advantages, especially in speeding the privatization process, as it will be easier to dispose of debt-free enterprises. It also has dangers (as well as fiscal cost) because, without adequate measures to impose commercial discipline on clients and without improving lenders' capacities to apply commercial lending criteria, debt cancellation may simply encourage a new round of loans to problem clients. This is a possibility in Romania, which has implemented a strategy of debt cancellation and write-off. It also removes a potential lever to force economic restructuring.

42. This summary draws on Martinez Cuenca (1992) and *El Observador Economico*, May 1992.

43. It should be noted that three of these countries have suffered from extensive civil conflict and that one has been involved in war with a neighboring country; economic systems are therefore not the only factor contributing to their poor performance.

44. In this, Tanzania's experience resembles that of the USSR in 1987–91.

45. Ndulu (1992).

46. As in Eastern Europe and the former USSR, the question of who the new owners should be is one of the most difficult issues for privatization.

47. For East Germany, see Dornbusch and Wolf (1992). Assistance to Mongolia, at $150 million, constitutes perhaps 15% of its GDP. To take another measure of assistance, official capital flows plus debt relief to Poland, Bulgaria, Romania, and Laos funded respectively 40%, 53%, 36%, and 51% of imports in 1990 (see Leipziger 1991, Table 1); for Vietnam (which also has a heavy foreign debt burden), they funded only 6% of imports. The corresponding percentages for Mozambique and Tanzania exceed 100.

48. For reviews of Vietnam's reforms, see Dollar (1992), Ljunggren (1992), and Leipziger (1991).

49. Ljunggren (1992).

50. Jefferson and Xu (1992) report total factor productivity growth of 2.4% for state firms and 4.6% for collective firms in 1980–88. In this period, state firms' output grew at 8.5% and that of the collective firms grew at 16.9%. For an overview of China's reform program and its results, see Gelb, Jefferson, and Singh (1993).

51. See, for example, Xiao (1991).

138   Alan Gelb

52. Leipziger (1991).
53. See Jefferson and Xu (1992).
54. For example, the share of capital goods subject to planning shrank from over 80% at the start of the reforms to only about 20% by 1990.
55. For an analysis of the incentives for local governments, see Byrd and Gelb (1990). Comparing a more and a less developed township, the ratio of income per capita was 7 to 1; that of government spending per capita was 29 to 1; that of industrial output per capita was 662 to 1.
56. Naturally the progressive devolvement of control away from the center has not been free of problems. All too often increased local interventions substituted for reduced central intervention. Local governments sought to retain locally raised investable funds and to protect their industries, for example, by restricting the export of key inputs, and some have "optimized" subject to distorted incentives, in particular cheap credit. The small size of rural communities reduced the potential for protectionist measures, however, as most rural industry relies overwhelmingly on markets in other areas. Decentralization also weakened macroeconomic controls and contributed to a phase of macroeconomic disequilibrium in 1985–87 that widened differentials between plan and market prices. Distortions increased and stimulated corruption, a development that contributed to the political disturbances of 1988.
57. East German experience can be interpreted as a case of the "Dutch disease" where revenue from some booming sector (oil, aid) appreciates the exchange rate, causing the decline of other tradable sectors.
58. This is not to say that it requires exactly the big bangs of Eastern Europe; for a comparison with Israel, see Bruno (1992).
59. This problem is common even outside Eastern Europe. For example, during Vietnam's reform, fiscal revenues fell from 12% of GDP in 1986 to 6% in 1991, mostly because of lower tax receipts from enterprises (Leipziger 1991). Despite a VAT of 28%, a 2% reconstruction tax, 25% corporate profits tax, and 45% marginal income tax, Armenia's fiscal revenues are projected at barely 8% of GDP in 1992.

References

Anderson, John. 1992. "Liberalization of Russia's Foreign Trade." Paper presented to the SEEE Conference on Systemic Change in Russia, Stockholm, June 15–16.
Begg, David, and Richard Portes. 1992. "Enterprise Debt and Economic Transformation: Financial Restructuring in Central and Eastern Europe." CEPR. May.
Berg, Andrew. 1992. Paper presented to the Conference on the Macroeconomic Situation in Eastern Europe, Washington, D.C., June 4–5.
Brada, Josef. 1992. "Regional Integration in Eastern Europe: Prospects for Integration within the Region and with the European Community." Paper presented to the Conference on New Dimensions in Regional Integration, Washington, D.C., April 2–3.
Brada, Josef, and Arthur King. 1992. "Is There A J-Curve for the Economic Transition from Socialism to Capitalism?" Economics of Planning.
Bruno, Michael. 1992. Stabilization and Reform in Eastern Europe: A Preliminary Evaluation." Mimeo.
Byrd, William, and Alan Gelb. 1990. "Why Industrialize? The Incentives for Rural Community Governments." In William Byrd and Lin Qingsong, eds., China's Rural Industry. Oxford: Oxford University Press.
Calvo, Guillermo, and Fabrizio Coricelli. 1992. "Output Collapse in Eastern Europe:

The Role of Credit." Paper presented to the Conference on the Macroeconomic Situation in Eastern Europe, Washington, D.C., June 4–5.

Commander, Simon, and Fabrizio Coricelli. 1992. "Output Decline in Hungary and Poland in 1990/1991." Paper presented at the Conference on the Macroeconomic Situation in Eastern Europe, Washington, D.C., June 4–5.

Dabrowski, Janusz, Michal Federowicz, and Anthony Levitas. 1991. "Report on Polish State Enterprises in 1990." The Research Center for Marketization and Property Reform. Warsaw, February.

Dollar, David. 1992. "Vietnam: Successes and Failures of Macroeconomic Stabilization." In Borje Ljunggren and Peter Timmer, eds., *The Challenge of Reform in Indochina*.

Dornbusch, Rudiger, and Holger Wolf. 1992. "Economic Transition in East Germany." Mimeo. MIT, April.

Estrin, Saul, Mark Schaffer, and Inderjit Singh. 1992. "Enterprise Adjustment in Transition Economies: Czechoslovakia, Hungary and Poland." Paper presented to the Conference on the Macroeconomic Situation in Eastern Europe, Washington, D.C., June 4–5.

Fischer, Stanley, and Alan Gelb. 1991. "The Process of Socialist Economic Transformation." *Journal of Economic Perspectives* 5, 4: 91–105.

Gelb, Alan, and Cheryl Gray. 1991. "The Transformation of Economies in Central and Eastern Europe: Issues, Progress and Prospects." World Bank, Policy and Research Paper No. 17, June.

Gelb, Alan, Gary Jefferson, and Inderjit Singh. 1993. "Can Communist Economies Transform Incrementally? The Chinese Experience." *National Bureau for Economic Research Macroeconomics Annual*. Cambridge, MA: MIT Press.

Gray, Cheryl W., et al. 1993. "Evolving Legal Frameworks for Private Section Development in Central and Eastern Europe." World Bank Discussion Paper No. 209.

Havrylyshyn, Oli, and Lant Pritchett. 1991. "European Trade Patterns after the Transition." World Bank.

Jefferson, Gary, and Wenyi Xu. 1992. "Assessing Gains in Efficient Production among China's Industrial Enterprises." World Bank, WPS 877, March.

Kornai, Janos. 1992. *The Socialist System: The Political Economy of Communism*. Princeton: Princeton University Press.

Leipziger, Daniel. 1991. "Awakening the Market: Vietnam's Economic Transition." World Bank Discussion Paper No. 157, March.

Ljunggren, Borje. 1992. "Market Economies Under Communist Regimes: Reform in Vietnam, Laos and Cambodia." SIDA, Stockholm, May.

Marresse, Michael. 1991. "Hungary's Economic Transformation: Twenty-Five Years of Reform Finally Yield Fragile Fruit." Northwestern University, December.

Marresse, Michael. 1992a. "The Growth of the Private Sector in Hungary: Establishing New Firms and Privatizing State Firms." Northwestern University, April.

Marresse, Michael. 1992b. "Solving the Bad Debt Problem of Central and East European Banks: An Overview." Northwestern University, May.

Martinez, Cuenca, Alejandro. 1992. "The State and the Market: The Case of Nicaragua." Paper presented to SIDA Workshop on the Role of the State and the Market, Stockholm, June 15–16.

Milanovic, Branko. 1991. "Income Distribution in Late Socialism." CECSE Research Paper, March, World Bank.

Milanovic, Branko. 1992. "Social Costs of Transition to Capitalism: Poland 1990." CECSE Research Paper, June, World Bank.

Milanovic, Branko. 1993. "Cash Social Transfers, Direct Taxes and Income Distribution in Late Socialism." *Journal of Comparative Economics*.

Ndulu, Benno. 1992. "The Role of State and Market in Reformed Economic Management in Sub-Saharan Africa." Paper presented to SIDA Workshop on the Role of the State and the Market, Stockholm, June 15–16.

Ofer, Gur, and Joseph Peltman. 1991. "Soviet Military and Economic Aid to the Middle East and Africa." Mimeo. Hebrew University of Jerusalem and George Washington University.

Pohl, Gerhard. 1992. "Privatization in East Germany and Eastern Europe." Mimeo. World Bank, March.

Rodrik, Dani. 1992. "Making Sense of the Soviet Trade Shock in Eastern Europe: A Framework and Some Estimates." Paper presented to the Conference on the Macroeconomic Situation in Eastern Europe, Washington, D.C., June 4–5.

Schaffer, Mark. 1992. "The Polish State-Owned Enterprise Sector and the Recession in 1990." CECSE Research Paper, February, World Bank.

Sheng, Andrew. 1991. "Bad Debts in Transitional Socialist Economies." Mimeo. World Bank.

Thorne, Alfredo. 1992. "Issues in Reforming Financial Systems in Eastern Europe: The Case of Bulgaria." World Bank, WPS 882, April.

Webster, Leila. 1992. "Private Manufacturing in Poland." Mimeo. IENIN, World Bank.

Xiao, Geng. 1991a. "Managerial Autonomy, Fringe Benefits and Ownership Structure: A Comparative Study of Chinese State and Collective Enterprises." *China Economic Review* 2, 1.

Xiao, Geng. 1991b. "What Is Special about China's Reforms?" CECSE Research Paper, November, World Bank.

CHAPTER 6

Stabilization and Economic Reform in Russia

Stanley Fischer

Only a handful of events in this century are as important as the creation and eventual collapse of the Soviet Union. That the Soviet Union disappeared with minimal loss of life is as extraordinary as its demise. While the political changes have been exceptional, the pace and extent of economic change have been sweeping, too. Less than four months after the Soviet Union was dissolved, Russia had decisively liberalized most prices, and was on the road to macroeconomic stabilization and convertibility of the ruble. The budget deficit has been cut from 20% to less than 10% of GDP. The inflation rate has been declining, after a price level adjustment. At the end of April 1992, Russia joined the IMF and the World Bank. Well before the end of the year, Russia will be receiving IMF financial support to implement a stabilization and reform process that probably will include converting the ruble at a fixed rate.

Rapid stabilization in Russia—along with price and trade liberalization and currency convertibility—will be an extraordinary accomplishment, if it is achieved.[1] But both the emerging record of Eastern Europe and the early evidence from Russia suggest that the more challenging and ultimately more important difficulties lie elsewhere: in privatization; in the distribution sector; in financial, fiscal, and agricultural reform—in short, in the structural reform of the economy.

The cumulative decline in output in the Soviet Union in 1990 and 1991 was similar to that experienced in the major Eastern European countries (table 6.1). Supply disruptions in the oil sector, the breakdown of the state order system, and severe disruptions in inter-republican trade exacted their toll on economic performance. For the former Soviet Union (FSU), as for the Eastern European countries, exports and imports declined sharply in 1991. However, in the FSU, much of the decline—one-third of exports—resulted from domestic supply disruptions, particularly in the oil industry.

Russia embarked on its reform program at the end of 1991 facing an impressive array of problems. First, as already noted, output had fallen by nearly 20%. Moreover, the inflationary overhang produced a 350%–400%

TABLE 6.1   East European and Soviet performance, 1990–1991

		CSFR	Hungary	Poland	Romania	USSR
GNP/GDP growth	1990	−1	−4	−12	−7	−4
(% per annum)	1991	−16	−8	−8	−12	−13
		(−9)	(−8)	(−4)	(−10)	(−4)
Inflation	1990	18	33	249	5	20
(% per annum)	1991	54	33	60	223	100
Budget deficit	1990	0.3	0.1	−3.5	0.3	8.3
(% of GNP)	1991	2.1	3.9	6.5	1.4	20
Memo: Start of						
IMF program		1991	1991	1990	1991	

Sources: Bruno (1992) for Eastern Europe, supplemented by *PlanEcon*; for USSR, *PlanEcon Report* 7, pp. 43-44, Dec. 9, 1991. Data for 1991 are estimates based on the first three quarters of the year. Data in parentheses are estimates of the direct impact of the decline in exports on growth (i.e., fall in exports as a share of GNP), taken from Bruno (1992) except for the USSR, which is based on *PlanEcon* data.

increase in prices within a month after prices were liberalized in January 1991. Second, the Group of Seven industrialized democracies (G-7) was intent on getting the fifteen republics to recognize their "joint and several" responsibility for the Soviet Union's $80 billion external debt and seemingly uninterested in providing direct financial support for economic reform.

Third, the incoming policymakers had to assemble a civil service and administration from the remnants of the Soviet system at the same time as they were planning their reforms. (In this respect, the Russian government, based in Moscow, was in much better shape than the other republics.) The breakdown of authority in the Soviet Union also has extended to authority within Russia, with its sixteen autonomous regions and subregional units reaching for greater independence—the more so the greater their resource riches. Even today, reports suggest that the reach of the central Russian administration is limited and that regional and local officials freely ignore instructions from the central authorities.

Fourth, trading and currency relations among the republics are in a state of flux. The republics of the new Commonwealth have agreed in principle to continue to use the ruble for two years, but there is no doubt that Ukraine is already implicitly introducing a separate currency through its coupon system and little doubt that it will explicitly introduce a separate currency later this year. In addition, the entire range of political issues following the breakup of the Soviet Union, including the disposition of the armed forces and nuclear weapons, as well as the ownership of assets and liabilities, must be dealt with.

The 20% decline of output in the republics of the FSU by the end of 1991 occurred even before reform had started. A key question is whether the republics of the FSU will have to pay a further poststabilization price similar to that of Eastern Europe-about 20% of output. Or, because the 1991 decline in output in both the FSU and Eastern Europe was heavily affected by the collapse of the Council for Mutual Economic Assistance (CMEA), is it more likely that most of the price has already been paid?

Other republics of the FSU generally lag behind Russia in their reform efforts (although there has been progress in some areas in some republics, such as privatization in Armenia). Because of Russia's dominance and to confine this chapter to manageable proportions, I will focus on stabilization and reform in Russia. First, I will briefly describe Russia's current economic situation. Then I will review Russia's reform strategy in light of the Eastern European experience. I will then take up in turn questions of inter-republican trade and policy coordination and the role of external aid.

The Russian Economy in the FSU

Russia accounts for three-quarters of the land mass and more than half the population of the FSU. The republic is the world's largest country by size and has the fifth largest population. Meaningful estimates of its real GDP at the time of transition are difficult to come by or credit. Use of the black market exchange rate implies numbers—such as $150 per capita a year—that are too low to be believable. More realistically, Abram Bergson estimates that on a purchasing power basis, per capita GDP in the Soviet Union in 1985 was somewhat below the CIA's estimate of 42% of the U.S. level, but well above 28% of the U.S. level.[2] Treating the estimate as 35% of the U.S. level would have put Russian per capita GDP at about 38% of the U.S. level, in the range of the low-income European countries as Greece, Portugal, and Spain. Given the subsequent declines in output in Russia and the increases in output elsewhere, Bergson's starting point would place Russian real (purchasing power) per capita GDP in 1991 at a level similar to Mexico's.

The World Bank, which uses estimates of dollar GDP to compare countries and establish eligibility for different programs and facilities, is likely to estimate a per capita dollar GDP for Russia in the same range as Poland— about $1,800 in 1989—which is also at about the same level as Mexico.[3]

Table 6.2 presents data on the five most populous former Soviet republics. The Russian economy, because of its size and resources, was the least dependent of the Soviet republics on inter-republican trade; its energy resources ensured that it had a greater share of exports outside the FSU than the other republics.[4] Russia is more urban and more industrialized and has a higher per capita income than most of the other republics. Table 6.2 also clearly shows the lower level of economic development of the Central Asian republics, represented by Kazakhstan and Uzbekistan.

TABLE 6.2 Basic data, republics of the former Soviet Union

	Russia	Ukraine	Uzbekistan	Khazakstan	Belarus	USSR
Population (m.)	148.0	51.8	20.3	16.7	10.3	288.6
(% of total)	51.3	18.0	7.0	5.8	3.6	
% urban	74.0	67.0	41.0	57.0	66.0	66.0
Per capita net						
output (index)	119.0	90.0	47.0	74.0	117.0	100.0
Per capita income						
(index)	110.0	96.0	62.0	93.0	102.0	100.0
Infant mortality[b]	17.8	13.0	37.7	25.9	11.8	22.7
Share of net						
output	61.1	16.2	3.3	4.3	4.2	100.0
Share of						
industrial						
output	63.7	17.2	2.4	2.5	4.2	100.0
Share of						
agricultural						
output	50.3	17.9	5.5	6.4	5.1	100.0
Exports/NMP:						
Inter-republic	18.0	39.1	43.2	30.9	69.6	29.3[a]
Abroad	8.6	6.7	7.4	3.0	6.5	7.5[a]

Source: JSEE (1991), Vol. I, various tables. Data are for latest available year, generally 1988 or 1989.

a. Data in these rows are for 1988. As a share of USSR GDP, inter-republican exports were 26.5%, and exports abroad 5.4%. GDP data are not available at the republican level.

b. Infant mortality is the number of deaths per thousand births.

The structure of employment in the Soviet Union was similar to that of other centrally planned economies. However, as table 6.3 shows, the Soviet system differed from market economies especially by the small share of resources in the distribution (wholesale and retail trade) sector and in the financial sector.[5] Economic transformation in Russia is certain to draw more resources into the distribution and financial sectors. It also will gradually draw workers out of the agriculture sector. Russia's share of employment in manufacturing is comparable to that in Western European countries and may not change much as economic restructuring occurs.

The domestic macroeconomic disequilibria facing the new Russian government at the end of 1991 are summarized in table 6.1. In the latter half of 1991, Russia took over obligations of the Soviet government, including the army payroll and the task of printing money.

Russia's balance-of-payments situation at the end of 1991 is difficult to appraise. Much trade with countries outside the FSU was carried out in nonconvertible currencies at artificial exchange rates and prices. Moreover, the prospects for trade with the other republics after the breakup of the Soviet Union are extremely unclear. Table 6.4 presents the most recent data.[6] These

TABLE 6.3   Structure of employment, 1988 (% of employment)

	USSR	USA	Germany[a]
Agriculture	20.2	2.9	5.3
Manufacturing	23.6	18.5	32.2
Construction	9.3	6.6	6.6
Wholesale and retail trade	6.1	22.1	15.1
Finance and insurance	0.5	11.3	6.7
Community services	25.9	31.4	25.9
Other	14.4	7.2	8.2

Source: IMF, IBRD, OECD, EBRD, *Joint Study of the Soviet Economy* (henceforth described as JSSE), 1991, Vol. 2, p. 196. Data are adjusted to ensure comparability.
a. German data are for 1986.

show the Soviet Union sharply reducing its current account deficit between 1990 and 1991 and Russia moving from a current account deficit to a sizable surplus between 1990 and 1991. The improvement in the current account results mainly from a greater collapse of imports from the CMEA countries than exports to them; however, imports from the countries with convertible currencies also declined sharply. During 1991, the Soviet Union received net credits larger than its balance-of-payments surplus.

Omitted from the trade data for Russia in table 6.4 are any estimates of inter-republican trade in 1990 and 1991. Russia's current account in inter-republican trade, evaluated at actual prices, was probably in surplus in 1991; at world prices, Russia would have had a large surplus in inter-republican trade.[7] However, the volume of inter-republican trade certainly declined sharply in 1991. For 1992, the questions must be at what prices inter-republican trade will be carried out, what capacity the other republics will have to pay for imports, and how much mutual credit republics can extend to one another to support trade. Inter-republican trade is likely to continue to implode.

The export and import rows in table 6.4 show a large decline in trade in the nonconvertible area between 1990 and 1991.[8] Some of the key export and import commodities are shown in table 6.5. Exports of the single most important commodity—oil—declined by nearly half, a rate of decline that well exceeds the estimated percentage decline in oil production of 10%–15%.[9] Thus the decline in oil exports in 1991 must have resulted from both supply disruptions in the Soviet Union and demand disruptions in the former CMEA countries. Corresponding to the decline in exports (which, as noted above, was mainly in the nonconvertible area) are sharp falls in imports of machinery and raw materials (not shown), as well as consumer goods. Imports of basic foodstuffs did not drop as sharply.

TABLE 6.4 Balance of payments, USSR and Russia, 1990 and 1991 ($ billion)

	1990 Total Soviet Union	1990 Total Russia	1990 Convertible Soviet Union	1990 Convertible Russia	1991 Total Soviet Union	1991 Total Russia	1991 Convertible Soviet Union	1991 Convertible Russia
Current a/c	−24.1	−6.1	−7.8	−1.7	−5.7	4.6	−5.6	0.9
Gold sales	2.7	1.8	2.7	1.8	3.8	2.5	3.8	2.5
Current a/c (incl. gold)	−21.4	−4.3	−5.1	0.1	−1.9	7.1	−1.8	3.4
Memo items:								
Exports	103.9	80.9	33.5	26.1	70.2	54.7	31.8	24.8
Imports	−120.7	−82.9	−35.1	−24.1	−68.2	−45.6	−30.7	−20.0
Net interest	−4.0	−2.5	−4.0	−2.5	−3.7	−2.1	−3.7	−2.1
Capital flows	1.6	2.7	2.3	1.6	5.1	1.1	5.4	2.7
Memo item:								
Net credits	10.9	6.6	10.9	6.6	12.0	6.5	12.0	6.5
Overall balance	−19.8	−1.6	−2.8	1.7	3.2	8.2	3.6	6.1

Source: *PlanEcon Report*, VIII, pp. 9–10 (March 13, 1992). The difference between the columns "Total" and "Convertible" consists of trade with both the CMEA countries (in 1991 most of this trade was in convertible currencies) and trade with other countries with which the Soviet Union had barter (clearing) arrangements.

TABLE 6.5 Russian exports and imports, 1990-91

	Units	1990	1991	% change
Exports				
Crude oil	millions of barrels/day	2.2	1.1	−50
Refined oil	millions of barrels/day	1.0	0.9	−11
Natural gas	bcm	109.0	104.5	−4
Hard coal	million metric tons	35.4	23.9	−32
Wood	million cubic meters	28.0	19.0	−33
TV sets	million	1.7	0.7	−58
Imports				
Equipment for food and light industry				−80
Grain[a]	million metric tons	30.0	28.0	−7
Leather shoes	million pairs	136.0	40.0	−71
Pharmaceuticals	billion rubles	3.1	1.8	−43

Source: *PlanEcon Report*, VIII, 9–10, March 13 1992, p. 8. Units for crude and refined oil are in mmt in original, in millions of barrels per day in this table.

[a] Data for first nine months only

In the debt agreement reached with the G-7 at the end of 1991, the Commonwealth of Independent States (CIS) governments accepted "joint and several" responsibility for the Soviet Union's debts. This obligation must be more binding on Russia than on the small republics. Russia's share of the debt (if the other republics pay their shares) is 61%, or just under $50 billion. By the conventional criteria, Russia is not severely indebted. In 1991, Russian exports to the convertible currency area were $25 billion[10] and exports to the former CMEA countries were $17 billion. With a debt-to-exports ratio of 200% (this is an upper bound), the ratio for Russia for this indicator would be in the middle of the range of the moderately indebted countries, as designated by the World Bank; so too would be the interest-to-exports ratio.[11] The disorganization that will accompany economic restructuring will temporarily affect the economy's ability to export and increase its need for imports. However, in the medium run, Russia should be able to service its debts easily.

Russia's Reform Strategy

In formulating its economic stabilization and reform strategy, the Russian government, has been able to draw on the well-known Soviet reform plans that were intensively discussed (and rejected by President Gorbachev) between 1989 and 1991, as well as analysis by Western economists and the experience of Eastern European, Latin American, and other stabilization programs.[12]

The standard reform prescription is for a five-point strategy, moving as rapidly as possible on all fronts: macroeconomic stabilization, requiring both a budget that is nearly balanced and tight control over credit; liberalization of the prices of most goods; current account convertibility of the currency; privatization; and the creation of a social safety net.[13] At the same time, the government should be putting in place the legal framework for a market economy.

The best known of the Soviet reform plans is the Shatalin 500-Day Plan.[14] The Shatalin Plan proposed a detailed program that would have transformed the Soviet economy into a market economy within 500 days, starting on October 1, 1990: by now, the program would have been completed. The sequencing of the Shatalin Plan differs from the sequencing of plans now being implemented in Russia and Eastern Europe. The first 100 days would have been devoted to privatization and stabilization. Small businesses, housing, and vehicles would have been privatized and large companies corporatized. Revenues from privatization were expected to make a serious contribution to balancing the budget. A market infrastructure was to be put in place. Existing state orders and contracts were to run through the middle of 1991. Wages were to be indexed. The multiple exchange rate system was to be replaced by a single rate. Imports of consumer goods were to be increased. The Soviet Union was to have cut back foreign aid.

Prices were to have been liberalized only after macroeconomic stabilization had been assured and the market infrastructure—including privatization—had been put in place. Between days 100 and 250, prices would have been liberalized, larger firms would have been privatized, and the first stage of agrarian reform would have been completed. During the next phase, lasting to day 400, privatization would have continued, antimonopoly activity would have been strengthened, and prices would have been fully liberalized. Internal ruble convertibility was to have been achieved. The plan envisaged widespread bankruptcies and saw the need for measures to support the unemployed. The last 100 days were envisaged as the beginning of the upswing.

The Shatalin group believed that a price jump at the start of a reform plan would be politically unacceptable: one reason they started with privatization was their belief that asset sales could help remove the monetary overhang. The Shatalin Plan placed much less weight on the need for early convertibility than do most Western plans. The plan also did not emphasize external assistance, believing that the Soviet Union could manage largely on its own. The plan recognized the need for greater republican autonomy and expressed concern about maintaining a single economic space. Read in the light of hindsight, the plan did not recognize the imminence of the threat of the collapse of the Soviet Union. Moreover, the plan's 500-day target was unrealistically ambitious, although the notion of a sequenced program makes sense.

In any event, the Russian government started its reforms by liberalizing prices—well before it had any assurance that fiscal and monetary policy were consistent with macroeconomic stability. The normal prescription is first or simultaneously to establish macroeconomic control and then to liberalize prices. However, that prescription applies to countries where most resources are allocated through functioning markets and where price liberalization means removing incomplete price controls and reducing tariffs; this was not the situation in Russia. There, the choice was between liberalizing prices and risking hyperinflation or maintaining price controls and exacerbating shortages. In weighing its decision, the government no doubt took into account the fact that a growing proportion of transactions were being conducted in black markets, so that the effective choice to a considerable extent was between hidden and open inflation. The government must also have taken into account the unavailability of external resources to help finance the budget and stabilize the currency. Moreover, by taking a radical and virtually irreversible step, it signaled that it meant what it said about radical reform.

Obvious problems with the standard strategy derive from the difficulty of doing everything at once. The Shatalin Plan's intention to put the elements of a market system in place before liberalizing prices is based on the fear of perverse supply responses by managers of state-owned enterprises (more accurately, enterprises whose ownership is not well defined). But privatization before liberalizing prices is also problematic because it is impossible to value firms for sale when current prices and profits provide little guide to future performance.

I will turn now to other elements of the standard strategy, leaving aside the safety net.

Macroeconomic Stabilization

Much still must be done to secure macroeconomic stabilization in Russia. The two essentials are fiscal consolidation and a tightening of monetary and credit policy. The Russian government was able to reduce the budget deficit by more than 10% of GDP by cutting subsidies, defense expenditures, and investment spending. But its efforts to collect taxes have been less successful, so that a planned budget deficit of 1% of GDP in the first quarter of 1992 will become an actual deficit of near 10%.

As table 6.6 shows, the Soviet tax system relied primarily on profits and turnover taxes, the former collected mostly at the union level, the latter more at the republican level. On the expenditure side, subsidies—provided mostly at the republican level—took up about 20% of the budget and 10% of GDP.

TABLE 6.6   Soviet fiscal system, 1989

Revenues 393 b.rubles (41% of GDP)

	As share of state budget (%)	As share of row		
		Union budget	Republican budget	Local budget
Total revenue	100.0	53	26	21
Tax revenue	94.6	53	27	20
Income taxes	41.0	54	17	29
Profit taxes	30.4	59	20	22
Personal income tax	10.6	39	11	50
Turnover tax	28.2	14	59	27
Alcohol	10.3			
Social insurance	8.4	84	16	0
Taxes on foreign trade	14.8	100		

Expenditures 480 b.rubles (50% of GDP)

	As share of state budget (%)	As share of row		
		Union budget	Republican budget	Local budget
Total expenditure	100.0	51	33	16
Economy	41.7	37	51	12
Investment	14.2	61	20	19
Price compensation[a]	13.8	29	67	3
Procurement prices[a]	6.6		100	
Social and cultural	29.0	26	37	37
Defense	15.7	100		

Source: JSSE (1991), Vol. 1, various tables.

a. These are both subsidy items. Most subsidies went to agriculture, mostly to support basic food prices. Cross-subsidization among firms is not recorded in the budget.

The Russian government, in its initial attempt at macroeconomic stabilization, cut subsidies and relied on a generalized 28% sales (or value-added) tax to close the budget gap. The sales tax should have been collectible through the same channels as before, and profits and export taxes also should have been paid to the Russian government. However, revenues have fallen short of projections, partly because of the decline in exports, partly because the parliament exempted food from taxation, and partly because of poor tax compliance.

In the short run, fiscal stabilization will require further spending cuts and increased revenues. The key to budget balances lies in taxing oil exports. The deficit could be closed if a planned 40% export tax could be collected, especially if recent declines in oil production could be reversed. Over the longer run, structural fiscal reform is needed to move away from the fiscal structure inherited from the Soviet Union. Given the inevitable weakness of tax administration at the early stages of reform, simplicity and collectibility are key criteria.[15] As part of the reform, penalties for tax evasion will have to be strengthened so that Russia does not descend into the former Latin American trap where no one pays taxes, no one is punished, the budget is chronically in deficit, and inflation is perennial.

The issue of monetary or credit policy in Russia is mired in a dispute between the Central Bank of Russia and the finance ministry over the need for tight credit. The central bank, with the support of parliament, has argued that tightening credit now will merely lead to unemployment and bankruptcies without achieving any positive results. The finance ministry wants the central bank to tighten credit as part of the stabilization program.

Much of what happened in early 1992 was standard buck-passing. However, there are also important issues of the reform strategy. Budgetary stabilization alone cannot stop inflation if the central bank continues to expand the stock of credit by lending to the private sector. Both the quantity and cost of central bank credit matter: the Central Bank of Russia has so far been lending at a very negative real rate, which is not surprising when a price level change is occurring. However, there is no sign that the central bank is willing to move the real interest rate to a positive level even when and if inflation recedes.

The central bank has argued that it is essential not to starve existing firms of finance. The argument for generous credit at this time would start from the view that credit policy cannot be divorced from issues of enterprise reform and regional policy at this stage. Enforcement of tight credit constraints could lead to the closing of enterprises. In the current distorted price and financial systems, the wrong firms might close. Further, given the geographical concentration of industry, such closings—even if they were justified on economic grounds—could devastate the economies of entire regions, as happened, for instance, in the shipbuilding regions of the former East Germany. The standard prescription—to formulate a regional policy and finance it through the budget—is unrealistic, given the government's inability to raise revenues. The provision of cheap credit is a substitute for an articulated and financed restructuring and regional policy.

This argument is not in principle incorrect. It certainly increases the urgency of moving ahead on economic restructuring—primarily privatization —and the formulation of regional policies. However, there is no doubt that credit policy should be tightened now. Prices have been liberalized and firms need to begin to face a financial bottom line. This would encourage normal supply responses, including the disgorging of inventories—a process that would help reverse expectations of rising prices and move goods into distribution channels. The argument that a tightening of credit policies will lead to massive unemployment may become relevant within a year if no industrial restructuring takes place. However, the fact is that few firms in the reforming Eastern European countries have been closed and unemployment has increased only slowly.

In the near term, monetary policy will have to support the stabilization effort if stabilization is to succeed and to attract Western financial assistance. Several possibilities exist. First, the central bank may already be tightening credit; there are some reports that credit growth was slow in February 1992. Second, an explicit monetary policy rule—such as a limit on domestic credit creation—or maintenance of a fixed exchange rate, could be embodied in the expected IMF agreement. Third, the interest rate may be raised to positive real levels—although this is not a sufficient policy unless accompanied by central bank refusal to roll over debts. Nonetheless, if the policy conflict continues, President Yeltsin will have to come down one way or the other on the issue.

Incomes Policy

Taxes on excess wage increases have been used in Poland. One argument for such tax-based incomes policies advanced in the 1970s is that these taxes mitigate an externality in the wage-setting process.[16] A stronger argument in reforming socialist economies is that so long as the ownership of enterprises is ambiguous, firms will tend to pay out excessive amounts to workers and other stakeholders. The requirement in Poland that firms pay dividends to the government also responds to this concern, but would not by itself prevent decapitalization of the firm. An equally powerful argument derives from the potential dynamic inconsistency of anti-inflationary policy. A government committed to controlling inflation should not accommodate wage-cost pressures on prices. However, if wages do rise, the government that resists such pressures has to create unemployment, which it is loathe to do. Rather than allow itself to be put in that position, the government seeks to prevent it by taxing excess wage increases.

Opponents argue that market forces should be left to determine wages. But wage setting in government-owned firms is not a market process. As in Poland, the tax should not apply to firms in the private sector, thereby providing an incentive to privatize. It is also true that because firms can compensate workers in many ways, evasion will be widespread. Nonetheless, the balance of the argument favors the use of a tax on excess wage increases in Russia.[17]

The Exchange Rate and Current Account Convertibility

One attraction of currency convertibility at a fixed exchange rate—the third element in the standard package—is that there would then be a clear monetary policy rule: to conduct monetary policy so as to maintain the exchange rate.[18] This would certainly help, but it would not be sufficient; as experience all over the world shows, countries can hold an exchange rate fixed for some time, even though they pursue policies that ensure it will have to be devalued at some future point. Thus, the nominal anchor of the exchange rate would have to be supplemented by a nominal anchor on, say, domestic credit, so that domestic inflation would not first erode competitiveness and then force a devaluation, as often has happened—including in Poland in 1991.[19]

The usual argument for a fixed exchange rate rule during stabilization is that it ensures that the supply of money will adjust automatically to relevant demand shifts at a time when shifts in the demand function are difficult to predict.[20] However, this argument assumes that there are no capital controls and would not apply to the reforming formerly socialist economies. The relevant macroeconomic arguments in Russia are that the exchange rate rule is one that the central bank can understand, and that the fixed exchange rate provides direct stabilization to the price level—both because it is a highly visible price whose stability can help stabilize expectations, and because it ensures that the prices of imports will rise only at the foreign rate of inflation (changes in domestic markups aside).

Equally important is the microeconomic argument that convertibility allows the country to import the appropriate, world price system.[21] Essentially, current account convertibility is the same thing as trade liberalization. It allows individuals and enterprises to buy and sell foreign exchange freely as the counterpart to imports and exports of goods and services. Current account convertibility is not consistent with widespread quantitative restrictions on trade or foreign exchange licensing, but could be consistent with tariffs and export subsidies or taxes. In most reforming Eastern European countries, tariffs have been reduced to lower and more uniform levels than was typical in the reforming countries of Latin America.[22]

If the exchange rate is to be fixed, its level will matter for the subsequent course of inflation.[23] Relative wages at current market exchange rates are well below levels likely to prevail if the currency stabilizes: the market is thin; most of trade is not conducted at that rate; and the rate can be moved by small amounts of foreign exchange. Setting the initial exchange rate at about the current market rate (for example, 120 rubles per dollar) would create an inflationary shock and would not provide any competition from imports. It would be preferable to set the initial rate at a level that (while allowing for some subsequent inflation) would put dollar wages in the vicinity of $50 to $100 per month. Whether this can be done will depend on the availability of a stabilization fund and other external financing and on the authorities' ability to prevent capital flight by exporters.

There has been much discussion of the choice between gradualism and shock treatment in Eastern European reform. The issue is in most respects irrelevant in the case of Russia.[24] For countries that start with a massive macroeconomic disequilibrium, rapid stabilization is essential. So is rapid price liberalization when shortages are pervasive, as they were in Russia. Some elements of a social safety net must be put in place immediately to ensure that stabilization does not cause excessive hardship.

There are two areas in which gradualism is a viable option: trade liberalization and privatization. The case for using tariffs is twofold: first, they provide protection against imports; second, they provide revenue for the budget. Both factors imply gradualism in reducing tariffs. To minimize the inevitable political pressures for special treatment, tariffs should be uniform;[25] they could start as high as 30%–40% and be reduced over five years to low levels. That way, they would provide protection for domestic producers while the economy is reorganizing; generate revenue for the budget while a more sophisticated tax system is being set up; and still allow a foreign price system to be imported. The fiscal case for trade taxes is already accepted in Russia on the export side, where oil exports will be taxed. The case is also strong on the import side. While tariffs carry potential political economy dangers, so does a lack of budget revenue. Gradual tariff reductions can be built into programs with the international agencies.

Enterprise Reform and Privatization

Soviet industrial enterprises were very large and industry was correspondingly monopolized.[26] (See table 6.7 for a comparison of industrial concentration in the Soviet Union, the United States, and Poland.) In 1988, 47,000 industrial enterprises operated in the Soviet Union. In the first half of 1990, enterprises owned by local authorities and republics accounted for 35% of value added.[27] The private sector in the Soviet Union was minuscule. Nearly 90% of employment was in state enterprises, 8% was on collective farms, and less than 4% was in private activity (including cooperatives). The number of cooperatives surged at the end of the Soviet period, exceeding 250,000 (with nearly 40% in construction) in the middle of 1991, employing more than 6 million people and accounting for as much as 5% of GDP. However, 80% of these cooperatives were operating within existing enterprises[28]—a process that can be viewed either as the beginning of industrial restructuring through the spinning off of viable components of firms or simply as the ripping off of state assets.

In the debate over shock treatment versus gradualism, the pace of privatization and the development of the private sector are relevant issues that pit experts on China[29] against those involved in Eastern European reform. China's gradualist reforms, which started in agriculture, have not involved formal privatization and state firms have not been sold to private individuals. Nonetheless, a vibrant, essentially private, sector has developed in Chinese

TABLE 6.7 Size distribution of industrial enterprises (share of employees)

	1–99	100–499	500–999	1000+	of which 5–10,000	10,000+
Soviet Union (1988)	1.8	13.2	11.7	73.3	15.6	21.5
United States (1985)	27.6	33.8	12.7	25.8		
Poland (1986)	10.0	25.0	15.0	51.0		

Sources: USSR: JSSE, Vol. 2, p. 37; USA: *Statistical Abstract of the United States*, 1988, p. 499 (for manufacturing); Poland: Lipton and Sachs (1990), p. 84.

agriculture and industry and the reforms have been extremely successful by any economic measure.

In Eastern Europe, the stated preference has been for rapid privatization. In practice, Eastern European progress in privatization has been disappointing, especially in Poland, where sophisticated schemes for mass privatization have yet to be implemented.[30] Success has been considerable in small-scale privatization—the privatization of small (primarily retail) firms, whose purchase or lease is often financed by the governmental agency making the sale. Privatization of medium- and large-scale firms has been less successful, although the Czechoslovak voucher system could soon result in privatizating much of industry—and perhaps shortly thereafter could also bring widespread disillusionment with the promises of financial operators. Hungary, which has avoided grandiose schemes and encourages current management and workers to pursue the sale of their firms subject to approval by the State Property Agency, appears to be making some progress with privatization of larger firms.[31]

The circumstances in Russia, where the state and the state order system have collapsed, are different from those in China. The Russian government has been losing control over the enterprise sector and must clarify the ownership status of firms and the rules under which they are to operate, for the old rules no longer apply. In that sense, gradualism in the reform of the enterprise sector in Russia cannot occur. The new rules and the new strategy must be developed and implemented so that firms can again begin to operate with clear management objectives.[32] The government should also aim to move firms out of state control as soon as possible.

However, enterprise reform needs to be gradualist in recognizing that privatization of large firms will take time—perhaps up to a decade—until most of the largest firms have been mostly privatized. Gradualism also is needed to implement a strategy in which the state will be responsible for a significant, but diminishing, part of industry for years and not for months.

Such a strategy would look much like those being carried out in practice (although not in rhetoric) in Eastern Europe and the approach that is starting in Russia. The first Russian auctions of small firms took place at the beginning of April 1992, but local authorities are not showing much enthusiasm about the sales.[33] Small-scale privatization is both urgent—as a precedent and signal that the privatization effort is serious—and important, because the distribution sector in which such firms operate is vastly underdeveloped in Russia.[34] Growth in this area is likely eventually to come from new firms, but opening up the sector requires the privatization of the existing firms owned by the local authorities. As emphasized by Andrei Shleifer and Robert Vishny, existing stakeholders will have to be given incentives to obtain their support for privatization.[35] If rapid progress cannot be made in this easiest area of privatization, the entire privatization and reform progress will be severely set back.

Stories about spontaneous or *nomenklatura* privatization of larger firms abound. Case study evidence presented by Simon Johnson and Heidi Kroll suggests that firms' managers have generally strengthened their control and their residual property rights during the period since 1988, but that they have not obtained de jure ownership of firms.[36] Johnson and Kroll emphasize the part played by management and downplay the role of the *nomenklatura*. Newspaper and other reports of corruption in the transfer of property tend to emphasize the role of the bureaucracy. It is not inconsistent with Johnson and Kroll's evidence to argue that in many cities and regions, property rights are being (insecurely) passed from the state sector to others, to the benefit of the *nomenklatura*.

Both existing management and existing workers will have to support privatizations of larger firms if firms are to be moved quickly into the private sector. Thus privatization schemes that give existing workers and management significant shares of the privatized firm are more likely to succeed than those that ignore the current distribution of implicit property rights.[37] Shleifer and Vishny suggest that the shares be given in a way that directly encourages management and workers to privatize; for instance, shareowners could receive dividends only after privatization.

The first step in privatization of larger firms—and one that can come within months—should be corporatization: moving the firms out of bureaucratic control and into the control of corporate boards. Workers will have to be represented on these boards. Inevitably the boards' composition will have to compromise between the need for knowledgeable members and the need to keep out the *nomenklatura*. For the largest firms, it would be desirable to bring in Western experts, but they should speak Russian.

As in Hungary, Russia from the beginning should be encouraging privatization by existing firms, subject to state approval. This process can take place at any time while other privatization schemes are being developed and implemented.

A possible privatization strategy following corporatization starts with each board—for manageability, say, boards of firms with more than 2,500 employees—presenting a restructuring plan to the privatization agency. All firms whose boards present a plausible restructuring scheme that does not involve large externalities for a given region or city will go into a privatization pool. Ownership rights for the firms in the privatization pool should be distributed to citizens, as well as workers and managers, through a voucher scheme—perhaps one that gives individuals ownership in holding companies, rather than individual firms. Smaller firms could be privatized through vouchers in the same or a separate scheme. The Eastern European evidence is that such schemes can get stuck, which is all the more reason for urgency.

It will be necessary during the restructuring process for the state to decide how to deal with existing financial assets and liabilities in firm balance sheets. There is a real attraction in a widespread write-down or even write-off of debts and corresponding assets, an action that would have to involve the banks. The banks could be compensated by being given claims on a diversified portfolio of firm equity, and by being given government bonds as reserve assets.

The large size of the enterprises and the concentration of industries creates both advantages and problems for boards considering restructuring. On the benefit side, the large firms are too vertically integrated; each provides its own complete range of ancillary services, such as catering, haircutting, and manufacturing spare parts in machine tool shops. Restructuring can begin by peeling off viable parts of firms. Similarly, because the firms are in many cases monopolies that hold most of the country's technical knowledge to produce that commodity, it is likely that some part of the firms will survive in the new regime.

The prime disadvantage of largeness is that rapidly closing down a giant firm that dominates the economy of a city or region will not be politically possible. Such giant firms will not go into the privatization pool; for them Russia will have to develop regional and restructuring policies. To state the point clearly, this arrangement borders on industrial policy. But there is no point in pretending that the Russian government will be able to do what most other governments—most obviously the German government—cannot, which is to leave such restructurings to the market, particularly because the market for corporate restructuring does not yet exist.[38] To put the point succinctly, privatization is not an adequate restructuring policy. Pretending that restructuring will take place if left to the market only delays doing what has to be done. An agency, operated with external financial and expert support, should be set up to deal with those firms that do not go into the privatization pool, to develop restructuring plans (and, if necessary, phased steps to shut down firms).

Within a few years, the Russian private sector will grow more through the creation of new firms than through privatization. Thus an essential element of the enterprise reform strategy consists of developing the legal, financial, and educational systems and infrastructure to support new enterprises.

Eastern European governments have been concerned that at the current over-devalued exchange rates, foreigners could buy up too much of their countries at too low a price. A similar concern seems to have arisen in the FSU in the recently completed negotiations over a Chevron investment in the Tengiz oil field, which revealed a Groucho Marx-like fear on the former Soviet side of accepting any deal to which the other side agreed. Despite such concerns, foreign direct investment, which brings not only finance but also management expertise and technology, should be and is being welcomed by the Russian government. Russia has hired foreign advisers to help develop and appraise potential foreign investments; this is an area in which the international agencies such as the World Bank, which presumably can operate more as honest brokers, might play an active role. At present, the real problems with foreign investment are that there is too little rather than too much of it, and that much of that is going into deals that are often corrupt. While foreign investors are obviously extremely interested in Russia, foreign direct investment will not flow on a substantial scale, such as the scale on which it is now flowing to Hungary (where it is more than 3% of GNP), until some sense of stability returns.

Of course, foreign expertise can be obtained without foreign investment. There is no reason why foreign management should not be imported on contract, even if foreign firms do not want to invest directly.

The Financial Sector
The creation of a viable private sector depends on the availability of financing both to purchase existing firms and to create new firms. To some extent, financing for privatization can come from the state sector—for example, in small-scale privatization, by leasing rather than immediately selling firms—and by setting the prices of firms low enough, through voucher schemes. The development of new firms depends more on the development of the banking system, through restructuring of existing balance sheets and the creation of new banks or units within existing banks. The possibility of canceling existing debts between firms and banks and replacing them with bank claims on a diversified range of firms has already been noted. Implicit or explicit state guarantees would be needed to ensure that banks do not go under if firms fail on a large scale.

Financial sector reforms have lagged in Eastern Europe, except in Hungary. Many new and specialized banks have been set up in Russia, but the existing banks have not yet been reformed.

The Agricultural Sector
Attention in privatization focuses on industrial enterprises. However, improving the agricultural sector is one of the highest reform priorities. Improvements in the availability and quality of food would not only benefit the population, but also bring strong political support to the reform process. Thus the priority being put on agricultural reform by outside agencies providing technical assistance is well directed.[39] It appears that many farmers on collectives do not want privatization; however, there must be many farmers who do. The development of private ownership of land and the extension of private agriculture are areas in which rapid progress is possible and would have a high payoff.[40]

**New Currencies, Inter-republican Trade,
and Economic Coordination**

The dissolution of the Soviet Union will lead to a decline—at least in the near term—of inter-republican trade and the introduction of independent currencies in some republics of the FSU. At present, the fifteen republics of the FSU continue to use one currency and have agreed in principle to allow the free passage of goods among them. But the Baltics and Ukraine have already announced that they intend to introduce their own currencies and other republics are preparing to do so. Ukraine's coupons are close to being a new currency. Moreover, goods are not flowing freely among republics.

Would the republics be better off staying in the ruble zone or introducing their own currencies? If Russia continues to move ahead on price liberalization, stabilization, and convertibility, there would be advantages for the other republics to staying in the ruble zone and automatically acquiring a more stable and convertible currency. In addition, inter-republican trade would probably hold up better if the ruble zone were maintained.[41] Offsetting these advantages is the certainty that there will have to be major changes in relative wages among republics; these would be easier to attain if exchange rates among the republics' currencies could be adjusted. Republics with less developed tax systems may want to use seigniorage more than others; this too requires an independent currency. Of course, operating an independent currency would require improving the quality of central bank management.

By virtue of its size and relative wealth, Russia would be less affected by the breakdown of inter-republican trade and the ruble area than the other republics. At the first stage of its reform program, Russia was able to force price liberalization on the others because they were not prepared to introduce their own currencies and manage their own economies. Russia's progress in achieving macroeconomic stabilization has put pressure on other republics by reducing the availability of rubles to cover their budget deficits and meet payrolls. Russia hopes to tighten fiscal and monetary policies and move toward convertibility within a few months. The other republics will either have to stabilize at the same time or introduce independent currencies. Beyond this defensive motive, some republics view an independent currency as a necessary attribute of sovereignty.

In any case, Ukraine and perhaps the Baltics are planning to introduce their own currencies later this year; other western republics are likely to follow. Presumably these republics would want their currencies to be convertible as soon as possible, but because reforms have been slow, convertibility will be delayed. The Central Asian republics will probably want to stay in the ruble area as long as they continue to receive transfers from Russia. Those transfers could be made explicitly through budgetary transfers or trade credits or by pricing Russian exports at internal Russian prices (that is, net of export taxes). For 1992, Russia will not levy export taxes on oil sent to other republics. Thus at least temporarily, Russia is seeking to maintain the wider trading zone. In the longer run, Russia's decision on whether to provide transfers must be mainly political.

New currencies can be introduced cooperatively by retiring an equivalent volume of rubles held within the territory or owned by citizens of the republic and replacing them with the new currency. A more confrontational approach would be to ignore the existing stock of rubles, leaving citizens to dispose of them as best they can. There is a mutual interest in avoiding a confrontation on this issue, so that new currencies are likely to be introduced cooperatively.

Republics other than Russia lag in the reform effort, not only because they are not yet committed to moving toward a market system, but also because they lack the qualified personnel needed to manage a reform program. Even Ukraine, which is politically committed to genuine independence and therefore has to develop an independent economic policy management ability, is only now beginning to pull an economic team together—and Ukraine has a large population, financial resources, and diaspora on which to draw. Economic management will be a real problem for other republics, even with the assistance of the international agencies.

Inter-republican Trade

The breakup of the ruble zone would speed the decline of inter-republican trade, especially if currencies are not convertible. It is often said that the republics of the FSU were extremely closely integrated, more than market economies are likely to be. Table 6.2 includes some data on the extent of trade, showing Belarus's exports at 70% of net material product (NMP). Because table 6.2 presents data for the largest republics, it understates the importance of trade for the representative republic. The average 1988 export

TABLE 6.8   Inter-republican and foreign trade balances, 1987 (% of NMP)

	At domestic prices			At world prices		
	Inter republican	Abroad	Total	Inter republican	Abroad	Total
Russia	0.9	−8.3	−7.4	7.4	3.3	10.7
Ukraine	1.6	−7.7	−6.2	−3.9	−1.5	−5.4
Uzbekistan	−20.6	−0.5	−21.1	−23.6	0.5	−23.1
Khazakstan	−20.0	−7.8	−27.8	−24.4	−4.1	−28.5
Belarus	11.8	−7.6	4.2	−8.3	−0.8	−9.5
Lithuania	−4.5	−7.9	−12.3	−37.0	−2.2	−39.2

Source: JSSE (1991), Vol. 1, pp. 226–227.

ratio (exports/NMP) in inter-republican trade for the other ten republics was 57%. For the Soviet Union, the GDP/NMP ratio was 1.34, so the average inter-republican export/GDP ratio for the smaller republics would be 40%–45%.[42] This is about the same as the dependence of the smaller European economies on intra-European trade. But because of the extreme specialization of production in the FSU, the republics must be more mutually dependent for vital production inputs than they will be after economic reform.

The massive changes in relative prices that have to occur will disrupt production all over the FSU. They will also impose huge adverse balance-of-payments shocks on many of the republics, particularly the energy importers. Table 6.8 presents estimates of the balance-of-payments shift caused by moving to world prices for the five largest republics and for Lithuania, one of the worst hit former republics.[43] These impacts are being cushioned by Russia's agreement to maintain a relatively low price of oil (compared to world prices) for inter-republican trade for 1992. Nonetheless, the data indicate the macroeconomic adjustments that must be made over the next few years.

The republics appear to be moving toward a series of bilateral trade deals for 1992. These agreements would avert the worst outcome—a complete collapse of trade along with the Soviet Union. However, the danger remains of a sharp reduction of the volume of trade as bilateral balancing—requiring the double coincidence of wants—replaces the multilateral trade that took place in the FSU. In a simple calculation, using a matrix of inter-republican trade, I assumed that with bilateral clearing, trade between each pair of countries would settle at the lower of imports or exports in 1988. The volume of trade would decline to 44% of its previous value under this constraint, a huge shock with potentially dangerously disruptive effects on trade.

There is no question that trade patterns within the FSU have to change drastically over the next few years. It is thus tempting to argue that whatever decline in trade takes place is part of a process of creative destruction that will lead more rapidly to an efficient pattern of output. This is wrong in two respects. As a matter of theory, trade that must ultimately disappear may nonetheless be desirable in a second-best situation. As a matter of political economy, a very rapid decline in production—even production that must ultimately disappear—may stop a reform program in its tracks. The recent experience of Eastern Europe provides suggestive evidence that trade-related shocks can produce a too rapid decline in output.

The Inter-republican Payments Mechanism

What can the republics do to mitigate and smooth these shocks? They have much to gain by collaborating on questions of trade and macroeconomic reform—on matters of inter-republican payments and, if necessary, in the introduction of new currencies. At present, the republics lack a framework of collaboration. The case for the introduction of a mechanism like the European Payments Union (EPU) has been made by Rudiger Dornbusch and Daniel Gros, among others.[44] The case for a payments mechanism includes: the need for a collaborative framework; the potential gains from multilateral, rather than bilateral, clearing of trade; and the fear that without such a mechanism, trade could spiral downward as each republic imposes restrictions on other republics that they fear cannot pay. The case against introducing a new mechanism views a payments union as a mechanism that will maintain central planning of trade and impose quantitative restrictions, rather than promote rapid convertibility—a charge given some plausibility by the fact that current account convertibility was attained in Western Europe only in 1958.

Much of the controversy over a payments union and the apparent Russian opposition to it stem from the emphasis on the EPU precedent. The EPU Board did play a major role in managing trade and payments among its members, in many respects taking the place of the IMF.[45] That is not needed in the FSU, where the IMF and the World Bank already are active, nor is the necessary experience available in the FSU. Rather, the need is for a more modest organization, the Inter-republican Payments Mechanism (IRPM). This group would have three tasks: to operate as a technical organization to clear payments; to provide a mechanism to extend credit among republics, and to economize on reserves; and to provide a convenient focus for broader inter-republican cooperation.

The issue is usually posed as convertibility versus a payments union. But components of an IRPM would be needed even with convertibility. The banking systems in the republics of the FSU are underdeveloped and explicit arrangements for inter-republican payments will need to be worked out, with the help of outside agencies. The arrangements would involve relations among the central banks of the republics, as well as among the nascent private banking systems. This is the first necessary function of an IRPM. Second, credit could be extended among the republics to try to prevent credit constraints from, in effect, imposing bilateral balancing on trade. The central banks of the republics will have to agree on mutual credit limits, to be administered through the IRPM. As in the case of the EPU, increasingly onerous settlement provisions will have to be imposed as imbalances increase, and upper bounds should be set on imbalances. Convertibility is not a full substitute for such arrangements because the republics will be short of reserves. An IRPM can be viewed as a means of economizing on hard-currency reserves, setting up an alternative means of financing temporary imbalances among the republics, even after convertibility is attained.

The IRPM should be thought of as a source of transactions balances to finance current transactions, not as a source of long-term financing. Given the adjustments some republics must make, they will run current account deficits for some years. Financing plans for those deficits will involve agreement with the IMF and may include separate intergovernmental agreements among republics for the extension of longer-term credit. Those agreements could be negotiated at IRPM meetings, but they are not an inherent part of an IRPM.

Some framework for continuing inter-republican collaboration and economic relations is clearly needed. The republics need to collaborate not only in developing payments mechanisms and providing the associated credits, but also to prevent potentially destructive trade and currency reforms. To this point, they have been collaborating on an ad hoc basis, including negotiating bilateral trade agreements. A more permanent multilateral arrangement, in the context of the IRPM, possibly with external technical assistance, would be constructive. It is not inherent in the creation of an IRPM that it would slow progress to a market system; the inclusion of international agencies would help ensure that it moves in the right direction.

There is one other potential role for an IRPM. It could be seen as a mechanism through which external assistance could be funneled to the republics and conditionality for such assistance could be imposed. There might be a case for using IRPM in this way if the republics were not members of the IMF and the World Bank. Because they are members, bilateral assistance can be provided through cofinancing of IMF and Bank programs, with conditionality agreed upon in direct negotiations among the agencies and the republics. The need for donor coordination remains.[46]

In the area of inter-republican coordination and payments, as in privatization, the best is the enemy of the good, and the transition has to be managed. The "best" in this case would be full convertibility, with adequate reserves, for all currencies in the FSU. The current structure of inter-republican trade must be destroyed. But convertibility with adequate reserves will not happen anytime soon, and trade can be destroyed too rapidly if nothing is developing in its place. These difficulties make the case for an IRPM that goes beyond the necessary minimum of a technical organization to manage the payments mechanism.

External Assistance for Russia

Maintaining the pace and direction of political and economic reforms in the FSU is certainly in the interests of the West. The West has recognized this interest by engaging the FSU through diplomacy, through defense arrangements, and with financial assistance and membership in the international organizations. In April 1992, the G-7 announced a $24 billion aid package for Russia, for 1992. Because aid remains controversial and the full details of the aid package are not yet clear, I will discuss the general case for financial assistance for Russia and the other republics.

For economic and political stability, the reforming republics need four types of assistance: humanitarian, technical, and general financial aid, as well as access to Western markets. Humanitarian and food aid is reaching the FSU. So is technical assistance, particularly as the international agencies, including the European Community, have moved decisively into the area. The technical assistance is so far concentrated on Russia, but is beginning to spread to the other republics, where it is needed even more. However, technical assistance from official agencies is usually provided in the visiting fireman form: in assisting the newly forming governments, it is important to station people in the republics for periods of a year or more, if possible. While technical assistance is now flowing, the FSU can easily and productively absorb more.

It is almost impossible to get accurate data on aggregate assistance that so far has been provided to the Soviet Union and the other republics of the FSU. Table 6.9 presents one set of data on total financial assistance commitments to the Soviet Union and the republics in the period between September 1990 and December 1991. The total committed in those sixteen months—more than $67 billion—is impressive; so are the facts that more than half that amount was committed by Germany, and so little was provided by the United States and Japan.

Unfortunately, table 6.9 is severely misleading. Least important, it is slightly misleading in categorizing food aid. Agricultural credits, the form of U.S. aid, are classified as export credits. The category of food aid in table 6.9 is probably aid provided by the donors in the form of food, rather than, say, credits. The more serious difficulty is that the table presents aid commitments over some future horizon, some of them in the form of ceilings on export credit agency exposure, some of which were withdrawn following the collapse of the Soviet Union, and some of which may represent debt outstanding rather than potential flows. The data do not represent aid disbursements. The

TABLE 6.9   Aid committed to the FSU (September 1990–December 1991, $billion)

	Food and medical assistance	Technical assistance	Export and other credits[a]	Troop withdrawal aid	Total
Europe	1.3	1.1	32.4	10.4	50.5
Germany	0.7	0.2	20.4	10.4	34.7
Italy			4.0		5.8
U.S.A.			4.1		4.1
Japan		0.2	2.5		2.7
S. Korea			3.1		3.1
Total	1.4	1.8	45.1	10.4	**67.6**

Source: *International Economic Insights*, Jan./Feb. 1992, described as based on unofficial figure compiled by the European Community.
Note: Data in source were in ECU; exchange rate of $1.25/ecu was used. Rows and columns do not add to totals because of omitted entries.
a. Sum of "Export guarantees and credits" and "Other credits."

republics could not access these amounts of finance within a year or even within several years. The more useful aggregate measure of Western assistance in 1991 appears in table 6.4—$12 billion in net credits. Russia's share of this sum is estimated at $6.5 billion. Even in this lower figure, the official credits were to a considerable extent replacing disappearing bank credits.

The package of financial assistance for Russia announced in April 1992 has two components. The first is a currency stabilization fund of $6 billion. The second is balance-of-payments support of $18 billion, including $2.5 billion of debt rescheduling. The currency stabilization fund is to come entirely from the IMF's General Arrangements to Borrow; about $4.5 billion of the remaining financing is expected to come from the international agencies; and $11 billion represents bilateral financial assistance, largely export credits, some of it already committed. The currency stabilization fund is intended to support the convertibility of the ruble, presumably at a fixed exchange rate. This step should be taken only when and if the Russian government tightens the budget and monetary policy. That could be before the end of 1992.

The balance-of-payments support must have been calculated on a needs basis, reflecting the amount of import financing Russia will need if some modest level of recovery in output—or at least only a small further decline—is to take place this year. In fact, the continuing disruption of inter-republican trade makes further deep declines in output this year very likely. This means (to answer a question raised at the beginning of the chapter) that Russia and the other republics are likely to suffer far worse recessions than Eastern Europe is now experiencing.

Opposition to the provision of financial assistance to Russia is based on several arguments. First, the type of advice and conditionality that accompanies IMF and World Bank assistance is generally wrong; for instance, it urges gradualism when shock treatment is needed.[47] Second, the money will be wasted because corruption is rife. After all, critics ask, what has happened to the $67 billion of assistance already provided? Third, the money would be better spent elsewhere, for instance, in Africa. Fourth, easing the financial constraint on the Russian (or any) government allows it to put off doing the right thing. In the Russian context, that would be to generate as much foreign exchange as possible by selling oil leases and other assets that the West wants. Fifth, we cannot afford it.

Some of these arguments are valid, and should find their reflection in IMF and Bank conditionality—for instance in developing oil leases, in requiring budgetary and credit tightening, and in other reform measures that are part of Russian agreements with the agencies. The argument about Africa is unfortunately wrong; the money would not be spent there either. Careful monitoring of IMF, World Bank, and other programs should prevent these particular funds from being misused; nonetheless the aid donors should be pushing hard on the corruption issue. However, there should be no illusion that the West provided $67 billion of assistance to the FSU last year. Rather, as noted above, the total was closer to $12 billion and some of that was used to repay debts to the West. The arguments about whether we can afford such assistance are too familiar to stand repetition.

The argument that governments perform best when left on their own is wrong. The correct argument is that programs forced on countries by the international financial institutions tend not to work. Programs that are chosen by governments, to which the government is fully committed, do tend to work well with external assistance. Despite claims to the contrary, the countries that reformed successfully during the 1980s reformed with external support. The programs were their own, but the reformers were not left to their own devices.

The issue in Russia is momentous. Russia will not always be weak and this is the time when the basis of a new relationship is being set. If the promised assistance materializes and works, Russia will need substantial aid for only a few years because Russia's balance of payments is fundamentally strong.

Of course, the aid must be conditional on economic policies. That is why the IMF and World Bank are involved. That is also why even bilateral assistance should be conditioned on an agreed-upon reform program (most simply through cofinancing of Fund and Bank programs). Similarly, the other republics should receive aid only when they pursue reformist policies. So far, they have been reforming very slowly.

The Need for a Long-Term Strategy

The drama of economic reform comes at the beginning, with political change, new governments, IMF agreements, convertibility, debates about the role and inadequacy of aid, and the rest of the scene that is increasingly familiar from Eastern Europe and the FSU. This initital phase is crucial, exciting, and interesting. The issues are clear-cut and—thanks in large part to the policy-makers and advisers involved in the early stabilizations—the necessary policies are reasonably well understood.

Another crucial part comes later, when growth is not yet visible, when the industrial structure has not changed, and when early promises have not been fulfilled. This is what has happened in Poland, two years after the start of the reform. In Russia, the government has not overpromised, but its reform program also will face severe political difficulties in a few years if structural policies are not addressed as intensively now as stabilization and financial assistance.

The Shatalin Plan was right to set out a complete, phased restructuring plan, although wrong in its timing. What long-term restructuring policies should be pursued now so that they come on line in the next few years? The most important is the reform of the enterprise sector, through privatization, the development of the distribution sector, and industrial restructuring, as discussed above. Other sectors that deserve special attention in Russia are the energy sector (a potent source of foreign exchange), the agricultural sector, and the financial sector. The foreign private sector has a potentially important role to play in all these sectors.

Government action would be useful in one other area. Infrastructure is crumbling in Russia, as it is in the rest of Eastern Europe. Infrastructure investment complements private investment and private investment will take some time to develop. Now is the time for governments to begin upgrading infrastructure, if necessary, with external assistance, for instance from the World Bank. Such investments do not always need public funding. Telecommunications investment is taking place in Eastern Europe with private external financing. Transportation infrastructure can also be developed with the assistance of private capital. With a little imagination, so can other parts of infrastructure. As government gets out of areas in which it does not belong, it should move into areas where it does belong. Upgrading infrastructure early in the program makes eminent sense as part of a growth-oriented reform strategy.

Notes

This chapter originally appeared as "Stabilization and Economic Reform in Russia," *Brookings Papers on Economic Activity* 1 (1992), and is reprinted here with permission.

I am grateful for comments by Michael Bruno, William Nordhaus, and Lawrence Summers; research assistance from Ruth Judson; and research support from the National Science Foundation.

1. Stabilization from the current situation should be judged to be reasonably successful if the inflation rate is reduced to less than 30% to 40% a year; the budget deficit is sustainable with noninflationary financing, implying a level of 4% to 5% of GDP or less; and the current account deficit is covered by orderly external financing.

2. Bergson (1991).

3. Joint Study (1990, p. 51) estimates the Soviet Union's 1989 per capita GDP at $1,780, using the exchange rate that prevailed at the time, 1.8 rubles to the dollar. This number was chosen in part because it put the Soviet Union at about the same level as Poland.

4. The data may exaggerate Russia's share of exports abroad because goods from other republics tended to be marketed through Russia.

5. The same statement applies to Russia, although it is more industrialized and less agricultural than was the Soviet Union. Data comparable to those in table 6.3 are not available for Russia. An alternative data set, which shows industry and construction together employing 38% of the Soviet labor force, puts Russian employment in that sector at 42%. Comparable data for the agriculture/forestry sector are 19% for the Soviet Union and 14% for Russia. See Joint Study (1991, vol. 1, p. 219).

6. From *PlanEcon Report*, March 13, 1992 (nos. 9–10), based on data that *PlanEcon* describes as having been prepared by the Russian government in accordance with standard IMF methodology and the cooperation of IMF experts. However, *PlanEcon* warns that the data may exaggerate the strength of Russia's export performance. Note also that the share of imports and exports attributed to Russia in table 6.4 is constant. (I am grateful to William Nordhaus for pointing this out.)

7. Joint Study (1991, vol. 1, p. 227) shows a small Russian surplus in inter-republican trade for 1987 that turns into a massive surplus when trade is evaluated at world prices. See table 6.8.

8. As pointed out by Larry Summers, this shift may be exaggerated by the move of the former East Germany from the nonconvertible to the convertible area.

9. The absolute decline in production appears to have been about the same as the decline in exports.

10. *PlanEcon Report*, March 13, 1992 (nos. 9–10), table 20.

11. The World Bank categorizes a country's indebtedness on the basis of four criteria: debt-to-GNP ratio (30% to 50%); debt service-to-exports (165% to 275%); debt service-to-exports (18% to 30%); and interest-to-exports (12% to 20%). A country is severely indebted if at least three of its four debt indicators exceed the upper limit of the moderately indebted range. (See World Bank, *World Debt Tables, 1991–92*.)

12. In his review of Eastern European reform experiences, Bruno (1992) identifies six key issues; the extent of the initial price jump; the output decline; the fiscal balance and its sustainability; the problem of financial reform; the problem of the interim regime for socially owned enterprises; and macroeconomic policies, including the choice of the exchange rate regime and income policies.

13. See, for example, Fischer and Gelb (1991), Joint Study (1990), and Lipton and Sachs (1990).

14. The Shatalin Plan is also called *Transition to Market* and has been translated into English and published by the Cultural Initiative Foundation of Moscow.

15. Largely on these grounds, McLure (1991) argues for a consumption-based tax. See also Kopits (1991).

16. Seidman (1978).

17. Blanchard and Layard (1991) discuss some difficulties in the implementation of the Polish excess wage tax, particularly that it allowed a period of slower-than-permitted wage in-

creases to be followed by a catchup, in which wages could increase temporarily at more than the target inflation rate. This difficulty could be handled by rebasing the reference wage each month. (I am grateful to Olivier Blanchard for discussion of this issue.)

18. See Greene and Isard (1991) for a review of the role of convertibility in transforming socialist economies. .

19. However, I am not arguing that the exchange rate should be held fixed no matter what. The exchange rate anchor is most needed in the early stages of stabilization and reform and may have to be moved to a crawling peg or other system after some time. The most important objectives of exchange rate policy must be to avoid significant overvaluation of the currency.

20. Fischer (1986).

21. Strictly speaking, this argument does not require a fixed exchange rate. However, exchange rate fluctuations would weaken the role of convertibility in helping determine domestic relative prices.

22. Rodrik (1992) reviews Eastern European experience. He does not find much evidence for the view that foreign competition disciplines domestic price rises (which is an essential part of the view that trade liberalization helps import a price system). He attributes this result to excessive devaluations of the domestic currency.

23. Bruno (1992) suggests that Poland set too high an exchange rate at the start of its stabilization. In Israel, a slightly overvalued exchange rate was used as part of the anti-inflation strategy.

24. It was more relevant to countries like Hungary and the Czech and Slovak Federal Republic that did not start with large disequilibria.

25. There is a theoretical case for reducing all tariffs proportionately, such that the ratio of domestic-to-foreign prices approaches unity gradually. I assume that such tariffs are too liable to manipulation to be a useful baseline.

26. Joint Study (1991, vol. 2, p. 40) lists products for which industrial concentration by producer is high. They include sewing machines (100% of output is produced by a single enterprise); hydraulic turbines (100%), steam turbines (95%) (with hydraulic and steam turbines being produced by the same company); freezers (100%); and many more.

27. Data are from Joint Study (1991, vol. 2, pp. 15–40), which provides a succinct description of the enterprise sector and reform strategies.

28. Johnson and Kroll (1991).

29. See, for example, Singh (1991) and McMillan and Naughton (1992).

30. Berg (1992).

31. Fischer (1991b).

32. In the New Economic Policy (NEP) in the 1920s, large firms, which were kept under state ownership, were told to behave like commercial enterprises. They formed themselves into large trusts and presumably maximized profits like good monopolists should.

33. Shleifer and Vishny (1992).

34. Much of the success of the NEP in the 1920s resulted from permitted private enterprise into the distribution sector. Private firms' activities brought the sector that predominated at the time—the rural sector—actively back into the economy. See Fischer (1992).

35. Shleifer and Vishny (1992).

36. Johnson and Kroll (1991).

37. Shleifer and Vishny (1992).

38. On the active role of the Treuhandanstalt in managing the industrial transition in East Germany, see Carlin and Mayer (1992).

39. The World Bank is coordinating a major study of reform of the agricultural sector.

40. For a preliminary view of reform priorities in agriculture, see Joint Study (1991, vol. 3, chapter V.5).

41. This argument is not analytically clear-cut. If a country had an independent currency and was trying to maintain free trade, it would have one more instrument with which to attain its free trade goal—exchange rate changes. However, more often, countries introduce trade restrictions to protect the value of the currency.
42. Joint Study (1991, vol. 1, p. 225). I assume in making this calculation that the services that are responsible for the gap between NMP and GDP are not traded.
43. Similar data are presented in *PlanEcon Report*, March 13, 1992 (nos. 9–10).
44. Dornbusch (1992); Gros (1991).
45. Kaplan and Schleiminger (1989).
46. Fischer (1991a).
47. See, for example, Eberstadt (1991).

References

Berg, Andrew. 1992. "The Logistics of Privatization in Poland." Paper presented at NBER conference on Transition in Eastern Europe, February.

Bergson, Abram. 1991. "The USSR Before the Fall: How Poor and Why." *Journal of Economic Perspectives* 5, 4 (Fall): 29–44.

Blanchard, Olivier J., and Richard Layard. 1991. "Post-Stabilization Inflation in Poland." Mimeo, MIT, May.

Bruno, Michael. 1992. "Stabilization and Reform in Eastern Europe: A Preliminary Evaluation." Mimeo, IMF.

Carlin, Wendy, and Colin Mayer. 1992. "The Treuhandanstalt: Privatization by State and Market." Paper presented at NBER conference on Transition in Eastern Europe, February.

Dornbusch, Rudiger. 1991. "A Payments Mechanism for the Soviet Union and Eastern Europe." Mimeo, MIT, November.

Eberstadt, Nicholas N. 1991. "How Not to Aid Eastern Europe." *Commentary* (November): 24–30.

Fischer, Stanley. 1986. "Exchange Rate versus Money Targets in Disinflation." In S. Fischer, *Indexing, Inflation, and Economic Policy*. Cambridge, MA: MIT Press.

Fischer, Stanley. 1991. "Privatization in East European Transformation." Cambridge, MA: NBER Working Paper No. 3703, May.

Fischer, Stanley. 1991b. "Economic Reform in the USSR and the Role of Aid." *Brookings Papers on Economic Activity* 2: 289–301.

Fischer, Stanley. 1992. "Russia and the Soviet Union Then and Now." Paper presented at NBER conference on Transition in Eastern Europe, February.

Fischer, Stanley, and Alan Gelb. 1991. "The Process of Socialist Economic Transformation." *Journal of Economic Perspectives* 5 (Fall): 91–106.

Greene, Joshua E., and Peter Isard. 1991. "Currency Convertibility and the Transformation of Centrally Planned Economies." IMF Occasional Paper No. 81 (June).

Gros, Daniel. 1991. "A Soviet Payments Union?" Mimeo, Centre for European Policy Studies, Brussels, November.

IMF, IBRD, OECD, EBRD. 1990. *The Economy of the USSR. Summary and Recommendations.* Washington, D.C.: World Bank. (Referred to as JSSE 1990; JSSE = Joint Study of the Soviet Economy.)

IMF, IBRD, OECD, EBRD (1991). *A Study of the Soviet Economy*, Vols. 1, 2, 3. Paris: OECD. (Referred to as JSSE 1991.)

Johnson, Simon, and Heidi Kroll. 1991. "Managerial Strategies for Spontaneous Privatization." *Soviet Economy* 7, 4: 281–316.

JSSE (1990, 1991). See IMF et al.

Kaplan, Jacob J., and Gunther Schleiminger. 1989. *The European Payments Union*. Oxford: Clarendon Press.

Kopits, George. 1991. "Fiscal Reforms in the European Economies in Transition." In P. Marer and S. Zecchini, eds., *The Transition to A Market Economy*. Paris: OECD, Vol. II.

Lipton, David, and Jeffrey Sachs. 1990. "Creating a Market Economy in Eastern Europe: The Case of Poland." *Brookings Papers on Economic Activity* 1: 75–133.

McLure, Charles E., Jr. 1991. "A Consumption-Based Direct Tax for Countries in Transition from Socialism." World Bank Working Paper WPS 751 (August).

McMillan, John, and Barry Naughton. 1992. "How to Reform a Planned Economy: Lessons from China." *Oxford Review of Economic Policy* 8, 1 (Spring).

Rodrik, Dani. 1992. "Foreign Trade in Eastern Europe's Transition: Early Results." Paper presented at NBER conference on Transition in Eastern Europe, February.

Seidman, Laurence S. 1978. "Tax-Based Incomes Policies." *Brookings Papers on Economic Activity* 2: 301–348.

Shleifer, Andrei. 1992. "Privatization in Russia: First Steps." Paper presented at NBER conference on Transition in Eastern Europe, February.

Singh, Inderjit. 1991. "Is There Schizophrenia about Socialist Reform Theory?" Transition, Socialist Economic Reform Unit, World Bank, July–August, 1–4.

Postscript

I am grateful to the editors for allowing me to add a postscript to my April 1992 article on Russian stabilization and reform. That article was written a few months before the El Escorial conference at which the other chapters in this volume were presented, and it represents a near consensus view on the prospects for Russian reform at the time.

In this postscript I shall first describe the current situation, then reflect on the views expressed in the article, and, unchastened by past forecasting errors, discuss the current outlook for Russian stabilization.

The Current Situation

The political struggle between the economic reformers and the remnants of the Soviet system represented in the congress and the Central Bank of Russia (CBR) has continued unabated over the past year. President Yeltsin's victory in the April 1993 referendum has strengthened the position of the reformers and weakened that of the congress, but the president has not given economic reform the highest priority. He has consistently supported the cause of reform and has come to the rescue of the reformers several times, he has pursued Western financial assistance resolutely, but he has not yet committed his prestige to a comprehensive stabilization and reform program.

By mid-1992, it was already clear that the extraordinary rates of credit expansion by the CBR were both fueling inflation and delaying the restructuring of the economy. The CBR's inability to process payments efficiently, combined with the continued production by enterprises of unsalable products that generated no revenues, created a massive arrears crisis. The crisis was eventually dealt with by expanding credit to enterprises, and by improving the payments system. CBR credit expansion in 1992 amounted to 40% of GNP: 22% to enterprises; 10% to other republics; and 8% to the government budget.

In November, a year after he had taken office, the leading reformer, Acting Prime Minister and Finance Minister Yegor Gaidar was forced out of office by the congress. The industrial lobby in congress, which had effective control over the CBR, seemed to be winning on all fronts, especially when industrialist Viktor Chernomyrdin became prime minister. By the end of the year inflation was running at 25%–30% per month, and the possibility of hyperinflation was in the air.

Since then, and until the end of July 1993, the reformers gradually regained the upper hand. They were helped by the G-7's April announcement of a $28 billion aid package (plus $15 billion in debt relief), a package that seemed more solid than the $24 billion package of April 1992. Deputy Prime Minister and Finance Minister Boris Federov reached an agreement with the CBR to reduce the rate of growth of credit to 10% per month by the end of the year, with a target rate of inflation of 5%. Later the CBR and the prime minister, who turned out to be a cautious supporter of reform, agreed that interest rates would be raised.

The creation by the IMF of its Structural Transformation Facility (STF), which would allow it to make some funding available before a full standby agreement had been negotiated, made it possible to get over the catch-22 situation in which the Russians would be able to stabilize with financial assistance, but financial assistance could only flow if stabilization were under way.

In mid-1993, it seemed quite likely that Russia would be able to stabilize by October, moving to an exchange rate peg to bring inflation down rapidly.[1] The late July decision by the CBR to undertake a confiscatory currency recall of old ruble notes has thrown this promising scenario into doubt. The CBR claimed that the move would reduce inflation, fight corruption, and hasten the introduction of independent currencies by other republics. Only the third reason makes any sense—and there were much better ways to proceed. It is hard to escape the impression that the CBR's motive was to set back reform, both directly by reducing confidence in the ruble, and indirectly by showing that the government was disunited. The dismayed reactions of the international community suggest that the CBR succeeded in the latter goal.

In mid-1992, it was still unclear whether the ruble area would survive, and whether the Russian government wanted it to. The IMF originally opposed the introduction of independent currencies, partly because the West did not want to encourage centrifugal forces in the FSU. Gradually it became clear that maintenance of the ruble zone was severely complicating Russian attempts to control money and credit growth. By mid-1993 the ruble area was disintegrating, with Russian encouragement: five republics have already introduced their own currencies; another four have announced that they will do so soon; and others including Kazakhstan are expected to follow. Inter-republican trade has declined along with the ruble area, and as the price of oil in inter-republican trade has been raised toward the world level.

Despite the difficulties confronting the reformers, and in the face of congressional opposition, the Russian voucher privatization program is succeeding. Vouchers were distributed to all Russians; they can be traded in both formal and informal markets. The privatization plan was designed to garner the support of current stakeholders, management, and workers, by giving them a significant ownership share with ownership rights exercisable only after privatization. By the middle of 1993, firms employing 18% of the industrial labor force had been sold in voucher auctions. Although the impact of privatization on firm behavior remains to be studied systematically, encouraging anecdotes abound. Meanwhile, the auctions continue apace. Firms in the defense sector and public utilities are not being privatized, but Western assistance for their restructuring is being made available.

The effects of small-scale privatization are visible everywhere in Russia. So is the creation of new retail firms, which start on sidewalks and rapidly becoming more substantial.

Then and Now

My 1992 article was too optimistic about the progress of the Russian reform program. It turned out that price liberalization had been quite incomplete, the society was not ready to begin a radical restructuring of industry, and macroeconomic stabilization was more tenuous than I had recognized.

In early 1992 the G-7 was intent on securing the repayment of Soviet debt, insisting on the "joint and several responsibility" of the republics for servicing the debt. The April 1992 aid package never seemed likely to materialize. The 1993 aid package was better crafted to meet Russian needs, and debt relief was included.

The unanswerable question remains of whether a more active Western and international agency role in support of the Russian reformers could have accelerated stabilization and the reform process. For instance, would the invention of the STF in April 1992 instead of April 1993 have led the Gaidar government to attempt a comprehensive stabilization program in the late summer or early fall of 1992? We cannot know, but we do know that the past year has vastly increased both the understanding of the Russian government about the operation of the economy and the experience of Russians with markets, including the crucial foreign exchange market. Even leaving aside President Yeltsin's enhanced authority, the chances for success of a stabilization program are greater now than they would have been a year ago.

The emphasis on the potential importance of the agriculture and energy sectors in 1992 was entirely warranted then and continues to be warranted. But very little has been done to develop their potential. Oil remains the main export, but although oil production is declining, Russia has made it extremely difficult for foreign investors to enter the industry. The strong sentiment against foreign ownership is being exploited by the Russian oil industry, to their own eventual disadvantage. The real prices of oil and other sources of energy have been increased, but oil is still priced well below world levels. In agriculture, private ownership of land is now permitted and the number of farms has expanded rapidly, but the great bulk of production is still taking place in the state sector. The private financial sector is expanding, but no adequate supervisory system is in place and long-term financing for firms is scarce.

The 1992 paper contains a lengthy discussion of the proposal for a payments union for the FSU republics. It recommended against an intrusive system like the EPU, but supported coordinated efforts to improve the payments mechanism among the republics. The payments union idea now appears to be dead, except for its espousal by Grigory Yavlinsky, the most respected proreform critic of the government. The republics are on the way to operating with independent convertible currencies, a better solution than a payments union. The IMF and OECD central banks have been helping improve the payments system within and among republics.

The emphasis in the 1992 paper on the need for an industrial policy to restructure the largest firms would remain in a 1993 version. Defense firms are not being privatized, and it remains to be seen whether the large privatized firms will be able to restructure themselves. So far, the official unemployment rate in Russia remains extremely low, suggesting that very little restructuring has taken place.

Prospects

Will the Russians attempt a big-bang, exchange-rate-based stabilization this year? The resources—the second tranche of the STF, an IMF standby, the stabilization fund, World Bank and EBRD loans, and an enterprise fund—are there. Now it is up to the Russian government to show that it can bring credit expansion and the budget under control. Until the middle of July 1993 it seemed to be doing just that. Now the signals from the CBR's currency recall, the congress's recent budget with a deficit of 25% of GNP, and rumors that the actual budget outcome is worse than the planned deficit of 8% of GNP suggest that the reformers are losing ground.

Quite likely the actions of the CBR and the congress are the dying gasps of the ancien régime that is set to lose power in the first election under the new constitution. After the election, the Russian government will probably undertake a major stabilization program within the next year, perhaps even by the end of 1993.

In the meantime, real reforms are taking place on the ground as privatization moves ahead, Russian entrepreneurs develop their abilities, the financial and foreign exchange markets expand, and individual Russians learn to live in a market economy.

Relative to the situation a year ago, there has been less macroeconomic reform and more real microeconomic change than it was reasonable to expect.

Note

1. See Stanley Fischer and Jeffrey Sachs, "Remove Roadblock to Russian Reforms," *Financial Times*, July 6, 1993.

CHAPTER 7

China's "Gradual" Approach to Market Reforms

Dwight Perkins

China's market-oriented economic reform efforts began earlier than in most other former Soviet-type economies except Hungary, have progressed further, and have been carried out despite the absence of radical political reform. Furthermore, by any reasonable yardstick, China's economic reforms have been a success. There ought to be, therefore, lessons for others that can be learned from China's experience—unless, of course, the underdeveloped nature of China's economy, its location in East Asia, and other special characteristics make the Chinese experience unique.

Some former Soviet-type economies, notably Vietnam, have observed what has been transpiring in China and have learned from it; occasional references will be made in this chapter to Vietnamese economic reform efforts. There is also some interest in China's reform experience in such Central Asian republics as Uzbekistan. But are there any lessons for the more industrialized nations of Eastern Europe, Russia, or the Ukraine?

The economic success of China's reforms cannot be seriously challenged by anyone with any kind of comparative perspective. The GNP growth rate data in table 7.1 are a part of the story. Since 1978 China's GNP has averaged a growth rate of 8.5% per year. There has been no 15% or 20% decline in output during the transition period. Even in the aftermath of the Tiananmen tragedy in 1989 and 1990, China's GNP growth rate averaged 4.5% annually. There are some problems with these figures, to be sure.[1]

Adjustments for overstated small-scale enterprise growth, prices not reflecting market forces, and the like would probably reduce these GNP growth rates slightly, but not by enough to change the basic story.

China's ability to expand exports has been equally notable. Chinese exports rose from U.S. \$2.3 billion in 1970 to U.S. \$9.8 billion in 1978 to over U.S. \$70 billion in 1991. In real terms this amounted to a 12% increase per year over the eighteen-year period 1970–1988 (see table 7.2), and that growth has continued through 1991 at more or less the same rate. Three-quarters of the 1991 exports from China were manufactured products, and a high proportion of these were destined for Western markets. Taiwan Province

178   Dwight Perkins

TABLE 7.1   Growth rate of GNP (billion renminbi, constant 1990 prices)

	GNP	Primary sector	Secondary sector	Tertiary sector
1978	655	252	253	150
1979	703	268	274	162
1980	746	264	311	171
1981	782	282	317	183
1982	852	315	334	203
1983	938	341	369	229
1984	1,075	385	423	267
1985	1,204	392	501	312
1986	1,303	405	552	346
1987	1,456	424	628	404
1988	1,592	434	719	438
1989	1,647	448	748	451
1990	1,738	476	789	473

Growth rates (percent per year)

	GNP	Primary sector	Secondary sector	Tertiary sector
1979–80	6.7	2.4	10.9	6.8
1981–83	7.9	8.9	5.9	10.2
1984–88	11.2	4.9	14.3	13.8
1989–90	4.5	4.7	4.8	3.9
1991	7.0	—	14.2	—
1978–90	8.5	5.4	9.9	10.0

exports, by way of comparison, grew from U.S. $13.4 billion in 1978 to U.S. $64 billion in 1990, while those of the Republic of Korea grew from U.S. $12.7 billion to U.S. $65.0 billion over the same period.[2] In short, China's foreign debt by September 1991 had also risen to U.S. $52.55 billion, but foreign exchange reserves had increased to U.S. $40 billion (not including gold holdings worth another U.S. $4–$5 billion).[3] Given the rapid rise in exports together with the (probably excessive) clampdown on import growth, China had no problem whatsoever servicing its foreign debt.

Perceptions are that income distribution became substantially more unequal during the reform period. By 1990 there were apparently a handful of people with a net worth of over 100 million yuan (over U.S. $20 million) and a few hundred more with wealth of over 1 or 2 million yuan (U.S. $200,000 or $400,000).[4] Before 1978 almost no one had a net worth of more than a few tens of thousands of yuan. Politically this handful of wealthy people may have been significant, but in terms of Gini coefficients or some other objective measure of inequality, these "millionaires" were of little consequence. During the first period of reform through 1984, the size distribution of income almost certainly became less unequal largely because farmer incomes rose much

TABLE 7.2   The growth of foreign trade

	Exports		Imports	
		Indexes (1970=100)		
	Nominal	Real	Nominal	Real
1970	100.0	100.0	100.0	100.0
1975	321.4	162.2	321.8	170.5
1978	431.2	182.2	468.3	264.4
1980	808.6	275.2	840.5	326.0
1983	982.3	398.2	796.6	366.3
1985	1,146.6	474.7	1,475.9	773.6
1988	1,798.3	735.6	1,712.9	724.7
		Growth rates (percent per year)		
1970–78	20.0	7.8	21.3	12.9
1979–83	17.9	16.9	11.2	6.7
1984–88	12.9	13.1	16.5	14.6
1989–90	14.3	—	−1.8	—

Sources: China Foreign Economic Relations and Trade Computation Committee, *Zhongguo duiwai jingji maoi nianjian, 1984*, pp. 1v–5 and *1989–90*, p. 303.
Note: These indexes are based on the trade data of the ministry of foreign economic relations and trade (MOFERT) rather than the more generally published trade data from customs. Before 1981, the state statistical bureau also used MOFERT, data but switched over to customs figures in that year. The growth rates of the customs figures are higher than those of MOFERT after 1983.

faster than incomes in the richer urban areas.[5] After 1984 agricultural output growth slowed, and those with the greatest gains in income were in suburban areas of large cities where much of the boom in small-scale industry was occurring. Remote rural areas did not share much in the rural industrial growth. Still, a large share of China's people saw major improvements in their standard of living. Housing conditions improved markedly in both urban and rural areas, most urban residents and a large number of rural people had television sets where few existed before 1978, and food was plentiful in all but the poorest mountainous regions.

Despite these accomplishments, there was considerable discontent in the urban areas by 1988 and 1989. Inflation was one of the reasons. The official retail price index rose by 18.5% in 1988 and another 17.8% in 1989, and prices on the free markets rose by 30.3% in 1988 according to official estimates, which may understate the true rate of increase.[6] These figures will seem modest to those familiar with East Europe or the republics of the former Soviet Union, but the Chinese were used to rates of under 1% a year. The hyperinflation of the 1940s had undermined the political strength of the Guomindang government and sensitized a generation of Chinese leaders to the dangers of rapid price increases. Corruption was also perceived as a major problem by 1988 and 1989, and the reforms were seen as one of the causes. Connections (*guanxi*) and outright bribes became the common route used to bypass officials. The dual price system, described below, provided opportunities for easy profits for those who could get allocations of goods at state prices and then resell them at the much higher market prices. Objectively it would be more accurate to say that corruption resulted from the continuation of unreformed government regulations and state-set prices rather than from the reforms themselves. If the dual price system had been replaced by a single market-determined price system, that source of corruption, at least, would have disappeared. But the widely held perception was that corruption had risen sharply during the reforms, and so the reforms got the blame. Student demonstrators in the spring of 1989 were able to tap into this well of discontent.

One lesson from the Chinese economic reform effort therefore is that a rising standard of living does not guarantee support for the government in power during the period of ascent. One could learn this lesson from a variety of other historical episodes, however, such as the experience of South Korea in the 1980s. The more interesting lessons from China's experience lie elsewhere.

The Sequencing of Reforms

There is a growing body of literature on which reforms should be tried before others.[7] The Chinese, however, did not start out with any particular sequence in mind. Most Chinese leaders did not even have a clear reform objective. Those leaders who may have had a concrete plan—Chen Yun is a case in point—mainly wanted to make the system of central planning and state ownership work more efficiently by increasing the role of market forces in peripheral areas where central planning worked poorly. The market for household-produced goods and private plot crops, for example, was the first area to be liberalized after the December 1978 Party Plenum.

No one realized it at the time, but reforms in China started with certain important advantages over the kind of situation that was later to face Eastern Europe, the republics of the former USSR, and Vietnam. First, China's effort to increase the role of the market domestically was not intertwined with the breakup of the country's international trading arrangements. China had once been a part of the Soviet trading system, but that had come to an end with the Sino-Soviet breakup of 1960. As the data in table 7.3 indicate, China had to sharply curtail imports beginning in 1961, and recovery of the previous capacity to import was not achieved until the mid-to-late 1960s. Not only did it take time for China to convert its exports to convertible-currency countries as the

Table 7.3 The foreign trade transition

	China (million U.S. dollars)					
	1957	1959	1961	1963	1965	1967
Exports	1,600	2,260	1,490	1,650	2,230	2,140
with USSR	747	1,118	536	407	222	55
Imports	1,500	2,120	1,450	1,260	2,020	2,020
with USSR	618	979	292	194	186	56

	Vietnam (millions of dollars or rubles)				
	1986	1987	1988	1989	1990
Ruble exports	438.9	487.9	590.7	807.5	1,019.5
Ruble imports	1,659.4	1,953.8	2,028.5	1,725.9	1,353.7
Balance	−1,220.5	−1,465.9	−1,437.8	−918.4	−334.2
Dollar exports	384.0	361.5	434.7	1,138.2	1,169.7
Dollar imports	495.7	501.3	728.5	839.9	1,241.7
Balance	−111.7	−139.8	−293.8	298.3	−72.0

Sources: General Statistical Office, Ministry of Trade, *Economy and Trade of Vietnam, 1986–1990*, p. 141, and SSB, *Statistical Yearbook of China*, 1981, pp. 357 and 363.

share of total exports to the USSR fell from 49% in 1959 to 2% in 1964;[8] China also faced an American embargo that extended to most of America's allies. In addition, China had a debt to the USSR, which it paid off during the 1960s by running a trade surplus with the USSR through 1965. For both similar and different reasons, Vietnam faces an equally daunting task today, more daunting because of the American embargo than that faced by Eastern Europe or Russia.

By the time the worst excesses of China's Cultural Revolution were finished in 1970, and the embargo had begun to lift, China had fully converted to a trading system oriented toward Japan and Western Europe. Beginning in 1970, in fact, China began an export drive, albeit one of more modest proportions than what was to occur after reforms began in earnest in 1978.

China also had no foreign debt of any consequence in 1978. Chinese leaders had made a virtue of necessity by refusing to borrow from abroad, unlike several Eastern European states, among others, which sustained growth in domestic consumption with foreign loans. China therefore started its domestic economic reforms from a relatively strong balance-of-payments position. China's first trade deficit of over U.S. $1 billion was in 1978. In most previous years China had run modest trade surpluses.

Second, China began its reform period without any significant degree of inflationary pressure, other than that which is inherent in the Soviet-type command economy because of such phenomena as "investment hunger."⁹ There was no government budget deficit equivalent to 10% or more of GNP hemorrhaging new money into the system. In 1978 there was actually a very modest budget surplus. Nor was the banking system issuing credit in an uncontrolled manner. As reforms proceeded, this situation would change, but on the eve of efforts to free up prices China's consumers were not standing in long lines waiting for state-supplied goods that more often than not were simply unavailable.

China therefore did not have to begin reforms with an across-the-board stabilization effort, unlike Vietnam, the former Soviet Union, and much of Eastern Europe. That stabilization effort is not the only reason for the decline in GNP that is occurring in these other former Soviet-type economies except for Vietnam, but it is an important reason. If China had had rampant inflation plus a large current account deficit and a sizable foreign debt, it would have had little choice but to start with stabilization. For historical reasons it did not have to make that decision.

Where, in fact, did China begin the reform process? It began principally on two fronts, agriculture and foreign trade. In certain respects foreign trade reform began first with efforts going back well into the 1970s to expand the exports of manufactures and petroleum. But these measures largely took place within a Soviet-type foreign trade system dominated by state corporations with monopolies over particular products. An attempt to free up imports in 1977 and 1978 came to naught when state enterprises went on a buying spree, signing letters of intent to purchase hundreds of billions of dollars worth of foreign imports. The letters had to be torn up and the control of imports recentralized. From that point on, the government began to revamp the foreign trading system in a step-by-step process that will be described below.

It was in agriculture that China's reformers first began to fundamentally overhaul the Soviet-type system and move toward a market economy. The action began with the freeing up of rural markets for most rural produce except grain and a few other key commodities. These rural markets existed in the early 1970s, but operated under the tight strictures of local cadres. In 1979 these strictures were removed and the local markets blossomed.

The end of the commune-production team collective system did not begin until 1981, and it was not a systematically planned effort. Initially certain poor areas were allowed to experiment with household farms. The motive, as in the case of all the early rural reforms, was to find a way to overcome persistent rural poverty. Per capita agricultural output in 1978 was essentially the same as in 1955–1957, and there were large areas containing over 100 million people where malnutrition was a chronic problem. What started as a special program to alleviate difficulties in pockets of poverty, however, began spreading to other areas. Local cadres often tried to halt the movement to household agriculture, but at critical times Beijing, with the backing of Deng Xiaoping, endorsed the changes. By the end of 1983 collective agriculture had ceased to exist. Within teams land had been divided up on an egalitarian basis, although no attempt was made to redistribute land among communes or teams.

Redistribution of the land did not involve going back to some older way of raising crops. Labor-intensive Asian-style agriculture had been the method under the collective teams as under the precollective household system. Nor did previous owners of the land lay claim to it. After twenty-six years in a collective, too much had changed for that to be even considered, unlike in the southern half of Vietnam, where the collectives existed for only a few years before the country returned to household farming. And new organizations for the supply of agricultural inputs, notably chemical fertilizer, were not required. The old organizations continued, only now they sold to households rather than teams.

The return to household agriculture laid the foundation for a further expansion of market forces in rural areas. The state had always used prices to a limited extent to influence which crops were planted, but the key device was a contract signed with the team and with higher levels of the commune. The contract was in turn based on the central plan. There was some flexibility, but the contracts were not voluntary. The team was required to plant so much land in a particular crop or to deliver a certain amount of that crop to the state in exchange for cash and key inputs. The contract system was cumbersome enough with 50,000 communes and 5 million teams; with over 170 million households, the contract system was not only cumbersome but unnecessary.

Contracts were not done away with, but they did become progressively more voluntary as more and more agricultural prices were freed up and allowed to reach market-clearing levels. After 1984 the government was even talking about freeing up grain prices. The primary motivation was the fact that government subsidies designed to keep urban sales prices low and farm purchase prices high were growing at a rate that threatened fiscal stability. From a modest 3.9 billion yuan in 1978, state grain subsidies ballooned to 11.9 billion yuan in 1980 and 23.4 billion yuan in 1984.[10] Successive bumper harvests in 1982, 1983, and 1984 also created favorable conditions for reliance on market forces, and increasing amounts of grain as well as most lesser crops were sold at market-clearing prices. But China's leaders could not quite bring themselves to go all the way to a pure market system for the rural areas. As grain output stagnated after 1984, and with the increasing strength of conservative forces within the top leadership in 1988 and 1989, price controls over state grain purchases and sales were retained.

By the latter half of the 1980s, therefore, China had an agricultural economic system much like that found in other parts of Asia. Farm households managed most of agricultural production and sold their produce at market-clearing prices except for a few key commodities such as grain, for which the state continued to set prices below market-clearing levels on a portion of the crop. Over a period of roughly five years China had converted the agricultural sector from a bureaucratic command system to a market system. While this conversion was taking place, value-added in agriculture rose in real terms at the extraordinarily high rate of 7% a year (see table 7.1). Analysts have not yet sorted out all of the elements that went into this 1979–1984 agricultural growth spurt. Improved farmer incentives to work harder and manage better were part of the story, as was movement toward better allocative efficiency in the choice of which crops to plant where. Chemical fertilizer use rose from 8.8 million tons (88 kilograms of nutrient per hectare) to 17.4 million tons (174 kilograms per hectare), and the rural use of electric power in 1984 also rose by 83% over 1978.[11] This increase in inputs would have accelerated agricultural growth even if collective agriculture in the form of production teams had been retained. Using a similar line of reasoning, the slowdown in the agricultural growth rate in the subsequent six years, 1985–1990, from 7.6% to 4.5% per year, can be seen in part as a modest slowing down in the growth rate of inputs, but mostly the exhaustion by 1984 of what could be accomplished with harder work, better management, and improved allocative efficiency.[12] The stagnation in grain output until the bumper harvests of 1990 and 1991 was also caused in part by the state's efforts to keep state purchase prices below market-clearing levels.

The boom in agricultural output and incomes that accompanied the 1979–1984 rural reform efforts gave great credibility to those who, in the Chinese context, were considered radical reformers. The urban reforms that accelerated beginning in late 1984 would have taken on a different and less market-oriented tone if agricultural output in general, and grain in particular, had not done well prior to 1984.

What made the conversion to a market system in rural China such a smooth and crisis-free process? A large part of the answer is that it is much easier to make a market system work in agriculture than it is in an industrial sector dominated by large firms. There are five elements required by a well-functioning market system:

1. Prices must be stable, in the sense that inflation must be low enough to avoid politically induced state price fixing and to encourage farmers and traders to make money by producing and marketing, not by speculating on price changes. As indicated above, China did not have to worry that much about price stability in the early 1980s, in part because prices prior to 1979 were stable and in part because fiscal and

monetary policy in the period from 1981 through 1983 was relatively conservative.

2. Goods must be made available through the market rather than allocated through the channels of the government bureaucracy. Many agricultural inputs were sold rather than allocated to farmers even prior to 1979–1984. Part of agricultural output was sold on markets in earlier periods as well, and it was a straightforward process to expand the scope of goods allowed onto these markets.

3. Prices must reflect relative scarcities in the economy. Chinese agricultural output and input prices were distorted by state interventions, but state price setting had always had to take into account that severely distorted prices led to undesirable production responses, even when farmers were organized into production teams and brigades. Thus prices, while distorted, were not as far out of line as those in industry. Furthermore, the direction of the distortion was clear, certain crop prices were too low, and hence the solution was to allow these prices to rise. The political dangers of passing on higher grain prices to urban consumers did lead to increasingly costly state subsidies, but these distortions affected only a few crops and only a portion of the marketed output of those crops.

4. There must be competition, or there is little point in moving to a market system; competition drives the productivity gains that are the object of reform. Farmers, however, are the textbook example of the perfectly competitive producer. Whether as individual households or production teams, they are price takers.

5. Decisionmakers in producing units must behave according to the rules of the market; that is, they must maximize profits by cutting their costs or increasing sales, not by inducing the state to provide them with subsidies or monopoly prices. This condition is sometimes described as being a question of property rights or privatization. Property rights changes and privatization are often part of the solution to the absence of appropriate behavior by producing units, but the key problem is to change that behavior by whatever means will bring it into line with the requirements of the market. The early literature on market socialism assumed that this change in behavior could be accomplished by the government issuing an order. Privatization advocates assume everyone will behave properly once they are owners of the property in question. Reality in the urban industrial sector is considerably more complex, but not in agriculture. Once farming has been turned back to individual households, agriculture is in the hands of natural profit or net income maximizers. The connection between effort and reward is direct. Even in the twenty- to thirty-family production teams that

existed prior to 1981, there was a substantial connection between effort and reward, but social pressures within the team plus outside state and party pressures on leadership cadres diluted the connection. The return to household farming reestablished it.

Because agriculture in China was so readily convertible back to a market system, the reforms worked as advocates of marketization hoped they would. Because the reforms worked in this critical consumer goods sector, the quantity, quality, and variety of food products available in the shops and markets improved dramatically and prices remained fairly stable. As food made up over half of the expenditures of urban consumers, and clothes (where much of the value added came from cotton) made up another 13%, the quality of life in urban areas improved in a way that all could see.[13] In the rural areas, where three-quarters of the population lived, the improvement in living conditions was even more pronounced. According to household survey data, real consumption levels in rural China by 1985 were 81% above the per capita levels of 1978.[14]

These reforms were not accomplished in a year or 500 days. They were accomplished in the relatively brief period of five years, but some issues remained to be tackled. Long-term household rights to the land, for example, were not defined with sufficient clarity to encourage adequate levels of investment in the land. And the absence of a land market meant families held on to their plots even when most members left for urban jobs. Despite these limitations, farm consumption per capita continued to rise after 1984 at around 4% per year through 1990.

Opening to the Outside World

The rapid expansion of Chinese exports during the reform period has already been mentioned, but what role did the reforms play in this process? And what made possible the imports of large amounts of foreign capital in the form of loans and private direct investment? Early on, prior to 1979, Chinese leaders thought they could solve their foreign exchange needs through the rapid expansion of petroleum exports at high OPEC prices. Ten new Daqing oilfields were anticipated both offshore and onshore, and the one existing Daqing field produced 1 million barrels a day of crude oil.[15] Even large state monopoly corporations have little difficulty exporting basic commodities such as petroleum, and several million barrels a day available for export at $30 a barrel would indeed have met most of China's immediate foreign exchange needs. As it turned out, China did not discover even one new giant field, and petroleum exports rose only slowly to a quarter of a million barrels a day and later to half a million barrels a day, but at the much lower prices of the latter half of the 1980s. Agricultural exports were also not the solution, mainly because with only 100 million hectares of land, or 0.1 hectare per capita, China—like most of East Asia—was probably destined to be a net importer of agricultural crops, although the balance of agricultural trade in the late 1980s was modestly positive (exports exceeded imports by about U.S. $5 billion). If exports were going to meet China's foreign exchange needs, growth had to come primarily from the export of manufactures. But China's foreign trade corporations under the ministry of foreign trade were not known for their skill in marketing Chinese manufactures or in getting Chinese industrial enterprises to produce what the more discerning foreign markets required. Many of China's export contracts were negotiated at the semiannual Canton Trade Fair, and there was virtually no contact between the Chinese manufacturer and the foreign purchaser.

China had one big advantage in its initial efforts to expand exports of manufactures: the example of its East Asian neighbors, which had already demonstrated what a resource-poor, labor- and skill-rich people could accomplish. Hong Kong, the Republic of Korea, and Taiwan had shown that the markets existed. The problem for China was how to get into the competition for those markets. The Chinese groped their way to a solution on a trial-and-error basis. There was no well worked-out plan at any stage, but there was also never a retreat from the basic objective. Even during the height of the conservative reaction to the events in Tiananmen in June 1989, the opening up of the economy to foreign trade was not seriously questioned.

The initial steps taken after 1978 involved the partial breakup of the monopoly control of foreign trade by the state trading corporations and the creation of rules designed to promote foreign direct investment. Later, as world prices were increasingly passed through to the Chinese domestic market, the government gradually became aware of the importance of avoiding an overvalued exchange rate.

The end of Beijing's trade monopolies was accomplished by decentralizing authority to hundreds of provincial and lower-level foreign trade organizations. Although many of these organizations were in a sense the subordinate units of the central corporations, provinces in China in the 1980s—and to some degree even earlier—acquired a substantial degree of autonomy from Beijing. As the provincial leadership achieved freedom of action from central dictates, so did these regional organizations.[16]

Foreign direct investment also began to play some role in exports. Special economic zones (basically export processing zones) were created in three areas of Guangdong and one in Fujian Province. Initially these zones were seen as something of a failure, involving large Chinese infrastructure investments but relatively little foreign investment or production for export markets. By 1988, however, Shenzhen, the largest of the zones and located in a former rural area next to Hong Kong, had exports of U.S. $1.85 billion, up from U.S. $11 million in 1980 and still only U.S. $250 million in 1985.[17] Many of the rules that initially only applied to these special zones were then applied to other cities with foreign trade potential. Guangdong exports for the whole province, for example, rose from U.S. $1.4 billion in 1978 to U.S. $8.2 billion in 1989, the latter figure accounting for 15.5% of national exports.

The first steps designed to promote foreign direct investment involved writing a joint-venture law. The initial rather unspecific joint-venture law was followed by numerous other commercial laws, many of which were applied to domestic as well as foreign firms. China, it should be noted, had for all practical purposes eliminated most commercial law during the Cultural Revolution period, along with all of the lawyers. A legal system suitable for an international trading country had to be rebuilt from scratch, and that did not happen overnight.

Data on foreign investment in China are presented in table 7.4. As the table indicates, foreign direct investment was quite modest during the first four years of reform, averaging only U.S. $291.5 million per year, but rose to over U.S. $3 billion a year in the 1988–1990 period, despite the Tiananmen tragedy. What the table does not show is the central role of Hong Kong in this growth. In 1988 and 1989 Hong Kong alone accounted for 63% of all foreign direct investment utilized. Japan and the United States, the next two largest sources, together accounted for only 21%.[18] By 1990 and 1991 the other significant trend was the rapid increase in investment from Taiwan. In effect, Hong Kong and Taiwan were moving their labor-intensive industries such as shoes and toys out of their own increasingly high-wage territory to the low-wage areas of Guangdong and Fujian Provinces, where the local people were not only still Chinese, but in some cases even relatives.

TABLE 7.4   Foreign capital utilized (million U.S. dollars)

	Total foreign capital	Foreign loans		Foreign direct investment	Other foreign commercial investment
		Total	Official		
1979–82[a]	3,114.3	2,672.5	603.3	291.5	150.3
1983–86[a]	4,147.8	2,513.3	—	1,199.9	277.3
1987	8,452.0	5,805.0	—	2,314.0	333.0
1988	10,226.0	6,487.0	5,074.3	3,193.0	546.0
1989	10,059.0	6,286.0	2,327.0	3,392.0	381.0
1990	10,289.0	6,534.0	2,612.0	3,755.0[b]	—

Sources: SSB, *Zhongguo tongji nian jian, 1990*, p. 653, and SSB, *Zhongguo tongji zhaiyao, 1991*, p. 102.
a. Annual average.
b. This figure includes "other foreign commercial investment."

No understanding of China's trade performance is possible without bringing in the special role of Hong Kong. That role went well beyond the provision of foreign direct investment or supporting infrastructure for the Shenzhen Special Economic Zone. Prior to the reform period, about 20% of China's exports were sent to Hong Kong, and most of these exports were retained and consumed in the colony. In 1970 and 1975, for example, only 4% of China's total exports were reexported through Hong Kong. That figure later rose to 11% in 1984 and to an extraordinary 40% in 1990.[19] Hong Kong had become the primary trade intermediary between China and Taiwan Province, and it was a major player in China's trade with much of the rest of the world. There is no way of estimating what the growth of China's foreign trade would have been in the absence of Hong Kong, but it would certainly have been slower. Shanghai, for example, the most logical competitor for Hong Kong, saw its exports peak in 1980 and then stagnate for the next six years and more, while the share of Shanghai exports in China's total exports fell from 29.7% in 1978 to 11.6% in 1986.[20] It was Hong Kong that knew how to market products in the United States, Europe, and Japan. Shanghai was learning, but slowly.

More difficult to assess is the role of the spreading marketization in the Chinese economy on the growth of exports. In 1991 the exports of rural industries and foreign investment enterprise were over U.S. $10 billion each,[21] and neither of these two sectors would have experienced dynamic growth if across-the-board central planning had been retained. They would not have been able to get the necessary inputs, nor would they have had much incentive to export. In the early stages of reform, the incentive to export was in fact quite weak. There was what has been called an "air lock" between foreign and domestic prices. The Chinese currency was overvalued, but that did not matter to the producing enterprises because they neither purchased nor sold goods at world prices. The trading corporations lost money on exports, but they made money on their imports, and profits weren't that important anyway.

By the late 1980s not only were profits important, but world prices were increasingly being passed on to producers. In addition, export earners were allowed to retain a portion of their foreign exchange earnings and use them to buy imports. To deal with the complaints from foreign investors that they could not obtain the foreign exchange required to repatriate profits or even to buy imported inputs, the government opened foreign exchange adjustment centers, or "swap markets." Initially only foreign investors could use them, but then domestic firms began to be allowed into these markets as well. By 1991 these markets accounted for a substantial share of all foreign exchange transactions. Furthermore, the exchange rate on these swap markets in 1991 was less than 10% above the official rate. The official rate was devalued in both 1990 and 1991, and China's large trade surplus combined to bring the two rates into line. All that remained was for the government to take the final step of making the renminbi fully convertible, but that the government couldn't quite bring itself to do, although moves toward a single exchange rate were under way in 1992. The increasing role of the swap markets is one of a number of examples of a reform measure designed originally only for foreigners that came in time to have a big impact on domestic businesses.

In addition to making the renminbi more nearly convertible, the government also took steps to remove its overvaluation. As the data in table 7.5 indicate, from 1978 to 1980 Chinese currency actually became more over-valued, but from that point on the government began a process of gradual devaluation that probably by 1985 reached a point where the renminbi could no longer be described as overvalued. At least that is what the indexes in columns 7 and 8 of table 7.5 seem to indicate, if one takes the view that the currency was not overvalued in 1991 and work backward from there.[22]

This brief discussion cannot do justice to all of the measures undertaken by China to promote foreign trade. China took its seat in the IMF and World Bank, and beginning in 1981 received its first loans from those sources. China obtained most-favored-nation status from the United States, although it was in danger of losing that rating in 1991 and 1992. China was also gradually bringing its trade practices in line with GATT, so that it would become eligible for membership. In essence China started its export drive with only modest alterations in the Soviet-type trading system that had been in place for more than two decades. A temporary spurt in the dollar value of oil exports helped out at this early stage, just as it did in Vietnam in 1990 and 1991. But step by step China has altered its trading system to where it now can plausibly argue that it will soon be in compliance with GATT rules, although it had not gotten all the way there by 1992. Not all of the steps were forward. Occasionally China recentralized controls when the foreign exchange situation seemed to be getting out of hand, as in 1985 and 1986 when the cumulative balance-of-trade deficit in those two years reached U.S. $27 billion. But these steps backward were the exception, not the rule.

Reforming Industry and Services

Petty urban services such as hawkers and small restaurants were freed up early on, but the major urban reform effort was not announced until October 1984. Prior to that time, the Chinese government had experimented with urban reforms in a number of cities, but not on a nationwide basis.

If one refers back to the four elements needed to make a market work (in addition to stabilization, which was not a serious problem in the mid-1980s), China made substantial progress on three and some progress on the fourth. Only a few of the key changes will be described here.

TABLE 7.5 China's foreign exchange rate

	(1)	(2)	(3)	(4)	(5)	(6)	(7)	(8)
	Foreign exchange rate (US$1 = RMB-)	index	Retail price index (1980 = 100)	Chinese export US$ price index (1980 = 100)	Chinese import US$ price index (1980 = 100)	NMP deflator index (1980 = 100)	(3) ÷ (2)	(6) ÷ (2)
1978	1.68	112.0	92.5	74.3	66.2	93.0	82.6	83.0
1979	1.55	103.3	94.3	85.8	83.0	96.7	91.3	93.6
1980	1.50	100.0	100.0	100.0	100.0	100.0	100.0	100.0
1981	1.71	114.0	102.4	103.1	103.5	101.9	89.8	89.4
1982	1.89	126.0	104.4	96.9	91.1	101.8	82.9	80.8
1983	1.98	132.0	105.9	86.4	77.1	102.9	80.2	80.0
1984	2.33	155.3	108.9	88.3	78.6	108.2	70.1	69.7
1985	2.94	196.0	118.5	82.2	74.0	118.3	60.5	60.4
1986	3.45	230.0	125.6	71.7	73.5	123.0	54.6	53.5
1987	3.72	248.0	134.8	76.1	72.2	132.3	54.4	53.3
1988	3.72	248.0	159.7	83.2	91.7	149.8	64.4	60.4
1989	3.77	251.3	188.2	n.a.	n.a.	162.1	74.9	64.5
1990	4.78	318.7	192.1	n.a.	n.a.	167.9	60.3	52.7
1991	5.30			n.a.	n.a.			

1. An increasing share of intermediate inputs as well as output destined for final demand was made available through market channels rather than through the administrative channels of the central government. There are various ways to measure this increasing role of the market. One measure is the number of products at least partially subject to state allocation. In 1978, for example, 689 kinds of producer goods were distributed through the state plan, and 837 in 1982. By 1990 or 1991 that number was down to only 20.[23] The total number of kinds of materials and equipment under a substantial degree of state control in 1990 was only 72, down from nearly 300 as late as 1988.[24] This process was already well under way by 1984. According to a survey of 424 enterprises, the proportion of raw and semifinished materials obtained on the market or through direct purchase from other enterprises rose from 27% of the total supply at the end of 1984 to 44% by June 1985. The proportion of "planned supply" of state enterprise in 1984 was still 87%, but that of urban and rural collective enterprises was only 6.5% and 3.0% respectively.[25] The relationship between an expanding market and the development of collective enterprises is a subject we shall return to below. The central point here is that the role of the market rose steadily but gradually over a period of at least eight years. As late as 1990 the state still distributed 49% of the steel and 43% of the coal produced, but only 12.6% of the cement, much of which was produced by small enterprises.[26] There was no sudden decision to abolish state allocation and throw everything onto newly evolving markets. The state system continued to operate, but its scope shrank steadily, and that reduced activity faced ever-increasing competition for goods from the market. By late 1990, Liu Suinian, the minister in charge of the ministry of materials and equipment, was calling on the 1.05 million employees of the state distribution agencies to turn their agencies into "competitive dealers" so that they could hold onto market share.[27]

2. As intermediate as well as final goods became increasingly channeled through the market, the state had to decide at what prices these goods would be sold. The old state-set prices were, for the most part, far below market-clearing levels, and maintaining these low prices throughout the economy would have made the development of markets impossible. Excess demand would lead immediately to long queues of both consumers and enterprises and to a return to state allocations. But China's leaders weren't prepared to let all prices just float up to market levels either. There were too many powerful interests prepared to resist loss of their privileged access to low-priced inputs. The solution chosen in 1985 was a dual price system. The substantial but shrinking portion of goods allocated through government channels would be sold at state-set prices, while those goods sold on the market would be priced closer to market-clearing levels. Over time this market became more and

more like a true market with freely determined prices, but initially the state frequently interfered in price setting.

The dual price system accomplished two things. It did create market prices, and increasing numbers of enterprises were making their marginal decisions on the basis of these prices. In fact, most enterprises purchased substantial quantities of inputs on the market, but a few key inputs, notably electric power, were in chronic short supply and only available at state prices. The second accomplishment of the two-price system was increasing opportunities for corruption. It was not long before those with the political influence to get access to supplies at state prices discovered they could make large amounts of easy money reselling them on the market. Companies sprung up to take advantage of this opportunity; some, it should be noted, were trying to help enterprises without political clout—foreign joint ventures, for example —to get around the strictures of the state bureaucracy. It was the corruption in the form of large earnings to well-connected individuals and their children, however, that drew the most notice from the urban population and increased their support for the student demonstrators in 1989.

Immediately after the June 1989 tragedy in Tiananmen, there was support for getting rid of the dual price system in favor of a return to a single state-set price not necessarily related to market forces. By 1991, however, reform measures were mostly oriented toward raising state prices all or part of the way to the market price level, or removing goods from state allocation altogether. On April 1, 1991, for example, the dual price system for cement was abolished in favor of one market-determined price.[28] State coal prices, on the other hand, were raised, but only enough to reduce coal mine losses and relieve pressure on the state budget. But the expansion of market prices by 1991 was no longer under effective state control for a wide range of goods. It was simply too easy for firms to raise prices by claiming that the product in question was new or by working out its own trading arrangements with its customers. By one estimate, 75% of goods were distributed through the market, and that percentage was rising steadily.[29]

3. Competition was introduced into Chinese industry in the early 1980s as well. Prior to the reform period, virtually every Chinese industrial enterprise had a monopoly of its local market and was not allowed to sell outside of that market. County farm machinery plants, for example, would produce plows for the county market. When the local market for plows was saturated, the plant was converted to the production of some other kind of machinery. These monopolies were formally abolished and enterprises were allowed to sell throughout the country, and began in fact to do so. Where there were buyers' markets, this change had the predictable result. Enterprises such as the Chongqing clock and watch factory found themselves in direct competition

with the high-quality products of Shanghai and had to cut their prices and lower their costs.[30] Where there was excess demand and hence a suppliers' market, the competitive pressures were largely absent. Excess demand or "target planning" is a common feature of centrally planned economies and hence suppliers' markets are common, but China to some uncertain degree appears to have been different. Plans in China even early in the reform period appear to have been considerably less taut (excess demand was less often present) than in the Soviet Union and Eastern Europe, and hence buyers' markets were more common.[31]

As a higher portion of goods was sold on the market, competitive pressures rose. An additional source of competitive stimulus was foreign trade. Manufactured exports by 1990 amounted to over 200 billion yuan, or nearly 10% of the gross value of industrial output, up from about 4% in 1985.[32] On the other hand, some industrial products such as electric power had natural monopolies, and others retained state-determined monopolies (the regional airlines, for example). In still other cases, provinces and even counties often erected trade barriers to the influx of goods from elsewhere in China when they threatened a local enterprise. The central government disapproved, but could not necessarily stop the practice.

4. Making enterprise decisionmakers behave according to the rules of the market has proved to be the most difficult challenge, as it was in Eastern Europe. Farmer families, as pointed out above, are natural profit maximizers through raising output and sales or by cutting costs. In a Soviet-type system, managers of large industrial enterprises, in contrast, are really lower-level department heads within the government bureaucracy. Success is achieved by following the lead of their bureaucratic superiors within the government ministries, and these superiors are typically interested in many goals in addition to increasing sales or cutting costs. As with state-owned enterprises all over the world, the enterprise objective function is muddled by the inclusion of goals that significantly inhibit the enterprise from concentrating on profit maximization through its own efforts. The enterprise will be asked to employ far more workers than it needs or to deliver its output to favored customers at low prices. In return, profits are ensured not by efficient production, but by state subsidies ranging from cheap loans to government-guaranteed markets.

The essence of achieving reform in this fourth sphere is to break the umbilical cord that connects enterprise managers to the government bureaucracy. The principle is easy enough. Enterprises should be told to maximize profits, not gross value output or employment, and they should have a free hand in deciding how to do that. If they fail to do well in raising profits, managers should be replaced. If the enterprise as a whole runs losses over a long enough period of time, it should go out of business. Applying these principles in practice, however, is not so easy.

The Chinese, for example, have a bankruptcy law, but there have been only a handful of bankruptcies among the larger enterprises, despite the fact that many of these enterprises have consistently made losses. In 1991 some of these losing enterprises were forced to merge with more successful firms in the same sector, but these mergers may have penalized the successful firms that have been pressured to take on a weak partner rather than penalizing the loss-making firm itself. In practice, governments around the world are reluctant to allow large enterprises employing tens of thousands of people to go under, and this is particularly true of socialist countries. In China, as in a number of socialist countries, the difficulty is compounded by the fact that the urban social welfare system is tied to the enterprise. There is no unemployment insurance, and housing is provided by the enterprise, as is day care for children and many health services. The Chinese are gradually trying to change this system, and large-scale experiments to privatize urban housing are under way, but there is a long way to go before urban workers can lose one job and still have a safety net to tide them over until they find another. Banking reform, which cuts off enterprises' easy access to credit with only a weak obligation to repay, is another element in forcing industrial enterprises to survive on their own.

If allowing a firm to fail is difficult, at least the managers of the enterprise could be made to pay the price of failure. Bonuses tied to performance is the traditional Soviet-style way of dealing with this issue, but this arrangement has never worked very well. A major problem is that managers are appointed and promoted by the government bureaucracies and, not surprisingly, see themselves as mainly responsible to those bureaucracies. In recent years in China they have also seen themselves as responsible to their workers, which creates another set of problems.[33] One solution to the issue of making managers responsible for their performance is to privatize the enterprise. Much of the discussion of privatization takes the simplistic view that this step automatically forces enterprises and their managers to survive on their own. As anyone familiar with import-substituting strategies of industrialization knows, there may be very little diminution in government support when the enterprise becomes private. In China, however, the issue is moot, for the time being at least, because the government is not even considering the privatization of large enterprises.

If privatization of large enterprises in not acceptable, is there a public substitute that accomplishes some of the same ends? China in a very modest way has begun experimenting with selling shares in public enterprises. The owners of these shares can be other enterprises, workers, and individuals who are not workers in the enterprise. There are a number of objectives behind share ownership, but if really applied on a nationwide basis, it would provide a vehicle for creating boards of directors that would be primarily concerned with the profitability of the enterprise. These boards could appoint managers who would focus on that goal rather than on whatever their superiors in the supervising ministry wanted. These share ownership experiments, however, are just that—experiments.[34] In 1989 there was some question as to whether the experiments would even be allowed to continue, but by 1991 they were once again under way and being vigorously debated.[35] Enterprise managers, however, are still appointed by the government bodies they serve.

The reform picture among industrial enterprises, however, is not as limited in scope as the discussion to this point would lead one to believe. The basis for this statement is the rapid rise of small-scale industrial enterprises, many of them based on collective ownership. In some cases these small enterprises are privately owned and in others the state is still the formal "owner," but, regardless of the ownership type in a formal sense, these small enterprises come much closer than do large enterprises to behaving according to the rules of the market.

The rising share of collective enterprises in total industrial output are presented in table 7.6. If small-scale state enterprises were separated out, the

TABLE 7.6   Growth rates of state and collective/private industry

	Gross value of industrial output	Gross value of state industry	Gross value of collective/private industry
Growth rate (% per year)			
1979–1984	9.6	7.0	16.6
1985–1988	16.7	10.0	26.4
1989	8.5	3.9	13.7
1990	7.6	2.9	12.4
1991 (11 months)	13.5	9.0	17.8
Share (in %)			
1978	100.0	77.6	22.4
1980	100.0	75.0	25.0
1984	100.0	67.5	32.5
1988	100.0	52.6	47.4
1990	100.0	48.2	51.8
1991 (11 months)	100.0	46.3	53.7

Sources: These figures differ slightly from those most commonly published. Official data were first converted into constant prices (for 1978) and the shares and growth rates calculated in terms of these constant prices. The estimates for 1990 and 1991 are based on newspaper reports of SSB announcements and are somewhat less reliable than the earlier data.

share of large-scale state enterprises would be even smaller. As it is, the share of the state sector fell from three-quarters to less than half in just twelve years. None of this declining share was due to privatization. It was all due to the more rapid growth of the small-scale and collective sector, despite the government's preference for the large-scale enterprises. This collective small-scale development was a surprise to the planners. The technical foundation for this boom had been laid in the 1970s with the rise of rural industries designed to provide agriculture with inputs such as farm machinery and cement. When industrial inputs were increasingly made available on the market rather than through state-planned allocation, the entrepreneurial energies of rural and suburban entrepreneurs were unleashed. The inability of urban enterprises to expand their labor force or get access to land also encouraged these large enterprises to subcontract with collective suburban firms.

There is considerable variation in the behavior of these township and village enterprises, as they are now called, but there are important common threads. The government units to which these enterprises relate are not the ministries in Beijing or even the provinces, but the local county and township governments. In some cases these enterprises are formally owned by the counties—that is, they are state-owned firms in a formal sense. But even if they are collective or even private, they make tax payments and other contributions to their local governments and receive government support in return. Government support, for example, can be instrumental in getting bank loans for these small enterprises. These enterprises, therefore, are sometimes almost as closely tied to their local government units as the larger enterprises are to the national ministries. But the soft budget constraint is not the problem for these small enterprises that it is for the large ones. The reason is simple: the county and township governments do not have the resources to bail out chronic money losers for long. Although the banks are not always repaid, a losing county or township enterprise ultimately must be funded out of the profits of another enterprise in the county or township. Local officials, unable to print money, soon decide to jettison the losing firm through reorganization or putting it out of business. In effect, the local government entity, dependent on local enterprises for much of its revenue, behaves more like a mini-conglomerate than a government bureaucracy. The rules of the market, with many deviations to be sure, are obeyed.[36]

What is true of industry is also true of other sectors such as construction, transport, and wholesale and retail trade. Small collective enterprises play a major and rising role in each of these sectors. They fill niches not covered by the large enterprises, but they also compete directly for market share with those enterprises. If one adds up all of the small-scale producing units in agriculture, industry, and services, they account for nearly three-quarters of total GNP. Put differently, three-quarters of Chinese output is produced by units oriented primarily toward the market. Only one-quarter is closely tied to the central government bureaucracy.

Has this change in the way industry is organized had any impact on performance? On the basis of recent studies of both the state and the collective industry sectors, the answer is clearly in the affirmative. The data for the pre-1978 period are of low quality, but numerous partial indicators suggest that productivity growth in industry was unlikely to have been positive. Studies of the post-reform period based on more reliable figures—particularly figures for the capital stock—show positive and rising total factor productivity. In one important set of estimates, total factor productivity in the state sector rose from 1.8% per year in the 1980–84 period to 3.0% per year in 1984–88. Collective industry total factor productivity in the two periods rose from 3.5% annually to 5.9%.[37] Increasing factor inputs still accounted for over two-thirds of industrial output growth, but productivity growth presumably generated by the increasing marketization of the economy accounted for the other third. And increasing marketization may also have made it easier to mobilize factor inputs, the reverse of what one would expect, as a strength of the command economy is its capacity to mobilize inputs. Some of the inputs into collective industry may have been diverted from the large-scale state sector, but some were in the form of local labor and capital that the state system may not have been able to mobilize.

Partial Reform and Macro Stability

While the discussion to this point makes clear that industrial reforms in the 1980s had a major positive impact on the growth of industrial output and productivity, the partial nature of those reforms also presented problems for the managers of the Chinese economy. These problems manifested themselves in part through rising inflationary pressures that led the government to brake the economy in 1989 and to call for a more moderate rate of growth in the future.[38]

Inflation began accelerating from the beginning of the urban industrial reforms in late 1984, as the figures in table 7.7 indicate. By 1988, price increases had reached a level politically unacceptable to most of the leadership. What accounted for this change?

Data on the government budget deficit are presented in table 7.8. As these figures indicate, accelerated inflation in 1980 is correlated with a rising government budget deficit, but that was not the case after 1984. The government deficit as a share of GNP actually fell to a minuscule 0.8% in 1985 and was only 2.5% of GNP in 1988, as contrasted to 5.2% in 1979 and 3.8% in 1980.

**TABLE 7.7 Consumer price indexes
(% increase over the previous year)**

	Retail prices	Collective market prices	Worker cost of living
1978	0.7	−6.6	0.7
1979	2.0	−4.5	1.9
1980	6.0	1.9	7.5
1981	2.4	5.8	2.5
1982	1.9	3.3	2.0
1983	1.5	4.2	2.0
1984	2.8	−0.4	2.7
1985	8.8	17.2	11.9
1986	6.0	8.1	7.0
1987	7.3	16.3	8.8
1988	18.5	30.3	20.7
1989	17.8	10.8	16.3
1990	2.1	−5.7	1.3
1991	2.9	n.a.	5.1

Sources: SSB, *Zhongguo tongji zhaiyao, 1991*, p. 38; SSB, *Zhongguo tongji nianjian, 1990*, pp. 249 and 268; SSB, *Statistical Yearbook of China, 1986*, pp. 535 and 544; and SSB, "Statistical Communique on National Economic and Social Development in 1991," February 28, 1992.

Data on the money supply in table 7.9 get closer to the nature of the problem. Bank deposits plus currency in circulation between the end of 1984 and the end of 1988 grew at an annual rate of 23% a year. What accounted for this increase, more than any other single factor, were bank loans to state and collective enterprises that were increasingly out of the control of those at the center responsible for price stability. The starting point was the high levels of investment of enterprises large and small. The rate of investment, or accumulation in Chinese terminology, was "held down" to under 30% of net material product in the 1981–83 adjustment period, but jumped to 35% in 1985 and stayed above 34% thereafter. This high rate was financed by bank loans at interest rates well below any market-clearing interest rate. Subsidies to loss-making enterprises were financed in a similar manner. If the banks were reluctant to lend, political pressure was brought to bear and the banks more often than not gave in. After the commercial banks had been separated from the central bank, the central bank continued to support the commercial banks' demand for funds just as it had when the commercial banks and the central bank were the one and same People's Bank of China.

The central bank had the power to stop the rapid increase in money

200   Dwight Perkins

TABLE 7.8   Government revenues and expenditures (million yuan)

	Expenditures		Revenue (− debt income + deductions for price subsidies)	Deficit		
	including price subsidies	budgeted price subsidies		(million yuan)	(as % share of NMP)	(as share of GNP)
1978	112,214	1,114	113,224	+1,010	+.003	+.003
1979	135,370	7,920	114,719	−20,591	−.061	−.052
1980	133,041	11,771	115,990	−17,051	−.046	−.038
1981	127,441	15,941	117,583	−9,858	−.025	−.021
1982	132,552	17,222	121,236	−11,316	−.027	−.022
1983	148,987	19,737	136,696	−12,184	−.026	−.021
1984	176,474	21,834	164,290	−6,825	−.022	−.018
1985	210,659	26,179	203,834	−20,875	−.010	−.008
1986	233,080	25,748	212,205	−20,875	−.027	−.022
1987	244,850	29,460	219,935	−24,915	−.027	−.022
1988	270,660	31,682	235,722	−34,938	−.030	−.025
1989	304,020	37,034	267,360	−36,660	−.028	−.023
1990	339,520	n.a.				

Sources: State Statistical Bureau, *Zhongguo tongji nianjian, 1990*, pp. 229, 232, and 244, and State Statistical Bureau, *Zhongguo tongji zhaiyao, 1991*, p. 33.

Note: Chinese budget statistics subtracted price subsidies on certain commodities, notably grain, from total revenue up through 1985, but then changed and added prices to total expenditures from 1986 on. Chinese revenue figures also include income from foreign and domestic borrowing and these have been removed from the revenue totals in this table.

supply, and it more or less did so by cutting off the supply (reducing the growth rate) in 1989, thereby bringing down the rate of growth of the money supply and inflation. At the user end, quotas were set that cut off credit to efficient and profligate borrowers alike. The result was a sharp drop in the growth of industry and increasing layoffs.

If a full market system had been in place, the central bank could have raised the cost of borrowing to the commercial banks, and they in turn could have passed on that cost to the enterprises. The enterprises with rates of return on their investments below the cost of capital would have stopped borrowing, while those with higher rates could have continued to borrow. But Chinese enterprises still suffered from what Janos Kornai calls "investment hunger" and the "soft budget constraint." If they made losses on their investments, they were still inclined to invest more, knowing the government would bail them out with low-cost loans, a negotiated lower tax rate, or some other kind of subsidy. One way to keep this situation from occurring would be to tighten the budget constraint of the commercial banks themselves, thereby forcing them to tighten their loans to the enterprises. But tightening the budget con-

TABLE 7.9 State bank deposits plus currency in circulation

	Currency in circulation		Bank deposits		Urban savings deposits	
	(million yuan)	% increase over previous year	(million yuan)	% increase over previous year	(million yuan)	% increase over previous year
1979	26,771		134,004		20,256	
1980	34,620	29.3	166,107	24.0	28,249	39.5
1981	39,634	14.5	203,540	22.5	35,414	25.4
1982	43,912	10.8	238,622	16.3	44,733	26.3
1983	52,978	20.6	276,159	16.7	57,258	30.0
1984	79,211	49.5	338,613	22.6	77,662	13.6
1985	98,783	24.7	393,648	16.3	105,781	36.2
1986	121,836	23.3	538,187	36.7	147,145	39.1
1987	145,448	19.4	657,205	22.1	206,402	40.3
1988	213,403	46.7	742,562	13.0	265,916	28.8
1989	234,402	9.8	901,385	21.4	373,480	40.5
1990	264,437	12.8	1,164,483	29.2	519,258	39.0

Sources: State Statistical Bureau (SSB), Zhongguo tongji nianjian, 1990, p. 666; SSB, Zhongguo tongji nianjian, 1987, p. 639; SSB, Zhongguo tongji zhaiyao, 1991, p. 35; SSB, Statistical Yearbook of China, 1986, p. 530.

straint of a few large banks may be just as hard to accomplish as doing so for the enterprises.

Because rationing credit to all enterprises across the board was such a crude device, it proved difficult to maintain for long. Between 1984 and 1988 the Chinese labor force grew by 61.4 million people. Of that huge number, 48 million (78%) were employed outside of agriculture. In 1989 and 1990 the labor force increased by 24.1 million, and 18.5 million (77%) had to be absorbed by agriculture. One uses the word absorbed rather than employed because 100 million or more members of the agricultural labor force were already in some sense superfluous.[39] By the year 2000 the Chinese labor force will increase by another 150 million people, and China cannot afford politically to add three-quarters of these to the surplus labor pool in the countryside. To avoid this, China's GNP must grow at a rate that is at least 6% to 8% per year. But a high rate of growth in an unreformed economy could retrigger inflation, followed by a renewed round of credit rationing. To avoid this kind of stop-and-go growth, China needs a market-oriented financial system as well as a marketized industry. In 1991, however, China did achieve 7% growth in GNP with inflation of only 4%.

Conclusion

China, as this account makes clear, has largely abandoned the Soviet-type command system and has replaced it with a system run more by market forces than administrative controls, but still with a heavy dose of the latter. It achieved this change over more than a decade while maintaining an average GNP growth rate for thirteen years of around 8% per year.

The key characteristics of this reform were:

1. China began by marketizing where the process did not involve a fundamental reorganization and retraining of the producing units, that is, it began with agriculture and services.
2. Reformers in the more complex urban industrial sphere began with experiments in specific regions, which were then gradually tried on a nationwide basis. Where the rural reforms took three to five years for the essentials to be completed, urban reforms have been in process for seven years, and that process is still ongoing. The interests of the government bureaucrats or of other conservative political forces have not succeeded in stopping or reversing the process for long, as some analysts feel happened in Eastern Europe prior to the collapse of the communist parties in that region. Even the 1989 tragedy in Tiananmen stopped the spread of market forces for one year at the most.
3. Marketization has been achieved to the degree it has been without

formal privatization of state-owned enterprises. Much of this success in the industrial sphere was due to the rapid expansion of small-scale industrial enterprises that behaved according to the rules of the market. Large-scale enterprises have consistently lagged behind, but competition in and changes in the way the large-scale sector does business have also been profound.

4. China followed as best it could the East Asian model for expanding the export of manufactures. The country's strong foreign exchange earnings situation made all other changes easier to manage.

Will this process continue until China has achieved full marketization of its economy—at least to the degree achieved by Japan in the 1950s, or the Republic of Korea in the 1960s and 1970s? It is doubtful that the economic bureaucracy in Beijing has the power to hold back the market incentives now driving hundreds of millions of people. The Communist Party may not be present one or two decades from now, but Marxist-Leninist-Maoist ideology has little discernible influence on economic policy, so it is not apparent that it would make much difference whether China was ruled by the Communist Party, a military government, or some third alternative. Any one of these forms of government could be led either by people who understood the forces that have been unleashed and try to guide them, or by people who resist these forces and divert the process for a time along some unproductive channel. No one is going to try, let alone succeed, in turning back the clock to Soviet-style central planning.

Notes

I wish to thank Linda M. Koenig for her comments on this paper at the El Escorial conference at which it was presented.

1. China's estimates of the growth rate of township and village enterprises, for example, may include some figures that are in current rather than constant prices, which would bias the GNP growth estimates upward.
2. National Statistical Office, *Major Statistics of Korean Economy* (Seoul: 1991), p. 203, and Council for Economic Planning and Development, *Taiwan Statistical Data Book, 1991* (Taipei: 1991), p. 208.
3. *China Daily*, December 31, 1991, p. 1.
4. There is no hard public evidence of the wealth of these people, but informed people feel that such wealthy people in more or less these numbers exist.
5. Between 1978 and 1984, per capita consumption among the agricultural population according to survey data rose by 68%, while that among the nonagricultural population rose by 30%. State Statistical Bureau (SSB), *Zhongguo tongji nianjian, 1990* (Beijing: Statistical Publishers, 1990), p. 291.
6. The weights for the construction of the price indexes, for example, may be biased toward goods sold at state prices, but the degree of bias would not fundamentally alter the picture of inflation portrayed by the official indexes.

7. For a review of some of the literature, see Michael Roemer and Stephen C. Radelet, "Macroeconomic Reform in Developing Countries," in Dwight Perkins and Michael Roemer, eds., *Reforming Economic Systems in Developing Countries* (Cambridge: Harvard Institute for International Development, 1991), pp. 56–80.

8. SSB, *Statistical Yearbook of China, 1981* (Hong Kong: Economic Information and Agency, 1983), p. 363.

9. The term is used here in the way Janos Kornai uses it in *Economics of Shortage* (Amsterdam: North Holland, 1980).

10. Qiao Rongzhang, *Jiage butie* (Beijing: China Price Publishers, 1990), p. 28.

11. China had roughly 100 million hectares of land under cultivation. In addition to chemical fertilizer, Chinese farmers used great quantities of organic fertilizer, so the amount of fertilizer nutrient per hectare was comparable to that found in other East Asian heavy users of fertilizer.

12. One requires reliable estimates of an agricultural production function to properly sort out the contribution of productivity versus increased inputs to growth. However, a crude estimate of the contribution of fertilizer (and complimentary inputs) to grain output can be obtained by assuming a yield response of 8 kilograms of grain for one kilogram of fertilizer nutrient, and that 80% of fertilizer was used on grain. Fertilizer using these figures would have been responsible for an increase in grain output of 54 million tons between 1978 and 1984 (out of a total increase in grain output of 102.5 million tons, or 53% of the total), and an increase in grain output of another 54 million tons between 1984 and 1990 (out of a total increase in grain output of 28 million tons, or 193% of the total). Either weather was substantially worse in 1990 than in 1984, or yield responses to fertilizer fell because of heavy use, or there is some third explanation for the drop in the grain output growth rate after 1984, despite the large increase in fertilizer use.

13. SSB, *Zhongguo tongji nianjian, 1990*, p. 300.

14. These figures were derived by taking the increase in per capita consumption in current prices for rural areas and dividing by the rural retail price index. Incomes and consumption rose faster than agricultural output in part because of an improvement in the rural-urban terms of trade, and in part because of increased income from rural nonagricultural enterprises.

15. The ten-year plan was first discussed in 1975, then attacked by the "Gang of Four," and then revived by Hua Guofeng and others in February 1978. Hua Guofeng, "Report on the Work of the Government," February 26, 1978, in *Beijing Review*, March 10, 1978.

16. China's trade reforms are discussed at length in Nicholas Lardy, *Foreign Trade and Economic Reform in China, 1978–90* (Cambridge: Cambridge University Press, 1992).

17. China Foreign Trade and Economic Relations Compilation Committee, *Zhongguo duiwai jingji maoi nianjian, 1989/90* (Beijing: 1989), p. 247; and Guangdong statistical office, *Guangdongsheng tongji nianjian, 1987* (Hangzhou: China Statistical Publishers, 1987), p. 332.

18. These figures are based on data whose coverage is not as broad as that for the official estimates of total foreign direct investment. SSB, *Zhongguo tongji nianjian, 1990*, p. 654.

19. Yun-wing Sung, "The Economic Integration of Hong Kong, Taiwan, South Korea and Mainland China," in Ross Garnaut and Liu Guoguang, eds., *Economic Reform and Internationalization: China and the Pacific Region* (forthcoming), p. 31.

20. Shanghai Statistical Office, *Shanghai tongji nianjian, 1987* (Shanghai: Shanghai People's Press, 1987), p. 295.

21. Rural industry exports were expected to reach U.S. $12.8 billion (Wang Dongtai, "Record Output of Rural Firms to Continue," *China Daily*, January 8, 1992, p. 1). Foreign-funded firms had exports of U.S. $8 billion in the first nine months of 1991 (Ying Pu, "Foreign Investment Set to Increase with Access to New Areas," *China Daily*, November 25, 1991, business section, p. 1).

22. Detailed commodity-by-commodity price comparisons to establish that China's potential exports were priced competitively and didn't require subsidies is not possible, but it is unlikely that China's rapid export growth to more than U.S. $70 billion in 1991 was still being fueled by large subsidies to exporting firms.

23. Lu Zheng, "China's Economic Reform and Development: Historical Review and Future Prospects," in Ross Garnaut and Liu Guoguang, eds., *Economic Reform and Internationalization: China and the Pacific Region* (forthcoming), and Tang Zongkun, "Supply and Marketing," in Gene Tidrick and Chen Jiyuan, eds., *China's Industrial Reform* (Oxford: Oxford University Press, 1987), p. 229.

24. Li Hong, "Materials Ministry to Take on Market Role," *China Daily*, December 4, 1990, p. 1.

25. Zhang Shaojie and Zhang Amei, "The Present Management Environment in China's Industrial Enterprises," in Bruce Reynolds, ed., *Reform in China: Challenges and Choices* (Armonk, NY: M.E. Sharpe, 1987), pp. 48 and 53.

26. Li Hong, *China Daily*.

27. Li Hong, *China Daily*.

28. Li Hong, "State Narrows Two-Tier Price Gap," *China Daily*, May 17, 1991, p. 1.

29. Chen Xiao, "Price Reform Pacing under Debate," *China Daily*, May 17, 1991, p. 1.

30. William Byrd and Gene Tidrick, "Adjustment and Reform in the Chongqing Clock and Watch Factory," World Bank Staff Working Paper No. 652 (Washington, D.C., 1984).

31. David Granick, *Chinese State Enterprises* (Chicago: University of Chicago Press, 1990).

32. These figures were derived by taking the percentage share of manufactured exports measured in dollars and applying that percentage to the export total in renminbi, and then comparing that figure with gross value of industrial output in current prices. A more accurate figure based on exports valued in Chinese domestic prices was not available.

33. These and other issues of the nature of the enterprise objective function as of the mid-1980s are discussed in William Byrd and Gene Tidrick, "Factor Allocation and Enterprise Incentives," in Gene Tidrick and Chen Jiyuan, eds., *China's Industrial Reform*, pp. 60–102.

34. The early debates over these issues are covered in Robert C. Hsu, *Economic Theories in China, 1979–1988* (Cambridge: Cambridge University Press, 1991).

35. A securities market was established in Shenyang in 1986, and subsequent markets were set up in Shanghai, Shenzhen, and elsewhere, but the volume on these markets is small. Yuan Zhou, "Shareholding in Focus," January 7, 1991 (business weekly), and Jiang Yiwei, "Further Economic Reforms Urged," *China Daily*, October 26, 1990, p. 4. The most prominent advocate of a shareholding system is Li Yining of Beijing University.

36. The best studies for getting into the microbehavior of township and village enterprises are in William Byrd and Lin Qingsong, *China's Rural Industry: Structure, Development and Reform* (Oxford: Oxford University Press, 1990).

37. These studies also indicate that returns to factors between the two sectors were converging, suggesting improved allocative efficiency. Gary Jefferson, Thomas Rawski, and Yuxin Zheng, "Growth, Efficiency and Convergence in China's State and Collective Industry," (July 1990, forthcoming), and Gary Jefferson and Xu Wenyi, "The Impact of Reform on Socialist Enterprises in Transition: Structure, Conduct and Performance in Chinese Industry," Brandeis University, 1990, No. 242.

38. See, for example, Chen Xiao and Zhang Xiaogang, "Economists Urge Slower Growth Rate," *China Daily*, December 27, 1990, p. 4, and Lao Zhang, "Minister Outlines Key Tasks for Development," *China Daily*, March 27, 1991, p. 1. The GNP growth rate target for 1991 announced by Planning Commission Chairman Zou Jiahua was 4.5%.

39. The 100 million figure is a crude calculation based on the size of the rural work force and an estimate of the number of workdays required to farm a hectare of arable land (375) and a work year per person of 200 to 250 days. The resulting figure of 150–188 million employed

206   Dwight Perkins

farm workers compares with a total agricultural labor force (excluding rural enterprises) of around 300 million. The term surplus labor, as used here, does not imply that the marginal product of that labor is zero, only that the marginal product is extremely low, probably below a subsistence wage. See Chen Xiao and Zhang Xiaogang, "Surplus Workers in the Spotlight," *China Daily*, June 21, 1991, p. 4.

CHAPTER 8

Cuba, A Unique Case of Antimarket Reform: The Rectification Process Experience

Carmelo Mesa-Lago

Cuba provides a unique case of economic counter-reform in the midst of a socialist world that is disappearing or introducing market-oriented reforms. Throughout the revolution, Fidel Castro has been a dominant figure and has strongly endorsed antimarket policies most of the time. Six stages can be identified in terms of economic organization in revolutionary Cuba: (1) 1959–60, liquidation of capitalism and market erosion; (2) 1961–65, failed attempt to introduce an orthodox (Stalinist) central planning model; (3) 1964–66, debate over and test of alternative socialist models (the idealist Guevarist approach versus a Liberman-type reform supported by pro-Soviet communists); (4) 1966–70, adoption and radicalization of the Guevarist approach by Castro; (5) 1971–85, introduction of a moderate (pre-Gorbachev) model of economic reform; and (6) 1986–1992, the Rectification Process, a movement away from the market, although there has been an opening to foreign investment since 1990.[1]

From 1976 to 1985, Cuban leaders gradually introduced a modest program of market economic reform (the System of Direction and Planning of the Economy: SDPE) that resembled the Soviet reform of the mid-1960s. Characteristics of the SDPE were: some decentralization in decisionmaking (giving more power to managers of enterprises), use of some market mechanisms (such as profit as a major indicator of managerial performance, free peasant markets, private self-employment—particularly in services), self-financing of enterprises based on bank credit, and expansion of economic incentives (e.g., wage differentials, production bonuses, prizes). Although the SDPE had serious flaws and was never fully implemented, the Cuban economy grew vigorously in this period. However, the deficit in the trade balance rapidly expanded and had to be covered with huge Soviet credits, while some inequality, bureaucratism, and corruption increased. These problems, combined with the change in leadership and growing economic limitations in the USSR, as well as Fidel Castro's politico-ideological objections to the SDPE, set the scene for a dramatic change in economic policy.

In 1986 Castro launched the Rectification Process (RP), which set Cuba against the worldwide socialist trend of market-oriented reform. But the RP has not produced an integrated economic-organization model to substitute for the previous SDPE. Theoretically, the RP is expected to find a middle point between the "idealistic errors" of the Guevarist-Castroist model in 1966–70 and the "economicist mistakes" of the SDPE in 1976–85. Several laws have been enacted and policies launched, but no comprehensive model of the RP has been published. As a result, there has been significant confusion and contradictions on the role of economic tools (for example, the nature of the central plan, the role of profit as a major indicator of managerial performance, price reform, the ways to measure efficiency, and so forth). As in 1966 when Castro took over many functions of the Central Planning Board (JUCEPLAN), in 1986–92 he launched and personally supervised numerous economic projects, but failed to produce an integrative model fundamental for a socialist economy, especially one that eschews markets.[2]

In 1990 Cuban social scientists cautiously began to call for definitions and a blueprint. According to the vice-president of the Center for Study of America (CEA), "criticism of the SDPE has not been accompanied by a new model . . . there is a lack of definition of the new system." Another CEA scholar has acknowledged that the search for a new system is in its initial stages and that surveys conducted among enterprises, cadres, workers, and political leaders have detected uncertainty and a clamor for concrete guidelines such as decentralization of management and investment: as in 1966–70, the "lack of definition" has provoked losses in economic structure and conscience. And José Luis Rodríguez, the vice-president of the Center for Research of the World Economy (CIEM), has said that the overall scheme for enterprise administration has not been finished and there must be a global system in which to insert it; the new system of incentives is still pending and experiments with new payment formulas are being applied to only 1% of the labor force; and there is an urgent need for a price reform: "we are waiting for definitions on all these issues."[3]

At the end of 1990 Castro recognized the necessity to "create our own system of economic direction and planning," despising the current approach as a "sore nag." He argued that the concepts and principles of such a system could not be applied today because "really what we are implementing are emergency measures."[4] In the same year the Central Committee of Cuba's Communist Party acknowledged the importance of the problem, but postponed the solution to its 4th Congress. The latter did not fulfill that promise and simply reiterated the need for searching for "new forms of organization and economic management, as well as the structure and functioning of enterprises."[5]

Economic Features of the Rectification Process
and the System of Direction of the Economy

There are little data available on the economic characteristics of the RP. In 1986 a new National Commission of the System of Direction of the Economy (SDE; which dropped the word "planning" from the SDPE title) prepared several proposals for modifying the old system, which were approved by the party in 1988. Declaring that their work was guided by Castro's ideas, Joaquín Benavides, the new president of the SDE, also warned that improvement of the system could not become an obstacle to the RP: "We should not adjust the RP to the SDE but just the opposite. [Our] fundamental criterion is that the economic mechanisms cannot replace the role of politics, ideology and conscience."[6]

State Ownership of the Means of Production

The RP has further restrained private property and the market: abolition of free peasant markets; acceleration of the process of integration of small private farms (8% of total agricultural land) into state-controlled cooperatives; elimination of activities of small private manufacturers, truck owners, and street vendors; reduction of self-employment (at least until 1991); and restrictions on private construction, selling, rental, and inheritance of housing.

The vacuum left by the elimination/reduction of the private activities was expected to be filled by the state through the expansion of procurement (*acopio*), marketing agencies, the parallel market, and production of state enterprises, as well as the resurrection of construction minibrigades and new construction contingents (state-managed, militarized-style groups of construction workers centrally assigned to priority targets). However, those mechanisms do not seem to have been successful, for several reasons: (1) the system of *acopio* continues to be inefficient, and state enterprises and farms, as well as cooperatives, have not been able to increase production; (2) the parallel market has virtually disappeared, and rationing expanded to all consumer goods; and (3) construction minibrigades and contingents have been criticized as inefficient.[7]

Asked if the state had been able to fill the output vacuum created by the elimination of the free peasant markets, a government official answered positively in terms of quantity but not in assortment and in effective supply, because organizational deficiencies have resulted in spoilage and losses; he also acknowledged that a majority of the population wanted the reintroduction of those markets.[8] But Castro forcibly opposed that action in a long speech delivered at the 4th Party Congress, arguing that the state and cooperative sectors were the proper vehicles for increasing agricultural production. Subsequently the congress voted negatively on the markets, but agreed to authorize individuals to cultivate produce in urban gardens, given the proper permit and adherence to regulations.[9] On the other hand, the congress approved the reintroduction of self-employment in private activities but with significant restrictions: it should be performed after regular working hours in the public sector, be supplementary to the role of the state, be confined to minor service activities, and be strictly regulated to ensure that it does not conflict with socialism. In addition, the self-employed cannot hire anyone outside of the immediate family. Reportedly these restrictions (and the fresh memory of harsh public criticism and curtailment of self-employment in 1982 and 1986 respectively) have impeded a noticeable resurrection of this type of work.[10]

Continuous Planning

According to Castro, the central plan should be kept under the SDE but become more flexible. Following this guide, an experiment of "continuous planning" began in 1988. The objectives were to avoid theoretical formal planning and promote active participation of managers and workers "who should not wait for directions from above but exercise their own initiative in elaborating the plan." Despite the lack of data on future supplies, the enterprise staff was encouraged to use past figures, work with projections, and maximize whatever resources were available. In addition, they were expected to correct those problems (e.g., shortages) that might emerge during the implementation of the plan and incorporate those solutions in the next plan period. A journalist asked the director of plan methodology and processing how different these techniques were from the previous approach. He candidly responded that continuous planning was "just a name, almost a pretext" because the features mentioned above were inherent to any planning process.[11] Later he said that by the end of 1990 this method would be operative in 36% to 41% of the total number of enterprises helping in the elaboration of the 1991 plan.[12] However, the national assembly extended the 1990 laws of the plan and state budget to the year 1991 (the first time this had occurred under the Revolution) and authorized the executive to adapt such laws to the changing situation throughout the year.[13] The 4th Party Congress ratified planning as a key economic instrument, but did not define its nature and failed even to mention "continuous planning"—probably because it was not successful.

Investment, Directive Indicators, Prices

Castro has asserted that centralized decisionmaking will totally control investment, the use of hard currency, and other key economic tools. The 4th Party

Congress ratified that statement (adding central control of enterprises) and granted exceptional powers to the party's central committee, presided over by Castro, to make economic decisions, enact laws (in lieu of the national assembly), and take any needed actions during the current crisis.[14]

The Cuban president has warned that profit cannot be the most important goal of an enterprise, but that it should be subordinated to the "national interest." But the latter has not been operationalized into substitutive practical indicators. An article published in Cuba's principal economic journal argued that the plan is not the key element of the SDE, because all directive indicators are not combined in a system. Toward the end of 1989, the 500 indicators previously used (among which profit was predominant) had been reduced to 90, but the SDE's president acknowledged that a new system of indicators was still needed. In 1990 another planning officer asserted that the system of directives was more important than "continuous planning," but four years after the RP had begun, they were still working on such a system and thinking of introducing "net production and productivity" (not defined) as better indicators than profit. At almost the same time, the newspaper of Cuba's association of economists asserted that physical indicators (e.g., weight, volume, etc.) were predominant and criticized them as flawed, leading to distortions in production and not taking into account demand, quality, and punctuality in deliveries. The 4th Party Congress ratified that "private interest" could not replace the "national interest," but again failed to operationalize the latter.

Prices are highly distorted in Cuba, as they were frozen from 1962 to 1981; in the last year there were some increases in wholesale and retail prices, but they remained distorted and state subsidies huge. Full price reform was expected to be accomplished by the SDPE in 1986, but it was not. Castro's statements on price reforms are confusing and contradictory, but at one point he announced a wholesale price reform in 1990, which did not take place. Many Cuban economists believe that such reform is urgently needed, but there is little public discussion on this important issue.[15] The 4th Party Congress postponed price reform until the current economic crisis is overcome; in the meantime, central physical allocation has been generalized to virtually all of the economy.

Enterprise Financing

Under the former SDPE, the financing of enterprises was to be changed from budgetary to self-financing (*cálculo económico*) by 1986. In budgetary financing, the state directly supports enterprises through budgetary allocations; year-end deficits are canceled and any resulting profits transferred to the central government. Under self-financing, enterprises receive repayable loans with interest and can retain part of their annual profits; enterprises running steady deficits are expected to be shut down. Castro has said, "I am not against these mechanisms [self-financing and profitability] provided that we understand that political work . . . is what makes efficiency possible."[16] After two years of secret debate, the party politbureau approved in 1988 the extension of self-financing; however, the publication of that resolution in the official gazette was delayed by one year.[17] In 1990 I asked Cuban Vice-President Carlos Rafael Rodríguez how many enterprises were self-financed; he said it was impossible to determine, but that serious inefficiencies impeded progress. He added that in most of the economy there was not budgetary financing but something between it and self-financing; he neither wanted to elaborate on this nor give any concrete figures on the scope of both methods.[18] The 4th Party Congress ratified the principle of self-financing, particularly in enterprises that operate in hard currency (a tiny minority), but allowed the continuation of centralized budgetary financing.

Enterprise Mergers

The RP has given a push to the vertical merging of state enterprises into trusts (*uniones lineales*). In the 1970s there was a movement to disaggregate enterprises whose number increased from 700 to 3,000. In the 1980s the opposite occurred, first with the aggregation of agricultural enterprises (such as sugar, rice, and citrus) and since the mid-1980s, with the organization of bigger trusts and agricultural and construction brigades intertwined with factories and transportation facilities. The system was regulated in 1988,[19] and one year later there were sixty-one *uniones* that produced 60% of agricultural, industrial, construction, and transportation output and employed one-third of the labor force. A few of these trusts have linkages with foreign trade agencies. The tendency is to continue the merging process and increase the size of the trusts. This movement has paralleled macroeconomic recentralization since 1986. By the end of 1989, however, the president of the SDE recognized the need to establish better linkages between *uniones* and JUCEPLAN.[20] In tourism, however, there has been decentralization of enterprises.

Integral System of Enterprise Improvement

The most important innovation under the RP is the "integral system of enterprise improvement." It began in the Che Guevara weapon factory of the armed forces (MINFAR); from there it was extended to other military enterprises and then tested in a group of civilian enterprises.[21] Under this system the administrator is "the production sergeant" who is fully in charge of the enterprise, and with the advice of a committee of experts, makes all decisions. The manager is encouraged to reject any false sense of brotherhood, solidarity, or friendship with the workers, who must stick to the duties stipulated under their labor contracts. A worker who fails to fulfill the output quota (norm) receives a basic salary. If the worker exceeds the quota, he or she receives a 10% bonus. This method is allegedly designed to avoid deterioration in quality. (Under the previous SDPE the granting of bonuses for over-fulfillment rapidly spread, but under the RP it was criticized and reduced by Castro, who complained at the end of 1990 that such "garbage . . . has not been legally changed yet.")[22] The worker who repeatedly falls below the quota is demoted or dismissed.

The colonel in charge of MINFAR enterprises was asked if they did not have an advantage over their civilian counterparts because the former could get around hundreds of limiting labor regulations. He answered that current labor legislation overprotects the bad worker and demoralizes the good one; hence it must be changed: "Job security should be granted only to workers who fulfill their duties." A subsequent question was whether enterprise efficiency should be increased at the cost of firing surplus labor. The colonel replied that 258 workers had been dismissed in the Che Guevara enterprise and assigned to other factories or labor brigades in agriculture; transferred workers now produce food for Che Guevara enterprise workers who, in addition, enjoy a restaurant/bar and a video arcade, and some have received houses.

Another element in the "integral system" is a change in the "quality inspector" who accepts or rejects goods produced according to quality standards. Previously this job was badly paid and did not attract skilled personnel. The new inspector "must be well qualified, experienced and paid according to the responsibility of his job." (Quality committees also supervise standards: more than 1,000 such committees had been established by the end of 1989.) Finally, the leaders of an "integral" enterprise must change the arrogant "take it or leave it" attitude toward their clients and start responding to their interests.

It is difficult to assess the extent of the "integral system." At the end of 1989, the SDE president presented two contradictory sets of figures: 400 to 500 civilian enterprises had the system in operation in 1987, but only 177 in October 1988 (8% of the total number of enterprises). In 1990 the colonel in charge of MINFAR enterprises said that 100 civilian enterprises would start using the system in 1991. All enterprises (about 2,200) should be under the system in 1992 or 1993.[23] The 4th Party Congress praised the MINFAR experiments, but did not provide any overall evaluation of the "integral system" results.

Labor, Construction Brigades, and Contingents

The RP launched a series of measures to increase control of labor productivity and wages, and to fight corruption: reduction of surplus labor; tightening of labor output quotas or "norms" (usually increasing them); revision of wages, production bonuses, prize funds, and overtime payments (normally reducing them); renewed emphasis on unpaid voluntary labor and nonmaterial or "moral" incentives (although with selective use of material incentives, for example, in tourism and construction contingents); and the defining of new economic and administrative crimes, to fight corruption. The process of reviewing all labor norms is behind schedule. According to an article published in 1989, 81% of 2.5 million norms had not been revised, without which it was not possible to establish cost systems programmed by the SDE for 1990, thereby halting or badly affecting the process.[24] The 4th Party Congress did not give specifics on this subject.

Construction minibrigades were first tried in Cuba in 1970 but— according to Castro—were eliminated by the SDPE because of their inefficiency: enterprises had to pay wages to brigade members whose output was not accounted for within the enterprise, hence reducing its profitability. In 1987 the Cuban president reintroduced the minibrigades as a keystone for solving the construction deficit (in housing, industry, etc.) and argued that the previous inefficiency problem was solved because: minibrigades were composed of surplus labor released from enterprises; the remaining workers kept up production at the enterprise and fulfilled the output targets without charging overtime; and the state reimbursed the enterprise for wages paid to minibrigade members and provided them with input and supplies. In 1987–88 Castro praised the minibrigades because by creating a new labor spirit, they were "working miracles," but at the end of 1989 he dramatically reversed his previous optimistic judgment: the brigades were disorganized, fell apart, were anarchic, mishandled the equipment, lacked cost control, spent 2.40 pesos for every peso produced (most members were not professional construction workers); in summary, they were "a mess." After Castro's initial assertion that minibrigades would build 100,000 houses annually, statistical series were changed, but overall housing construction declined in 1985–87, and scattered data suggest that only 18,315 units were built in 1986–89.[25]

In view of the inefficiency of minibrigades, Castro decided that construction contingents would be the solution. Instead of recruiting redundant workers from enterprises, contingent members were carefully selected and very well paid, fed, housed, and provided with other special privileges. In return, they were expected to work very hard: "It is no secret that Fidel designed, created and personally supervises the contingents . . . and they have not failed him . . . they have produced great feats, labor miracles." The target for 1990 was 100 contingents with 50,000 workers, but in that year, only 72 contingents with 37,852 workers were in operation. Initially, contingents were rapidly organized, then it became mandatory that they be authorized by the council of ministers. Eventually, new contingents were not established (because of lack of supplies and to avoid being "discredited" by the re-creation of "old vices"), and finally, some workers were sent home or to work on other projects. Castro first claimed that the contingents were very productive (0.70 cost per peso produced), but problems soon appeared. Members were paid higher wages than most workers, hence their production costs were also higher. (Castro argued that this was not a problem because costs still were below one peso.) Special food, air-conditioned housing, and other perquisites, many of which are imported, added to salary costs. Shortages of construction materials caused bottlenecks, an obstacle initially pinpointed by Cuban technicians but disregarded by Castro. And hidden costs were inflicted on other sectors of the economy. Castro has not clarified whether these extra expenditures are taken into account in the calculation of costs per peso of the contingents, and he has discredited criticism against his project as being made by "worms" who only look "at the negative side" of things. When the new secretary general of the Confederation of Cuban Workers (CTC) complained in 1990 that contingent workers earned more than the minister of construction, Castro replied that "ministers don't have to break stones or drive bulldozers" and their work cannot be compared to that of the contingents.[26]

Results and Modification

The SDE committee was expected to perform monthly checks on the evolution of all elements in the new system, but to the best of my knowledge, not one report was publicized in four years since the reform proposals of the committee were approved by the party. (Conversely, annual evaluations of the SDPE's progress were publicized.) At the end of 1989, the SDE president was asked the concrete results of all the related experiences and experiments. He first apologized, saying that they had been working only for one year and a half; then he admitted that of a total of 213 tasks, they had worked on only 139; 20% of those had been completed and 30% were "practically finished" by November of that year. He added that even if all 139 tasks were fulfilled (an obviously unattainable goal), it would not mean that the problems had been solved because the tasks would then have to "go into real action," a process that would take more time.[27]

In February 1990 the party's central committee met and declared that the results of the RP in economic development were "fruitful and promising." Paradoxically, it added that "in view of these results . . . the time has come to deal with the improvement of the . . . system in practical and concrete terms . . . under the leadership and with the enormous guiding effort of Fidel, who is . . . at the peak of his mastery to deal with the crisis of socialism." Finally, the central committee acknowledged the need to correct mechanisms that "have lost freshness and assumed bureaucratic forms."[28] This declaration was followed by important changes in the leadership of the political bureau, the national assembly, mass organizations, and—last but not least—in the removal of the president of the national committee of the SDE. The new president said in February that the SDE had to be restructured, its transformation completed by June. Starting in January 1991, 100 enterprises would be chosen for restructuring in agriculture, agro-industry, and principal industries according to MINFAR's experience. He also stated that all regulations that might inhibit such action would be abolished.[29]

The 4th Party Congress ratified the RP and its programs but failed to design a new economic model. Paradoxically, in his speech opening the congress Castro referred to some of the RP programs as something that belonged to the past, measures of great promise that had been paralyzed or hurt by the collapse of socialism elsewhere and the economic crisis at home.[30]

Factors That Conspire Against SDE's Success

Clear indicators show that the SDE is in serious trouble: (1) the RP lacks a comprehensive economic model; (2) its backbone, the SDE, is entirely subordinated to politics; (3) several key elements of the SDE are either not clearly defined, not operationalized, or are being introduced slowly; (4) available data on actual SDE implementation and progress are scarce and contradictory; (5) the SDE leadership has been replaced and the system itself is being transformed; and (6) the 4th Party Congress has neither developed an integrated new economic system nor evaluated SDE performance. In this section additional domestic and external factors are presented that conspire against SDE success, all of which are discussed by Cuban economists, technocrats, and leaders.

Absence of Public Debate on Economics

An article published in the University of Havana newspaper in 1990 analyzed the problems Cuba faced in the fields of economics and accounting, and pinpointed as most important the lack of public economic debate: "Never has our press published a debate on a given plan or economic policy or method . . . never has the validity of a plan or investment project been questioned." This is a reflection of what happens in enterprise meetings. As an example, the article noted that the last congress of Cuba's National Association of Economists—which took place in October 1989, when socialism in Eastern Europe was collapsing—neither discussed this crisis nor the island's serious economic problems or issues (such as whether a centralized economy leads to stagnation). Instead, the debates focused almost exclusively on a "safe" topic: the ethics of the economist.[31]

Poor Skills and Initiative among Economists, Managers, and Accountants

Cuba's Vice-President Carlos Rafael Rodríguez told me in an interview in mid-1990 that Cuba badly needed people with entrepreneurial skills; he noted that the USSR had been unable to help on that front and indicated that the United States could help. The former SDE president admitted that if current serious deficiencies in accounting and managerial control were not resolved, it would be impossible to advance in other areas.[32] And yet, there are more than 25,000 economists and accountants in Cuba (out of a total population of 11 million), and 37,000 are projected for 1995. The University of Havana article cited above shrewdly observed that with so many professionals, one would expect greater economic efficiency in Cuba. The article gave explanations for that paradox: educational flaws, lack of connections between the university and enterprises, and poor initiative.

Most students in economics chose this discipline because they were not admitted to others; hence they lack interest and are "the worst students in higher education." To make things worse, university training in economics is deficient. Curricula are usually reduced to political views and omit the study of most bourgeois economists, forgetting that "in an open economy such as Cuba's it is vital to know about them." The course on capitalist accounting does not cover domestic nor international capitalist institutions, their problems, and solutions ("we have to guess about them"). Subjects are presented in a dogmatic manner rather than encouraging critical viewpoints. Students are taught about an ideal economy instead of being provided with practical skills to solve real entrepreneurial problems. The university has arranged student internships in some enterprises, but its staff is not interested in the students' work. Economists and accountants are discriminated against, and they do not take part in the managerial councils of enterprises. "There is constant talk of the need to have people with skills to handle international market prices, open new markets abroad and understand stock markets, but to fill those needs, it is a must to infuse creativity, aggressiveness, initiative in the individual . . . an experience we lack in Cuba . . . We have failed in developing a look to the future . . . even our best graduates are frustrated."[33]

The former SDE president elaborated on the pervasive lack of initiative: "One obstacle that we face is that, historically, our cadres have always waited for orders from above: we need a revolution in the minds of our management." Emphasizing this issue, another economist said that there is no initiative nor autonomy in most enterprises: "Everything is guided from above and then checked and rechecked."[34]

The best-selling book of 1990, which quickly went out of print, was a rudimentary manual for administrators of state enterprises. It reported generalized ignorance, incapacity, and lack of discipline among them and noted that managers are afraid to make decisions and mistakes; hence there is a tendency to postpone actions while waiting for instructions from above, which combined with the lack of delegation of functions provokes slowdown or paralysis of decisionmaking.[35]

A somewhat different view is that there are indeed skilled professionals in Cuba, but they are denied access to positions of responsibility because such jobs have long been occupied by the aging leadership and their loyalists, who lack proper training. An article published in the youth newspaper in 1990 depicted that situation in surprisingly blunt terms: At the beginning of the Revolution the leadership was young, economically inexperienced, and voluntaristic, and hence they made mistakes: peasants became sugar mill administrators, and physicians became ministers (an allusion to Che Guevara). Fidel has been "like a father" and we are proud of his "defects and virtues, errors and triumphs." For more than thirty years we have made war and not paid enough attention to the warning that "a nation cannot be governed like a military camp." We have to devote ourselves to the full development and application of the skills we have gained thanks to the Revolution. There is a generation of technicians and experts in all fields who should play an active role in economics because "the war for development is much more complex than a military war." And yet, there is a "hidden resistance [to that role] of which we are not always conscious." Thus many positions are not filled with the available cadres and "political loyalty and historical merits count more than proper skills." Until we change that habit, "we will remain attached to the old mentality that could be justifiable in old times but not now." We must "open the way to the most skilled to avoid the cause of so many problems."[36]

Uncertainty in Planning but Increase in Centralization

The SDE is either in serious trouble or has been discarded without replacing it with another planning mechanism. The vagueness of the domestic economic model of organization is compounded by external uncertainty concerning imports, exports, etc. In the "Special Period in Time of Peace" (a euphemism for the stage of emergency that began in 1990; see section on adjustment policies) a highly centralized strategy to cope with the crisis, maximize resources, and establish priorities has been forged, but it can hardly be equated with a plan. Furthermore, market tools have been reduced even more except for foreign investment enclaves.

Some Cuban economists concur with the view of a few foreign experts who claim that the RP has not reversed the decentralization process initiated in the mid-1970s under the SDPE.[37] A top official at JUCEPLAN asserts that there is central planning and decisionmaking in many areas, and it will continue in the future partly due to the current shortage of resources. One of these areas is investment, according to the director of the Institute of Economic Research in Havana. And yet, "continuous planning" allegedly increases the role of enterprise, managers, and workers vis-à-vis the central planners, and party-approved rules in 1988 endorsed decentralization measures such as self-financing.[38]

A journalist asked how there can be decentralization in Cuba if even the most trivial issues can end up with the executive council of ministers (concrete examples of this are the approval of the inception of each construction contingent and discussion of petty robbery on buses). Another journalist asked the same JUCEPLAN official cited above how could he reconcile scarcity of resources and "continuous planning" with the goal of increasing initiative at the enterprise level without waiting for instructions from above. Under current conditions, the official answered, there is no possibility for significant annual changes in the volume of supplies, output, etc., since these elements are "clearly determined" and repeated year after year; alas, there is no need to wait for instructions. He then acknowledged that in the implementation of the enterprise planning proposals, difficulties have arisen due to the lack of resources, poor skills of cadres, and low participation of workers.[39] The CTC in its 1989 Congress pinpointed the "inadequacy of mechanisms set up for workers' participation in drawing up, monitoring and implementing plans"; the CTC complained that managers do not give importance to that issue and consider production assemblies "mere formalities."[40] The increasing trend since the mid-1980s toward merging enterprises is another indication of recentralization. Furthermore, the need and importance of information has become greater. In 1990 Cuba's most popular magazine reported that 550 million pesos worth of desperately needed industrial equipment was found unused in a warehouse. "This situation made clear the lack of information between those who produce and those who need goods." However, the former president of SDE said that "intermediary" enterprises that connect producers and consumers are "parasites" and should be suppressed. Finally, the party's decision on self-financing has not been implemented partly because the group that endorsed it lacked political muscle to enforce such a decision, and also because the emergency situation has been used as an excuse to continue centralization of financing.[41]

Persistent Corruption

The RP intended to correct corruption, which allegedly had flourished under the SDPE. Scarce and contradictory official data indicate that total crime declined slightly in the first half of 1987 compared with the 1980–86 average, but serious crime increased in 1987 over 1986. The crime rate leveled off in

1988, but rose in the first half of 1990. In the provincial party meeting of Isle of Youth held in 1991, crime was said to be gradually growing, particularly robbery; similar concerns were voiced in the provincial meetings of Cienfuegos and Matanzas. Some of the crimes reported were rustling, pig butchery and selling, forest tree cutting, hunting or raising wild animals, and not handing in tips received by employees of tourist facilities. Castro has acknowledged that the tough measures enacted to fight corruption and crime have not been entirely successful. The economic police reports continued violations of the penal code, fraud, and robberies: in 1990 an unaccounted 25 million pesos were uncovered in ninety-one enterprise audits. According to Castro, merchandise scarcities are not only due to external factors (cut in imports), but also to domestic lack of control and stealing, "an evil we have not conquered": "There are some who would be willing to die in battle, and yet, when they are assigned to manage a store, they steal money from the till . . . this is a shortcoming of our culture." He has reported that poor financial performance in transportation is caused by passengers who fail to pay the fare, which he blamed on "ideological deficiency."[42] A public survey conducted in 1990 on People's Power revealed that its delegates were using their power to obtain crucial goods or services that the population lacked: "In our block the sewage system is clogged and infected water enters our houses; the government says it lacks resources to correct these problems. But our delegate has gotten a house and on his block there are sidewalks and good sewage."[43]

At the end of 1990, Cuba's state news agency (AIN) asserted that crime and corruption were more dangerous than the Central Intelligence Agency. Citizens were exhorted to help the government fight corruption through constant vigilance even of leaders and members of the security ministry (MININ). Those people who show expenditures or a living standard above their positions and normal earnings (e.g., buying a car or a motorcycle, expanding their homes or furnishing them with electric appliances) should be denounced—and not only the butcher or the grocery employee, but also administrators and leaders who engage in these extravagant expenditures soon after being appointed to jobs.[44]

In 1991 Castro complained that there were obstacles to putting offenders in jail: "Softness, pettifogging and bureaucratic procedures must end . . . If laws are not tough enough, then enact new laws . . . Shameless people who demoralize others must be repressed."[45] The 4th Party Congress demanded a tougher policy to fight the increase in crime, and by the end of 1991, the national assembly responded by enacting new laws for the integration of all "forces of order" into a United System of Vigilance and Protection, the modification of criminal procedures to expedite the trial of delinquents, and the selection of judges who will take a tougher stand with criminals.[46]

Termination/Reduction of Trade and Aid
with Eastern Europe and the USSR

In 1985, 83.1% of Cuban trade was with the CMEA: 70.5% with the USSR and 12.6% with Eastern Europe. Cuban trade with the USSR systematically ended in deficit, which grew rapidly. The RP external policy aimed at reducing the external disequilibrium with their socialist partners through export promotion (establishing investment priorities), import cuts, and an increase in domestic production of foodstuffs.

From 1960 to 1990 Cuba received an estimated $65 billion in Soviet economic aid alone, without counting Soviet military aid and Eastern European economic aid. More than 60% of Soviet aid was in the form of nonrepayable price subsidies and less than 40% in repayable loans. (My estimate of subsidies is based on world market prices; if preferential prices are used, both the size of such subsidies and total aid are reduced but still remain enormous.) At the end of 1989 the Soviets disclosed that the Cuban debt was 15.5 billion rubles, or $27.5 billion at the Soviet official exchange rate in 1990. I have conservatively estimated the Cuban debt with Eastern Europe at $2.5 billion in 1990; and the debt in hard currency was $7.3 billion that year. Therefore in 1990 Cuba's total external debt was $37.6 billion, the highest per capita in Latin America and the Caribbean. Until the 1990s the RP did not include any policies aimed at reducing the debt.[47]

The collapse of socialism in Eastern Europe and the USSR has resulted in termination or dramatic reduction in trade and aid. No five-year trade agreement was signed with the USSR for 1991–95, and Cuba confronts medium-term uncertainty on placing island exports, securing key imports, and determining prices of both. A trade pact signed for 1991, although making some concessions to Cuba, left for contract negotiation the determination of specific quantities and prices of most commodities, adding uncertainty in the short run as well. The disappearance of the USSR has forced Cuba to negotiate individually with CIS independent republics; at the time this chapter was finished, trade agreements for 1992 had been signed with only half of the republics, and the pact with Russia was for just the first quarter of the year, optionally renewable in the remaining quarters. The CMEA was dissolved at the beginning of 1991, and there was a radical shift from mutually agreed subsidized prices and payment in transferable rubles to world prices and payments in hard currency. As 84% of Cuban trade was with the CMEA and 92% was in nonconvertible currency or barter, such a shift has had an enormous impact on the island's economy. The trade pact of 1991 maintained a preferential price for sugar, but left all other commodities to be set at world prices and in hard currency (U.S. dollars) starting on April 1; since 1992 sugar prices have been set at world market levels. The trade turnover between the two countries declined by 11.5% in 1985–89; this was due to a 28% decrease in the value of Cuban exports while the value of Soviet imports were stagnant. But the value of the latter fell by 70% in 1989–91 and possibly by another 50% in 1992. Cuba's trade deficit increased by 144% in 1985–89; no data are available for 1990–92. The USSR terminated two special concessions to Cuba in 1990: "reexporting" in hard currency of crude oil supplies exceeding the island's needs, and a guarantee of the Cuban debt with a French firm that provided credit to buy sugar in the world market to meet the island's export commitments. The terms of trade with the USSR continued their deterioration against Cuba in 1986–88, at least concerning three major trade products. Despite such deterioration, Cuba still enjoyed an estimated net gain of $10 billion in 1986–90, but it was 36% lower than in 1981–85. Although not enough data are available, the deterioration in the terms of trade against Cuba must have worsened in 1991–92, particularly because the Soviet price paid for sugar was cut to one-fifth of the 1990 level. The amount of total Soviet aid granted to Cuba declined only slightly in 1986–90 (compared to the previous five years), but its composition shifted from 29% in repayable loans and 71% in nonrepayable subsidies to 54% and 46% respectively. All Soviet economic aid to Cuba was terminated in 1992. Cuba's debt with the USSR kept growing in 1990–91; the USSR apparently has requested that the debt be repaid at an exchange rate to be mutually agreed upon or with exports. Cuban centralized enterprises must deal with increasingly decentralized, competitive, and profit-maximizing Soviet counterparts. Under the 1991 trade pact, Cuban sugar exports were handled by one central Soviet institution, which in turn contracted with numerous enterprises inside the USSR for key supplies to the island; the rest of foreign trade was conducted with thousands of decentralized enterprises. Under the previous system, 80% of the contracts were ready at the time of signing the annual trade pact, but in 1991 all contracting started after signature. Since 1992 the central buying/selling mechanisms have virtually disappeared. These problems, combined with the complexity of the new contracts (to be set at world prices and in hard currency), take considerably more time to negotiate and have been one cause in the delays of Soviet deliveries. Additional limitations to Cuban trade with the USSR are a dramatic decrease in the number of Soviet merchant ships available to carry that trade (since 1992 virtually none) and insufficient capacity of Cuban docks. In 1989–91 Cuba reported delays and cuts in numerous Soviet supplies; in the last year close to half of planned imports were not delivered. The most important cut has been crude oil and oil products, which decreased 36% in 1987–91 and were expected to further decline by another 53% to 70% in 1992. Information for 1992 is fragmentary but indicates that Cuba would export about two million tons of sugar to CIS, one-half of what it used to export, and import a maximum of 4 million tons of oil and oil products, less than one-third of what was imported in 1987. Cuba will probably sell less nickel and citrus than before, and an expansion of biotechnology exports cannot compensate for the huge losses from other exports. Cuba's trade relationship with the CIS will probably continue in the immediate future, but at drastically reduced levels and without the previous advantages and facing increasing difficulties and challenges.

Cuban trade with the former German Democratic Republic and Czechoslovakia (the two major trade partners in Eastern Europe), as well as with Hungary and Poland, has either stopped or been reduced to a trickle. Trade with Bulgaria and Romania continues, but at a very low level. Estimates indicate that by 1992 Cuba might have lost $1.8 billion or 95% of trade turnover with Eastern Europe. The latter include about $800 million in export value, mostly sugar (a loss of exports of 1 million tons), at twice the price of the world market. The loss of key East European imports has created serious disruption in the Cuban economy. Trade deficit financing with Eastern Europe has stopped altogether. An agreement to pay Cuba's debt to Eastern Europe is a precondition set to resume trade by some of these countries.

In 1986 Cuba suspended payments on the service of its hard-currency debt. The Paris Club immediately suspended new credits—a situation that prevailed in mid-1992. Trade has declined due to the lack of trade credit and Cuba's heavy reliance on sugar exports. The island's official position is that fresh credit is needed to restart paying the debt service; but debtors request that servicing of the debt precede the granting of new credits; hence there is a stalemate.

Effects on the Cuban Economy and Society

From 1986 to 1992 the Cuban economy deteriorated and entered the worst crisis under the Revolution. There is no doubt that since 1990 such deterioration has been principally the result of the collapse of socialism in the USSR and Eastern Europe. However, the negative economic performance began in 1986 when the RP was launched—long before the collapse of socialism. There has been a debate on whether the economic worsening from 1986 to 1990 was caused by the RP or external factors, or a combination of both. Furthermore, the antimarket features of the RP have possibly played a negative role in the 1991–92 crisis.

Official Cuban publications and economists have blamed exogenous, conjectural variables as exclusive causes of the 1986–90 deterioration, such as adverse climate conditions (drought), deterioration of world prices (e.g., sugar) and of the terms of trade with the USSR, and lack of fresh hard-currency credit from market economies (after Cuba suspended debt-service payments in 1986), while arguing that the RP has had a positive, compensatory effect. Most U.S. scholars, including myself, without disregarding external variables have noted serious inconsistencies in the official argument and have pinpointed the importance of negative effects of the RP, such as the decline in private output and services, state inability to substitute the eliminated market mechanisms, and lack of a coherent new model. Recently a few Cuban economists have acknowledged that the crisis cannot be explained by external factors alone; for instance, they admit that the state—overburdened with too many functions—has been unable to fully fill the vacuum left by the eradication of free peasant markets and reduced self-employment. On the other hand, the third most powerful political figure in Cuba declared in mid-1991 that the crisis (and particularly rationing) is "not a consequence of inefficiency or incompetence on our part but has been imposed on us by external factors beyond our control."[48] As it is impossible to separate the causes of the crisis, we focus, hereafter, on the evaluation of its socioeconomic effects.

Macroeconomic Indicators of the Crisis Effects

Table 8.1 summarizes the state of the Cuban economy in the year prior to the introduction of the RP and compares the booming performance of 1981–85 with the economic deterioration of 1986–90: (1) the global social product (GSP, based on the Soviet material product system instead of the Western system of national accounts) grew at 41.6% in 1981–85, but declined by 6.3% in 1986–90 (in per capita terms there was an increase of 36% and a decline of 10% respectively); (2) labor productivity grew at 41.4% in 1981–85, but declined 10.3% in 1986–89; (3) the average annual nominal wage in 1989 was at the same level as in 1985 (no data are available in constant prices); (4) there was a cumulative budgetary surplus of 287 million pesos in 1981–85, but a cumulative deficit of 5.5 billion pesos in 1986–90 (the deficit increased 645% in 1985–90); (5) housing construction increased 17.8% in 1981–85, but declined 6% in 1985–87 (aggregate comparable data have not been published after 1987); (6) total merchandise trade increased 63% in 1981–85 and declined 6.6% in 1985–89; (7) the growth rate in the trade deficit slowed significantly (from 209.5% in 1981–85 to 33.6% in 1986–89), but the deficit level remained above 2 billion pesos (official data for 1990 are not available); (8) the trade deficit with the USSR increased from 44.2% in 1981–85 to 144.5% in 1986–89; (9) the trade deficit in hard currency worsened by 148% in 1981–85, but only by 18.3% in 1986–89; this was achieved not by increasing exports (which were stagnant), but by reducing hard-currency imports and shifting the trade deficit to the USSR; (10) international reserves declined 13.2% in 1981–85, but decreased further, by 74.8%, in

TABLE 8.1 The deterioration of the Cuban economy in 1980–90

Indicators	1980	1985	1986	1987	1988	1989	1990	% Comparison 1985/80	% Comparison 1989–90/85
	(in millions of pesos)								
GSP[a]	19,111	27,070	27,390	26,350	26,921	27,208	25,360[h]	41.6	-6.3
GSP per capita[a,c]	1,971	2,681	2,685	2,558	2,585	2,586	2,406[h]	36.0	-10.2
Labor productivity[b,d]	6,626	9,373	9,235	8,826	8,677	8,404	n.a.	41.4	-10.3
Average annual wage[b,c]	1,774	2,252	2,255	2,208	2,242	2,260	n.a.	26.9	0.4
Budget balance[b]	n.a.	(253)	(188)	(609)	(1,146)	(1,624)	(1,985)	n.a.	684.6
Housing units[e]	60,576	71,367	70,914	67,099	n.a.	n.a.	n.a.	17.8	-6.0
Total merchandise trade[b]	*8,594*	*14,027*	*12,894*	*13,013*	*13,098*	*13,516*	*13,000*	63.2	-6.6
Exports	3,967	5,992	5,322	5,401	5,518	5,392	5,932	51.0	-7.9
Imports	4,627	8,035	7,596	7,612	7,579	8,124	7,068	73.6	-5.6
Balance	(660)	(2,044)	(2,274)	(2,211)	(2,061)	(2,732)	(2,015)	209.5	33.6
Trade with USSR[b]	*5,158*	*9,901*	*9,248*	*9,363*	*9,047*	*8,753*	*8,978*	92.0	-11.6
Exports	2,654	4,482	3,935	3,867	3,683	3,231	4,064	68.9	-27.9
Imports	2,904	5,419	5,337	5,496	5,364	5,522	4,914	86.6	-1.9
Balance	(650)	(937)	(1,402)	(1,629)	(1,681)	(2,291)	(850)	44.2	144.5
Trade in convertible currency	*2,295*	*2,473*	*2,082*	*1,915*	*2,020*	*2,287*	*n.a.*	7.8	-7.5
Exports	1,284	1,171	896	975	1,049	1,066	n.a.	-8.8	-8.9
Imports	1,011	1,302	1,186	940	971	1,221	n.a.	28.7	-6.2
Balance	273	(131)	(290)	35	78	(155)	i	-148.0	18.3
International reserves[b,f]	403[g]	350	242	196	234	88	i	-13.2	-74.8
Hard-currency debt[b,f]	3,170	3,621	4,985	6,094	6,450	6,165	7,300	14.2	101.6

Source: C. Carmelo Mesa-Lago. "Economic Effects on Cuba of the Collapse of Socialism in USSR and Eastern Europe." *Cuba After the Cold War* (Pittsburgh Press, 1993).

a. Constant 1981 prices.
b. Current prices.
c. Pesos.
d. Productive sphere only (exclude commerce).
e. Built by the state, coops and population; 1981 instead of 1980 (no comparable data available).
f. December 31, except international reserves in June 1989 and debt in September 1990; reserves in 1981 instead of 1980 due to lack of data.
g. 1981.
h. Based on information provided by a Soviet scholar. Miami, November 1991.
i. Daniel Legra an official of Cuba's National Bank, reported a decline vis-à-vis 1990.

1986–89; and (11) the hard-currency debt increased 14% in 1981–85, but 101.6% in 1986–90. Foreign trade figures for 1990 are rough estimates by a Cuban economist and have not been used in the comparison; these figures indicate a decline in the total trade turnover but a reduction in the global deficit, mostly due to a sharp decrease in imports; the turnover with the USSR increased and the deficit was cut dramatically due to an increase in exports and reduction in imports. None of the annual planning targets set in 1986–90 were met (for GSP growth, productivity, average wages, imports and exports, housing construction); real performance was half of the target.[49] Specific objectives of the RP, such as reduction of the budget and trade deficits, have not been realized either.

Cuba has not released any data on macroeconomic indicators after 1990, thus it is not possible to accurately calculate the impact of the collapse of socialism in USSR/East Europe on the Cuban economy. I have roughly estimated that, in 1989–92, Cuba's GSP declined 23%, based on the loss of Soviet/Eastern European economic aid alone, without taking into account the reduction of Cuba's imports from and exports to those countries and their impact on domestic production.[50] Other estimates of GSP decline are: 22% in 1989–91 plus an additional 9% in 1992, and 35% to 40% in 1989–91 plus 7% to 12% in 1992.[51]

Adjustment Policies

In August 1990 the Cuban leadership launched a "Special Period in Time of Peace," a euphemism for a national economic emergency, which had included, until early 1992, three rounds of adjustment measures. Many factories have been either shut down or drastically reduced production: a Soviet-built nickel plant; an oil refinery; a bus factory; textile, cement, and construction material factories; 347 factories of the ministry of light industry; production of books, magazines, and newspapers. Cuts in the use of energy have been: 50% in the supply of gasoline and fuel deliveries to the state sector and 30% to the private sector; 10% in electricity consumption (40% of private consumers who exceeded their quotas are being deprived of electricity from three to ten days, and public violators are forced to shut down their businesses); 80% in the number of buses; 50% in the total number of taxis (state taxis are constrained to the most essential services such as medical emergencies and funerals, while private taxis are totally deprived of gasoline); 70% in the supply of gasoline to cars belonging to professionals, and a further cut by 30% to private and public vehicles. There is a massive use of bicycles for urban transportation (close to 1 million are being imported from China), and draft animals are being substituted for fuel-operated machinery in agriculture. In addition, there are reductions of street lighting, shutdown of air conditioners, and rationing of cooking gas. The work week has been decreased from 5.5 to 5 days, and there is talk of a further cut to 4 days; the party bureaucracy has been halved and administrative workers are being reassigned to agriculture. Rationing of 28 food products and 180 consumer goods has been reintroduced, and social consumption of food (in state enterprises, schools, etc.) has been cut; prices of agricultural products began to be raised early in 1992. Television transmissions have been shrunk from 129 to 48 hours weekly, many cinemas and restaurants have been closed, and sports activities are scheduled only during daylight hours.[52]

A fourth round of adjustment measures is expected to take place in 1992 if Soviet deliveries are lower than expected. Castro has warned, "We should be prepared for greater difficulties . . . even for the 'Zero Fuel Option' in the most extreme case." At the end of 1991 and early in 1992, he added that Cuba has not entered "the most critical phase of the Special Period . . . the worst is not here yet."[53]

Social Effects: Rationing, Inflation, Unemployment, Crime

In 1979 before the liberalization measures introduced in 1980–85 (e.g., free peasant markets), a series of goods were freely sold and others could be bought in the state parallel market at higher prices than the rationing price. By the end of 1991, not only were there some 200 consumer goods added to the rationing list (hence none was freely sold in the market), but the rationed quotas of two-thirds of the goods had been cut (they barely guaranteed subsistence), and the parallel market had disappeared. Medicine was in very short supply as well. The quality of the goods has also deteriorated; for instance, coffee was mixed with green peas. The quotas are not guaranteed, and long queues form in the early hours of the morning (reducing the population's leisure time), and many products disappear from the state shop for months.[54]

Cuba has one of the most egalitarian systems in the world, but the crisis is conspiring against it. The rationing system has always been justified as a measure designed to protect low-income groups. But the severe scarcity of consumer goods has produced a phenomenal expansion of the black market, with skyrocketing prices: for example, the official price of a pound of chicken is 0.70 cents, but a two-pound chicken is sold on the black market for 20 to 30 pesos; other goods such as cigars and rum are sold from seven to ten times the official price. The average monthly salary is 190 pesos and the minimum salary is 100 pesos, while the minimum pension is 90 pesos. Therefore the lowest income groups cannot supplement the meager rations by buying in the black market. Furthermore, since February 1992 official food prices began to increase: for instance, 150% for potatoes, 125% for tomatoes, 75% for plantains. The elite has always had access to goods and services not available to the masses, such as special stores, separate hospitals, medicines, cars and gasoline, social clubs, recreational villas, and trips abroad. The gap between the elite and the masses is therefore expanding.[55]

Inflation in Cuba is probably the lowest in Latin America, but price increases in 1992 should generate some degree of inflation. There is a more perverse trend, however: as consumer goods become increasingly scarce, the surplus money in circulation has grown, as there is nothing to buy with it outside of the rationing system except for items available on the black market. In 1970 the monetary surplus per capita peaked at 388 pesos; it declined to 216 pesos in 1980 and then began to climb again. In 1988 it reached 347 pesos and kept rising, thereafter probably surpassing the 1970 level. At the end of 1990, Castro asserted that there was "an abundance of money which has many disadvantages," then he asked "what should be done with all that money in the hands of the population?"[56] The 4th Party Congress declared that it was urgent to cut the monetary surplus because of its negative effects on labor productivity and absenteeism. In 1970 the latter reached 20% of the labor force, and that situation is rapidly approaching now. Some Cuban economists have said that "inflationary pressures" are "derived from the insufficiency of consumer goods production and the impossibility of covering that gap with imports." Domestic managerial inefficiency is given as a major cause of output insufficiency: "increases in prices cannot be used to promote equilibrium after a certain point [because they will cut down consumption among the lowest income stratum], hence it is necessary to increase supply."[57]

Since it is not possible to expand the supply of consumer goods to reduce the monetary surplus, the government is encouraging the people to save by increasing the interest rate from 2% to 4% and 5%, according to different plans. But this measure cannot make a dent in the surplus: in 1991 net savings totaled 600 million pesos, but that sum probably put apart no more than 15% of the monetary surplus. Hence the government is attempting to control labor discipline, waste of work hours, and labor absenteeism by increasing the rigor of sanctions levied against violators. Even some of the celebrated labor contingents are now being subject to criticism because of their inefficiency and have been threatened with dissolution.[58]

In 1990 one of the top Cuban economists pinpointed the domestic financial disequilibrium as among the most serious problems faced by Cuba.[59] The budgetary deficit has steadily increased since 1986, and in 1990 it was eight times higher than in 1985. (The state budget for 1991 was not published in the Cuban press for the first time since 1967–77.) State revenue is insufficient. More than half comes from the circulation tax, but it declined in 1987–88, reportedly due to a decrease in domestic output and import limitations. One-fourth of revenue comes from enterprise surpluses, but losses have been increasing; to reverse the situation, it is necessary to improve efficiency, and yet labor productivity declined 10% in 1986–89. On the expenditure side, the average wage was stagnant while productivity decreased, hence there is more money in circulation but fewer products available. In 1986–87 state subsidies to enterprises and for rationed consumer goods (sold below cost) increased almost twofold (from 362 to 678 million pesos) and were the major culprits of the budget deficit in 1987–88. (The total might be higher: in 1988 the province of Pinar del Rio alone received a subsidy of 280 million pesos, more than half due to enterprise losses.) The size of the subsidy in 1989–90 was not revealed, but it was said to be huge and largely covered by foreign exchange.[60] The increase of agricultural prices in 1992 has been justified for the following official reasons: (1) such prices have been kept very low for many years in spite of increases in the cost of inputs and imports (fertilizers, seeds, pesticides, herbicides), hence they are well below real costs; (2) state subsidies to cover the price gap, although reduced in 1980–81, steadily increased thereafter (the state subsidy for nonsugar agricultural products was 447 million pesos in 1991, excluding distribution costs); according to a survey conducted by the ministry of agriculture, 84% of agricultural products are subsidized; and (3) a portion of the subsidized agricultural products are used to feed animals in the private sector.[61] An article in a Cuban economic journal explains that budgetary deficits in socialist countries can be financed with domestic resources (population savings in fixed-term deposits), external debt, or/and printing currency. Since 1986, when Cuba stopped its hard-currency debt service, fresh credits have not been available. Soviet loans have stopped since 1992, and savings are relatively small. Thus deficit financing is made increasingly through printing additional currency. The latter must have been higher than growth in the economy and in savings accounts, thereby fueling inflation.[62]

Open unemployment in Cuba rose from 3.4% to 6% in 1981–88 and should be higher now due to the shutdown of enterprises and reductions in economic activities.[63] Unneeded workers (*sobrantes*) have two options: retraining or transferring (temporarily or permanently) to other "useful" jobs, particularly in agriculture. In the first case, the worker receives 70% of the corresponding salary, at a minimum of 100 pesos monthly. If the worker cannot be transferred due to lack of a job, he or she receives 100% of the salary in the first month and 60% in subsequent months, until a job is found (payments are stopped if the worker refuses a proper job offer). The government is also encouraging job swaps to get workers closer to their places of work, thus reducing transportation costs and time wasted on trips. Young graduates who cannot find jobs are placed in a "skilled labor reserve": middle-level technicians are paid 75 pesos monthly and go to retraining courses; university graduates can opt for continuation of their studies or retraining and be paid 130 pesos monthly, or wait for a job offer and receive 100 pesos monthly.[64] The level of frustration and disappointment among youth is rising as they are unable to get adequate jobs. Furthermore, as the surplus labor expands, the burden to the economy in terms of both the subsidy and the fall in labor productivity is becoming heavier.

The claim that the RP would reduce crime and corruption has not been borne out; conversely, the growing scarcity of consumer goods has become a fertile ground for robbery, black-marketing of goods and exchange of pesos for foreign currency, and even prostitution. Despite the introduction of harsh penal sanctions in 1988, there are many reports of people stealing food from state farms and cooperatives, assaulting warehouses and cafeterias, attacking trucks, and even stealing a huge container from the docks. Castro himself has denounced some of these crimes and requested that the army, the police, security forces, and groups of armed workers and peasants protect the food.[65] We have noted that new harsher measures against crime were implemented in 1992.

Policies to Confront the Crisis

Cuban Policies

These policies involve diversification of trade partners and exports, opening to foreign investment, search for alternative energy sources, and the Food Program (FP).[66]

The prospects of Cuba's replacing its former trade with Eastern Europe and the USSR by expanding trade with China as well as with developed and developing market economies are not promising, at least in the medium term. China cannot export to Cuba most of the capital goods, manufactures, and spare parts that Eastern Europe and the former USSR used to send. The increase in sugar buying by China is small, limited by that nation's growing self-sufficiency and other factors, and it has absorbed only a tiny fraction of the sugar surplus left by Cuba's former buyers in the vanished CMEA. Trade with Western Europe, Canada, and Japan steadily declined through the 1980s and particularly since 1986, due to lack of Cuba's salable exports and fresh credit; in addition, the European Community is a growing net exporter of sugar. In Asia, competition by Australia, Thailand, and other more efficient sugar producers, which also offer cheaper freights, is presenting a serious challenge to Cuba. Trade with Latin America is very small and has resulted in a deficit difficult to finance, as many potential partners are either sugar exporters or self-sufficient. Cuba's expansion of trade in the region is also obstructed by U.S. dominance, poor competitiveness of Cuban exports, and U.S. free trade agreements with Canada and Mexico. Foreign investment has been recently growing in Cuba, lured by more attractive conditions, but we lack data to measure its overall magnitude and economic impact. Finally, the United States is tightening the embargo on the island, and it is possible that U.S. subsidiaries abroad will be prohibited from trading and investing in Cuba.

A necessary condition for Cuba's reinsertion into the capitalist market is export diversification, a frustrated dream for almost 100 years of the Cuban Republic. But Cuba's potential for significantly expanding traditional and nontraditional exports is quite limited, at least in the medium run. Natural and technical barriers impede a substantial increase in sugar output well beyond the 1986–91 average output of 7.5 million tons, and the 1992 harvest is expected to be 5.8 to 6.5 million tons due to domestic and external constraints. The grandiose plans to triple nickel output have not materialized, and after a modest increase in output in 1988–89, there has been a decline due to the shutdown of a large new plant and the fuel shortage. The lack of advanced technology and the poor quality of Cuban nickel ore, combined with the fuel shortage, are serious obstacles. Output of tobacco leaf has oscillated with a tendency to decline, and production of the famous Havana cigars has halved—this before the major international buyer of Cuban tobacco ended its dealings, alleging a deterioration in quality. "Reexports" of Soviet oil, the main source of hard currency in the 1980s, ended in 1990.

The most promising sources of revenue are citrus, seafood, and biotechnological-medical exports, as well as tourism. In spite of dramatic increases in domestic output and export shares (ten and seven times), citrus and seafood face limitations: the low quality of citrus and strong competition in the world market, and the universalization of the maritime zone, combined with an aging fleet and fuel shortages for fishing boats. Both products suffered a significant decline in output in 1989. Reportedly, biotechnical and medical exports are rapidly increasing and appear to be most promising; however, we lack solid data on the profitability of this industry, quality of products, and value of total exports. Although biotechnical exports to the USSR were expanding fast, fierce competition in the world market will have to be overcome to make this a successful source of hard currency. Finally, tourism has the potential to become a dynamic source of revenue, but in 1990, yielded only 0.6% of GSP; optimistic plans project a four- to fivefold increase of tourists and revenue in 1991–95, but Cuba will have to substantially improve the quality of services to increase the rate of return of tourists, keep attracting foreign investors, and expand its world marketing to make that dream come true. The combination of additional annual revenue from new nontraditional exports plus tourism ($1.5 billion at best) is grossly insufficient to offset the annual losses in trade and aid resulting from the collapse of socialism (more than $6 billion). The island must develop an "export culture" to improve the quantity, assortment, quality, and stability of its exports, but to achieve that end it needs to transform domestic management, making it more responsive to world demand and prices.

The probabilities that in the medium term Cuba finds either domestic or external sources of oil to replace the 45% to 70% cut in Soviet supply are poor. Domestic oil output declined 31% in 1986–91, and Cuban crude is of poor quality. Despite various oil exploration/production contracts signed with international petroleum corporations, results are disappointing so far, and if good-quality oil in large quantities is found, it would take from four to six years to have oil produced. Cuba's nuclear plan in Juraguá is either paralyzed or progressing very slowly; it is doubtful that the first unit will start operating in the next few years. Production of alcohol from sugar is not an option due to the poor prospects for good crops in the immediate future. And the leaders of three major oil-exporting countries in Latin America have recently stated that they do not intend to export oil to Cuba at subsidized prices.

The Food Program (FP) attempts to make the provinces of Havana and Santiago self-sufficient in the production of tubers, vegetables, rice, plantains, bananas, beef, milk, poultry, eggs, and fish, as well as to increase the output of export crops (mainly sugar and citrus). The FP makes good sense, and it is urgently needed. What is questioned is the huge size of this program and its costs, the way in which it was designed and is being implemented, its unrealistic targets, and the underestimation of the severe limitations imposed by the worst crisis endured by the Revolution. For instance, FP goals are to increase output in 1991–95 from 14% to 121% in products that suffered declines of 1% to 15% in 1984–89, and to expand the area under irrigation in 1991–95 by 1 million hectares, more than the irrigated area developed in 1959–89. It is probable that the FP will increase output in some lines of production and in some provinces or municipalities; it might even reduce somewhat the foodstuff dependency of Havana and Santiago. But the overall FP targets are so ambitious that they are not feasible. The question then is whether the partial gains coming from the FP would justify its enormous investment of capital and human resources, and surpass as well the potential damage that such an ambitious program could inflict on the rest of the economy.

The Other Alternative: Market-Oriented Reform

Faced with the island's desperate need to reinsert itself in the world capitalist market, raise domestic efficiency, and improve consumption, in 1990 a few Cuban economists began to look at economic reform as the lesser of two evils. There was an ongoing but nonpublicized discussion of the possibility of combining a socialist framework with market mechanisms—which the Cubans rushed to clarify are not exclusive of capitalism. My conversations and debates in Havana in 1990 were held with a small group of academic economists and other social scientists, hence they had a limited scope. My impression, however, was that the debate did not center so much on whether or not to use market tools, but to what degree they should be employed and how to avoid their negative consequences. Two of my counterparts argued that if such mechanisms are ignored or repressed, they emerge anyway, as the black market demonstrates. Another point made was that the satisfaction of urgent needs of the population should be more important than the desire to curtail profiteering by a small groups that could help to meet those needs. Finally, there was the argument that if the state were unable to satisfy an urgent and important need, a regulated market or private activity should be allowed to fulfill it.[67]

In the fall of 1990, mid-level technicians were calling for privatization of personal services that the state is unable to provide, and the reintroduction of free peasant markets, production bonuses, and other mechanisms abolished or greatly reduced under the RP. Such technicians, however, did not want a global market reform, but small gradual changes to avoid further economic decline and promote some improvement.[68] A well-known Cuban economist told a U.S. journalist, "Why should the state concern itself with running things like ice cream stands and barber shops?" He went on to say that state taxi drivers offer bad service, do not take care of the cabs, and pocket part of the earnings, but if the state sold the cabs to the drivers, they would provide excellent service and take good care of the cars.[69]

Open-minded Cuban economists and technicians nevertheless harbor many reservations and fears about the use of market mechanisms, many of which have resulted from their observation of the unintended consequences of market reforms in Eastern Europe and the USSR. For instance, they see the private sector as capable of playing positive roles: eliminating the state monopoly and offering healthy competition to improve state efficiency. But there could be a snowball effect as the private sector demands increasing inputs, accumulates wealth, and presents a frontal challenge to the state. The disappearance or sharp reduction of the safety net is a major preoccupation: (1) high unemployment (apparently the Cubans have not discussed remedies such as unemployment compensation and retraining); (2) significant inequalities (one argument was that equality is the cement that keeps the Cuban people together, but when I rebutted that there were inequalities under socialism—in housing, access to special stores, automobiles—there was no reply); (3) price increases that would sharply reduce consumption of low-income groups (an interesting suggestion was to substitute subsidies to people for subsidies to goods); and (4) reduction of social benefits such as free education, health care, and social security. Private ownership of the means of production seemed to be a taboo, as it was never directly discussed.[70]

But the most important obstacle to a market-oriented reform in Cuba is

Castro's stern opposition even to the type of reform implemented in countries that still are socialist, like China. In numerous speeches, he has systematically rejected privatization of even small family enterprises, ownership by groups of workers, contracts of state farms and factories with families, free peasant markets, street vendors, and tiny producers, etc. Conversely, he has promised that the Revolution will progressively socialize more, battle against the remaining private farmers, and solve all economic problems through the state.[71]

Since 1990 Castro's speeches increasingly include attacks on individuals and groups of people inside Cuba who are "skeptical," "disaffected," "demoralized," "critical," or "defeatist." Economic reformers have become the president's target, as he has accused them of being "imperialist puppets," "political snipers," "fifth columnists," and "traitors," and threatens them with harsh retaliation. As already discussed, the 4th Party Congress laid to rest any illusion that there could be a market-oriented reform in Cuba, not even of the Chinese variant that has managed to combine political repression with economic progress. Castro's speeches in 1990–92 unequivocally show his aversion to any market reform, willingness to smash those who oppose him, and disposition to die entrenched in his ideas, taking the whole nation with him.[72]

And yet such reform is the only realistic alternative Cuba has to overcome the crisis because the old command-economy model has proved ineffective all over the world, and in Cuba specifically. Furthermore, without the enormous aid provided by the former USSR and CMEA, the probability of survival of such a model is virtually nil, even with the current economic strategy. Hence the forthcoming scenario is gloomy: gradual economic deterioration and increasing frustration and discontent of the people. The worsening situation could eventually create on the island the conditions required for the type of change that occurred in the USSR and Eastern Europe.

Throughout 1992 and the first half of 1993, Cuba moved to open its external sector, aggressively pursuing foreign investment and expanding hard-currency tourism. Nevertheless, the total amount of this capital and earnings appears to be relatively small: somewhere between $500 million and $1 billion cumulative in investment (although statistics are not available) and about $250 million in net revenue from tourism in 1992. On the other hand, in 1989–1993 Cuba's GSP declined at least one half, for a loss of about $13 billion, while imports declined to one fourth, for a loss of $6 billion. Obviously, investment and other hard-currency revenue represents only a fraction of those losses. Furthermore, by the end of the summer of 1993, the structure and organization of the domestic economy basically remained in state hands and centralized except for the few enterprises connected with the external sector. There has not been privatization in agriculture or industry or basic services, and government leaders assert that although they have accepted external capital under state control, they will not decollectivize the internal economy. In the summer of 1993 a team of Spanish economists visited Cuba, and Castro traveled to Colombia reportedly to seek advice on market-oriented reforms. But he fears that if he chooses that path, the prospects for losing economic and political control will increase. He probably will introduce minor changes, but resist structural market-oriented reforms in the domestic economy—unless he perceives that his regime is going to fall, in which case he might try a radical economic reform out of desperation.

Notes

1. See C. Mesa-Lago, *The Economy of Socialist Cuba: A Two Decade Appraisal* (Albuquerque: University of New Mexico Press, 1981) and "Cuba's Economic Counter-Reform (*Rectificación*): Causes, Policies and Effects," *The Journal of Communist Studies* 5:4 (December 1989): 98–139. This paper is based partly on two previous works of mine: "Economic Effects on Cuba of the Collapse of Socialism in USSR and Eastern Europe," and "Cuba's Economic Policies and Alternatives to Confront the Crisis," forthcoming in *Cuba After the Cold War*, University of Pittsburgh Press, 1993.
2. For divergent viewpoints on the RP, in addition to my works cited above, see: Mesa-Lago, "On Rectifying Errors of a Courteous Dissenter," *Cuban Studies* 20 (1990): 87–108, and "Rectification Round Two: An Answer to Eckstein's Rebuttal," *Cuban Studies* 21 (1991): 193–198; José Luis Rodríguez, "Aspectos económicos del proceso de rectificación," *Cuba Socialista* 44 (April–June 1990): 86–101; Susan Eckstein, "The Rectification of Errors or the Errors of the Rectification Process in Cuba," *Cuban Studies* 20 (1990): 67–85, and "More on the Cuban Rectification Process: Whose Errors?" *Cuban Studies* 21 (1991): 187–192; and Jorge Pérez-López, "The Cuban Economy: Rectification in a Changing World," *Cambridge Journal of Economics* 16 (1992): 113–126.
3. Discussions with Julio Carranza, Havana, meeting at CEA, July 11, 1990; Pedro Monreal and J. L. Rodríguez, Havana, meetings at CIEM, July 10, 1990.
4. "Resumen de los debates de la Asamblea Nacional," *Granma*, December 29, 1990, p. 4.
5. Central Committee of the Communist Party of Cuba, "On to the 4th Party Congress," *Granma Weekly Review* (hereafter *GWR*), March 25, 1990, p. 203; and "Resolución sobre el desarrollo económico," *Granma*, October 23, 1991, p. 6. Subsequent references in the text to 4th Congress resolutions are based on this source.
6. "El momento no es de teoría sino de resolver problemas" [interview with Joaquín Benavides], *Tribuna del Economista* 1:6 (November 1989): 16.
7. Mesa-Lago, "Cuba's Economic Policies."
8. "P'atrás ni para coger impulso (Entrevista con Darío Machado)," *Areíto*, 3:9 (June 1991): 27–28.
9. F. Castro, "Intervención sobre el mercado libre campesino en el IV Congreso," *Granma*, October 29, 1991, pp. 3–6; and "Cuba: Congreso elige . . . ," *El Nuevo Herald*, October 15, 1991, p. 4-A.
10. "Resolución sobre el desarrollo," p. 6; Gillian Gunn, presentation at UCLA Seminar on Cuba, Los Angeles, February 28, 1992.
11. Sara Mas Farías, interview with Idalberto León, *El Militante Comunista*, no. 4 (April 1990): 68–72; see also interview with Benavides.
12. Idalberto León, "El perfeccionamiento de un método: La planificación continua," *Tribuna del Economista* 1:8 (January 1990): 8–9.
13. "Resumen de los debates," p. 3.

236   Carmelo Mesa-Lago

14. "Resolución que faculta al Comité Central," *Granma*, October 23, 1991, p. 6.
15. For Castro's statements, see my "Cuba's Economic Counter-Reform," pp. 109–110. Other sources are Alma Hernández, "La planificación como mecanismo de dirección de la economía en Cuba," *Economía y Desarrollo* 18:4 (July–August 1988): 6–15; interview with Benavides, p. 17; Mas Farías, pp. 68–72; and "El contrato económico en los resultados empresariales," *Tribuna del Economista* 1:11 (April 1990): 4.
16. F. Castro, "En la clausura de la decisión diferida del III Congreso del Partido Comunista de Cuba," *Cuba Socialista* 25 (1987): 20.
17. CNSDE, "Decisiones adoptadas sobre algunos elementos del Sistema de Dirección de la Economía," March 1988, and "Decisiones . . . II," June 1988; quoted by J. L. Rodríguez, "Aspectos económicos," p. 95. (He does not give any details about the document's content.) The journal *Cuba Economía Planificada* (January–March 1989: 145–201) published an article on those decisions, but provided little concrete data.
18. C. R. Rodríguez, interview, Havana, July 12, 1990.
19. Comisión Nacional del SDE, *Normas sobre la unión y la empresa estatal* (La Habana: April 1988).
20. Miguel A. Figueras, "Empresas estatales latinoamericanas y la amenaza de las privatizaciones," La Habana, December 1989; interview with Figueras, Havana, July 11, 1990; and interview with Benavides.
21. Julio Casas Regueiro et al., *A problemas viejos soluciones nuevas: El perfeccionamiento de las empresas del MINFAR* (La Habana: Editora Política, 1990).
22. F. Castro, "Discurso de Clausura del Congeso de la FEU," *Granma* (Suplemento Especial), December 31, 1990, p. 7.
23. Alberto Pozo, "A nado en nuevas aguas," *Bohemia*, July 20, 1990, pp. 20–25; and interview with Benavides, pp. 18–20.
24. José Yanes, "Hay que crearles condiciones al costo," *Tribuna del Economista* 1:4 (September 1989): 11.
25. For Cuban sources, see Mesa-Lago, "Cuba's Economic Counter-Reform," pp. 116–118, and "On Rectifying Errors," pp. 104–105; see also *GWR*, November 12, 1989, pp. 4, 12.
26. *GWR*, October 15, 1989, pp. 2–4 and December 11, 1989, p. 12; F. Castro "Speech at the Closing of the 16th Congress of the CTC," *GWR*, February 11, 1990, p. 4, and "Speech at the Ceremony to Present the Blas Roca Contingent" *GWR*, June 17, 1990, p. 3; and *Granma*, August 13, 1990, p. 6.
27. Interview with Benavides, pp. 18–19.
28. "Special Plenum of Central Committee," *GWR*, February 25, 1990, p. 9.
29. "Principales líneas de trabajo del SDE," *Trabajadores*, May 23, 1990, p. 6.
30. F. Castro, "Discurso en la Inauguración del IV Congreso del Partido Comunista de Cuba," *Granma*, October 14, 1991, pp. 7–12. He repeated these ideas in "Discurso de Clausura del V Congreso del Sindicato de Trabajadores Agropecuarios," *Granma*, November 26, 1991, p. 5.
31. José León, "Una llave que gotea," *Alma Mater*, July 1990, pp. 23–27.
32. C. R. Rodríguez, interview; and interview with Benavides, p. 18.
33. José León, pp. 23–27.
34. Interview with Benavides, p. 20; and *Tribuna del Economista* 1:11 (April 1990): p. 5.
35. Armando Pérez Betancourt et al., *Cacería de brujas* (La Habana: Editorial Ciencias Sociales, 1990).
36. Soledad Cruz, "Eliminar las causas de los azares," *Juventud Rebelde*, July 8, 1990, p. 2.
37. Andrew Zimbalist and Claes Brundenius, *The Cuban Economy: Measurement and Analysis of Social Performance* (Baltimore: Johns Hopkins University Press, 1989), pp. 140, 142; Eckstein, "The Rectification," pp. 71–72; and J. L. Rodríguez, "Commentary" at the International Congress on Cuba, University of Pittsburgh, April 27–28, 1992.

38. Mas Farías, interview with Gerardo Trueba, Havana, July 11, 1990; and José León.
39. Mas Farías.
40. "Trade Unions Actively Participating in the Rectification Process," *GWR*, October 8, 1989, p. 3.
41. "Substitución de importaciones," *Bohemia*, July 13, 1990, pp. 25–26; interview with Benavides, p. 18; and conversations at a seminar on Cuba at the University of Warwick, May 11–13, 1989.
42. Mesa-Lago, "Cuba's Economic Counter-Reform," pp. 102–103, and "On Rectifying Errors," p. 106; *Tribuna del Economista* 1:5 (October 1989): 9; *GWR*, July 22, 1990, p. 9; *Granma*, January 8, 1991, p. 3, January 15, p. 3, and January 17, p. 4; and Castro, "Discurso en la Clausura del Congreso," p. 4.
43. "¿Qué piensa el pueblo de su poder?" *Bohemia*, July 6, 1990, p. 6.
44. "Cuba lucha contra corrupción oficial," *El Nuevo Herald*, November 3, 1990, p. 4A.
45. "Fidel en la clausura de la Asamblea Provincial del Partido en La Habana," *Granma*, February 26, 1991, p. 3.
46. "Elaboran proyectos legislativos en la Asamblea Nacional," *Granma*, December 27, 1991, pp. 1–3.
47. This section is a summary of Mesa-Lago's "Economic Effects on Cuba."
48. The first view is from two Cuban economists who participated in a LASA-sponsored seminar held in Havana, CIEM, July 10, 1990; the second view is from Carlos Aldana, "Anyone Who Wants Can Leave the Country," *Granma International*, July 21, 1991, p. 2.
49. Annual targets in the economic plans for 1986–90 were published in *Granma*, January 12, 1986, p. 8 and December 29, 1986; *Gaceta Oficial*, December 30, 1987, p. 96; *Granma*, December 24, 1988, p. 3, and December 26, 1988, p. 4; and *Gaceta Oficial*, December 30, 1989, pp. 1, 110.
50. Mesa-Lago, "Economic Effects on Cuba."
51. "Siege Economy," *Oxford Analytica*, February 5, 1992; and Andrew Zimbalist in "Cuba and the Future," Donald E. Schultz, ed., U.S. Army War College, January 16, 1992, p. 3, and quoted by Richard Boudreaux, "Can Castro Weather the Storm?" *Los Angeles Times*, April 6, 1992, p. A-8.
52. Summarized from Mesa-Lago, "Economic Effects on Cuba."
53. F. Castro, "Discurso en la Clausura del Congreso de la FEU," pp. 2–3, "Discurso en la Inauguración del IV Congreso," pp. 7–12; and "Discurso en la Clausura del VI Foro Nacional de Piezas de Repuesto," *Granma*, December 18, 1991, pp. 3–6.
54. Mesa-Lago, "Economic Effects on Cuba," Table 9; F. Orgambides, "La tristeza hace presa entre los cubanos," *El País*, August 5, 1991, p. 9; and Ana E. Santiago, "Libreta en Cuba abastece poco," *El Nuevo Herald*, January 19, 1992.
55. "Lucha contra el auge del mercado negro," *El Nuevo Herald*, November 22, 1991, p. 3-A; and Anne Marie O'Connor, "Fidel's Last Resort," *Esquire* (March 1992): 104, 156.
56. Excess money in circulation from *Anuario Estadístico de Cuba 1986* to *1988*; and Castro, "Discurso en la Clausura del Congreso de la FEU," p. 4.
57. Ramón Martínez Carrera, "Cuba: Crecimiento económico e inestabilidad externa," *Economía y Desarrollo* 1 (January–February 1990): 26–28; and Estela Espinosa and Dinio Quintana, "Consideraciones acerca de la evolución de ingresos y los gastos monetarios de la población," *Compendio de Investigaciones* 7 (August 1989): 129.
58. "Nuevas medidas del Banco de Ahorro Popular," *Granma*, February 11, 1992, p. 2.
59. José Luis Rodríguez, "Los cambios en la política económica (1986–1989)," Washington, D.C., Woodrow Wilson Center, 1990, p. 19.
60. Mesa-Lago, "Cuba's Economic Counter-Reform," p. 122; Eugenio Balari, "The Supply of Consumer Goods in Cuba," in S. Halebsky and John M. Kirk, eds., *Transformation and Struggle: Cuba Faces the 1990s* (New York: Praeger, 1990), p. 164; Rafael Calcines, "Rec-

238   Carmelo Mesa-Lago

tificación: El camino es aún largo," *Tribuna del Economista* 1:4 (September 1989): 12; "Radio Rebelde," Havana, January 25, 1990; and Joaquín Infante, "El excedente económico y los ingresos del presupuesto," *Tribuna del Economista* 1:2 (May 1990): 2.

61. "Adecuación de precios agrícolas a los costos de producción," *Granma*, February 14, 1992, p. 4.

62. Joaquín Infante, "El déficit presupuestario y la inflación," *Tribuna del Economista* 1:3 (August 1989): 9. Infante does not specifically mention Cuba, but his discussion obviously applies to the island.

63. Mesa-Lago, "Cuba's Economic Counter-Reform."

64. "Precisiones acerca de las implicaciones laborales y sociales de las últimas medidas acordadas," *Granma*, February 1, 1992, p. 2.

65. "Fidel en la reunión del Comité Ejecutivo," p. 3; Castro, "Intervención sobre el mercado libre," pp. 3–6.

66. This section is a summary of Mesa-Lago's "Cuba's Economic Policies."

67. This is my interpretation of views expressed by several Cuban social scientists in two roundtables held in Havana in July 1990.

68. Reported by Fulton Armstrong, member of the U.S. Interest Section in Havana, conference in Washington, D.C., October 19, 1990.

69. José Balari, quoted by O'Connor, p. 57.

70. See note 67.

71. F. Castro, "Closing Speech at the Second National Meeting of Production Cooperatives," *GWR*, June 1, 1986, p. 3; "Speech to Close Pedagogy 90 Congress," *GWR*, February 5, 1990, p. 2; "Speech at the Session Closing the 16th Congress of the CTC," *GWR*, February 11, 1990, p. 4; and "Fidel en la Clausura de la Asamblea Provincial," p. 3.

72. F. Castro, "Speech at the Session Closing the 16th," p. 4; "Speech at the Closing of the 5th Congress of the FMC," *GWR*, March 18, 1990, p. 11; *GWR*, March 25, 1990, p. 2; "30th Anniversary CDRs," *GWR*, October 7, 1990, pp. 1,9; "Discurso en la Clausura del Congreso," p. 6; and "Discurso en la Clausura del IV Congreso del PCC," pp. 8–10.

Part III
The Postdirigiste Transitions

CHAPTER 9

Latin American Adjustment
and Economic Reforms:
Issues and Recent Experience

Patricio Meller

Latin American Overview

The 1980s have been called "the lost decade" in Latin America. Latin American average annual economic growth rates were 5.7% for the previous two decades (1960–80); Latin American gross domestic product grew by 1.3% per year during 1980–90. Given the relatively high population growth rates (2.2% during the 1980s; 2.5% during the 1960s and 1970s), the average Latin American income per capita level of 1990 is 9% lower than the one of 1980; in some countries like Argentina, Bolivia, Peru, and Venezuela, the 1990 income per capita level is even lower than the 1970 level (table 9.1).

During the 1980s, most Latin American countries experienced sharp internal and external disequilibria; the time sequence shows an inverse relationship between these two types of disequilibria, that is, the cost of reducing external disequilibrium has been generally associated with an increased internal disequilibrium.

Several indicators of external disequilibrium show the following pattern (table 9.2): At the beginning of the 1980s, most Latin American countries had a trade deficit; the average (1980–81) trade deficit for the region was 1.4% of GDP, and there were a few countries such as Argentina and Chile with trade deficit figures larger than 4%. For the same period, current account deficits were much larger; the average current account deficit for the region was 5.1%, with many countries having deficit figures larger than 6%. Given the drastic contraction of external credit, current account deficits had to be deeply reduced by the end of the decade; Latin America's current account deficit reached less than 1% by 1990. Moreover, the region began to generate large trade surpluses, for example, 8.5% in 1990. The external debt problem affected most Latin American countries during the whole decade; by 1990, many countries such as Argentina, Bolivia, Brazil, and Peru showed an external debt stock/export coefficient larger than 3.

242   Patricio Meller

TABLE 9.1 Economic growth and income per capita in Latin America

| | Economic growth (annual average, %) | | | Income per capita | | | Population (millions) |
	1960–70	1970–80	1980–90	(1980 = 100) 1970	1990	US$/capita[a] 1990	1990
Argentina	4.3	2.6	−1.2	91.3	77.2	2461	32.3
Bolivia	5.6	3.9	−0.1	88.0	76.8	552	7.2
Brazil	6.1	8.6	1.6	55.3	94.5	1973	150.4
Chile	4.2	2.5	2.9	91.6	112.3	2075	13.2
Colombia	5.2	5.4	3.7	74.3	117.5	1859	33.0
Mexico	7.0	6.5	1.6	71.5	92.8	2425	85.1
Peru	5.0	3.9	−1.1	89.6	71.7	1041	21.6
Venezuela	6.0	1.8	0.3	118.0	78.6	3746	19.7
Latin America	5.7	5.6	1.3	73.6	91.1	1994	423.2

Sources: CEPAL 1990 and World Bank.

Note: The eight Latin American countries selected represent more than 85% of the Latin American GDP, exports, and population.

a. World Bank income per capita of year 1985 has been used as a benchmark; then, real output per capita of CEPAL plus U.S. CPI has been used for updating for year 1990.

On the other hand, indicators of internal disequilibrium exhibit the following pattern (table 9.3): Several Latin American countries showed increasing and even explosive inflation rates throughout the 1980s; some countries that had a two-digit annual inflation rate during 1980–81 experienced three-digit and four-digit annual rates by the end of the 1980s (Argentina, Brazil, Peru).[1] Other Latin American countries such as Bolivia, Chile, Colombia, and Mexico have been successful in controlling inflation. The trend of Latin American unemployment during the 1980s is mixed; in some countries (Argentina, Peru, and Venezuela), unemployment has increased significantly, while the opposite trend is observed in Chile and Mexico. Most Latin American countries show a critical fiscal deficit situation (including interest payments on debt) during the 1980s, with deficits larger than 6% (and even 10%) in a few years[2;] only Chile, Colombia, and Venezuela had reached a balanced fiscal budget by the end of the decade.

In the following sections, using country experiences selectively, some of the following issues will be examined: What are the difficulties that Latin American countries have faced in the reduction of the fiscal deficit? What explains the success and failure of anti-inflationary stabilization programs? How were trade deficits transformed into surpluses? What are the problems related to increase investment and growth resumption? What are the social costs related to the required economic reforms?

TABLE 9.2 Indicators of external disequilibrium for Latin America (1980–90)[a]

	Trade deficit[b] (% GDP)			Current account deficit (% GDP)			External debt/exports (N°)		
	1980–81	1982–84	1985–90	1980–81	1982–84	1985–90	1980–81	1982–84	1985–90
Argentina	1.8	−8.5	−8.3	5.7	3.2	1.7	3.0	4.8	5.5
Bolivia	−1.8	−4.7	0.0	5.7	5.0	10.5	2.5	3.6	4.9
Brazil	0.8	−4.3	−5.9	2.6	0.9	0.3	3.2	4.0	3.7
Chile	7.1	−6.1	−8.7	12.6	8.2	3.5	2.5	4.1	3.0
Colombia	1.9	3.3	−4.3	3.1	7.1	0.4	1.6	2.6	2.4
Mexico	2.9	−9.4	−9.4	3.1	−0.7	1.0	2.5	3.0	3.5
Peru	−0.5	−2.9	−2.3	4.8	5.3	5.7	2.2	3.2	4.1
Venezuela	−8.1	−9.7	−17.4	−8.5	−4.4	−1.4	1.5	2.0	2.7
Latin America	1.4	−5.9	−7.9	5.1	2.2	1.2	2.4	3.4	3.5

Source: CEPAL.
a. Percentages are measured with variables expressed in US$ 1980.
b. Including goods and services.

TABLE 9.3 Indicators of internal disequilibrium in selected Latin American countries, 1980–90

	Annual inflation[a] (%)			Unemployment[b] (%)			Public sector deficit[c] (% GDP)		
	1980–81	1982–84	1985–90	1980–81	1982–84	1985–90	1980–81	1982–84	1985–90
Argentina	108.3	406.9	564.2	3.6	4.7	6.4	11.5	14.9	5.8
Bolivia	24.5	628.7	151.7	8.4	8.8	8.6	7.7	16.4	6.3
Brazil	93.3	157.6	566.4	7.1	6.7	4.1	6.6	4.8	5.1
Chile	19.9	22.4	21.0	11.5	19.0	11.0	-3.4	3.6	2.2
Colombia	26.6	19.5	25.5	9.0	11.5	11.8	2.9	7.1	1.8
Mexico	29.2	78.9	65.6	4.4	5.5	3.7	11.3	11.8	14.5
Peru	66.6	101.9	746.2	8.8	9.5	7.3	6.6	9.7	4.5
Venezuela	15.2	10.9	33.2	6.7	10.9	10.7	-0.3	3.1	-4.7

Source: CEPAL.

a. Geometric average values of December–December figures. If the 1987–90 period is used for Bolivia, annual inflation is 16.6%. If the 1988–90 period is used for Argentina and Brazil, annual inflation values are 1,424% and 1,435% respectively.

b. Urban unemployment. See CEPAL for specific cities included in each country.

c. It includes public debt interest payments. For specific references, see tables 9.6; 9.4; 9.5.

Closing the External and Internal Disequilibria

The traditional view relates the external disequilibrium to the internal one; the excess of domestic expenditure (absorption) over national income generates a deficit in the current account. Standard policy prescriptions suggest the combination of expenditure-reducing policies (adjusting expenditure to income restriction) and output-expenditure switching policies through relative price changes (for example, a devaluation would increase the production of tradables while discouraging tradables consumption, helping in this way to reduce the external disequilibrium).

Moreover, if the private sector budget is in equilibrium (or its expenditure–income deficit is relatively small), a fiscal deficit becomes the main factor generating the external disequilibrium. Then tight fiscal policy complemented by a devaluation become the policy package recommended for solving the external and internal disequilibria; furthermore, the complementary nature of these policies has been pointed out. To transform the nominal devaluation into a real one, it is necessary to have a contractionary fiscal policy to avoid an inflationary outcome, which would erode the real effect of the devaluation.

Recent Latin American experience demonstrates that there are three distinct problems with this standard view. The first includes the possibility that a nonsustainable external disequilibrium could coexist with a public sector showing an important surplus; in this case, the private sector expenditure–income deficit is generating the disequilibria. In Chile, the public sector had an annual surplus of the order of 2% during 1978–81, while the current account deficit was increasing, reaching almost 15% in 1981 (Meller 1990).

The second problem is related to the difficulties associated with a reduction of the fiscal deficit. In the short run, fiscal deficit reduction would crucially depend on the contraction of government expenditures; however, this situation is aggravated when there has to be an accommodation of increased external debt service. In other words, when multilateral organizations (the IMF and World Bank) assign first priority to full and punctual external debt service, and when there are increasing international interest rates, this fact increases the magnitude of the existing fiscal deficit (see table 9.4); then, stressing a drastic reduction of the overall fiscal deficit, independent of the level of contraction of government expenditures, generates a cumbersome political problem; that is, how much and how fast can government expenditures be reduced? This is the implicit discussion behind the alternative definitions of the fiscal deficit—primary, operational, and real (including internal and external debt interests—and (nominal) public sector borrowing requirements.[3]

The third problem is related to the fiscal difficulties (or benefits) generated by a devaluation when there exists an external debt service. Given the

TABLE 9.4   Public sector debt interest payments for selected Latin American countries (% of GDP)

	Total interest payments			External interest payments		
	1980–81	1982–84	1985–89	1980–81	1982–84	1985–89
Argentina	5.5	7.9	4.2[a]	1.5	4.6	3.6[a]
Bolivia	5.9[b]	13.0[c]	8.0	5.9[b]	13.0[c]	8.0
Brazil	3.8	6.1	5.7	1.8	2.8	2.4
Chile	1.5	3.6	4.1[d]			
Colombia	0.7	2.0	3.4[a]			
Mexico	4.4	11.1	14.6[d]	2.2	4.7	4.5[d]
Peru	5.8	6.5	5.5[d]			
Venezuela	4.1	5.3	5.6[d]			

Source: Barandiarán (1988) for Argentina, Chile, Colombia, Mexico, Peru and Venezuela.
Morales, J. A. 1991. "Determinantes del déficit del sector público en Bolivia," Serie Política Fiscal N°9, CEPAL, Santiago.
Morales (1991) for Bolivia; Damill, Fanelli, and Frenkel (1991) for Brazil.
a. 1985–87.
b. 1980–82.
c. 1983–84.
d. 1985–86.

international capital market situation, Latin American governments have to make an external transfer to meet external debt service requirements; for this purpose, they require foreign exchange. When the public sector is not an exporter (i.e., there are no state enterprises exporting goods), an internal transfer of foreign exchange from private agents to the government is required. Then, when a devaluation is implemented, there is a corresponding increase in the magnitude of this internal transfer, and in this way there is an augmentation of government expenditures; that is, a devaluation *reduces* the fiscal deficit. Moreover, economic authorities face the additional problem of sterilizing the acquisition of foreign exchange; this is one of the factors related to the increase of domestic public debt. The opposite situation is generated when there exists publicly held export firms (for example, petroleum in Mexico and Venezuela, and copper in Chile); in this case one tool, the (real) devaluation, helps simultaneously to reduce the fiscal deficit and the external disequilibrium. In other words, the existence of public export firms facilitates the internal transfer problem; moreover, the devaluation acts like a tax instrument increasing government revenues (see table 9.5). Furthermore, it is relatively easy to sterilize the monetary impact generated by the foreign exchange of public export firms without increasing public debt; a special stabilization fund could be used.

TABLE 9.5   Fiscal revenues provided by export public firms (% of GDP)

	1980–81	1982–84	1985–90
Chile (copper)	8.5	8.0	15.0
Mexico (petroleum)	7.8	14.1	11.1[b]
Venezuela[a] (petroleum)	18.5	17.4	12.8[c]

Sources: Romaguera (1991) for Chile; Ortiz and Noriega (1990) for Mexico; Velázquez (1992) for Venezuela.

a. From 1983–87 it includes exchange rate profits, which were (annual averages): 5.6% (GDP) for 1983–84 and 4.6% (GDP) for 1985–87.

b. 1985–89.

c. 1985–87.

The initial conditions related to the magnitude of the fiscal deficit at the beginning of the 1980s (prior to the external debt shock) plus the two problems mentioned above—the external transfer (accommodation of increased debt service) and the internal transfer (the negative relationship between devaluation and fiscal expenditures)—are behind the difficult stabilization experiences and inflationary price explosions observed in several countries of Latin America.

Policy Reforms

The so-called Washington consensus stresses the following policy reforms (Williamson 1990)[4:] (1) State reforms that include: (a) Fiscal discipline (i.e., the fiscal deficit should not surpass the 1%–2% (GDP) range). To achieve this goal in the short run, the reduction of government expenditures (in real and relative terms) is most efficient. On the other hand, a tax reform should be oriented toward increasing its efficiency in providing revenues to the government; for this purpose a broad tax base with low marginal tax rates is required. (b) Privatization of state enterprises, as the private sector is considered much more efficient as a producer than the public sector. Moreover, the existence of fewer public firms will make it easier to achieve the objective of fiscal discipline. (2) Liberalization and deregulation reforms that would promote domestic competition; these include: (a) Domestic capital market liberalization, which would imply free interest rates; real interest rates should be positive but moderate. In this context, supervision of financial institutions is recommended. (b) Trade liberalization, where quantitative restrictions and discretionary measures should be replaced by tariffs; furthermore, tariffs should be reduced. (c) Positive treatment to foreign investment that provides capital, skills, and know-how. (3) High and stable real exchange rate to increase international competitiveness for export promotion.

Let us examine the issues involved in the implementation of some of these reforms; the scope of Latin American policy reforms will also be reviewed.

Fiscal Reform

The key issue in this respect is how to reduce fiscal deficits larger than 5%. Let us use a simple decomposition analysis of the fiscal deficit to examine the performance of several Latin American countries. Using $f = (T - G)/Y$ as the percentage of the fiscal deficit with respect to GDP (Y), where G and T are government expenditures and tax revenues respectively, then, by differentiation, df will be the change observed in f: $df = fY' - \alpha_T \xi_{TY} Y' + \alpha_G G'$, where Y' and G' are the GDP and government expenditure growth rates, α_G and α_T are the GDP government and tax revenue shares, ξ_{TY} is the income tax elasticity. In the reduction of f there is a contribution of three distinct factors: government expenditure contraction, the positive contribution of taxes (mixture of the tax system and economic growth), and a third element that combines the initial conditions (the initial level of the deficit) and economic growth.

Let us assume that the initial fiscal deficit is 6% (GDP), $f = -6\%$. Standard Latin American IMF adjustment programs have used a simple rule for fiscal deficit reduction: "cut (in one year) the fiscal deficit to half" (see Ground 1984); in this case, $df = 3\%$. Using $\alpha_G = 26\%$, $\alpha_T = 20\%$, $\xi_{TY} = 1$, and assuming that the economic growth rate is 4%, then, employing the df expression, the required government expenditure contraction becomes -7.5%. More than 60% of the reduction of the fiscal deficit is related to government expenditure contraction.

The previous calculation underestimates the effective reduction of government expenditures that had to be implemented by Latin American economies. If the required increased external debt service is added, which introduces pressures for expenditure enlargement, then the effective primary government expenditure contraction becomes[5]: $G_P = (G' - \alpha_S S')/\alpha_{GP}$, where S' is the growth rate of external debt services, α^S and α^{GP} are GDP shares of external debt service and primary government expenditures. Assuming that α_S increases from 2% to 3%, then G_P becomes -9.5%, the required real contraction of (primary) government expenditure is close to -10%.

Table 9.6 provides information related to the performance of the Latin American public sector during the 1980s. Latin American governments have had to impose the fiscal discipline principle; at the end of the 1980s most Latin American economies show primary fiscal surpluses. In spite of this fact, many governments face a critical fiscal disequilibrium; when public sector debt interests are considered, some countries (Argentina, Bolivia, Brazil, Mexico, and Peru) still have operational deficits around 5% (see table 9.3).

TABLE 9.6 Government expenditure and revenues (% of GDP)

	Public sector deficit[a]			Government expenditures[b]			Tax revenues		
	1980–81	1982–84	1985–89	1980–81	1982–84	1985–89	1980–81	1982–84	1985–89
Argentina	6.1	7.7	1.6	21.6	23.1	22.8	19.7	17.6	20.7
Bolivia	3.2	11.3	2.0	31.5	22.8	22.6	9.4	4.2	10.8
Brazil	2.8	−1.2	−0.6	12.5	11.5	13.5	24.7	24.1	23.0
Chile	−5.1	−0.1	−1.9	12.4	11.1	9.1	26.1	23.4	23.0
Colombia	2.2	5.2	−1.6	8.8	8.9	7.9	12.2	11.4	15.7
Mexico	6.9	0.8	−0.9	7.1	7.3	7.6	17.5	18.2	15.7
Peru	0.8	3.2	−1.0	35.4	35.5	29.1	16.4	13.6	12.5
Venezuela	−4.2	−2.3	−5.4	15.0	15.2	13.7	28.7	23.3	17.9c

Sources: Same as table 9.4 and 9.5—IMF for rest of tax revenue, figures (Argentina, Chile, Colombia, Peru).
a. Excluding public debt interest payments.
b. Including public consumption excluding social security transfers and public debt interests payments.
c. 1985–87.

Government expenditures (excluding social security transfers and interest payments) were reduced throughout the decade by 9% in Bolivia, 6% in Peru, 3% in Chile, and around 1% in Colombia and Venezuela. If the GDP share of these government expenditures is considered to be around 15%, a reduction of a 1% corresponds to a 6.7% contraction of expenditures. When these government expenditures were reduced, it was done abruptly (independent of their magnitude); in most cases, this type of government contraction persisted.

Tax revenues (direct and indirect taxes) experienced erosion in those countries given accelerating inflation; for example, the Peruvian economy shows a 4% tax revenue reduction during the decade. Capital flight is another factor influencing tax revenues. With the exception of Bolivia, only a few things were done with respect to tax reform in Latin America; Williamson's summary (1990) shows that Mexico eliminated corporate tax loopholes, Brazil perfected financial assets income indexation, Chile and Colombia broadened the tax base, and Argentina and Venezuela started to discuss tax reforms. In Bolivia a special gasoline tax (1985) and the value-added tax (1986) were introduced; gasoline taxes provided 75% of total taxes (or 8% of GDP) at the end of 1985; (Bolivian) government tax revenues increased 7% (GDP) between 1984 and 1989. During the Latin American adjustment efforts, economic reforms were oriented toward a reduction of the role of the state and the government; therefore, tax reforms were in general excluded from the agenda, to avoid a negative effect on the dynamic role of the private sector on the recovery and growth process.

When government consumption expenditures are difficult to reduce significantly and tax revenues cannot be increased, fiscal disequilibrium adjustment involves a contraction of public investment on the one side, and to "increase" government revenues, accelerating inflation or privatization.

Anti-inflation Stabilization Programs

Latin American governments faced a very difficult situation: they had to correct a sharp fiscal disequilibrium while the domestic social situation was deteriorating; moreover, tax revenues were diminishing and debt service (external and internal) was increasing. Furthermore, external credits to finance public deficits were not available.[6] This complex dilemma is behind the dramatic high inflation and hyperinflation that Latin America experienced in the 1980s.

The traditional orthodox stabilization program is based on the idea that inflation is essentially a monetary phenomenon: excessive money growth to finance the fiscal deficit generates inflation. Restrictive fiscal and monetary policies are seen as the recipe for stopping inflation. Orthodox programs have been applied many times in the same country and in many Latin American countries during more than two decades, generating high costs and only a partial and temporary reduction of inflation. The Brazilian experience at the beginning of the 1980s is a good example of an orthodox program failure. During 1980–82, Brazilian annual inflation was around 100%; an IMF standby fiscal and monetary program was implemented during 1983 with the following outcome: the annual inflation rate increased to 200% in 1983 and 1984, while the operational deficit was reduced from 7.3% in 1982 to 2.7% in 1984 (the primary fiscal deficit of 1.9% in 1982 was transformed into a fiscal *surplus* of 4.1% in 1984; see Damill, Fanelli, and Frenkel 1991). These strange results led some Latin American economists to arrive at a strange conclusion: budget deficits and inflation were unrelated (see Cardoso and Helwege 1992, for specific details on the Brazilian and Peruvian economic discussion).

The heterodox view states that Latin American inflation has two components:[7] an original or fundamental one, such as a fiscal deficit or an external shock, which originates the inflationary process, and an inertial component that sustains price increases. Two factors explain the existence of inertial inflation:[8] indexation and expectations. The outcome is that agents forecast that future inflation will at least equal present inflation. When inflation is at the three-digit level, it is believed that the inertial component is much more influential than the fundamental component. For this reason, heterodox stabilization programs have stressed the importance of stopping the inertial component of inflation, often using the convenient tool of a generalized price control. In short, even when the government announces the implementation of a coherent stabilization macro program eliminating the fiscal deficit and reducing monetary expansion, it will not be advantageous to any agent to be the first to stop price increases; the generalized price control becomes the coordinating mechanism making all agents act simultaneously in their price behavior (Dornbusch and Simonsen 1987).

Heterodox stabilization programs implemented in Latin America (Argentina, Austral Plan, 1985; Peru, Inti Plan ,1985; Brazil, Cruzado Plan, 1985) had the following features:[9] (1) A generalized control of prices, wages, exchange rates, and public utility prices. (2) A tight fiscal program oriented toward a reduction of the fiscal deficit.[10] (3) A monetary reform, which had a special contractual debt conversion to avoid wealth transfers between creditors and debtors while the economy goes abruptly from high inflation (15% to 20% per month) to low inflation (1% to 2% per month); moreover, a new currency was introduced that suppressed three or six zeros of the old one. (4) An expansionary monetary policy to avoid sharp increases in the real interest rate, and to accommodate the (domestic currency) monetization of the economy; in this way, a higher seigniorage and a lower real interest rate would help to reduce the fiscal deficit.

These three heterodox stabilization programs were highly successful in reducing inflation in the short run (over two to three quarters; see Ocampo 1987; Bruno et al. 1988); moreover, it looked like the elimination of inertial inflation was a low-cost operation, inducing high growth rates very quickly; but on the other hand, the trade balance deteriorated quite fast, generating an unsustainable external disequilibrium. In short, heterodox stabilization programs worked in the short run, breaking the high inflationary spiral and gaining two to three quarters of crucial time; the big failure of these programs is related to the belief that the short-run success in price reduction (due to the generalized price control) had solved the long-run inflationary problem (i.e., inertial inflation was gone), and not much was left to be done. The initial success could have been used to introduce very quickly the deep reforms required to address the fundamental causes (the overall public sector deficit) contributing to inflation.[11]

The 1987 (December) Mexican stabilization program is an example of a successful heterodox program. A key component of this anti-inflationary package was the political agreement by three key agents (government, entrepreneurs, workers) in an income policy program ("Economic Solidarity Pact") that included (Ortiz and Noriega 1990; Ros 1992): a specific de-indexation mechanism (equivalent at the beginning to a freeze) for wages, public tariffs, and the exchange rate, while there was simultaneously an explicit voluntary agreement by entrepreneurs to avoid price increases. In addition there were specific public expenditure austerity measures complemented by a tax reform[12]; due to these measures, the primary fiscal surplus increased by 2.5% of GDP during the following years (1988–89). The outcome of this heterodox program was a reduction of the annual inflation rate from 159% (1987) to 18% (1989); at the same time annual GDP growth rates were 1.3% in 1988 and higher than 3% in 1989–90. The successful stabilization program has provided the political support to start deep structural reforms (liberalization of the external sector and privatization). It has been a general characteristic in Latin America that government popularity increases considerably when monthly inflation is reduced; this fact provides the scope for introducing economic reforms, but there should be care to avoid price-destabilizing effects.

The successful end of Bolivian hyperinflation in 1985 is being used as the key example for the implementation of a neo-orthodox stabilization program. Following Sargent (1982), a hyperinflation is mainly caused by a regime in which a large deficit is financed by money creation; then, if there is a change of regime in which the government is firmly committed to balancing the fiscal budget and stemming money creation, hyperinflation will disappear without much cost. The new feature with respect to the traditional orthodox view are the elements that have to be used to convince economic agents that there has truly been a change of regime.

The key components of the Bolivian program were (Sachs 1986; Morales 1987): (1) A drastic contractionary fiscal and monetary program. Public employment was cut by 10%; a nominal wage freeze, which generated a 60% real wage reduction in one month, was another tool to encourage voluntary public employment reduction; public investment was frozen for a full year. The fiscal and public firms' budget is balanced on a cash-flow basis; public firms' revenues have to be deposit at the central bank (on a special account), and the minister of finance has to approve the use of those resources to finance current public firm expenditures. Moreover, there was a sharp reduction of fiscal subsidies by increasing public tariffs and gasoline prices to international levels; even though gasoline taxes did not change, the new prices generated an increase of government revenues of 5.5%.[13] (2) There was a large devaluation of 93% (of the official exchange rate) implemented by the unification of the official and parallel exchange rates; a central bank foreign exchange auction was combined with a dirty-float system to guide and stabilize the exchange rate level. (3) Full price liberalization was established. (4) Several structural reforms were introduced: (a) Liberalization of the trade account (elimination of quantitative restrictions and nontariff barriers; establishment of a flat 20% nominal tariff). (b) Domestic financial liberalization (free interest rates; banks can receive dollar deposits, which have a low reserve requirement, and can provide dollar loans). (c) Sharp increase in labor market flexibility regulations (reduction of legal requirements for worker dismissals; elimination of wage indexation clauses; elimination of collective bargaining).

The Bolivian neo-orthodox stabilization program produced the following results: (1) Average monthly inflation, which had been 60% during 1985 prior to the stabilization shock (August), was reduced to less than 2% per month during 1986; annual inflation rates have been lower than 20% during 1987–90. (2) Tax revenues that were 3% in 1983–84 increased to more than 11% during 1987–90. (3) The main criticism of the stabilization program is related to its heavy social costs and its poor growth performance.

The Bolivian program suggests that there exists complementarity between stabilization and structural reform policies; these structural reform policies play the role of reinforcing the idea of the change of regime, that is, fiscal deficits are being eliminated in the short and long runs. However, the link between the specific structural reform components and the elimination of the long-run fiscal deficit, and/or the agents' perception of a change of regime is not clear. After the 1973 military coup Chile implemented all the structural reforms included in the 1985 Bolivian package, and added some others (privatization, tax reform, capital account liberalization); however, it maintained indexation clauses for wages, the exchange rate, financial debt, and taxes. The political and economic changes of 1973 were a clear signal to all Chileans that there had been a change of regime; the large 1973 fiscal and public deficits (10% and 22% of GDP respectively) were transformed into fiscal and public surpluses by 1978, but inflation was reduced to a one-digit level only in 1981 (after having for two years a fixed nominal exchange rate). After the change of regime, it took eight years to get inflation under control.

The recent 1992 Venezuelan experience is an example of the political danger surrounding a neo-orthodox stabilization package. The components of the 1989 Venezuelan macroeconomic adjustment program were very similar to the Bolivian program (for details, see Hausmann 1990): public adjustment (elimination of gasoline and food subsidies and increase in public tariffs), price liberalization, and exchange rate unification (which implied a 150% official exchange rate devaluation); moreover, there were measures related to external trade liberalization. Hausmann (1990) argues that the new Venezuelan government had the advantage of being able to make deep economic changes and blaming the previous government for the negative consequences. But this trick cannot be played two years later; programs with heavy social adjustment costs can very easily turn a fragile democracy into a tough dictatorship.

In the 1990s, Argentina is a good example of a new complex neo-orthodox/neoheterodox stabilization program with the following components (CEDES 1991; Canavese 1991; Kiguel and Liviatan 1992): (1) The neoorthodox components include: (a) The government and the central bank cannot arbitrarily increase the money supply. This principle is implemented through the *convertibility law*, which establishes a fixed nominal exchange rate (10.000 australes/U.S. $1)[14]; the monetary base has the requirement to have at the central bank a 100% backing of liquid international reserves; therefore, the central bank purchase of international reserves is the only available mechanism for monetary expansion. In short, a written law stating the value of the exchange rate and the 100% backing requirement of the domestic monetary base is being used to provide a clear signal of a change of regime in the fight against inflation. (b) Additional fiscal adjustment complemented by rationalization of public expenditures and an increase of public tariffs. (c) Implementation of structural reforms like privatization and external trade liberalization to provide additional signals of a "change of regime." (2) The neoheterodox components include: (a) A forced rescheduling of public domestic debt maturity and interest rates changes; government liabilities of seven days and more were all reprogrammed to ten-year bonds (linked to the dollar), with an interest rate equal to the LIBOR.[15] Government interest payments on its public debt were reduced by 4.8% in 1990 (Canavese 1991). (b) To eliminate inertial inflation, there was an explicit prohibition of indexation clauses in wages and financial contracts; moreover, there was an implicit incomes policy where workers and entrepreneurs were persuaded by economic and political authorities to abstain from increasing prices. (c) Tax administration and enforcement has been strengthened.

This Argentinian stabilization program has been successful so far in reducing inflation; the average monthly inflation rate of 1989–90 of around 30% was reduced to around 2% (per month) during the second semester of 1991 and first quarter of 1992. However, the fixed nominal exchange rate, which is the nominal anchor and a key component of the overall credibility stabilization effort, together with the import liberalization program, are generating an increasing trade disequilibrium; the real exchange rate had appreciated by 15% after a year, and the trade surplus diminished from a monthly average of U.S. $450 million during the first semester of 1991 to U.S. $170 million (per month) during the last quarter of 1991.

Trade Reforms

Prior to 1980, the ISI (industrialization based on import substitution) strategy prevailed in Latin America; industrial policy was mainly commercial policy, that is, high tariffs and nontariff barriers. Many horror stories have been told about the inefficiencies created by the ISI strategy; one of the principal problems has been related to the anti-export bias generated by the domestic incentive price structure.[16] In this respect it could be observed that at the overall level, Latin American exports had an annual average export growth rate of 3.2% during the 1960–80 period; this export (annual) expansion rate increased to 5.4% during the 1980s (table 9.7). Moreover, Latin American export per capita levels in 1990 for most countries is below U.S. $500 (Venezuela and Chile are the exceptions); this figure is about one-third and one-eighth of South Korean and Taiwanese export per capita levels, respectively.

On the other hand, during the ISI period Latin American annual GDP growth rates of 5.7% were reasonable (table 9.1). Furthermore, a few countries under the ISI trade regime, such as Brazil, had exports growing at 8.6% per year for twenty years (1960–80); another case is Mexico, with (annual) export growth rates of 10.2% (1970–80) (table 9.7). A completely different case is the Chilean example, where a drastic trade liberalization reform was implemented during the 1970s; Chilean annual export expansion increased from 3.5% during the 1960s to 6.9% during the 1970–90 period. There is wide consensus in Latin America that by the end of the 1970s the ISI strategy was exhausted; the external debt shock accelerated this fact.

During the 1980s there has been a profound change of focus in most Latin American countries; the ISI strategy (inward-oriented development) is being replaced by an export-oriented strategy (outward-oriented develop-

TABLE 9.7 Latin American exports

	Export growth[a] (Annual average, %)			Export/GDP[a] (%)			Exports[b] (Millions US$) (1990)
	1960–70	1970–80	1980–90	1970	1980	1990	
Argentina	6.1	2.1	5.4	9.9	9.4	18.5	12,354
Bolivia	9.1	−1.7	0.7	37.3	21.5	23.4	831
Brazil	8.9	8.2	5.9	8.6	8.3	12.5	31,414
Chile	3.5	7.4	6.4	11.5	18.2	26.2	8,310
Colombia	4.3	3.7	7.2	14.5	12.3	17.3	7,105
Mexico	3.0	10.2	9.5	6.3	8.8	18.6	26,773
Peru	1.5	2.3	−1.1	22.1	19.0	18.9	3,276
Venezuela	2.6	−5.1	2.2	64.5	37.5	42.7	17,278
Latin America	3.9	2.6	5.4	17.1	12.8	19.0	121,747

Source: CEPAL.

a. Exports (goods and services) are measured in US$ 1980.

b. Exports (FOB).

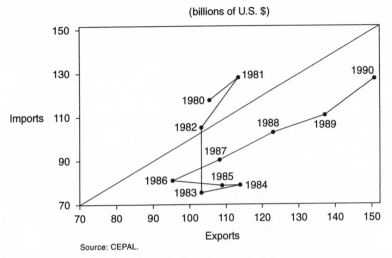

Source: CEPAL.

Figure 9.1 Latin American trade balance

ment). The example of the highly successful Asian export countries has become the pattern to follow; exports are encouraged to become the engine of growth. The new predominant rationale states that given their small relative size, Latin American economies should be open outward; the pursuit and increase of efficiency will be obtained by an integration of the domestic economy with the rest of the world. The transformation of the trade account deficits at the beginning of the 1980s into important trade surpluses at the end of the decade is a clear empirical indication that there has been an important effort by many Latin American countries to increase exports (see figures 9.1 and 9.2).

The Latin American trade regime that prevailed during the ISI strategy had a highly complex and messy structure; there were different types of nontariff barriers like import licensing, import prohibition, and quotas, together with a high level and large dispersion of tariff schedules, surcharges, etc.; moreover, there were special regimes and special exemptions, some related to geographic areas and some to type of firms (public firms). During the 1980s there was a clear trend toward a rationalization of the trade regime (see table 9.8); several features are included here: simplification and reduction of bureaucratic procedures related to external trade operations (exports and imports), elimination of most nontariff restrictions, diminution of the number of special regimes and special exemptions. With respect to tariffs, the following reforms have been undertaken: (1) in many countries there is a tendency toward the use of only a few tariff categories; Chile and Bolivia have a flat structure, Argentina and Peru have three tariff categories, Mexico and Brazil

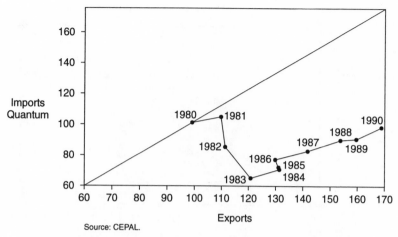

Source: CEPAL.

Figure 9.2   Latin American external quantum index (1980=100)

have six and seven respectively; (2) average and maximum tariff levels have been greatly reduced; nominal tariff rates larger than 30% are now considered large in most Latin American countries.

It is interesting to point out that George Bush's Initiative for the Americas (the creation of a free trade area) has been a strong stimulus to rationalization and liberalization of the trade regime in many Latin American countries; table 9.8 provides examples in this respect showing significant reduction of tariff levels implemented during the 1990s.

In short, there is a wide consensus in Latin America in support of a rationalized trade regime. However, there is a divergence between gradualist groups and those advocating abrupt change; Brazil and Colombia are following the gradualist approach, while Bolivia, Chile, and Mexico followed a relatively fast liberalization program. There is here a double concern. First, there is the issue of the import liberalization–export expansion relationship. There is general agreement on the need for a quick reduction of all sorts of barriers and tariffs related to imports (inputs and machinery) required by the export sector; but why would consumer-good imports help to increase export expansion? Second, given the asymmetry existing between the rapid expansion of imports and the relative slowness related to export growth, what ensures the maintenance of a sustainable trade balance in the short and medium run? Moreover, how is the import liberalization process connected to the anti-inflationary program? Furthermore, given the importance of tariff revenues in total tax collection, what will be the effect of tariff reduction on government revenues?

TABLE 9.8 Trade reforms in selected Latin American countries

	Nominal tariff levels (%)						Nontariff barriers
	Average tariff			Maximum tariff			(Changes during the 1980s; situation prevailing at 1990–91
	1980–84[a]	1985–89[b]	1990–91[b]	1980–84[a]	1985–89[b]	1990–91[b]	
Argentina	e		d	e	50	22	Large reduction of QR, simplification of the tariff structure.
Bolivia[c]		20	10		20	10	Elimination of QR and most exemptions by 1990.
Brazil	43[e]	39	32	73[e]	50	40	Gradual liberalization changes
Chile[c]	35	20	11	35	20	11	All nontariff barriers eliminated during the 1970s.
Colombia	42	27	21	87	74		Gradual liberalization changes.
Mexico	27[e]	10		80[e]	40	20	Import licensing which covered 100% of imports by 1982 are abolished by 1989.
Peru	e	43	d	e	100	50	Elimination of all QR, simplification of the tariff structure.
Venezuela	e	40		e	80	50	Elimination of most QR by 1989.

Sources: Williamson (1990); *Situación Latinoamericana*, several issues.

a. Maximum value of the period.

b. Minimum value of th period.

c. Flat tariff structure.

d. Three tariff categories: 0-11-22 for Argentina and 15-25-50 for Peru.

e. Predominance of QR (quantitative restriction) and nontariff barriers.

Exchange Rate Policies

Multiple exchange rates had been used in many Latin American countries during the ISI period as a complement to the complex trade regime; a dual exchange rate regime, with a controlled official rate for the trade balance components and a free rate for the capital account, has been used by a few countries. At the end of the 1980s, however, a unified exchange rate system prevails in most countries of the region. Strict exchange controls, which were a normal feature in most Latin American countries prior to 1980, have been considerably relaxed in many economies; foreign exchange transactions and dollar deposits are now legal operations to which most agents have an easy access in many countries.

Distinct exchange rate regimes have been used in Latin American countries; even the same country has changed the exchange rate regime many times. Prior to 1980, some countries like Mexico and Venezuela had a fixed nominal exchange rate (pegged to the dollar); to keep stable the level of the real exchange rate in an inflationary environment, Brazil and Colombia used a passive crawling peg for more than two decades; Argentina and Chile used an active crawling peg to guide inflationary expectations at the end of the 1970s; a fixed nominal exchange rate has been used as the nominal anchor in the stabilization programs of Chile (1979–82), Bolivia (1985–86), and Argentina (1991–92); free (or dirty) floating has been used by Venezuela (1989) and Peru (1990–91); a combination of a passive crawling peg with a float within a 10% band (increased from 2.5% to 5% and then to 10%) is being used by Chile during the 1990s.

The change of the exchange rate regime is related to the policy role assigned to the exchange rate. There are several different issues connected to the use of the exchange rate as the mechanism to change relative prices (price of tradables/price of nontradables) or as the nominal anchor of the general price level. The use of the exchange rate for resource reallocation plays an important role in trade liberalization and export expansion processes. Import liberalization accompanied by a compensated (real) devaluation helps to minimize the adjustment costs related to the reallocation process; given the fact that the reduction of tariffs and nontariff barriers is generally a lengthy process, this would require an equivalent matching devaluation throughout the liberalization process. However, a sustained increasing real devaluation is not a feasible policy, especially in an inflation-prone economy; therefore, it would seem more advantageous to have a large abrupt devaluation prior to the implementation of the import liberalization reform, and then make efforts to avoid real exchange rate deterioration while the next stages of the liberalization reform are implemented. This is the experience of Chilean trade reform during the 1970s; after a reduction of tariffs (and nontariff barriers) to a third

TABLE 9.9   Evolution of the real exchange rate for selected Latin American countries, 1970–91 (1980=100)

	Argentina	Bolivia	Brazil	Chile	Colombia	Mexico	Peru	Venezuela
1970–79	183.3	102.8	65.9	94.4	112.1	103.9	76.8	105.1
1980	100.0	100.0	100.0	100.0	100.0	100.0	100.0	100.0
1981	116.7	70.6	83.5	81.9	87.9	88.2	86.3	89.9
1982	178.3	100.0	78.0	93.1	81.8	127.6	77.9	81.8
1983	178.3	63.6	103.3	109.7	82.8	164.5	89.5	90.9
1984	155.0	64.3	108.8	112.5	88.9	123.7	88.4	104.0
1985	166.7	69.9	109.9	138.9	101.0	131.6	105.3	101.0
1986	175.0	87.4	112.1	162.5	132.3	152.6	88.4	119.2
1987	208.3	85.3	108.8	172.2	150.5	156.6	77.9	159.6
1988	228.3	93.7	101.1	180.6	151.5	126.3	88.4	154.5
1989	250.0	90.2	80.2	169.4	154.5	117.1	54.7	178.8
1990	188.3	109.8	67.0	175.0	175.8	115.8	40.0	189.9
1991	138.3	109.1	74.7	166.7	171.7	101.3	31.6	174.7

Source: CEPAL.

of their initial levels, domestic production kept the same external protection due to the complementary (initial abrupt) devaluation.

High and sustained real exchange rates are a necessary condition for export growth. Most Latin American economies have had higher real exchange rates during the 1980s (second half) compared to the 1970s (table 9.9); this is one of the key factors explaining the recent Latin American export expansion pattern. To keep this export growth trend, more physical and human capital investment will be required; changing the entrepreneurial mentality to consider the entire world as the market, and having the ability to compete outward where there are already many efficient producers, is a very slow process. Learning by doing is an important asset in a competitive world; therefore, the sooner a country starts, the better off it is.

Another important issue related to export growth has been how a nominal devaluation, in an inflationary environment, is transformed into a real devaluation. A nominal devaluation increases the price of tradables in local currency and thus the price of tradables relative to nontradables. This change in the relative price induces a substitution of production toward tradables and of expenditure toward nontradables; both responses clearly help to reduce a current account deficit. However, to prevent a nominal devaluation from being eroded by inflation requires several things. First, fiscal and monetary policies must validate the devaluation. This is considered a necessary but not sufficient condition. Second, in the short (and medium) run, a real devaluation requires a reduction of real wages; this means deindexation if wages are indexed. An income policy or unions agreement is required in a democratic regime. Third, the use of a crawling-peg regime after the devaluation has been shown empirically to be the most appropriate means of maintaining the new real value of the exchange rate (Edwards 1989).

The use of the exchange rate as a tool for resource reallocation seriously conflicts with the objective of price stabilization. Furthermore, establishing the exchange rate as a nominal anchor is considered the most fundamental part of a stabilization program (for example, the Argentinian convertibility law); the exchange rate has clear advantages over monetary targets as a nominal anchor; it is easier for any agent to monitor (and to understand) a fixed nominal exchange rate than changes in any of the monetary aggregates like M1, M2, or Mi. In the end, the overall credibility of the stabilization program becomes connected to the permanence of the nominal value of the exchange rate. Given the fact that inflation reduction takes time, there is eventually an appreciation of the exchange rate; internal disequilibrium is reduced at the price of increasing external (trade) disequilibrium.

In short, the internal disequilibrium–external disequilibrium situation cannot be solved by using only one tool, the exchange rate[17]; moreover, when the exchange rate is used to reduce one disequilibrium, it does so at the price of increasing the other. When the domestic interest rate is used to fight inflation while the exchange rate is used to promote exports, capital inflows attracted by interest rate differentials introduce pressures for exchange rate appreciation; moreover, their monetary impact complicates the price stabilization efforts. This is the situation observed in most Latin American countries during 1991, in which capital inflows have led to exchange rate appreciation (table 9.9).

Privatization

There are two key arguments for privatization. Private firms are considered to be more efficient than public firms; profits and the risk of losing their own capital provide incentives to private entrepreneurs to do their best in terms of efficiency; moreover, bankruptcy puts a floor on the level of inefficiency of private firms. The second argument is related to the public deficit; given the fact that public firms do not go bankrupt, they eventually become an important factor that increases the public deficit (see table 9.10). Therefore, the sale of public enterprises provides resources to finance the overall public deficit in the short run and will diminish it in the medium and long run; moreover, the increase in efficiency will generate higher growth rates.

Public enterprises have an important share of GDP in many Latin American countries; this share increased during the 1970s and beginning of the 1980s (table 9.10); even excluding the large Chilean state copper mines and the large petroleum firms of Mexico and Venezuela, public firms' expenditure

TABLE 9.10 Public enterprises expenditures and deficits for selected Latin American countries, 1970–85 (% GDP)

	Current expenditures			Overall deficit[a]		
	1970–71	1980–81	1984–85	1970–71	1980–81	1984–85
Argentina	8.3	10.8	15.2	1.9	2.2	2.9
Brazil	7.5	16.3	13.8	0.4	6.0	2.0
Chile[b]	10.2	15.3	19.8	3.3	0.6	−0.4
Mexico[b]	6.1	8.2	9.7	0.5	1.5	0.6
Peru	3.9	29.3	28.3	0.4	3.5	1.7
Venezuela[b]	5.6	12.2	n.a.	3.9	9.0	n.a.

Source: Larraín and Selowsky (1991).
a. Including current and capital accounts.
b. Excluding copper in Chile, and petroleum in Mexico and in Venezuela.

represented more than 10% of GDP in Argentina, Brazil, Chile, Mexico, Peru, and Venezuela by 1984–85.

What has been the economic rationale for having so many public enterprises in Latin America? There are several factors. First, to close the existing gap with respect to developed countries, many Latin American governments felt that they had to take a more active role, especially in an environment where there was a lack of private entrepreneurial management (in the 1940s, 1950s, and 1960s). Second, before 1970 the push for industrialization was related to the creation of big domestic basic industries (steel, petrochemicals, electricity, etc.), which required large investments; only the public sector had the needed resources. Third, at the theoretical level, market failures and market distortions were emphasized; in this type of environment, only the public sector would use social prices for long-run development planning; also, the government would act as the economic coordinator providing the "right" signals. And finally, any bankrupt private firms have been rescued by the Latin American public sector to avoid job destruction; in some cases, these firms either are the only ones existing in isolated regions or have large employment. This bankruptcy rescue policy explains the presence of the public sector in hotels, sugar mills, and manufacturing firms of all sizes.

After many years of a strong public sector presence in the productive sphere, there are many criticisms about it. Government failure is perceived as being much larger than market failure, due to political assignments of public firms' top and intermediate positions, public firms' large internal inefficiency due to lifetime job tenure and job rigidity, lengthy bureaucratic procedures, etc. Furthermore, a large public sector with a government that replaces the market in many aspects induces a rent-seeking attitude in the private sector; to increase private profits, having the right connection becomes much more important than increasing productive efficiency; this is especially valid in a highly protected economy.

During the 1980s there has been a pendulum swing in Latin America toward a larger use of the free-market price mechanism with a stronger role for the private sector; the Chilean case is an example in which abrupt price liberalization and a deep reprivatization (divestiture of public firms acquired by the state from the private sector to avoid their bankruptcy) and fast privatization (sale of public firms created by the state) processes have been implemented. Privatization is now being used in Latin America as the clearest signal of a change of regime for having higher future growth rates[18]; however, in spite of the rhetoric, only a few countries have been engaged so far in a real privatization process: Chile, Mexico, and Argentina (table 9.11; see Cardoso 1991 and Williamson 1990).

Mexican privatization has been a gradual process during which different divestitures procedures have been used (Ortiz and Noriega, 1990): liquidation (276 firms), merging of firms from the same sector (82 firms), transfer to municipalities and states (30 firms), and sale of 240 firms—all during the 1982–89 period. The firms included corresponded to small and medium-sized firms; in this way, the government acquired the know-how for divestiture. Large firms' privatization started in 1990. On the other hand, Chilean and recent Argentinian privatizations have been relatively rapid processes that include many large state firms; there are criticisms related to the lack of transparency of the divestiture procedures, which undermines the legitimacy of the operation, the divestment of natural monopolies without a clear regulatory framework, and unclear payment schedules by the new owners (for details, see Meller 1990 for the Chilean case, and Fanelli, Frenkel, and Rozenwurcel 1990 for Argentina).

Investment and Savings

A key assumption of the traditional stabilization and structural adjustment programs is that they are a necessary and sufficient condition for growth resumption; that is, after the successful implementation of the policy package, economic growth will start automatically. However, Latin American evidence shows that the way back to growth is not short (Dornbusch 1990); moreover, a country could be stabilized and adjusted structurally, and remain stagnant[19] (the recent Bolivian case could be an example).

Most Latin American countries showed a sharp decrease of (gross) investment during the 1980s (table 9.12); Chile and Mexico have started to show increasing relative investment levels in the second half of the decade. Comparing the 1970s and the end of the 1980s, Brazil, Bolivia, Peru, and Venezuela show a fall of around 4% of the investment level, while Argentina shows a reduction larger than 10%.

TABLE 9.11   Privatization in selected Latin American countries during the 1980s and 1990s

	Number of privatized firms (N^o)	Amount of sales (millions US$)	
Argentina	23	3,274	Drastic and abrupt privatization of large public firms has started from 1990 on.
Bolivia	—	—	No action. There are 67 small public manufacturing firms. Big public mining firms have political and constitutional constraints.
Brazil	20	1,470	Slow process and much rhetoric up to 1990. A big steel and an electric-mechanic company shares sold at the end of 1991.
Chile	46	3,042[a]	Deep and abrupt privatization implemented during 1985–89. There remain only a few public firms.
Colombia	—	—	Colombian public firms are not important in the economy; privatization is not an issue; reprivatization of a large bankrupt Grupo Gran Colombiano.
Mexico	615	10,000	Gradual privatization of small and medium firms during 1982–89. Large firms privatization from 1990 on.
Peru	5	39	Only a few cases where plants were transferred to employees. Recent legislation allows privatization of 23 of the 186 public firms; these 23 firms represent 2% of total public firms assets.
Venezuela	—	—	No action. Reprivatization of hotels, sugar mills, cement companies is discussed.

Sources: Cardoso (1991); Williamson (1990); Vial (1992); *Situación Latinoamericana*, several issues.
a. Corresponds to estimated net worth (see Larraín and Selowsky 1991).

One factor clearly connected to the reduction of investment is the drop in savings; available national savings[20] have been influenced by the fall in national income and by the real transfer related to external debt payments, while the drastic reduction of external credits has decreased the level of foreign savings. Peru and Venezuela show a diminution of national savings of more than 10% during the 1980s; national savings decreased more than 5% in Argentina, Bolivia, and Mexico. During the decade, foreign savings were reduced by 3% to 4% in Argentina, Brazil, Colombia, and Mexico (see table

TABLE 9.12   Gross investment for selected Latin American countries (% GDP)

	Argentina	Bolivia	Brazil	Chile	Colombia	Mexico	Peru	Venezuela
1970–79	20.9	17.1	22.4	147	15.9	21.4	22.0	23.2
1980	22.2	14.2	22.0	16.6	16.8	24.8	23.5	25.2
1981	19.6	13.8	19.8	18.5	17.3	26.5	26.1	26.3
1982	15.1	10.2	18.5	14.0	17.8	22.2	25.5	25.6
1983	14.0	11.0	15.7	12.0	17.6	16.6	20.5	19.9
1984	12.4	10.4	15.4	12.3	17.2	17.0	18.4	16.4
1985	11.5	12.5	15.9	13.8	15.7	17.9	16.1	17.1
1986	11.8	13.6	18.8	14.1	15.8	16.4	17.7	18.4
1987	13.1	13.7	17.6	15.5	14.9	16.1	18.9	22.7
1988	11.3	13.6	17.0	15.3	16.1	16.8	17.7	23.7
1989	8.7	13.7	16.6	16.9	14.7	17.3	16.1	19.2
1990	7.5	12.7	15.9	17.7	13.9	18.9	17.7	18.6

Source: CEPAL.
Note: Percentages are measured with variables expressed in US$ 1980.

9.13). Moreover, most countries were having an annual real transfer of resources of more than 4% during a large part of the 1980s (see trade deficit figures of table 9.2).

In short, the required external disequilibrium adjustment induced a fall of national income and in this way a drop of national savings; part of these savings had to be transferred out of the region to meet external debt payments. Moreover, Latin American economies had large capital flight flows, that is, an important percentage of domestic financial savings is intermediated abroad,

TABLE 9.13   National savings, foreign savings, and real resource transfer for selected Latin American countries, 1980–90 (annual average; % GDP)

	National savings			Foreign savings		
	1980–81	1982–84	1985–90	1980–81	1982–84	1985–90
Argentina	16.1	10.7	8.6	6.1	3.2	1.8
Bolivia	10.0	6.4	5.1	4.0	5.0	9.8
Brazil	17.9	13.5	16.9	5.0	3.0	1.2
Chile	9.9	3.6	12.1	12.8	8.2	3.3
Colombia	15.1	13.6	15.9	4.6	7.1	0.3
Mexico	21.0	19.2	16.2	4.7	−0.7	0.8
Peru	24.8	17.1	13.8	6.0	5.3	5.0
Venezuela	33.7	24.2	20.1	−8.4	−3.3	−1.2

Source: CEPAL.

generating a "squeeze" of domestic financial resources (for a deeper discussion of this issue, see Fanelli, Frenkel, and Rozenwurcel 1990).

Contractionary stabilization macroeconomic programs could generate a reduction of investment (see Taylor 1991; Servén and Solimano 1992). To induce a cut in the fiscal deficit, diminishing public investment represents the least politically costly measure; public investment represents from around 25% to 40% of total investment in Latin America. Moreover, the cut in real wages and restrictive monetary policies generate a domestic recession, reducing domestic expenditure and inducing lower output and private investment; the credit crunch and higher interest rates also directly discourage private investment. Finally, a real devaluation increases the price of imported capital goods (which in some Latin American countries represent more than 70% of total capital goods) and therefore affects private and public investment.

Another factor explaining lowered Latin American investment, pointed out by Dornbusch (1990), is the extremely cautious attitude of the private sector; that is, the private sector adopts the "wait and see" option to be sure that the stabilization and adjustment programs will be successful and the economy will not return to the previous unstable situation. There are several elements behind this "wait and see" stance. For one thing, the implementation of the stabilization and adjustment programs generates heavy social costs and important income redistribution; will the government be able to resist political pressures to stop or change the policies? The existence of uncertainty with respect to the future—given the irreversible nature of investment—induces entrepreneurs to wait for a reduction of uncertainty; it is assumed that good investment opportunities present now will be there tomorrow.

The consequence of the private sector taking the waiting option could be the failure of the stabilization and adjustment programs; in other words, the fate of these programs depends on showing a success in the short run, and this requires a fast injection of private investment. There is a sort of self-fulfilling prophecy; if private investors believe in the stabilization and adjustment program and start new projects, this will generate a successful outcome, whereas failure to invest will stall the programs. The same policy reform package therefore could take the economy to a "good" or to a "bad" equilibrium depending on the attitude of private investors (Dornbusch 1990); this is a case of coordination failure. Private entrepreneurs make decisions in a decentralized and isolated way; but there is a sort of herd behavior among them: if a few start investing, the others will follow. The government should offer a special prize to the first investors (Labán 1992); tax exemptions or subsidized privatization are some of the options.

Other suggestions for reducing the waiting period of private investors are: (1) sustained financial support by multilateral organizations *after* the stabilization and adjustment programs have been implemented (Dornbusch

1990); this helps create a favorable climate for private entrepreneurs; moreover, it has been observed that private investment is procyclical with external credit, as seen in Chile and Mexico. (2) The increase of public investment stimulates the domestic economy; some type of public investment tends to be complementary with private investment.[21] In the Chilean case, the sequence in the recovery and growth period was the following: there was a strong increase of public investment, which was followed by foreign investment; domestic private investors were the last to start investing when they realized that foreigners were taking the best available investment opportunities.

Social Costs

The implementation and the lack of implementation of policy reforms have had heavy social costs in Latin America; the main difference between both situations consists in the fact that for the countries that have implemented economic reforms, like Chile and Mexico, social costs are a part of the past and the future looks very promising; the reverse situation is observed in the other countries.

Distinct type of indicators show the magnitude of Latin American social costs incurred during the 1980s (table 9.14): (1) Consumption per capita is a better indicator than GDP or national income per capita of average Latin American welfare evolution. In Argentina, Bolivia, Peru, and Venezuela, consumption per capita has been reduced by more than 17%. (2) Unemployment reached the two-digit level in Bolivia, Colombia, Peru, and Venezuela; Chilean unemployment even surpassed the 30% level. It should be pointed out that in most Latin American countries there are no unemployment compensation payments. (3) Average wages show a reduction larger than 50% in Peru and Venezuela; in Argentina and Mexico wage cuts are larger than 20%. (4) Social expenditures (health and education) per capita dropped by 20% during the 1980s in many countries.

Chile and Mexico provide opposite cases with respect to the magnitude of social costs of a policy reform program. During the 1980s, to close the external disequilibrium gap, Chilean economic authorities applied a contractionary shock adjustment (GDP fell by 14.2% in 1982 and kept falling during 1983), which generated an increase of unemployment to over 30% (for an in-depth discussion, see Meller 1992); unemployment was higher than 24% over four years (1982–85); this was the mechanism by which real wages were cut by more than 20% for at least a five-year period; social expenditures per capita were reduced by 10%. In the Mexican case, the adjustment process was relatively more gradual; GDP fell by almost 5% (1982–83) and again by almost 4% (1986), then increased by less than 2% per year in the two following years; however, there was a large reduction of real wages, close to 30%

TABLE 9.14   Several social costs indicators for selected Latin American countries, 1980–90

	Consumption per capita (1980 = 100)		Highest unemployment rate during 1980–90 (%)	Average wages (1980 = 100)		Social expenditures per capita[a] (1980 = 100)		Social expenditure[a] (% GDP)		
	1985	1990		1985	1990	1985	1990	1980	1985	1990
Argentina	78.2	71.1	7.6	107.2	76.2	71.8	82.3[b]	2.4	2.1	2.3[b]
Bolivia	78.7	80.6	11.6			40.7		5.5	2.8	
Brazil	89.1	93.8	7.1	116.1[e]	102.9[e]			6.2	6.0	5.7[e]
Chile	83.7	98.2	30.0[f]	93.5	104.8	87.8	90.2[c]	6.2	6.0	5.7[c]
Colombia	104.2	111.0	14.1	114.6	118.4	107.7	96.5	7.3	7.7	6.0
Mexico	95.6	93.1	6.6	75.9	77.9	103.1	59.5[d]	3.5	3.7	2.3[d]
Peru	95.3	82.0	10.1	77.6	42.7	106.5	71.7	3.3	4.0	3.3
Venezuela	88.4	80.9	14.3	75.7	41.5	92.9	95.9[c]	5.4	6.4	6.3[c]

Source: CEPAL.
a. Social expenditures in health and education.
b. 1986.
c. 1987.
d. 1988.
e. Average of São Paulo and Rio de Janeiro indicators.
f. CIEPLAN data is used; official unemployment figures exclude unemployed workers receiving unemployment subsidies.

during a three-year period (1986–88), and 20% lower than the 1980 level over nine years (1983–91); this wage flexibility avoided the increase of Mexican unemployment, which remained below 5% from 1985 on.

With respect to these social adjustment costs, it should be pointed out that in a Latin American economy where unemployment subsidies are practically nonexistent, a fully free and flexible labor market produces economic insecurity and a sharp decline of the standard of living. Workers receive income only through wages and only if they are employed; during an adjustment, they have no means of protecting themselves, and their families could face a serious survival problem.

When neither the formal labor market nor the government provides jobs or income subsidies to the workers, subsistence requirements lead to the adoption of a survival strategy in which sharing of food, housing, and jobs becomes the main element of an informal economy. The main role of this informal economy is not related to its contribution to GDP; in fact, it is the "institutional" mechanism that solves the survival problem of the unemployed and their families.

The sharing economy of the informal sector fills the void left by the nonexistence of a social safety net, but the social costs of this solution are high and unfairly distributed: the unemployed and their families will live below the subsistence line. Employed workers and the rest of society should share part of their income, through taxation, with the unemployed. Austerity adjustment packages would be less often rejected if it were felt that everyone were contributing equally and sharing the sacrifices. Moreover, there is an additional fundamental principle: society should have a basic social safety net to keep people above the subsistence level.

There is no adequate web of social organization in Latin America. It could be said that, just as an adequate macroeconomic setting is a fundamental prerequisite for the success of a structural adjustment program, an adequate social organization should be established to address the distressing situation of the underprivileged. This social web would reduce the negative popular reactions and political explosions provoked by adjustment program that create unemployment and a drop in real wages in the short term, and it might make adjustment programs easier to sustain and more efficient overall.[22]

Final Remarks

There appears to exist a consensus with respect to policy reform sequencing; Selowsky (1989) states that "there is a logical sequence of stages," and moreover, "countries cannot jump stages and still sustain progress." Stage 1 would be devoted to macro stabilization, which implies fiscal adjustment and control of inflation; structural reforms will fail if they are implemented in an internal (and external) disequilibrium environment. Stage 2 would correspond to the establishment of correct relative prices and incentives through structural reforms like opening the economy, liberalization, deregulation, and privatization. Stage 3 would be the increase in investment and growth resumption period.

However, the optimal sequence of reforms is practically impossible to define, especially in a second-best world. Therefore it is important to learn from specific cases. The empirical evidence shows that macro stabilization and structural reforms are implemented simultaneously. On one hand, it seems that many countries have run out of time and would like to do everything fast; on the other hand, the macro stabilization process takes time, and in the meantime, structural reforms start to be implemented. In this respect, Bruno (1992) has suggested a fast or shock anti-inflation stabilization program complemented by slow structural adjustment reforms; rapid reduction in the rate of change of the general price level and slow changes of relative prices (to reduce adjustment costs related to resource reallocation).

Following Solimano (1992 and chapter 12, this volume), table 9.15 provides the number of *years* involved in the change of regime policies and

TABLE 9.15 Time period related to change of regime policies and to key economic indicators, Chile, Mexico, and Bolivia (number of years)

	Change of regime policies				Economic indicators			
		Trade reforms						
	Fiscal deficit reduction to finance-able level	Elimination of QR & special regimes	Tariff reduction to below 20%	Privatization	Inflation reduction to 20%	GDP recovering level previous to adjustment	Unemployment	Wages
Chile	3 (in the 70s) 4 (in the 80s)	3	3 ÷ 4	2 ÷ 3	8	4 (in the 70s) 6 (in the 80s)	4 years over 24%	20% cut for 5 years
Mexico	3 ÷ 3	4 ÷ 5	3 ÷ 4	More than 4	2 ÷ 3	4	Low (below 6%)	25% cut for 6 years
Bolivia	More than 5	1	1	None	1	2	3 years over 10%	n.a.

the evolution of key economic indicators in the three successful Latin American cases (Chile, Mexico, and Bolivia). The macro stabilization experiences provide the following: (1) Chilean experience shows that reduction of the fiscal deficit to a financeable level (even under a dictatorship) can take more than three years. (2) Even when there existed a fiscal surplus, it took more than three years in Chile to bring inflation to the 20% annual level; a similar period of two to three years is observed in Mexico for the reduction of inflation to the same level. On the other hand, Bolivian hyperinflation was reduced to 20% in one year; but the fiscal (operational) deficit has remained over 4% for more than four years. With respect to trade reforms, the elimination of nontariff barriers and removal of special exemptions took four to five years in Mexico, two years in Chile, and one year in Bolivia; tariff reduction to below 20% took three to four years in Chile and Mexico, and one year in Bolivia. The relatively fast Chilean privatization process took from two to three years; it is taking more than four years in Mexico. As a result of the combination of macro stabilization and structural adjustment programs, there was a fall of GDP; raising GDP to the level existing prior to the stabilization/adjustment program took four to six years in Chile, around four years in Mexico, and two years in Bolivia. Recovery of investment to preadjustment levels has taken more than four years in Chile and Mexico, and investment has stagnated in Bolivia (see table 9.12).

In short, the figures show that the implementation of policy reforms and the eventual positive economic outcome is a slow process measured in *years*. Moreover, macro stabilization and structural reforms generate important social adjustment costs that could last more than three to four years (see table 9.15). However, the alternative of doing nothing is even more costly in welfare and time terms. Therefore macro stabilization and structural reforms are necessary to start moving the economy into a higher growth path; but also, in a democracy, an income policy agreement is required to maximize the sustainability and the probability of success of the reforms (Dornbusch 1990). Given the high social adjustment costs, an income policy agreement should achieve an equitable distribution of those costs; this implies that the people have to feel that everyone is involved in sharing the adjustment costs and no privileged groups are exempted. In Latin America, real wage cuts would generate less political opposition if they were accompanied by an efficient and progressive tax reform. In other words, the long wait required for the positive effects of the reforms necessitates a long-run social–political agreement, so that all parties share the political costs related to the implementation of the economic reforms.

The type of policy reforms usually suggested (macro stabilization and structural reforms) are oriented toward a reduction of the role and size of the state and the public sector in the economy, that is, "the smaller the state and

TABLE 9.16 Direct taxes in selected Latin American countries in the 1980s (% GDP)

Argentina	Bolivia	Brazil	Chile[a]	Colombia	Mexico[a]	Peru	Venezuela[a]
2.3	0.6	4.0	3.1	3.3	4.9	2.7	3.3

Sources: IMF for Argentina (1988), Bolivia (1989), and Brazil (1988); Larraín and Selowsky (1991) for Chile (1985) and Peru (1985); CEPAL (1990) for Colombia (1989), Mexico (1989); Velázquez (1992) for Venezuela (1987).

a. Excluding state copper firms in Chile and state petroleum firms in Mexico and Venezuela.

the less it interferes in the economy, the larger will be the increase in social welfare." Therefore, it may sound like a logical contradiction to promote a tax reform in this type of environment. Price stabilization and trade liberalization will eventually decrease the inflation tax and tariff revenues; a tax reform is required to compensate for the reduction in government revenue sources. Fiscal adjustment requires a rationalization and reduction of public expenditures, but it should also include a minimum social network; taxes should generate revenues to finance minimum social expenditures; moreover, in a highly inequitable society, the tax structure has to be progressive; as an indicator of tax progressivity, the direct tax to GDP share of developed countries could be used as a benchmark. In most Latin American countries the highest 20% income group has a share larger than 50% of national income; on the other hand, total direct taxes represent around 3% of GDP in many Latin American economies (table 9.16). (Total direct taxation represents more than 10% of GDP in OECD countries.) Latin American governments have to solve the domestic political issue of taxing high- and middle-income groups. A flat 20% direct tax applied to the highest 20% income group could increase tax revenues by more than 3% of GDP; IMF standby arrangements concerned with the fiscal deficit and/or World Bank public sector structural reforms could use that tax figure (increase in direct taxes of 3% of GDP) as a target in their loan agreements; moreover, IMF and World Bank staff could help to establish an efficient tax system to close loopholes and minimize evasion; each country could decide on the preferred combination of personal income, property, wealth, and capital gains tax structure to be applied to the highest 20% income group in order to generate the additional tax revenue.

Finally, it should be pointed out that "there exists a strong complementarity between improved domestic policies and external financing" and "improved policies without extra financing jeopardize progress by making the adjustment politically and socially too costly" (Selowsky 1989). In Latin America, the most successful stabilization and adjustment experiences receive significant external credit support at the beginning, during, and after the implementation of policy reforms (Fanelli, Frenkel, and Rozenwurcel 1990). In the Chilean case, multilateral organizations (IMF, World Bank, IDB) provided credits equivalent to 3% of GDP per year over five years (1983–87), which was complemented by an equivalent amount provided by commercial banks during the first three years (1983–85); this external credit support was maintained in spite of the fact that during 1984 there was a policy reversal (expansionary aggregate demand policies), which lasted almost a year (Meller 1990). The 1985 Bolivian stabilization program had the support of the U.S. government and multilateral organizations (IMF, World Bank, IDB, Paris Club); multilateral and bilateral operations together provided an annual credit flow equivalent to more than 5% of GDP during a four-year period (1985–88) (Williamson 1990). During 1989 Mexico signed several agreements with multilateral organizations (IMF, World Bank, Paris Club) and with Japan which led to a substantial reduction of its external debt. The 1989–90 Mexican debt relief package reduced the external financial transfer by 2% of GDP per year (almost U.S. $4 billion per year) during a six-year period (1989–94). In addition, the eventual North American Free Trade Agreement has been a strong positive stimulus to private investment and reversals of capital flight flows; in this case, an external real anchor (the U.S. economy) has generated optimistic expectations with respect to future Mexican growth prospects, and in this way it contributes to the successful outcome of stabilization and structural reform policies.

In short, sustained external support, either financial or in the form of access to developed countries' markets, can support a successful implementation of required policy reforms.

Notes

The author acknowledges the useful comments received from Roberto Frenkel, Martin Paldam, Andrés Solimano, and the other participants at the El Escorial conference; moreover, the author appreciates the efficient research support provided by Andrea Repetto. All errors are the author's.

1. Bolivia and Nicaragua have had hyperinflation; Bolivian hyperinflation reached more than 28,000% (1985) and Nicaraguan hyperinflation was higher than 30,000% (1988).
2. In some countries, the quasi-fiscal deficits, that is, subsidies provided by the central bank to rescue domestic foreign exchange debtors and financial institutions, could reach deficit figures on the order of 4% to 6% of GDP in a few years. These quasi-fiscal deficits are excluded from table 9.3.
3. See Cardoso and Dantas (1990) for different measures of Brazilian fiscal deficits during the 1980s; see also Bacha (1992).
4. For a severe criticism of this Washington consensus, see Fanelli, Frenkel, and Rozenwurcel (1990).
5. Let total government expenditures be $G = G_P + S$, where G_P are the primary government expenditures (excluding debt services) and S are the debt services. Then, by differentiation: $G' = \alpha_{GP} G_P' + \alpha_S S'$.
6. However, Fanelli, Frenkel, and Rozenwurcel (1990) point out that differences in the external

financing received by the public sector is an important factor explaining the magnitude of the macroeconomic effects of the fiscal deficit among Latin American countries.

7. This heterodox view corresponds to the so-called Latin American neostructuralists. For an excellent discussion of stabilization theory, see Taylor (1991). For a review of the new and old controversy between neostructuralists and neomonetarists, see papers included in Meller (1991).

8. For a deeper discussion of inertial inflation, see Arida and Lara-Resende (1986) and Lopes (1986). Indexation is an institutional mechanism introduced in some Latin American countries during the 1960s with the purpose of keeping constant the distributive shares of national income in an inflationary environment; given its standard 100% backward-looking indexation rule, today's inflation is at least equal to yesterday's inflation. After a long history of inflation, agents form their expectations assuming that future inflation will be at least equal to present inflation. Any agent not doing so while others do will have a diminishing share of national income.

9. For a country-specific and deeper discussion, see Ocampo (1987) and Bruno et al. (1988).

10. This feature could be in some cases more rhetorical than real; this seems to be especially valid in the Peruvian case.

11. As Kiguel and Liviatan (1991) point out, the government has to take advantage of the initial "grace" period to show its real commitment to the elimination of the public deficit.

12. For details, see Ortiz and Noriega (1990). The 1987 tax reform included a reduction of the effective tax rate and a widening of the tax base; it also introduced the incorporation of inflationary accounting practices to the calculation of the tax base. In 1989, a 2% tax on corporate assets became effective.

13. The big advantage of the sharp increase of gasoline prices is that the government is able to collect tax revenues very quickly, with very low tax evasion.

14. This exchange rate was slightly higher than the free market rate at the moment of enacting the convertibility law (March 1991).

15. In Brazil, the Collor stabilization program included an eighteen-month period of financial asset blocking; this freeze implied that "overnight" public bonds were reprogrammed to eighteen-month bonds (in domestic currency) having an interest rate that included indexation plus 6% (per year). These Argentinian and Brazilian monetary reforms are different from the ones implemented during the heterodox stabilization shocks; they have a clear redistributive impact that helps the public sector to reduce its budget disequilibrium.

16. In some Latin American countries, the rationale for an anti-export bias was related to the fact that traditional commodity (natural resources) exports were controlled by foreign firms or by landed oligarchs.

17. However, as mentioned, when there are public export firms, one tool, the exchange rate, could help to reduce simultaneously the public deficit and external trade disequilibrium; moreover, the fact that public export firms are generating foreign exchange could help to make sterilization easier and in this way reduce pressures for exchange rate appreciation.

18. There is some validity to this argument. Public firms' investment decisions are generally included in the overall fiscal budget discussion, that is, they compete for resources with public employees wages and social expenditures; in general, public firms have restrictions on credits in the financial market. Privatized firms do not have that constraint; moreover, they can directly request credits in the banking system; in the Chilean case, privatized firms have shown important increases in investment.

19. When a Latin American economy goes into a deep recession, a frequent discussion is related to having reach the bottom of the recession; it is believed that this is important to know, because after reaching the bottom, the economy can only go up. However, an alternative not considered is that the economy can remain stagnated in the bottom for a long time.

276   Patricio Meller

20. For a specific review of the evolution of public savings, see Bacha (1992).
21. For a deeper review of this issue in Latin American economies, see Bacha (1992), and Servén and Solimano (1992).
22. The previous paragraphs have been taken from Meller (1992). For an in-depth discussion of social costs and income distribution issues during adjustment programs, see Bourguignon, de Melo, and Morrisson (1991).

References

Arida, P., and A. Lara-Resende. 1986. "Inflación inercial y reforma monetaria: Brasil." In P. Arida, ed., *Inflación Cero*. Bogotá: Ed. Oveja Negra, 11–42.
Bacha, E. 1992. "Savings and Investment for Growth Resumption in Latin America: The Cases of Argentina, Brazil, and Colombia." Mimeo. Catholic University, Rio de Janeiro.
Barandiarán, E. 1988. "The Adjustment Process in Latin America's Highly Indebted Countries." Mimeo. World Bank, Washington, D.C., March.
Bourguignon, F., J. De Melo, and C. Morrison. 1991. "Poverty and Income Distribution during Adjustment: Issues and Evidence from the OECD Project." *World Development* 19, 11 (special issue, November): 1485–1508.
Bruno, M. 1992. "Stabilization and Reform in Eastern Europe: A Preliminary Evaluation." Mimeo. IMF, January.
Bruno, M., G. Di Tella, R. Dornbusch, and S. Fischer, eds. 1988. *Inflation Stabilization. The Experience of Israel, Argentina, Brazil, Bolivia, and Mexico*. Cambridge, MA: MIT Press.
Canavese, A. 1991. "Hyperinflation and Convertibility Based Stabilization in Argentina." Mimeo. Instituto Torcuato di Tella, Buenos Aires.
Cardoso, E. 1991. "Privatization in Latin America." Paper presented at the annual meeting of the Red de Centros Latinoamericanos de Investigación en Macroeconomía. Cartagena, Colombia, April.
Cardoso, E., and D. Dantas. 1990. "The Brazilian Case." In J. Williamson, ed., *Latin American Adjustment*, 129-153.
Cardoso, E., and A. Helwege. 1992. *Latin America's Economy. Diversity, Trends, and Conflicts*. Cambridge, MA: MIT Press.
CEDES. 1991. "Situación económica en Argentina." *Situación Latinoamericana*. Madrid: Fundación CEDEAL.
CEPAL. 1990. *Anuario Estadístico de América Latina y el Caribe*. Santiago, Chile.
CEPAL. 1991. "Balance Preliminar de la Economía de América Latina y el Caribe." Santiago, Chile.
Damill, M., J. M. Fanelli, and R. Frenkel. 1991. "Shock externo y desequilibrio fiscal. Brasil." Mimeo. CEDES, Buenos Aires, December.
Dornbusch, R. 1990. "Policies to Move from Stabilization to Growth." *Proceedings of the World Bank Annual Conference on Development Economics*, 19–58.
Dornbusch, R., and M. Simonsen. 1987. "Inflation Stabilization with Income Policy Support: A Review of the Experience in Argentina, Brazil, and Israel." Group of Thirty, New York.

Edwards, S. 1989. *Real Exchange Rates, Devaluation, and Adjustment. Exchange Rate Policy in Developing Countries.* Cambridge, MA: MIT Press.

Fanelli, J. M., R. Frenkel, and G. Rozenwurcel. 1990. "Growth and Structural Reform in Latin America. Where Do We Stand?" *Documento CEDES* No. 57, Buenos Aires.

Ground, L. 1984. "Los programas ortodoxos de ajuste en América Latina: Un examen crítico de las políticas del FMI." *Revista de la CEPAL* 23 (August): 47–84.

Hausmann, R. 1990. "The Big Bang Approach to Macro Balance in Venezuela: Why So Sudden, Why So Painful?" Mimeo. Instituto de Estudios Superiores de Administración, Caracas, August.

Kiguel, M., and N. Liviatan. 1991. "Lessons from the Heterodox Stabilization Programs." *Working Papers* WPS 671, World Bank, Washington, D.C.

Kiguel, M., and N. Liviatan. 1992. "Stopping Three Big Inflations." Mimeo. World Bank, Washington D.C.

Laban, R. 1992. "Incertidumbre política, fallas de coordinación y repatriación de capitales." Mimeo. CIEPLAN, Santiago.

Larraín, F., and M. Selowsky. 1991. *The Public Sector and the Latin American Crisis.* San Francisco: International Center for Economic Growth.

Lopes, F. 1986. *O Choque Heterodoxo.* Río de Janeiro: Editoria Campus.

Meller, P. 1990. "The Chilean Case." In J. Williamson, ed., *Latin American Adjustment*, 54–85.

Meller, P., ed. 1991. *The Latin American Development Debate. Neostructuralism, Neomonetarism, and Adjustment Processes.* Boulder: Westview Press.

Meller, P. 1992. *Adjustment and Equity in Chile.* Paris: OECD.

Morales, J. A. 1987. "Estabilización y nueva política económica en Bolivia." In J. A. Ocampo, ed., *El Trimestre Económico*, 179–212.

Morales, J. A. 1991. "Determinantes del déficit del sector público en Bolivia." Serie Política Fiscal No. 9, CEPAL, Santiago.

Ocampo, J. A., ed. 1987. "Planes inflacionarios recientes en la América Latina." *El Trimestre Económico*, Vol. LIV, Número Especial, México City, September.

Ortiz, G., and C. Noriega. 1990. "Rationalizing the Public Sector: The Mexican Experience in 1982–1990." Paper presented at the World Bank-IESA Conference on "Latin America Facing the Challenges of Adjustment and Growth," Caracas, July.

Romaguera, P. 1991. "Las fluctuaciones del precio del cobre y su impacto en la economía chilena." *Notas Técnicas* 143, CIEPLAN, Santiago, October.

Ros, J. 1992. "Apertura externa y reestructuración económica en México." In J. Vial, ed., *¿A dónde va América Latina?*

Sachs, J. 1986. "The Bolivian Hyperinflation and Stabilization." National Bureau for Economic Research. *Discussion Paper* No. 2073, Cambridge, MA.

Sargent, T. 1982. "The End of Four Big Inflations." In R. Hall, ed., *Inflation. Causes and Effects.* Chicago: University of Chicago Press, 41–98.

Selowsky, M. 1989. "Preconditions Necessary for the Recovery of Latin America's Growth." Paper presented at the Latin America Meeting of the World Economic Forum, Geneva, June.

Servén, L., and A. Solimano. 1992. "Private Investment and Macroeconomic Adjustment. A Survey."*World Bank Research Observer* 7, 1 (January): 95–114.

Solimano, A. 1992. "Diversity in Economic Reform: A Look at the Experience in Market and Socialist Economies." Mimeo. CECMG, World Bank, Washington, D.C., March.

Taylor, L. 1991. *Varieties of Stabilization Experience*. Oxford: Clarendon.

Velázquez, E. 1992. *El Déficit Público y la Política Fiscal en Venezuela (1980–1990)*. Caracas: Banco Central.

Vial, J., ed. 1992. *¿A dónde va América Latina? Balance de las reformas económicas*. Santiago: Ediciones CIEPLAN.

Williamson, J., ed. 1990. *Latin American Adjustment. How Much Has Happened?* Washington, D.C.: Institute for International Economics.

CHAPTER 10

Economic Reform in Southern Europe:
The Spanish Experience

Miguel Angel Fernandez Ordoñez and Luis Servén

Over the last fifteen years Spain experienced a deep economic and political transformation. The democratic institutions were restored after four decades of dictatorship, and in the late 1980s the Spanish economy rebounded from a prolonged crisis. In many Latin American and Eastern European countries, the Spanish experience has come to be regarded as a model of successful political transition and economic reform, and the factors responsible for Spain's success are attracting renewed attention.

Spain's reform process was protracted and difficult. With the collapse of Francoist rule, the new democratic regime inherited an economy in deep crisis, with mounting inflation, large external imbalances, and a highly inefficient productive structure plagued with government interventions. In a scenario reminiscent of today's Eastern Europe, the consolidation of the democratic institutions had to proceed along with the economic adjustment.[1] Tackling the economic crisis in such a context required restrictive macroeconomic policies and deep structural reforms in almost every major area of the resource allocation system, with all their implied short-run social costs, while at the same time attempting to deliver the higher living standards and more equitable income distribution demanded from the democratic regime.

The economic adjustment process, interrupted by the second oil shock, extended over almost a decade, during which the Spanish economy stagnated and the employment cost of the crisis reached huge proportions. The turnaround finally arrived, along with full EEC membership, in the second half of the 1980s, with an investment boom and a strong recovery of growth and employment. But the recovery came under threat in the early 1990s. The persistence of high unemployment along with renewed inflationary pressures are clear evidence of the need for further reforms. In turn, the reappearance in recent years of large external imbalances and a real exchange rate appreciation call for a new macroeconomic adjustment.

This chapter provides an overview of the process of economic adjustment and reform in Spain in the 1970s and 1980s, and attempts to identify the policy lessons that can be drawn from the Spanish experience.

TABLE 10.1   Spain: Main economic indicators (percentage, period averages)

	1965–1974	1975–1977	1978–1985	1986–1990
Real GDP growth	6.3	2.3	1.3	4.8
Unemployment rate	2.8	4.9	14.8	18.8
Inflation: GDP deflator	8.6	18.7	13.4	7.3
Priv. cons. defl.	8.3	18.6	14.0	6.5
Nominal labor cost growth	14.9	24.0	15.3	7.3
Profitability index (1970 = 100)	98.4	73.4	67.3	112.4
Real interest rate[a]	0.8	−6.0	2.8	6.0
Investment/GDP	25.9	25.5	21.2	22.2
Public deficit/GDP[b]	−0.4	0.3	4.1	3.8
Curr. acct. deficit/GDP	0.6	2.8	0.7	1.2
Foreign debt/GDP[c]	7.1	12.4	17.0	9.1
Memo items (EEC-12):				
Real GDP growth	4.3	2.2	1.9	3.1
Inflation (priv. cons. defl.)	6.1	12.6	9.8	4.2
Unemployment	2.5	4.6	8.1	9.6

Sources: Bank of Spain, Ministry of Finance, and EEC.
Notes: a. In terms of the GDP deflator.
    b. 1970/74.
    c. End of period.

The Political and Economic Crisis of the 1970s

By 1973 Spain had experienced over a decade of rapid economic expansion. Real GDP had grown by over 6% per year in 1965–73, well above the European average, and the economy was virtually in a state of full employment (table 10.1).[2] This outstanding performance was to a large extent the result of the structural reforms introduced by the Stabilization Plan of 1959, which had opened the economy to foreign trade and investment, and of the favorable international environment prevailing in those years.

But this rapid growth concealed important weaknesses. The industrialization process had been largely inward-oriented, biased toward heavy, energy-intensive industries (basic metals, chemicals, shipbuilding), sheltered from foreign competition by a still markedly restrictive trade regime[3]—which made extensive use of nontariff barriers—whose viability depended critically on the maintenance of low wages. Economic activity was characterized by pervasive administrative interventions, from price controls[4] to comprehensive regulation of the financial system (interest rate controls, mandatory credit allocation schemes, and even a ban on the creation of new banks). The move toward liberalization had lost momentum with the "development plans" of the 1960s, which again replaced competition with tax exemptions and credit subsidies to "strategic" industries. In the labor market, the ban on free trade unions and the limited scope for collective bargaining (with wages and major work conditions determined largely by administrative decisions) were matched by regulations aimed at job protection, among them tight restrictions on layoffs. In turn, the government sector was quite small by international standards, with the coverage of essential social services and the provision of basic infrastructure severely limited by an insufficient tax system.

In the early 1970s Spain entered a prolonged economic crisis. The adverse effects of the first oil shock and the ensuing world recession were compounded by a strong wage push and the deep political crisis that marked the final years of Franco's dictatorship.

Wage growth had proceeded at a brisk pace since the late 1960s, under the impulse of the still illegal but increasingly powerful trade unions and favored also by the relatively tight labor market. The varied administrative interventions in wage setting became increasingly ineffective in containing workers' demands in the early 1970s; when the authorities resorted to wage ceilings starting in 1973 in a timid attempt to control inflation, the ceilings (given by past inflation plus a productivity allowance to be awarded only exceptionally) automatically became the minimum demanded by the illegal unions, and therefore were amply exceeded by actual wage settlements. Fueled also by a parallel rise in employers' Social Security contributions during the 1970s, the real labor cost per worker rose by over 30% in 1972–77[5] (figure 10.1); moreover, this was accompanied by a steady reduction in

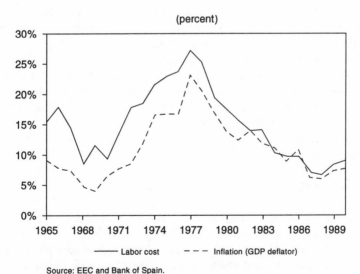

(percent)

Source: EEC and Bank of Spain.

Figure 10.1 Nominal labor cost growth and inflation (percent)

working hours. In addition, the wage boom was associated with a significant narrowing of wage differentials across occupations, as workers typically demanded that a large fraction of pay increases be equally (as opposed to proportionally) distributed to all employees.

When the first oil shock hit, the last governments of Franco's regime, with their political base crumbling, were unable to adopt adjustment measures to the terms of trade loss—which, among other things, would have required a moderation of real wage growth to preserve employment. Aided by the initially comfortable position of the external accounts, macroeconomic policy opted instead for accommodating the rise in wages and energy prices. The latter was, up to 1975, largely absorbed in the budget by appropriate tax/subsidy changes—at a fiscal cost that in 1974 alone was estimated at about 2% of GDP[6]; the modest surplus that the public sector had maintained before the oil shock was wiped out. Energy prices were adjusted later on, but to a lesser extent than in other OECD countries[7]; this underpricing of energy, which persisted throughout the 1970s, in fact encouraged the continuation of investments in energy-intensive sectors (e.g., steel), and resulted in a steady increase in energy use per unit of real GDP during the decade, in sharp contrast with the reductions achieved in almost every other industrial country.

The attempt at accommodating the wage and energy price hikes led to a rapid deterioration of the basic macroeconomic balances. Measured by the GDP deflator, inflation rose from 11% in 1973 to close to 25% in 1977 (figure 10.1), well above the European average. The current account surplus of 1970–73 gave way to growing deficits, which by 1976 exceeded 4% of GDP; to a pileup of external debt—whose initial level was, however, quite low (see table 10.1)—and to a rapid loss of foreign reserves, with the increasing threat of a balance-of-payments crisis (figure 10.2).

The worsening growth and employment performances were also apparent. The increase in labor and energy costs led to a profitability squeeze and a sharp rise in bankruptcies (figure 10.3). Combined with the unstable political situation, the result was a decline in investment (which had reached very high levels in the early 1970s) starting in 1975, which would continue almost without interruption for a decade; likewise, aggregate employment started in the same year the free fall that would extend until 1985.

The Stabilization of the Economy, 1978–85

The correction of these imbalances did not begin in Spain until late 1977, when most industrial countries were already enjoying a transitory recovery between the two oil shocks. The macroeconomic adjustment process effectively lasted until the mid-1980s, and comprised two stabilization attempts. The first was carried out by the Center governments of 1978–82; after some

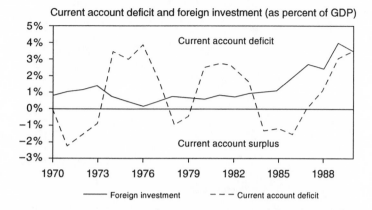

Figure caption/title (above chart): Current account deficit and foreign investment (as percent of GDP)

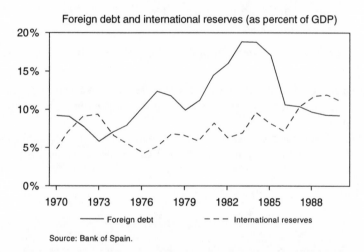

Figure 10.2 **(a) Current account deficit and foreign investment (as percent of GDP); (b) Foreign debt and international reserves (as percent of GDP)**

initial achievements, it was curtailed by their political fragility and by the second oil price hike. The second episode corresponded to the Socialist administration of 1983–85.

Nevertheless, the essential features of macroeconomic policy remained basically unchanged throughout the 1978–85 period. The centerpiece of the stabilization was a money-based disinflation, implemented through a gradual reduction in money growth targets, which were preannounced to curb inflationary expectations—and, in general, met with remarkable accuracy (table 10.2). This was complemented by an incomes policy applied through nation-

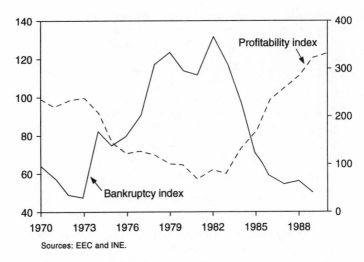

Sources: EEC and INE.

Figure 10.3   Profitability and bankruptcy indices (1970=100)

wide wage agreements, often with direct government participation (and always with its support), aimed at facilitating the moderation of wage growth (table 10.3).

As shown above (see table 10.1), and contrary to the experience of other reforming countries, Spain did not have a fiscal imbalance at the onset of the

TABLE 10.2   The monetary disinflation[a]

Year	Money growth (percent)		Memo item: GDP inflation
	Target	Actual	
1978	14.5–19.5	20.3	20.2
1979	15.5–19.5	19.6	16.7
1980	16.0–20.0	16.1	13.7
1981	14.5–18.5	15.7	12.0
1982	13.5–17.5	15.3	13.8
1983	11.0–15.0	12.8	11.6
1984	11.0–15.0	14.0	10.9
1985	11.5–14.5	13.2	8.5
1986	9.5–12.5	11.9	10.5
1987	6.5–9.5	14.3	5.9
1988[b]	8.0–11.0	11.0	5.7

Source: Ariztegui (1990).
Notes: a. Until 1983, the figures correspond to M3; in 1984–88, to ALP (total liquid assets).
    b. After Spain's entry into the EMS in 1989, exchange rates rather than money growth targets became the main priority of monetary policy.

TABLE 10.3   Centralized wage setting during the disinflation

Year	Agreement and participants	Wage settlement (%) Target	Actual[a]	Memo item: CPI inflation[b]
1978	Moncloa agreements—Government and political parties	20–22	20.6	19.8
1979	No agreement	—	14.1	15.7
1980	AMI—labor and business organizations	13–16	15.3	15.6
1981	Ibid.	11–15	13.1	14.5
1982	ANE—government, labor, and business organizations	9–11	12.0	14.4
1983	AI—labor and business organizations	9.5–12.5	11.4	12.2
1984	No agreement	—	7.8	11.3
1985	AES—government, labor, and business organizations	5.5–7.5	7.9	8.8
1986	Ibid.	7.2–8.6	8.2	8.8

Source: Lorente (1990) and Palacios (1989).
Notes: a. Wage settlements underestimate actual wage growth because of wage drift.
   b. Year average.

crisis. On the contrary, the public deficit emerged as a result of the political transition, which placed increasingly large social demands on an archaic tax system. This factor, together with the slow progress of tax reform and the action of automatic stabilizers during the prolonged growth slowdown of the late 1970s and early 1980s, accounts for much of the observed deterioration in public finances in those years (table 10.4). The initially low levels of public debt made it possible to avoid a full-blown fiscal crisis despite the mounting public deficits incurred during the adjustment process.

In turn, the exchange rate played a minor policy role in the adjustment process. With high de facto wage indexation, the real effects of nominal depreciations were very limited, as a failed devaluation episode had shown in 1976. On the other hand, achieving separate monetary and exchange rate targets proved increasingly difficult, despite the formal existence of capital controls (which were oriented more toward preventing outflows than inflows). Thus monetary targets took priority, and the exchange rate was left on a managed float during most of the adjustment period—except for two discrete depreciations undertaken at the early stage of the two stabilization attempts.

The First Stabilization Attempt and the Deepening of the Economic Crisis, 1978–82

With the restoration of democratic institutions in 1977, halting the deterioration of the economy became the top political priority for the consolidation of

TABLE 10.4 General government revenues and expenditures (percent of GDP)

	1975	1976	1977	1978	1979	1980	1981	1982	1983	1984	1985	1986	1987	1988	1989	1990
Current revenues	24.3	25.2	26.4	27.0	28.3	29.7	31.2	31.3	33.5	33.5	34.3	34.7	36.4	36.3	38.0	37.7
Taxes on production and imports	6.7	6.6	6.7	6.2	6.4	6.6	7.5	7.9	8.8	9.3	9.8	10.8	10.5	10.5	10.4	10.0
Taxes on income and wealth	4.4	4.7	4.9	5.5	5.9	6.8	7.0	6.6	7.6	8.1	8.2	7.9	10.1	10.3	11.9	11.8
Social security contributions	10.3	11.0	11.8	12.5	13.1	13.2	13.4	13.3	13.7	13.1	13.0	12.8	12.8	12.5	12.7	13.0
Other	2.9	2.9	3.0	2.8	2.9	3.1	3.3	3.5	3.4	3.0	3.3	3.2	3.0	3.0	3.0	2.9
Current transfers	12.0	13.0	13.7	15.7	15.9	16.5	18.2	18.7	19.6	20.6	22.0	21.6	20.7	20.8	21.0	21.5
Social security benefits	9.3	10.0	10.4	12.0	11.9	12.3	13.8	13.6	14.0	14.0	14.4	13.9	13.8	13.9	14.0	14.6
Interest on public debt	0.5	0.5	0.5	0.5	0.6	0.7	0.8	1.0	1.4	2.1	3.4	4.0	3.5	3.3	3.4	3.5
Subsidies	1.1	1.3	1.4	1.9	2.0	2.0	2.1	2.6	2.6	3.0	2.5	2.0	1.8	2.1	1.9	1.9
Other	1.1	1.2	1.4	1.3	1.4	1.5	1.5	1.5	1.6	1.5	1.7	1.7	1.6	1.5	1.7	1.5
Public consumption	9.2	9.8	10.0	10.4	12.2	13.6	13.9	14.2	14.8	14.6	14.7	14.6	15.1	14.7	15.0	15.3
Wages	7.2	7.8	8.1	8.4	9.3	9.8	10.3	10.2	10.6	10.5	10.6	10.3	10.4	10.4	10.5	10.9
Purchases of goods and services	1.6	1.6	1.5	1.6	2.1	2.9	2.7	3.0	3.2	3.1	3.1	3.3	3.7	3.3	3.5	3.3
Fixed capital consumption	0.4	0.4	0.4	0.4	0.8	0.9	0.9	1.0	1.0	1.0	1.0	1.0	1.0	1.0	1.0	1.1
Public investment	2.7	2.4	2.7	2.1	1.8	1.9	2.3	3.1	2.8	2.6	3.7	3.6	3.4	3.8	4.3	4.9
Capital revenues	0.2	0.2	0.2	0.2	0.2	0.2	0.2	0.2	0.2	0.3	0.4	0.5	0.4	0.6	0.6	0.5
Taxes on capital	0.2	0.2	0.2	0.2	0.2	0.2	0.2	0.2	0.2	0.2	0.2	0.2	0.2	0.3	0.2	0.2
Other	0.0	0.0	0.0	0.0	0.0	0.0	0.0	0.0	0.0	0.1	0.2	0.3	0.2	0.3	0.4	0.3
Capital transfers	1.0	1.0	1.2	1.1	1.2	1.5	1.9	2.2	2.2	2.0	2.3	2.3	1.8	1.7	2.0	1.6
Gross savings	3.5	2.8	3.1	1.3	1.0	0.5	0.0	-0.6	0.1	-0.7	-1.4	-0.5	1.6	1.8	3.0	2.0
Primary surplus (+) or deficit (−)	0.5	0.1	-0.1	-1.2	-1.4	-1.9	-3.0	-4.6	-3.4	-3.1	-3.5	-2.0	0.3	0.1	0.7	-0.5
Overall surplus (+) or deficit (−)	0.0	-0.3	-0.6	-1.7	-2.0	-2.7	-3.9	-5.6	-4.8	-5.3	-6.9	-6.0	-3.2	-3.2	-2.7	-4.0
Memo items:																
Cyclically adjusted primary surplus (a)					0.3	0.0	-0.5	-1.7	-0.4	-1.1	-0.6	0.4	1.7	0.4	-0.5	-1.1
Total public debt (b)					16.0	18.4	24.4	31.3	40.1	38.7	44.6	44.9	45.2	41.4	42.9	43.0

Source: Ministry of Finance
Notes: a. From Gonzalez-Paramo et al. (1991).
b. Including credits from the Bank of Spain.

the newly installed regime. The first democratic government and all political parties[8] adopted the Moncloa agreements of 1977, a comprehensive adjustment program that combined stabilization measures aimed at containing inflation and the external deficit with structural reforms of the tax system, the labor market, and the financial system; the reform agenda would be extended to include the reorganization of the energy sector as well as preliminary steps toward industrial restructuring.

The basic ingredient of the stabilization was a restrictive monetary policy, accompanied by a discrete devaluation of the exchange rate. They were complemented by the replacement of the existing wage indexation to past inflation with indexation to *anticipated* inflation; thus wage settlements were to be made within a band around the inflation forecast, itself guided by the preannounced slowdown in monetary growth. Among the measures offered in counterpart for this wage deceleration,[9] the key element was a tax reform aimed at raising fiscal revenues to finance a significant increase in public expenditures in the social sectors (pensions, unemployment compensation, etc.) and at making the tax system more equitable.

The sharp monetary deceleration succeeded in achieving an immediate reduction in the inflation rate, which between 1977 and 1979 declined by almost ten percentage points. Ex post real interest rates, which had been large and negative since 1973, rose to positive levels by 1979–80 (figure 10.4). The current account balance turned into surplus in 1978–79, and the reserve outflow was reversed. But the adjustment effort quickly ran out of steam. Progress in the implementation of the structural reforms was minimal, especially in the areas of industrial restructuring and increasing labor market flexibility, as the increasingly weak minority governments of the Democratic Center (which never enjoyed a parliamentary majority) were unwilling to assume the associated political costs. The inability to tackle the industrial crisis was reflected in the takeover by the public sector during 1978–82 of a substantial number of loss-making private enterprises—especially in the industries worst hit by the crisis, such as the basic metal and shipbuilding sectors—to avoid the political costs of further employment losses. The second oil shock, and the ensuing world recession, further complicated the continuation of the adjustment process.

In addition, the rapid expansion of the public deficit, which grew from 0.6% of GDP in 1977 to 5.6% in 1982 (figure 10.5), introduced another destabilizing element. The growing public imbalance reflected a large increase in current expenditures, from 23% of GDP in 1977 to 32% in 1982 (table 10.4), partly due to the overall deterioration in macroeconomic performance—unemployment compensation and subsidies to troubled public enterprises were among the most rapidly growing items; however, cyclically adjusted measures of fiscal stance also reveal a (more moderate) deterioration

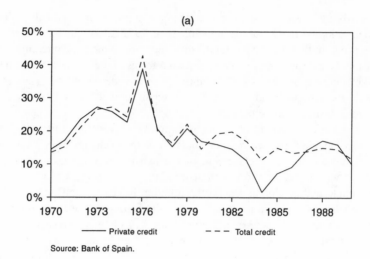

Source: Bank of Spain.

Note: The real interest rate is the long-term nominal rate minus the one-period ahead rate of GDP inflation.

Figure 10.4   (a) Credit growth; (b) Ex post real interest rate

in the fiscal balance in those years (see the line at the bottom of table 10.4).[10] Given the slow progress of tax reform, by 1982 public savings had turned negative and the primary deficit had reached its historical high at 4.6% of GDP.[11] The fiscal imbalance was financed basically by printing money, implying that if the monetary restraint initiated in 1977–78 was to be maintained, an increasingly sharp squeeze in credit to the private sector would be

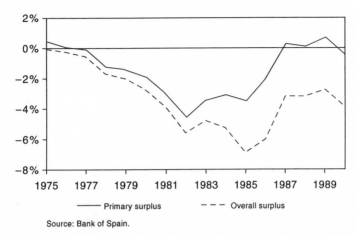

Source: Bank of Spain.

Figure 10.5   Primary and overall fiscal balances (as percent of GDP)

needed[12]—something that the Center governments were increasingly reluctant to do.

Against this background, the centralized wage agreements continued the wage deceleration initiated in 1978, albeit at a very slow pace (table 10.3). Their major contribution probably was helping to avoid an overt social confrontation, whose consequences could have been unpredictable in the climate of increasing political instability that culminated in the attempted coup of 1981. However, despite the moderation of real wages, real labor costs kept rising through 1981, partly due to a sustained increase in employers' Social Security contributions (see figure 10.1).[13]

The new terms of trade loss and the lack of decided policy action led to a repetition of the 1975–76 scenario in the early 1980s, with a marked worsening in economic performance and the reemergence of large external imbalances. Real GDP growth averaged less than 1% in 1980–82, and inflation stabilized in the 15% range, leading to an increasingly misaligned real exchange rate (figure 10.6).[14] The current account turned again into deficits exceeding 2.5% of GDP, and Spain's foreign asset position showed a rapid deterioration (see figure 10.2).

Performance was particularly adverse on the employment front: between 1977 and 1982 employment declined by over 10%, and the unemployment rate consequently jumped from 5.6% to over 16% (figure 10.7). The compression of profit margins due to the wage boom of the 1970s was now compounded by tightened credit and higher real interest rates,[15] along with the increase in energy costs (and possibly also by the intensified external competition resulting from some partial trade liberalization measures adopted since

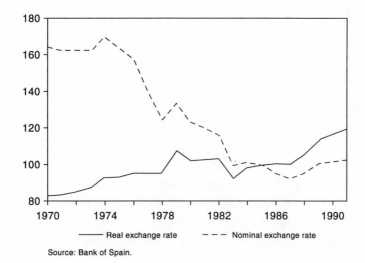

Source: Bank of Spain.

Figure 10.6 Nominal and real exchange rate indices vis-à-vis the EEC (1985=100)

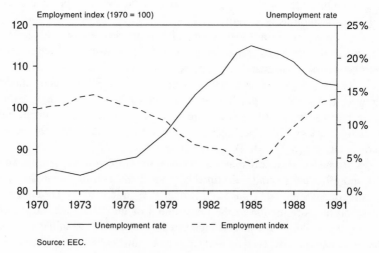

Source: EEC.

Figure 10.7 Employment index and unemployment rate

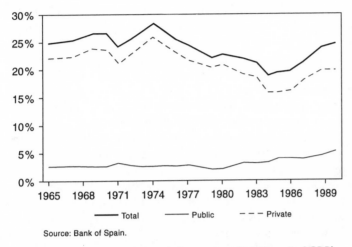

Source: Bank of Spain.

Figure 10.8   Gross domestic investment (as percent of GDP)

1977). This was reflected in record-high bankruptcies from 1978 on (see figure 10.3), with the associated layoffs, and in the continued decline of investment—by close to 12% in real terms between 1977 and 1982 (figure 10.8).

Macroeconomic Adjustment under the Socialist Administration, 1983–85

The Socialist party came to power in late 1982 on an electoral program with Keynesian overtones that emphasized the protection of real wages and the recovery of growth and employment as the basic priorities of its economic strategy. However, the "Mitterrand experiment" had just shown that independent attempts to revive growth and employment through aggregate demand management were doomed to failure. Thus after some initial hesitation, the new administration decided instead to resume the adjustment effort initiated in 1977–78, adopting an economic program that in its basic respects was entirely similar to that contained in the Moncloa agreements. It combined stabilization measures with structural and institutional reforms, giving priority to disinflation and the restoration of the external balance; it also identified the excessive growth of real wages as a leading cause of the employment collapse; finally, integration in the EEC was repeatedly underscored as the final objective of the adjustment program. In summary, the diagnosis and the intended remedies were not different from those reached in 1977–78; rather, the main new factors were the wide parliamentary majority that the Socialist party enjoyed, and the international economic recovery started in 1983, both of which contributed greatly to facilitating the actual implementation of the reforms.

Although the government's economic program emphasized the need to contain the growing public sector imbalance, in practice stabilization largely remained a monetary matter. As in 1977–78, the initial step was an 8% nominal depreciation to halt the alarming reserve losses—which by late 1982 were close to $500 million per day—and a new monetary tightening (figure 10.4), which led to a drastic deceleration in domestic credit to the private sector (it declined in real terms every year between 1983 and 1985) and to a further rise in interest rates.

In contrast, the fiscal deficit remained at high levels, with the primary deficit above 3% of GDP—but to a large extent as a reflection of the persistent growth slowdown.[16] However, as the money financing of the deficit was replaced after 1983 with debt issue—largely placed with financial intermediaries through portfolio restrictions—the overall deficit escalated to almost 7% of GDP in 1985 under the increasing burden of interest payments (see table 10.4).

Like previous administrations, the Socialist government also tried to encourage wage moderation through nationwide wage agreements—although no compromise was reached in 1984, and the government only participated directly in the Social and Economic Agreement of 1985–86. The fact that 1984 was the only year in which real wages actually fell casts some doubt on the effectiveness of the agreements as a wage-moderating device.

Nevertheless, these policies succeeded in containing domestic absorption and turning the current account into surplus in 1984–85. Inflation also decelerated further, to about 8% in 1985. Despite the decline in domestic demand—which was still led by falling real investment—real GDP growth actually rose due to the strong performance of exports, aided by the international recovery and also by the real depreciation of the peseta in 1983. Employment, however, continued to decline, and the unemployment rate escalated to almost 22% in 1985. But by that year profitability indicators already showed a significant rise from the depths of 1979–82 (see figure 10.3), setting the stage for the recovery of employment and growth.

Macroeconomic Policy during the Recovery

With Spain's entry into the EEC in 1986, economic policy in 1986–90 was devoted to the implementation of measures derived from the accession treaty and the preparation for the single European market in 1993. Macroeconomic policy focused on the achievement of inflation convergence with EEC partners and on the reduction of the fiscal imbalance. The first objective was pursued by continuing the gradual deceleration of monetary targets; however, monetary policy also paid increasing attention to the stabilization of the peseta against the ECU in preparation for its formal integration in the exchange rate mechanism of the European Monetary System, which took place in 1989. In turn, improvements in the tax administration and progress in the reform of the public enterprise sector, as well as the action of automatic stabilizers derived from the ongoing recovery, and the decision to absorb the 1986 decline in oil prices in the budget led to a sharp improvement in the fiscal accounts up to 1987: the primary balance turned into surplus and the overall public deficit declined by almost four points of GDP (table 10.4).

But the process of fiscal consolidation came to a halt in 1988[17] with an expansion of public investment, partly aimed at upgrading basic infrastructure in preparation for the European market of 1993, and also of current transfers, which largely resulted from unions' demands for increased unemployment compensation (that had led to a general strike in 1988). The expansionary change in fiscal stance[18] greatly complicated Spain's incipient recovery by leading to an absorption boom, which had to be eventually halted by a sharp monetary tightening. Thus, the late 1980s were characterized by a markedly unbalanced policy mix of fiscal expansion and monetary contraction, with strong upward pressure on interest rates and on the peseta (see figure 10.6). Given the impossibility of achieving two targets (monetary and exchange rate) with a single instrument (monetary policy), various capital controls and direct restrictions on domestic credit growth were introduced—with the paradoxical consequence that Spain's entry into the EMS was transitorily associated with a reduction, rather than an increase, in the degree of openness of the capital account.[19]

The other major policy development of the late 1980s was the end of Spain's experiment at neocorporatism and of the cooperative climate between the government and the trade unions, as no new nationwide wage agreements were reached in these years, and a recent government proposal (the Competitiveness Pact) for a new agreement setting real wage growth below productivity growth was flatly rejected by the unions.

The Structural Reforms

The counterpart to the macroeconomic stabilization was a comprehensive program of structural reforms in most areas of the economy: the external trade regime, the financial system, the labor market, the industrial sector, and the tax system. The reforms were broadly aimed at removing distorting interventions and barriers to the operation of market forces, to raise efficiency and increase the growth potential of the Spanish economy.

As with stabilization policies, the structural reforms were implemented in two stages, which followed the complete halt of the liberalization process during the final years of Francoism: first, as part of the adjustment attempt by the Center governments in 1978–82, and second, by the Socialist administration in 1983–85. In turn, the period of EEC membership (1986–90) was mainly devoted to the implementation of the reforms required by the accession treaty. For reasons of space, we do not attempt to provide a thorough description of the reform measures; instead, we summarize below the main developments.

Reforms under the Center Governments

Under the Center governments, reforms concentrated on five areas: the tax system, the energy sector, industrial restructuring, the financial system, and external trade. By contrast, no significant measures were adopted in the labor market or in the public enterprise sector.

Tax reform was devoted to the modernization of the archaic direct taxation system, and focused on the personal income tax. It led to a rapid increase in direct tax revenues (table 10.4), but was hampered by the failure to develop an adequate tax administration system and by the absence of parallel progress in the reform of indirect taxation, both of which would not be undertaken until the Socialist administrations.

The reform measures in the energy and industrial sectors were more limited. The 1979 Energy Plan represented the first comprehensive attempt at rationalizing the energy sector, but was based on a gross overprediction of energy demand that led to excess capacity.[20] The politically costly process of industrial restructuring was persistently delayed, and its legal framework would not be completed (not to say implemented) until 1981; as a result, the industrial crisis continued to deepen. Moreover, as noted before, the lack of action was complemented by the acquisition by the public sector of a number of loss-making enterprises, which quickly became a heavy burden on the budget. By 1983, the losses of these newly acquired nonviable firms exceeded 0.5% of GDP, and represented the vast majority (over 60%) of industrial public enterprise losses.

Progress was more significant on financial reform. The overprotected banking sector was opened up to foreign competition, forcing the domestic banks to start a process of productivity improvement, and interest rates were partially liberalized. The Bank of Spain's regulatory powers were also enhanced. But the measures necessary to strengthen the banking system were not adopted, and this would prove very costly: the growing industrial crisis had caused a sharp decline in the banking system's solvency, and from 1980 to 1981 led to the failure of an increasing number of banks.[21]

In turn, the trade reform measures of this period represented a unilateral attempt to accelerate EEC integration. They included tariff reductions and the elimination of some licensing requirements.[22] However, the liberalization was halted by the second oil shock and did not resume until Spain's entry into the EEC.

Reforms under the Socialist Administration, 1983–85

The reform process accelerated under the Socialist administration. Nevertheless, in conflicting cases stabilization took priority over structural reform. Thus trade reform was postponed until the completion of the macroeconomic adjustment, and financial liberalization partially backtracked when it threatened to raise excessively the cost of financing the public deficit.

In addition to continuing the reforms initiated in 1977–78, the policy actions extended to the labor market and the public sector. A new Energy Plan tackled the reorganization of the energy sector. The industrial restructuring process was finally initiated, with the adjustment of the excess capacity in the sectors worst hit by the crisis (e.g., steel, shipbuilding, textiles).

The gradual reform of the financial system also continued during this period, with further liberalization of interest rates; however, the shift to an orthodox financing of the mounting public deficit after 1983 was accompanied by renewed restrictions on banks' portfolios. The restructuring of the insolvent banks was also tackled, as the banking crisis had reached huge proportions.[23]

Perhaps the most significant among the reform measures was increasing the flexibility of the labor market. Until 1984, the restrictions on flexible labor contracts dating from Franco's regime had remained largely untouched, except for some timid relaxation attempted under the Center administrations. Thus for practical purposes labor contracts continued to be of indefinite duration, and layoffs, when permitted, involved high severance payments. The generalization of flexible labor contracts was agreed to by the government and the unions as part of the 1985–86 Social and Economic Agreement, which removed most of the remaining restrictions on temporary contracts of up to three years; this would greatly contribute to the employment boom of the late 1980s.

In turn, numerous reforms were introduced in the public sector, according to a medium-term program whose objective was the reduction of the fiscal imbalance. Among them, the reform of the pension system was particularly important to halt the mounting deficit of the Social Security system. The medium-term program was also useful in providing a framework of discipline and identifying the necessary specific reforms; it helped single out many small reform measures that reduced both expenditures and distorting interventions at the same time.

An important step was the initiation of the reform of public enterprises, which had become a heavy burden on the budget. The large nonfinancial public enterprise sector (which by 1982 contributed over 7% of total GDP, and over 15% of aggregate gross fixed investment) was heavily concentrated in some of the industries worst hit by the crisis. In 1982, the financing of its losses and of its investment absorbed over 3.5% of GDP in current and capital transfers from the general government. In this context, the reform had the double objective of reducing the fiscal burden of public enterprise losses and eventually diminishing the public sector's direct involvement in industry. Thus the acquisition by the public sector of nonviable private firms was halted,[24] and the Socialist administration opted for the privatization of large segments of the industrial public enterprise sector. Restructuring of loss-making enterprises began, and by 1985 a first group of enterprises was privatized.

These reforms, however, carried significant costs. This applies in particular to the fiscal and quasi-fiscal burden associated with the rescue of the private banking system, perhaps the most expensive sectoral operation of the whole adjustment process.[25] Similarly, the cost of industrial restructuring was probably magnified by the slow pace and the overly generous terms of its implementation—largely dictated by the government's desire to avoid a confrontation with the labor organizations. Even increasing the flexibility of labor contracts entailed significant fiscal costs, because it was achieved in exchange for an expanded coverage of unemployment compensation and for other government commitments, ranging from the indexation of pensions to the introduction of fiscal incentives to investment; the fiscal cost of all these measures could represent as much as 1 percentage point of GDP in 1985 (Segura 1990).

Reforms from within the EEC

After Spain's entry into the EEC, structural reforms concentrated on the implementation of the measures required by the accession treaty, and "autonomous" reforms became relatively less significant, with the financial system representing perhaps the main exception to this rule.

Needless to say, for the Spanish economy the accession treaty implied an exceptionally thorough liberalization[26] and one of the most important structural reform packages in recent history. Its most obvious components are the liberalization of trade and capital flows vis-à-vis the EEC. The former involves the gradual reduction of tariffs until their complete elimination in 1993, along with the dismantling of quantity restrictions. Likewise, the latter requires the removal by the same date of all barriers to capital movements.[27]

The liberalization of the external sector was accompanied by the continuation of reform measures in other areas. In the tax system, the value-added tax replaced the old excise tax. The privatization of industrial public enterprises continued, accompanied by the market sale of minority equity holdings in some large public firms. Industrial restructuring was extended to new productive sectors. Finally, the reform of the financial system was also completed, with measures aimed at strengthening competition and with the complete liberalization of all interest rates. Portfolio restrictions on the banking system were eased and a timetable for their eventual elimination was established; and measures to strengthen the stock market and increase its transparency were also adopted.

The Results of the Adjustment and the Challenges Ahead

By 1985, the process of adjustment and reform of the Spanish economy had advanced significantly. The external accounts were in surplus, inflation had declined to single-digit levels, and profitability indicators showed a marked improvement.[28] Aided by the world recovery and by the important impact on expectations of the accession to the EEC in 1986, Spain entered a phase of sustained expansion. The recovery also unveiled new challenges, however, and underscored the need for further policy action in some key areas.

The Recovery of 1986–90

Growth resumed strongly after 1985. Real GDP growth rose to an average of 4.5% in 1986–90. Most important, the improved growth performance was led by a private investment boom, which reflected the sustained recovery of profitability: following a decade of almost uninterrupted decline, private fixed investment rose from 15.9% of GDP in 1984 to 19.6 in 1990 (see figure 10.7).

An important factor behind the private investment recovery was the sharp increase in foreign investment.[29] From a historical average of less than 0.5% of GDP in 1970–85, direct foreign investment (in net terms) rose to about 2% in 1990—or close to 9% of total private investment in that year. The increase was led by a steep rise in the flows originating within the EEC.[30] Its role was particularly important in the recovery of manufacturing investment, of which it represented close to 50% in 1986–90.[31]

Employment also showed a spectacular recovery in 1986–90, following eleven consecutive years of decline; by 1990, total employment was almost 20% above the level of 1985, and close to its historical high of 1974 (figure 10.8). The rise in employment was led by a rapid increase in the number of workers on the newly introduced flexible labor contracts, while those on indefinite-term contracts declined somewhat.[32] The parallel decline in unemployment, from 21% in 1985 to 16% in 1990, was also significant, although it was moderated by an increase in participation rates largely associated with the ongoing improvement in the employment situation.

Additional progress in the reduction of inflation was also achieved. The inflation differential vis-à-vis EEC/EMS countries (the key target of Spanish policymakers, especially after the peseta's formal integration in the EMS in 1989) also declined further to about 1%–1.5% in 1989–90 (figure 10.9), aided by the dismantling of trade barriers associated with the accession treaty and by the nominal appreciation of the peseta after 1987. But efforts to eliminate the remaining inflation differential proved unsuccessful. Despite the seemingly massive labor market slack, nominal wage growth rebounded by 1989–90. Analysis of sectoral inflation rates reveals that services prices failed to decelerate after 1986; by contrast, industrial prices slowed down considerably.[33] This reflects not only the obvious effects of the trade liberalization on industrial prices (mainly tradable) as well as the pressure from the demand expansion on services (nontradable), but also the insufficient deregulation and persistence of monopolistic practices in the latter sector.[34]

The potentially most troublesome developments of the late 1980s were the significant real appreciation of the peseta and the rapid deterioration of the current account. The real exchange rate (CPI-based) vis-à-vis the EEC appreciated by about 20% (see figure 10.6); vis-à-vis industrial countries, the appreciation was even larger. Combined with the trade liberalization measures, the appreciation contributed to a spectacular rise in imports.[35] The moderate current account surplus of 1984–86 gave way to rapidly growing deficits, which exceeded 3% of GDP in 1989–90. However, unlike the current account imbalances of the 1974–76 and 1980–82 episodes, the underlying

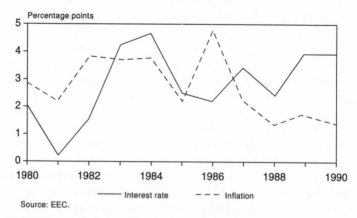

Source: EEC.

Figure 10.9   Inflation and interest rate differentials between Spain and the EEC

force now was an investment boom, rather than a saving decline. In addition, the financing of the external gap did not pose any immediate problem, as it was amply covered by foreign investment inflows alone; indeed, the stock of foreign reserves grew by over $40 billion in 1986–90, while in previous episodes the result had been massive reserve losses. But the fragility of the situation can be appreciated by noting that in 1990 the seemingly large foreign reserve stock represented less than one-third of Spain's total external liabilities.[36] Moreover, as figure 10.2 shows, direct foreign investment flows—which could be assumed to be the most stable component of foreign investment—had become clearly insufficient to finance the external gap after 1988.

Hence the sustainability of this cycle of appreciation and current account imbalance critically depends on the continuation of the massive capital inflows of recent years. While to some extent these may reflect a permanent portfolio reallocation associated with Spain's process of reform and its entry into the EEC,[37] there are good reasons to think that they are mainly a transitory phenomenon. A large portion of the capital inflow is just the result of the persistent interest differential associated with the unbalanced policy mix of recent years (see figure 10.9), and will vanish when the latter is corrected. In addition, the boom in direct foreign investment should subside once the international relocation process associated with the creation of the European market in 1993 is sufficiently advanced; indeed, the persistent deterioration in the competitiveness of Spanish production derived from the real appreciation should contribute to discouraging direct foreign investment in the future.

All these considerations suggest the need for policy action to correct the competitiveness loss, to avoid the possibility of a "crash landing" scenario that would require a drastic real depreciation in the face of a sudden drying up of capital inflows. To protect investment, the policy measures should aim at raising savings, especially in the public sector, thus continuing the fiscal consolidation process interrupted after 1987. This in turn would allow a relative monetary easing and a reduction in interest rates, alleviating the upward pressure on the exchange rate.[38]

The Employment Cost of the Adjustment

Spain's economic adjustment entailed an extremely high cost in terms of employment. Between 1975 and 1985 over 2 million jobs (close to 20% of total employment) were lost, and despite the recovery of 1986–90 the pre-crisis employment level has yet to be regained. As a result, the unemployment rate has roughly doubled the EEC average throughout the 1980s. Although high unemployment has been a generalized phenomenon in Europe in the last decade, its magnitude and persistence in the Spanish case are striking, as is the failure of real wages to decelerate more markedly given the apparently massive labor market slack of recent years.

The decline in labor demand during 1975–85 is easy to understand along the lines already described. The real wage rises of the 1970s discouraged labor demand directly and, through the adverse effect of the ensuing profit squeeze on investment, also indirectly; the policy of tight money and the rise in real interest rates in the early 1980s added further to the profit squeeze and the investment fall, and thus to the decline in labor demand. Likewise, the bankruptcies of loss-making firms also contributed significantly to the destruction of employment.

However, those factors do not explain the persistence of unemployment and its minimal contribution to wage moderation in recent years.[39] These two facts suggest that the high observed unemployment has largely become an equilibrium phenomenon.[40] The causes should be traced to the functioning of the labor market and, in particular, to those aspects that tend to reduce the pressure of the unemployed on wage formation.[41]

Recent studies have underscored the low degree of geographical and occupational mobility in the Spanish labor market. In some instances this reflects archaic regulations (such as the legal restrictions on functional mobility), but it may also result from the breakdown of labor market mechanisms in a context of high unemployment. For example, high average unemployment contributes to hamper labor mobility due to the poor prospects of finding work, leading to an increase in geographical mismatch and to reduced pressure on wages; there is evidence that this mechanism has been at work in reducing regional mobility in Spain in recent years.[42] In turn, the long-term unemployed may get discouraged and reduce their job search (or, alternatively, lose their human capital and become "unemployable"), thus exerting little pressure on wages; this agrees well with the observed high proportion of long-term unemployed in the total.[43]

The centralized wage agreements of the adjustment period may have also contributed to reducing the pressure of unemployment on wages. Apart from the likely possibility that wage setting by the unions may have reflected mainly the interests of the employed insiders, ignoring those of the unemployed outsiders,[44] the nationwide wage setting paid little attention to sector- or firm-specific factors, which must have been important at a time of intense sector-specific shocks and intersectoral reallocation. This contributed to a narrowing of wage differentials across industries; in addition, the "equal wage increases" demanded by workers in the 1970s also substantially narrowed wage differentials across categories. This process (which was reversed only partially after 1982) led to a rigid wage structure that could help explain the persistence of high unemployment among low-skilled workers.

Whatever the cause of its persistence, why did mass unemployment not result in a social explosion? The answer has to lie mainly in the composition of unemployment: at its peak in 1985, only about one-fourth of the unemployed were heads of households, and this proportion has since declined. Thus unemployment has affected mainly second-wage earners (especially the young), who have been able to subsist on the income earned by the head of household; this has probably contributed to mitigate the costs of mass unemployment and its consequences for Spain's social stability.

The Challenges Ahead

The above discussion shows that, despite the relative success of the process of adjustment and reform, Spanish economic policy still has to tackle two important problems. The first one is the restoration of macroeconomic stability, which requires reversing the fiscal expansion of the late 1980s, in order to ease the pressure on the external balance and the real exchange rate and to restore a more balanced policy mix. But the fiscal adjustment should protect infrastructure investments, an area in which Spain still lags behind its EEC partners. The limited scope for further tax hikes implies that the bulk of the adjustment should correspond to revenue increases arising from improvements in tax administration (especially measures aimed at reducing the still widespread tax fraud), and to current expenditures and noninfrastructure investments. Additional steps in the reform and privatization of the public enterprises should also help reduce the fiscal burden that many of them still represent.[45]

Second, further structural reforms are necessary, particularly in two areas. The first one is the labor market, some of whose regulations are still too restrictive. In particular, steps should be taken to increase geographical, sectoral, and functional labor mobility to make the wage structure more responsive to labor market conditions. Among these measures, adequate training programs for the unemployed are an important factor. These actions are especially necessary in view of the intense process of intersectoral reallocation that is likely to follow the creation of the European market. In addition, a revenue-neutral reduction in employers' Social Security contributions[46] matched by an increase in the value-added tax would help stimulate employment—which in Spain's situation should be the top priority. Finally, further reforms are needed to deregulate and increase the degree of competition in the services sector, which so far has remained largely sheltered from the liberalization process.

Some Key Factors in Spain's "Success"

By the end of the 1980s the Spanish experience of adjustment and reform would have been regarded as a success, were it not for the persistence of high unemployment. In retrospect, which are the responsible factors? We believe there are at least five: economic policies, the initial conditions, the "EEC effect," the international environment, and Spain's political background.

The economic policies of the adjustment period were quite standard. Their essential objectives were the restoration of macroeconomic stability and profitability. As already described, the stabilization was centered around a gradual money-based disinflation accompanied by heterodox wage targets. The reform measures shared a broad free-market orientation: liberalization of the financial and labor markets and external trade, along with public sector retrenchment, fiscal reform, and privatization.[47] Moreover, the stabilization measures generally took precedence over the reforms, especially in the second adjustment attempt (1983–85). Spain's performance in the late 1980s is proof that these conventional policies—with the important help of other factors listed below—did work.

One may wonder to what extent the government-supported wage agreements really helped the adjustment process, especially in view of its disproportionate unemployment cost (and also given the sharp deceleration of wages observed, for example, in 1984, a year without agreement). Would decentralized wage setting not have achieved the same result, perhaps more quickly (and without the associated distortion of a rigid wage structure)? The answer might well be affirmative, but the main role of the wage agreements should instead be found in their contribution to social and political stability—and thus to the viability of the whole reform process. Indeed, in the early years of the adjustment a head-on clash with the unions could have set the stage for the collapse of the democratic regime. Instead, a negotiated distribution of the costs of the reform process surely provided a much better economic environment, even if it did so at the cost of slowing down the disinflation.[48]

Second, Spain's reform effort started from initial conditions that in certain aspects were much more favorable than in the case of other reforming countries. As noted earlier, initial public debt levels were low not only by Latin American, but even by European standards. This made it feasible to run large fiscal imbalances, partly in an attempt to compensate losers from the reforms, without having to face a fiscal crisis. Foreign indebtedness was also low, which likewise allowed more leeway in the adjustment process. In turn, the seemingly rapid success of the external liberalization of the late 1980s is not the result of a sudden opening up of the economy; rather, the liberalization process had really started in the late 1950s and continued, at varying pace, for two decades.

Besides policy actions and initial conditions, a third key factor was the "EEC effect," which goes well beyond the specifics of the reform package associated with the EEC accession treaty. Even more important was the role of the EEC in providing an anchor for economic policy. Joining a powerful and well-established economic area not only meant ensuring access to a large market (in itself important); it also guaranteed the irreversibility of the liberalization process, with the reform measures specified in a treaty not open to modification by future governments, while providing at the same time a well-specified timetable for its implementation. This automatic guarantee of the permanent nature of the reforms must have made an extremely important contribution to the investment climate and to the recovery of capital accumulation and growth in the late 1980s.

Moreover, the timing of EEC accession was also particularly favorable. The first democratic government had applied for membership almost a decade earlier without any results, and by the early 1980s the hopes for a quick enlargement of the Community had almost faded. The enlargement arrived precisely when the adjustment process was well advanced, making it possible for the Spanish economy to benefit quickly from the liberalization without need for any drastic stabilization measures. Also, Spain joined the EEC when the customs union was undertaking its transformation into the full-fledged single market of 1993 and later the EMU, which implied an even more comprehensive process of liberalization and reform.[49]

Fourth, the improvement in world economic conditions begun in 1983 also made an important contribution to the success of Spain's second adjustment attempt. While the failure of the previous episode was partly due to the second oil shock and the ensuing world recession, the 1983–85 stabilization was favored by the international recovery and, after 1985, by the decline in oil prices. The windfall was particularly important in the Spanish case because, in spite of the energy sector reforms, Spain remains the industrial country with highest dependence on imported oil. This of course was a bit of luck, but it is also safe to assume that the windfall would have been wasted if the previous adjustment measures had not been implemented.[50] The government opted for absorbing the windfall in the budget, which contributed to an unexpectedly painless fiscal adjustment.

Finally, Spain's reform process benefited from an exceptionally favorable political environment. This could be best summarized in two facts: political moderation, and consensus on the "European project."

The degree of political moderation prevalent in today's Spain is truly remarkable for a country with a tradition of violence that suffered one of the bloodiest civil wars of this century. Today it is not easy to find important differences among the economic programs of the main political parties: the first democratic governments of the Center adopted progressive measures such as tax reform, while the Socialist governments implemented liberalization policies. In summary, the basic framework of economic policy is stable, which provides a favorable environment for investment. In addition, the consensus—or near unanimity—on Spain's integration in the European Community should also be underscored. Integration in Europe means liberalization and reform, and thus material short-term losses set against uncertain future gains. Yet so far it has encountered practically no opposition, contrary to the cases of other European countries. Just as moderation represents a break with the past, so does this attitude that runs against Spain's traditional isolation. Spain's backwardness was largely due to the protectionism and isolationism that characterized economic policy since the nineteenth century. It would seem as if Spaniards realized that their troubles were due to isolation and lack of moderation, and were ready to change their historical traditions.

Notes

We are grateful to Guillermo de la Dehesa, Mario Blejer, Osvaldo Sunkel, and to participants in the El Escorial conference for useful comments; to Juanjo Dolado for his advice on data issues; and to Raimundo Soto for valuable research assistance.

1. Obviously, this similarity between Spain in the 1970s and today's Eastern Europe should not obscure the abysmal differences between the two scenarios—for example, in terms of well-defined property rights or the existence of well-established (albeit far from perfect) goods, labor, and capital markets.

2. However, the low unemployment figures concealed a sustained labor migration toward EEC countries.

3. By the early 1970s, Spain ranked among the least open OECD countries in terms of import- and export-to-GDP ratios. See de la Dehesa et al. (1990).

4. By 1970, only about 20% of the CPI basket corresponded to goods with liberalized (or semiliberalized) prices. By 1973, this proportion had risen to two-thirds of the total. See de la Dehesa et al. (1990).

5. Although there is no doubt as to the rapid real wage increase of 1972–77, it is more difficult to establish its precise extent, due to the large discrepancies between alternative sources of wage information. The figure in the text reflects national accounts data, which provide a more conservative estimate of wage growth over this period than the alternative wage survey. See Albarracin and Yago (1986) for a critical discussion.

6. See OECD (1975).

7. See Martinez-Mendez (1982).

8. It is remarkable that the Moncloa agreements, with their important wage moderation component, were formally endorsed by the political parties and not by the trade unions (although the latter did participate in the discussions and effectively supported implementation). This was largely a reflection of the incomplete consolidation of the just-legalized labor organizations, whose affiliation rates were low and that, unlike the political parties, had not yet confronted an electoral process.

9. The effectiveness of the Moncloa agreements in slowing down wage growth can be appreciated by noting that in the months immediately preceding them, the unions were demanding nominal wage increases in the 35%–40% range for 1978 (Palacio 1989). With the application of the agreements, the increase effectively reached in wage settlements that year averaged only 21%; including wage drift, nominal wages rose by about 25%.

10. The cyclically adjusted deficit figures in table 10.4 are from Gonzalez-Paramo et al. (1991). Alternative measures of fiscal stance also indicate a marked deterioration since 1977; see, for example, Raymond and Palet (1990).

11. It is important to note that here and in the rest of the chapter the "public sector" figures refer

only to the general government, and exclude a large portion of the public enterprise sector. Thus, to the extent that the latter financed part of their saving-investment imbalance in the financial market (as happened during this period), the figures understate the true dimension of the consolidated public sector deficit.

12. See Ariztegui (1990) for a description of the growing difficulties encountered in implementing monetary policy during this period.

13. Since 1979, average wage growth in new settlements had fallen below CPI inflation, although because of wage drift effective real wages had kept rising in CPI terms. This declining trend of real wage growth was formally sanctioned in the National Agreement on Employment of 1982, signed by the trade unions, employers' organizations, and also by the government, in which for the first time the wage norm for the negotiations was set below the anticipated rate of CPI inflation (table 10.3).

14. See Dolado and Viñals (1990) for an empirical appraisal of real exchange rate misalignment in Spain in 1970–90.

15. The latter probably understate the extent of the financial tightening, given the widespread credit rationing prevalent in Spain in the late 1970s and the strong dependence of firms' financing on bank credit.

16. As shown in table 10.4, the cyclically adjusted primary surplus did show a modest improvement after 1982.

17. The seeming decline in the deficit in 1989 shown in table 10.4 reflects a change in the timing of tax reimbursements. Without it, the overall deficit would have equaled 3.5% and 3.6% of GDP in 1989 and 1990, respectively.

18. The increase in the observed public deficit (to 4% of GDP in 1990 in table 10.4) grossly understates the true extent of the fiscal expansion due to the strong cyclical effect of the economic upswing. The cyclically adjusted figures computed in Gonzalez-Paramo et al. (1991) suggest that the fiscal impulse actually raised the adjusted public deficit to record-high levels.

19. This is illustrated empirically by Viñals (1990), who also analyzes the effectiveness of capital controls in Spain in recent years. The restrictions were eventually lifted in 1991.

20. The overcapacity put the electricity sector in a delicate financial position, from which it was eventually bailed out by a general increase in electricity prices.

21. Cuervo (1988) provides a thorough description of the banking crisis in those years.

22. The average nominal tariff rate was reduced from 8% to 5%. The proportion of liberalized imports in the total rose from about 78% in 1976 to 88% in 1981–82. See de la Dehesa et al. (1990) for further details.

23. The liabilities of the banks affected by different degrees of insolvency during 1978–85 represented over one-fourth of the total liabilities of the banking system.

24. There were some exceptions, the most remarkable being the bizarre (and very costly) nationalization of a large financial conglomerate (Rumasa) in 1983; however, it was quickly reprivatized.

25. Cuervo (1988) estimates that the overall fiscal and quasi-fiscal cost of the rescue represented about 5% of 1985 GDP.

26. With some agriculture-related aspects as the main exception.

27. A thorough analysis of the implications of EEC integration for the Spanish economy is provided by Viñals et al. (1990).

28. The persistent rise in the profitability index in figure 10.2 in the late 1980s, to levels well above those of the early 1970s, may overstate the extent of the profitability recovery. Nevertheless, the upswing that it shows after 1982–83 agrees well with the sharp decline in bankruptcies, displayed also in the figure.

29. By contrast, it is interesting to note that the recovery of private investment took place before the expansion of public infrastructure investment, which only began in 1987–88.

30. Bajo and Torres (1992) provide a detailed description of the recent evolution of direct foreign investment in Spain. An econometric analysis of its determinants is presented in Bajo and Sosvilla (1991).

31. The recovery of industrial investment is analyzed by Gonzalez-Romero and Myro (1989). Simulations reported in OECD (1989) also suggest an important role of foreign investment in the improved performance of overall private investment after 1985.

32. The number of workers on fixed-term contracts rose from 15% of all workers in 1987 to 30% in 1990 (Segura et al. 1991). Econometric results reported by Bentolila and Saint-Paul (1991) also suggest that the introduction of flexible labor contracts explains an important portion of the rapid employment expansion of 1986–90.

33. The inflation rate of industrial prices declined sharply, from about 9% in 1985–86 to 4% in 1989–90, below EEC/EMS levels. By contrast, inflation in the services sector has remained practically unchanged from its 1985–86 levels (over 8%). See Banco de España (1991) and OECD (1992) for further discussion.

34. This is further confirmed by the failure of services inflation to decelerate even after the demand slowdown of 1990–91.

35. Econometric estimates reported by Fernandez and Sebastian (1989) and updated in Sebastian (1991) indicate that the real appreciation could explain a 30% increase in the volume of non-energy imports between 1986 and 1990. The total increase actually observed was over 150%.

36. Defined as the sum of the foreign debt stock, plus nonresident bank deposits, plus the stocks of equity and bonds held by foreigners.

37. Dolado and Viñals (1990) attempt to disentangle empirically the extent to which the persistent real appreciation represents an equilibrium phenomenon derived from these factors rather than a real exchange rate misalignment.

38. After this chapter had been completed (in June 1992), the urgency of such policy action became even more apparent with the international recession and especially, with the uncertainties that arose concerning the construction of the European Monetary Union. The ensuing loss of confidence in EMS parities brought into the open the fragility of Spain's macroeconomic situation, and the crash-landing scenario mentioned in the text began to materialize with a sudden reversal of capital flows which, after massive reserve losses, forced repeated depreciations of the peseta.

39. An international comparison of measures of real wage flexibility in Dolado and Malo de Molina (1985) highlights the high degree of wage rigidity in Spain relative to other countries.

40. Empirical studies support this hypothesis by finding a sharp increase in the NAIRU (nonaccelerating inflation rate of unemployment) in the 1980s. See Dolado et al. (1986).

41. For a recent analysis of the factors behind the persistence of Spain's high unemployment, see Bentolila and Blanchard (1990).

42. See Bentolila and Dolado (1990). There is also evidence that occupational mismatches have risen; indeed, in 1986–90 many firms were reporting their inability to find adequately qualified workers, which indicates that existing job training schemes for the unemployed are clearly insufficient.

43. In 1985, two-thirds of the unemployed had been out of work for at least 12 months; by 1990, the corresponding figure was about 50%.

44. This would be possible because of the existence of high firing costs that effectively make both groups of workers imperfect substitutes from employers' point of view (see Lindbeck and Snower 1988). However, the strength of this mechanism should have been significantly diminished by the generalization of flexible labor contracts after 1984.

45. In 1990, current and capital transfers to nonfinancial public enterprises from the central government alone still exceeded 1% of GDP.

46. Compared with other European countries, the rate of the Social Security tax (currently at about 30% in Spain) is in the high range.

47. The policy recipe that results from this mix is practically identical to that in World Bank (1991).
48. It is worth noting that the number of work days lost in strikes shows clear increases in the years with no agreement.
49. The fact that at the time of Spain's accession the EEC was starting to revise its most negative policy (on agriculture) provides yet another proof of lucky timing.
50. In Hemingway's words, "In life, luck is the most important thing. But one has to be ready for the moment when luck strikes."

References

Albarracin, J., and A. Yago. 1986. "La industria española en el período 1970–1984." *Boletin Económico del Banco de España.*

Andres, J., et al. 1989. "La inversión en España: un enfoque macroeconómico." *Moneda y Crédito.*

Andres, J., et al. 1990. "The Influence of Demand and Capital Constraints on Spanish Unemployment," Ministerio de Economía y Hacienda.

Ariztegui, F. J. 1990 "La política monetaria: un período crucial." In J. L. Garcia-Delgado, ed., *Economía Española de la transición y la democracia.* Madrid: CIS.

Bajo, O., and A. Sosvilla. 1991. "Modelling Direct Foreign Investment in Spain." Mimeo.

Bajo, O., and A. Torres. 1992. "El comercio exterior y la inversión extranjera directa tras la integración de España en la CEE (1986–90)." Mimeo.

Banco de España. *Informe Anual.* Various years.

Bentolila, S., and O. Blanchard. 1990. "Spanish Unemployment." *Economic Policy* 10: 233–281.

Bentolila, S., and J. Dolado. 1989. "Mismatch and internal migration in Spain: 1962-1986." Documento de Trabajo, Banco de España.

Bentolila, S., and G. Saint-Paul. 1991. "The macroeconomic impact of flexible labor contracts, with an application to Spain." Documento de Trabajo, Banco de España.

Cuervo, A. 1988. *La crisis bancaria en España.* Barcelona: Ariel.

de la Dehesa, G., J. J. Ruiz, and A. Torres. 1990. "The Timing and Sequencing of a Trade Liberalization Policy: The Case of Spain." In M. Michaely et al., eds., *Liberalizing Foreign Trade.* Oxford: Basil Blackwell.

Dolado, J., and J. L. Malo de Molina. 1985. "Desempleo y Rigidez del mercado de trabajo en España." *Boletin Económico del Banco de España.*

Dolado, J., J. L. Malo de Molina, and A. Zabalza. 1986. "Spanish Industrial Unemployment: Some Explanatory Factors." *Economica* 53: 313–335.

Dolado, J., and J. Viñals. 1990. "Macroeconomic Policy, External Targets and Constraints: The Case of Spain." Documento de Trabajo, Banco de España.

Fernandez, I., and Y. M. Sebastian. 1989. "El sector exterior y la incorporación de España en la CEE: análisis a partir de funciones de exportaciones e importaciones." *Moneda y Crédito* 189: 39–65.

García-Delgado, J. L., ed. 1989. *España Economía.* Madrid: Espasa-Calpe.

308   Miguel Angel Fernandez Ordoñez and Luis Servén

García-Delgado, J. L. 1990. *Economía Española de la transición y la democracia*. Madrid: CIS.

González-Paramo, J. M., et al. 1991. "Issues on Fiscal Policy in Spain." Documento de Trabajo, Banco de España.

González-Romero, A., and Y. R. Myro. 1989. "La recuperación de la inversión industrial en España 1985–88: sus objetivos y factores determinantes." *Moneda y Crédito* 188: 17–55.

Layard, R., and S. Nickell. 1987. "The Performance of the British Labor Market." In R. Dornbusch and R. Layard, eds., *The Performance of the British Economy*. Oxford: Clarendon.

Lindbeck, A., and D. Snower. 1988. *The Insider-Outsider Theory of Employment and Unemployment*. Cambridge, MA: MIT Press.

Lopez-Claros, A. 1988. "The Search for Efficiency in the Adjustment Process: Spain in the 1980s." IMF Occasional Paper.

Lorente, J.R. 1990. "Negociación colectiva y empleo en España." Mimeo.

Martínez-Mendez, P. 982. "El proceso de ajuste de la economía española 1973–1980." Estudios Económicos, nom. 23, Banco de España.

Novales, A., et al. 1987. *La empresa pública industrial en España*. Madrid: FEDEA.

OECD. *Economic Surveys: Spain*. Various years.

Palacio, J. I. 1989. "Relaciones Laborales y Tendencias Organizativas de los Trabajadores y los Empresarios." In J. L. Garcia-Delgado, ed., *España Economia*. Madrid: Espasa-Calpe.

Raymond, J. L and J. Palet. 1990. "Factores determinantes de los tipos de interes reales en España." *Papeles de Economía Española* 43: 60–69.

Revenga, A. 1991. "Economic Liberalization and the Distribution of Income: The Spanish Experience." Mimeo, The World Bank.

Sebastian, M. 1991. "Un análisis estructural de las importaciones y exportaciones españolas." *Información Comercial Española*.

Segura, J. 1990. "Del primer gobierno socialista a la integración en la CEE." In J. L. Garcia-Delgado, ed., *Economía Española de la transición y la democracia*. Madrid: CIS.

Segura, J., et al. 1991. *Análisis de la contratación temporal en España*. Madrid: Ministerio de Trabajo y Seguridad Social.

Viñals, J. 1990a. "Los riesgos de la libre circulación de capitales." *Papeles de Economía Española* 43: 74–83.

Viñals, J. 1990b. "Spain's Capital Account Shock." CEPR Working Paper, nom. 477.

Viñals, J. et al. 1990. "Spain and the 'EEC cum 1992' Shock." In C. Bliss and J. Braga de Macedo, eds., *Unity with Diversity in the European Economy: The Community's Southern Frontier*. Cambridge Cambridge University Press.

World Bank. 1991. *World Development Report*.

Part IV
Economic Reform:
Retrospect and Prospect

CHAPTER 11

Contemporary Economic Reform
in Historical Perspective

Osvaldo Sunkel

The Wider Context of Economic Reform

The macroeconomics of adjustment, restructuring, and the transition from socialism to capitalism is of critical importance to many countries and should be addressed in a historical and comparative way as well as from various perspectives. Given the formidable scope of the subject, which by its very nature trespasses disciplinary boundaries, let me offer some personal reflections that I trust will be provocative and useful.

With this aim in mind, it seems convenient to attempt to place the current worldwide and pervasive process of economic reform in a context wider than the specific policy changes being proposed. The application of a set of policies aimed at deregulating and liberalizing internal and international markets for goods, factors, and finance; at reducing substantially the size and roles of the state; and at privatizing public services and enterprises requires fundamental institutional changes and has profound social and political consequences for economic and social development.

These inevitably bring to the fore the ideological, political, cultural, technological, environmental, and other closely related dimensions of change and development, at various levels and layers of society, both national and international. We should therefore be open to exploring our subject from a multidisciplinary perspective as well as to placing it in its global and longer-term historical contexts. I will attempt to look at certain important aspects of the process of economic reform from this angle in the hope of helping to understand the nature of the changes taking place, and of contributing some useful background and insights to the developmental aspects of macroeconomic management of economic reform.

The basic argument that I want to put forward is that during these last decades of the twentieth century, we are in the midst of a period of epochal civilizational transformation, a sea change in the sociocultural affairs and arrangements of humanity, within and among societies, as well as between

311

them and their environmental life-support systems. The wave of economic reform that we are witnessing is part and parcel of this wider process, is largely conditioned by it, and will certainly influence it.

To attempt to single out from such a complex process some of the more relevant features, it seems convenient to compare it to another such phase: the interwar period during the first half of this century, about which we have sufficient historical perspective. It may seem farfetched to take such a long and wide view, but as will become apparent, it may be not only appropriate and useful, but perhaps even indispensable.

Long-Term Phases of Capitalist Development

To start with what is more familiar to our discipline, let us have a look at the long-term average trends of some basic economic aggregates and indicators: GDP, GDP per capita, fixed capital stock, volume of exports, and rate of unemployment. As can be seen in table 11.1, capitalist development over the last century or so has gone through distinct phases. There have been two periods of intense growth and low unemployment, one from around 1870 to 1913, and a second and exceptionally rapid one between 1950 and 1973. And there have been two phases of relatively slow growth and high unemployment, the first during the interwar period from 1913 to around 1950, and the more recent one since 1973, which still continues.

As one can gather from the relevant literature, the phases of rapid economic growth and development, sometimes labeled respectively as those of *Pax Britannica* and *Pax Americana*, seem to be associated, among other elements, with periods of relatively stable national power structures, international geopolitical arrangements, and dominant ideologies; waves of diffusion

TABLE 11.1 Growth characteristics of different phases, 1870–1989 (arithmetic average of figures for individual countries)

Phases	GDP	GDP per capita	Tangible reproducible gross nonresidential fixed capital stock[a]	Volume of exports	Average unemployment (% of labor force)
			Annual average compound growth rates		
1870–1913	2.5	1.4	3.4	3.0	4.5
1913–50	2.0	1.2	2.0	1.0	7.5
1950–73	4.9	3.8	5.8	8.6	2.6
1973–89	2.6	2.1	4.2	4.7	

Source: Augus Maddison, *Dynamic Forces in Capitalist Development*, p. 118, 119 (Oxford: 1991).

a. Refers to six countries; first period is 1880–1913, last is 1973–87. United Kingdom and United States, 1900–1913

of major technological innovations; and new forms of business organization and financial expansion, which tend to generate a stimulating and confident business and investment climate. In contrast, the periods of slow growth or relative stagnation are characterized by several kinds of shocks, acute crises, and abrupt transformations in these and other national and international socio-political structures and institutions, creating an atmosphere of uncertainty (Gilpin 1987; Maddison 1989, 1982, 1991).

As we seem to be immersed in one of the latter periods, it is particularly instructive to go beyond strictly economic trends to look into some of the more profound changes in several related fields during the interwar period, and attempt to explore certain similarities and differences with respect to the present time.

As is well known, the period comprising World War I, the turbulent decade of the 1920s, the Great Depression, World War II, and the beginnings of the Cold War was a time of profound crises in the capitalist system: runaway inflations, huge and prolonged unemployment, boom and bust in the U.S. economy during the 1920s while stagnation prevailed in Europe, collapse of the international trading and financial system. Moreover, this period was characterized by the transition from one epoch to another in the realms of ideology, values, social and political organization, culture, technology, and international relations.

Some of the changes that are more relevant to our current concerns were the following: the British Empire gave way to U.S. hegemony in international affairs; other nineteenth-century empires also collapsed, and decolonization led to the creation of numerous new states in Africa, Asia, the Caribbean, and elsewhere; fascist regimes rose to prominence and were eventually defeated; a new era of cheap and easily mobile energy based on oil and electricity allowed a technological and organizational revolution in industry, transportation, and communications; socialism took hold initially in Russia and eventually spread all over the world, becoming a powerful historical force that threatened the very existence of capitalism; within capitalism itself the persistent and severe economic and social crises of the period, including the socialist challenge, led to profound institutional changes, particularly regarding the role of the state.

The Interwar Crisis of Capitalism and the Rise of the State

As a matter of fact—and this will be the leitmotiv throughout this chapter— for the following several decades and all over the world, the state emerged from this period as the most powerful institutional actor. It expanded the traditional political role of governments to include economic, social, and cultural activities generally, and became the savior of the capitalist system through the creation of what was to become known as the public sector. It was also the crucial institution in leading the way to the establishment of an alternative socialist system in the Soviet Union and later in other countries.

In the newly established socialist economies, the state became the owner of the means of production and organized a centralized planning system to impose profound structural and institutional transformations and to force accelerated processes of modernization, particularly as regards industrialization and the provision of social services. What is seldom explicitly recognized is that the phenomenon of a vastly expanded and strongly interventionist state, though in a far less radical fashion than in socialist nations, swept the whole of the capitalist world as well. Liberal economists in the Austrian tradition and conservative thinkers became aware of this process early on and denounced it forcefully, as is perhaps best illustrated in Friedrich von Hayek's well-known *Road to Serfdom*, first published in 1944 and popular again since the 1970s.

Among the industrialized capitalist countries, the more extreme cases of the state becoming an overpowering economic and political reality were those of several European countries where national socialist or corporatist-fascist regimes emerged. These were followed, after their defeat in Germany and Italy, by social-market or mixed economies, where the state played a different but still significant and growing role. In the Scandinavian countries and the United Kingdom, the welfare state was established, and in the United States the New Deal and full employment policies took hold (Shonfield 1965). In Japan a state-organized and -managed market economy had been created long ago, after the Meiji Restoration in 1868, in order to modernize society, industrialize, and catch up with Western industrial countries. It was largely recreated after its defeat in World War II, and taken as a model by other very successful Asian followers. The institutional setup that emerged in these various cases and the policy mix that was adopted differed in each country in response to national conditions and strategic objectives. In the Scandinavian countries, the United Kingdom, and Canada the fundamental objective of state action was social welfare; this was also true in continental Europe, but with an additional emphasis on modernization and economic integration; in the United States the focus was on infrastructure building and full employment; and in the USSR and Japan it was on industrialization and modernization.

Last but not least, inspired by these models, various mixtures of state-led economic and social development strategies and policies were adopted in underdeveloped countries all over the world to overcome their backwardness and skewed economic structure. This was characterized in most cases by a specialized commodity export sector and a primitive domestic productive structure. It took different shapes according to the prevailing ideologies and power configurations, as well as other initial conditions, such as their resource base, cultural and institutional characteristics, and stage of development.

The main new functions of the state in these cases were: intervention in goods and factor markets to shift resources to industrialization and modernization; financing of long-term projects and programs to overcome the lack of a private financial market; redistribution of income, through the creation and expansion of infrastructure and services in the "social sectors" (health, education, culture, housing, urban development, and social security); generation of public investments in infrastructure, to provide the necessary physical support for the integration of the internal market by means of transportation, communication, and energy facilities; creation of public enterprises in activities that did not interest or were beyond the scope of private entrepreneurs; generation of employment opportunities in the above-mentioned spheres, which contributed substantially to the development of universities responsible for the training of the qualified personnel needed in all these new activities (Sunkel and Paz 1970).

One consequence of the newfound prominence of the state and the public sector was a substantial increase in the share of government expenditures in GDP, as shown in table 11.2. The increase was particularly strong during the 1960s and 1970s and then tended to level off and decline in several cases in the 1980s. The exceptions are a few special cases related mostly to the dismantling of war or socialist economies.

The state not only became a central institutional actor within the confines of the national economies of most countries. The collapse of the international economy during the Great Depression of the 1930s produced a catastrophic reduction in trade flows, a strong increase in protectionism, and the disappearance of private international finance and investments. The need to reconstruct devastated Europe and the weakened international economy at the end of World War II led respectively to the Marshall Plan and the organization of a state-supported multilateral system of public international institutions: the United Nations and some of its specialized organizations like the International Monetary Fund, the International Bank of Reconstruction and Development, and the General Agreement on Tariffs and Trade, in charge of reestablishing and equilibrating the international flow of goods, finance, and investments. Developed-country governments created public bilateral international mechanisms to foster exports, like the Export-Import Bank in the United States, the Kreditanstalt in Germany, etc., as well as multilateral and bilateral aid and technical assistance institutions designed to cooperate with the development of underdeveloped countries. In a way, these various organizations were the seeds of a "global state" and the establishment of an international public sector.

In these different ways during the postwar decades, at both the national

TABLE 11.2 State size indicators (% expenditure/GDP)

	1937/40	41/45	46/50	51/55	55/60	61/65	66/70	71/75	76/80	81/85	86/90
INDUSTRIAL COUNTRIES											
Germany	17.8			15.4	14.4	13.7	16.0	25.8	29.5	31.3	30.3
Canada		51.0	23.8	16.8	15.1	15.4	16.0	19.7	20.6	23.8	22.9
France				24.9	24.4	22.9	22.1	31.8	38.5	44.7	43.7
Italy				17.9	17.2	16.8	18.4	21.7	28.0	38.0	39.5
Norway	15.3	59.7	28.4	21.1	18.6	18.5	20.4	32.2	38.5	37.7	42.6
Sweden		25.4	18.8	19.1	20.7	20.3	28.0	28.2	36.2	43.9	41.0
U.K.	42.4	71.1	43.5	29.5	27.4	27.5	30.3	34.0	37.2	40.3	36.7
U.S.	11.8	35.5	20.6	18.4	19.0	18.0	19.2	18.4	21.2	24.2	23.6
SOUTHEAST ASIA											
Japan				21.6	19.7	14.1	12.0	11.4	13.7	18.1	16.8
Korea				7.0	12.3	13.8	17.1	15.4	16.3	17.3	15.8
Malaysia					15.6	19.5	22.5	24.9	29.3	35.2	30.2
Singapore						17.2	17.2	16.8	24.2	24.1	29.7
Indonesia							13.3	16.9	21.6	21.5	21.2

LATIN AMERICA

Argentina				8.8	11.0	12.3	12.5	18.1	17.5	21.1	19.0
Brazil				13.3	13.8	19.7	11.3	16.3	18.8	21.7	28.1
Chile				8.2	7.9	8.1	20.4	34.2	30.1	31.9	29.7
Colombia							9.0	12.4	11.9	15.1	13.5
Mexico							11.5	12.7	16.1	25.1	26.6
Venezuela							19.9	20.6	24.5	25.1	21.4
OCEANIA											
Australia	10.9	41.5	29.1	23.6	21.6	21.7	22.8	20.1	25.0	26.4	27.1
New Zealand				32.4	31.1	27.9	27.6	29.4	36.0	41.0	44.2
AFRICA											
Egypt								59.6	48.6	48.1	41.6
Nigeria						7.3	10.4	9.7	13.5	12.7	21.9
Kenya						15.6	16.3	20.3	24.1	25.9	26.6
Zambia						26.6	29.5	34.4	32.9	34.3	38.1
Morocco						20.3	22.0	26.1	36.5	33.8	28.4
Ghana						25.3	20.7	18.8	16.6	10.5	13.7

Source: International Monetary Fund.

and international levels, in the North and in the South, as well as in the East and in the West, the state promoted capitalist development and became the central pillar of socialist development, giving rise to an unprecedented phase of economic growth, as shown in table 11.1—so much so that it has been labeled the "Golden Age" (Maddison 1982, 1989, 1991) and the "Golden Years" (Armstrong, Glyn, and Harrison 1991).

We shall return to this phase of state-driven economic boom, but before doing so it is convenient to contrast it with the contemporary phase. With the important exception of several Asian countries, this period has again been characterized by slow and unstable growth, severe economic crises and uncertainty about the future, and profound transformations in the ideological, technological, institutional, geopolitical, and cultural realms, just as in the interwar crisis period.

The Emergence of Neoliberalism
and the Decline of the State

During the 1970s a considerable part of the national and international institutional setup that emerged out of the earlier period of systemic change and lasted for several decades has again been substantially reorganized. The worldwide process of economic reform started in fact in the late 1960s with the elimination of exchange controls on financial transactions that survived in some OECD countries from the postwar period (leaving, however, "import-substitution" agricultural protection and support schemes in place). Some modest decentralization and liberalization attempts were introduced in socialist countries such as Hungary, Poland, and China. A determined shift from import-substitution strategies to export promotion took place in Korea and Taiwan. Several policy shifts in that direction were adopted in Latin American countries: tariff simplification and reduction schemes, introduction of the sliding exchange rate, replacement of quantitative import controls by tariffs, reduction and simplification of exchange and price controls and subsidies, deliberate promotion of manufactured exports in Brazil and Mexico and other activities, as for example fruits, fisheries, and forestry products in Chile, flowers in Colombia, and so on. In some countries these reforms were soon frustrated by aborted attempts at socialist revolution, and later by the "Dutch disease" syndrome, brought about by the effects of the rise in oil prices in petroleum-exporting countries and more generally by the financial permissiveness and debt boom of the late 1970s.

The new era dawned dramatically at the international level with the collapse of the Bretton Woods system of international economic relations, the two oil shocks of 1973 and 1979, and the adoption of radical neoliberal policies by the Thatcher and Reagan governments. It is now clearly a central part of the overall transformation process. But the stunning events of the past few years, particularly those that erupted suddenly and unexpectedly in the former Soviet bloc countries, have been obscuring more fundamental forces at work over several decades, there and in other parts of the world.

Some of the most relevant phenomena for our purposes are the following: the United States has lost its earlier overwhelming economic predominance of over half a century, although retaining its uncontested military might; Europe, and especially reunited Germany, together with Japan are emerging as comparable or even superior economic powers and are beginning to seek to exercise the corresponding political clout (Thurow 1992); the former public multilateral system of international economic relations that emerged after World War II has been eroded by the expansion of multinational enterprises and the emergence of the global corporation, and by international financial deregulation and the eurodollar, petrodollar, and foreign direct investment booms; and it has been superseded by a reconstituted, closely integrated, and very powerful private transnational corporate sector, particularly in the investment and financial spheres, as well as by informal and highly elitist mechanisms of international economic management, with the IMF as their linchpin.

A new economic world order is emerging, reaching an advanced stage of globalization: just 600 transnational corporations, each with 1985 sales greater than U.S. $1 billion, were responsible for one-fifth of total nonsocialist bloc industrial and agricultural value added. More significant, in the contemporary stage of the information-communications revolution, ten of these TNCs controlled 66% of the world semiconductor market, nine accounted for 89% of the telecommunications market, and ten others took care of the vast majority of the computer market. But the world is simultaneously being reorganized around three main blocs led by the United States, Japan, and the EEC, where Germany has become the predominant economic actor. This new Triad of economic power accounts for two-thirds of world GDP, four-fifths of outward stocks of foreign direct investment, and one-half of world trade (UNCTC 1991, 1992; Mortimore 1992).

Socialism as it existed in the Soviet bloc countries has collapsed, taking with it the East-West confrontation that characterized the bipolar world system of the Cold War; the demise of the Second World has pulled the rug out from under the North-South confrontation, with the former Third World countries (the Group of 77), like the former socialist countries, being reabsorbed into the new tripolar system, or simply left in limbo and disintegrating economically, socially, and even politically.

Meanwhile, profound scientific and technological revolution has taken place: the development of microelectronics and the information revolution, robotics, biotechnology, and new materials has produced fundamental changes throughout economic, social, and political systems, including the nature of interfirm and labor relations and the work process as well as traditional international and locational comparative advantages (Freeman, Clark, and Soete 1982; Piore and Sabel 1984; Hoffman and Kaplinsky 1988; Castells 1989; Rodríguez 1991). Environmental degradation, natural resource exhaustion, and threats to local, regional, and global ecosystems have introduced a new dimension into human affairs: the need for a shift to sustainable development as proclaimed by the 1992 Rio de Janeiro Earth Summit.

Last but certainly not least, the predominant role of the state that emerged after World War II, under various socioeconomic and political guises, has been giving way to a renovated and strengthened civil society in the social, political, and cultural realms (Tomassini 1992; Keane 1988). It could be argued that the events of May 1968 and the Prague Spring that followed were early warnings, in the capitalist and socialist worlds, of the social movements that have gained strength and momentum since then, representing minorities, youth movements and women's rights, green power, decentralization, participatory democracy, the defense of human rights, etc., and leading to the corresponding proliferation of grassroots and nongovernmental organizations, and to the retrenchment of the state.

This has also been the case in the economic field, including most prominently the increased role of the market and the strengthening of private enterprise, with declining shares of public expenditure in GDP, massive privatization of public enterprises and services, and a shift from public to private investments (Bouin and Michalet 1991). This process has been reinforced by the great expansion of the transnational corporation, giving rise to an unprecedented globalization process and to new kinds of relations between the state and private international and local capital. All this is leading to a profound reorganization of public–private sector relations, both national and international (Lipietz 1987; Dunning 1991; Ostry 1990; Salazar 1991; Reich 1991).

With globalization and more complex forms of private economic penetration of markets, these phenomena generate new problems, for instance, those associated with different national practices that affect international competitiveness. This inevitably becomes part of the conditionality under which economic reform is pursued. Therefore, for example, the agenda of international and regional negotiations are at a turning point, as negotiations are shifting from the treatment of products to the treatment of policies. This is the reason behind the search for a wider mandate for GATT toward assessing policy and institutional differences as sources of "distortions" (Agosin and Tussie 1992).

Economic Reform in a Period of Transition

Philosophers, thinkers, and intellectuals of various stripes are groping for a way to describe the new phase, as testified by the frequent use of "post-" and "neo-" as prefixes in their attempts to generate labels: postcapitalism, postindustrialism, postmodernism, neoliberalism, neoconservatism, neostructuralism, and even "The End of History and the Last Man."

Recognizing and attempting to understand trends as well as possible future scenarios is crucially important in devising development strategies and policies and should be taken into account in the processes of economic reform. For the shape of the future will not only depend on these and other forces, but also—and very critically at this stage, when the situation is still in flux—on the wider and longer-term strategic visions and concrete institutional proposals that can be put forward both at the global and the national levels to confront, adapt, or otherwise react to these tendencies. Some public functions concerned with poverty, equity, the environment, and longer-term growth strategies are urgently required, at both the national and international levels. They could be performed in part by the private sector, perhaps at the behest of the state, or by the state alone, or, with the private sector, and also by international collaboration among states and private firms.

The need is there. For example, at the international level, will the three emerging blocs develop in collaboration or conflict, and what will either scenario mean for their mutual relations and those with the former socialist bloc countries and the developing world? Will this large group of developing countries have some say in international economic management? Will it be possible to reverse the net capital flows from debtor to creditor countries, provide access to highly protected markets, and share or otherwise take advantage of the rapidly changing technological know-how concentrated in global firms? Will there be new and more appropriate cooperation and aid to underdeveloped and former socialist countries, and if so, in what way: negotiation or imposition through various kinds of conditionalities? Moreover, how will we share and protect the increasingly threatened environmental life-support systems of the world? How will individual firms, groups of enterprises, industries, individual nations, and groups of nations respond to these challenges? Should they just trust the market to work it all out?

Similar questions need to be posed at the national level. If one were to believe the world financial press and what is published by the main international economic institutions as well as the mainstream economic journals, after having arrived at the end of history we would also seem to have reached the end of economics, especially the "economics of development" (Lal 1983). Neoclassical economics, and the more extreme neoliberal economic policy menu derived from it—deregulation, liberalization, openness, a minimal state, getting prices right, trusting the market and the animal spirits of private entrepreneurs, etc.—is being pushed with little variation everywhere, regardless of the country's initial conditions: size, resource base, location, culture, social structure, institutions, international relations, and historical evolution. It is presented as constituting the ultimate wisdom, a consensus from the right to the left—or at least the left that remains after the collapse of socialism.

Although there is undoubtedly much more agreement than in the past on several main economic policy issues, I submit that there is also a lot of confusion surrounding this prevailing view. Far from having reached the end of ideology—another contemporary slogan—I am afraid that we are in danger of becoming locked into an unprecedented ideological monopoly, a sort of undimensional ideology, to paraphrase Marcuse, or "monoeconomics," in Hirschman's characterization. To cut through this intellectually stifling ideology, I believe it is necessary to have a closer look at the convergences—but also the divergences—that exist about several critical issues of economic policy, particularly from the development perspective (ECLAC 1990, 1992; Colclough and Manor 1991; Sunkel and Zuleta 1990; Sunkel 1993). The latter consideration is crucially important because economic reform programs may create an institutional setup with lasting effects that may not be conducive to sustained economic growth, social development, and political democracy.

My views are admittedly colored by my Latin American, and particularly Chilean, experience of neoliberal dogmatism in the 1970s reaching extremes similar to those of Thatcher's United Kingdom and Reagan's United States in the 1980s. I believe, however, that such an examination has general relevance, particularly for countries that have not yet tasted the bitter medicine or have just started the medication and have swallowed uncritically the supposedly wonderful virtues of unbridled laissez-faire. This is not just a personal or academic view, but has become a hot political issue, as shown at one level by the debate on economic policy generated recently in the United Kingdom and by the presidential election in the United States, and at another by the opinions expressed by high-level Japanese officials in relation to the neoliberal economic reform policies endorsed by the World Bank (*Journal of Commerce* 1991).

To recognize the need for sufficient room for maneuver in the process of economic reform, it is indispensable to have an adequate diagnosis of how and why reform has become necessary and inevitable, while also realizing that there are different options and modalities.

The prevailing interpretation, put as succinctly as possible, is that past development has been a dismal failure because of excessive and misguided state intervention in and protection of the domestic economy. Therefore, economic reform tends to consist of swinging the pendulum fully in the opposite direction: minimizing government intervention and opening up to complete integration into the world economy. Discussion seems to be limited to questions that are critical in the short term, such as shock treatment versus gradualism, and reform sequencing; but there are also more fundamental development issues at stake, and they too must be examined.

From a development perspective, both of the above assertions about the past—the failure of development, and the naming of the state as the main culprit—as well as neoliberalism as the recipe for the future, seem to me questionable. The danger is of throwing out the baby with the bath water—that is, eliminating all state intervention, and running the risk of intolerable social suffering and protracted stagnation rather than making the effort to sort out the bad from the good. Let us then look more closely at the assertion about the disastrous past record of development. An examination of long-term historical trends offers a much more complex picture, both throughout various historical periods and within different countries.

The State and Development: A Reappraisal

We must start with the evolution of the world economy as a whole, an approach that is supremely important but is usually absent when judging individual country performance and policies (Prebisch 1950; Drucker 1986). After the near total breakdown of international trade, finance, and investment in the early postwar period, it is striking how favorable the global economic environment became in the 1950s and 1960s in almost all crucial aspects: an exceptionally rapid overall rate of sustained expansion of the world economy, even faster growth of international trade, a considerable reduction of protectionism, increasing public international finance (both multilateral and bilateral), substantial international technical cooperation and aid, small but growing private direct investment and the emergence of the multinational corporation, and a very low rate of interest. The exception was private international finance, which did not revive and gain momentum, at least for the developing world, until the 1970s.

The contrast in this global postwar picture with the decade of the 1980s is quite remarkable, as illustrated in table 11.3. Several of the variables mentioned lost their positive influence or became acutely negative, as in the case of global GDP growth and trade expansion, the rate of interest, protectionism in the principal world markets, the unfavorable terms of trade for commodities, the attitude toward international cooperation, and the proliferation of various conditionalities. As is well known, this situation became particularly grave for most countries of the developing world and several countries of the socialist bloc after the debt crisis erupted in 1982. The only variable that improved considerably and expanded very fast in the second half of the decade was foreign direct investment, but this was highly concentrated among the industrialized nations.

Looking at the long-term growth record of the postwar period by regions and individual countries, the sharp division into two subperiods, before and after the mid-1970s, is also clearly apparent, but with some interesting con-

TABLE 11.3 Long-term trends in the international economy before and after the 1970s

	Between 1950 and 1970	After 1980
World economy	Exceptionally rapid and sustained growth	Slow and unstable growth
International trade	Great expansion	Slow growth, instability
Terms of trade	Relatively low and stable (in relation to early 1950s)	Severe deterioration (in relation to 1980)
Public international financing	Rapid and sustained increase	Very limited and conditioned
Direct foreign investment	Rapid and sustained expansion	Strong increase among developed countries, very scarce for developing countries
Private financing	Exceptional expansion since late-1960s	Scarce, decreasing, and substantial negative net flow (debt servicing) during 1980's
Interest rates	Very low	Very high during most of 1980s
Protectionism	Decreasing	Strong increase
International cooperation	Very favorable attitude	Very negative attitude
External conditionality in economic policy matters	Short term, IMF	Short term: IMF, international banks, U.S. government. Long term: World Bank, U.S. government.

trasts (table 11.4). In the earlier period, economic growth proceeded almost everywhere at historically unprecedented levels: many countries exceeded an annual growth rate of 6% and only a few grew less than 4%, and all regions and most countries converged toward the 5.1% average recorded for the thirty-two countries examined. Since the mid-1970s the growth rate slowed by about half: from an average of 4.9% to 2.4% in the OECD countries, from 5.2% to 2.9% in Latin America, and from 5.0% to 2.1% in the USSR. There was considerable convergence in this relative stagnation. The notable exception is Asia, where the 5.4% average rate of growth of the 1950–73 period increased to 5.9%. I shall return to this most significant discrepancy.

Regarding the role of the state, it is interesting to examine the growth performance of different countries in which the state played a major role. Looking again at table 11.4, it can be seen that socialist USSR and several Latin American countries where the state played such a role—though in quite different ways—did in fact grow somewhat faster than the average of the OECD countries in the 1950–73 period. Moreover, Japan grew at an incredi-

TABLE 11.4 Real GDP growth, 1900–1987 (annual average rate of GDP growth at constant prices)

	1900–1913	1913–1950	1950–1973	1973–1987
Australia	3.1	2.1	4.7	2.9
Austria	2.4	0.2	5.3	2.2
Belgium	2.4	1.0	4.1	1.8
Canada	6.3	3.1	5.1	3.4
Denmark	3.2	2.5	3.8	1.8
Finland	2.9	2.7	4.9	2.8
France	1.7	1.1	5.1	2.2
Germany	3.0	1.3	5.9	1.8
Italy	2.8	1.4	5.5	2.4
Japan	2.5	2.2	9.3	3.7
Netherlands	2.3	2.4	4.7	1.8
Norway	2.7	2.9	4.1	4.0
Sweden	2.2	2.7	4.0	1.8
Switzerland	2.6	2.6	4.5	1.0
United Kingdom	1.5	1.3	3.0	1.6
United States	4.0	2.8	3.7	2.5
OECD average	2.9	2.0	4.9	2.4
Bangladesh	1.0	0.5	1.7	4.5
China	0.8	0.1	5.8	7.5
India	1.0	0.7	3.7	4.1
Indonesia	1.8	0.9	4.5	5.4
Pakistan	1.0	1.4	4.4	6.1
Philippines	4.4	1.8	5.0	3.2
South Korea	(2.0)	1.7	7.5	7.9
Taiwan	1.8	2.7	9.3	7.8
Thailand	1.7	2.2	6.4	6.2
Asian average	1.7	1.3	5.4	5.9
Argentina	6.4	3.0	3.8	0.8
Brazil	3.5	4.2	6.7	4.8
Chile	(3.4)	3.3	3.7	1.9
Colombia	(4.2)	3.8	5.2	3.9
Mexico	2.6	2.6	6.4	3.6
Peru	(3.5)	2.8	5.4	2.6
Latin American average	3.9	3.3	5.2	2.9
Developing country average	2.6	2.1	5.3	4.7
USSR	3.5	2.7	5.0	2.1
Thirty-two country average	2.8	2.1	5.1	3.4

Source: A. Maddison, *The World Economy in the 20th Century*, OECD, Paris, 1989, p. 36, up date to 1989: for OECD countries from Angus Maddison. *Dynamic Forces in capitalist Development*, OUP, 1991, South Korea, Taiwan, Thailand and Latin America from A.A. Hofman, ECLAC Economic Development Division, rest of Asian countries up-date provided by Angus Maddison.

ble rate of 9%, and the continental European countries between 4% and 6%, while the U.S. economy, with by far the weakest forms of state intervention, grew only 3.7%. As far as Asia is concerned, critics and defenders of the "market truth" find support for their views in the phenomenal growth of the Asian newly industrialized countries. Hong Kong and Singapore are often viewed as market successes, but the very special nature of their "city-state" economies closely integrated into much wider economic zones should be taken into account. South Korea and Taiwan, in contrast, are mentioned as state-driven winners.

Average social conditions as expressed in indicators such as life expectancy, child mortality, and literacy also improved substantially during the postwar period (table 11.5). "Developing countries reduced their average infant mortality from nearly 200 deaths per 1,000 live births to about 80 in about four decades (1950–1988), a feat that took industrial countries nearly a century to accomplish" (UNDP 1990). The relative number of families living in poverty in Latin America declined substantially during the postwar period, from 51% in 1960 to 35% in 1980; it started to increase again to 37% in 1986 as a consequence of the debt crisis and the adjustment and restructuring policies that followed. Absolute poverty followed a similar path, declining sharply from 26% to 15% between 1960 and 1980, and then increasing again to 17% in 1986 (Tokman 1991).

Although it may sound bizarre in light of present circumstances, what has been said above also applies to some extent to the centrally planned economies of Eastern Europe and the USSR. Economic growth was similarly fast, and until the last decade did not exhibit the gross inequality and widespread poverty of the underdeveloped capitalist world. Furthermore, these countries cannot have been as badly off as is claimed today, if their very backward living conditions in the prewar period rose to 1970s levels that were similar to those of countries like Spain and Portugal (Maddison 1989). Moreover, most socialist bloc countries are classified among the "high human development" group of countries as measured by the UNDP Human Development Index (table 11.5). The case of Cuba could be cited in this regards; its rapid economic growth and especially the substantial social improvements that took place, again until the mid-1980s, contrast dramatically with the rest of Latin America.

Postwar national economic development strategies and policies based on Keynesian theories of full employment and an active role of the state, Marxist and Harrod-Domar theories of capital accumulation, Prebisch-Singer and ECLAC theories of protected industrialization, Rosenstein-Rodan/Nurkse/Hirschman theories of public investment and planning, Schultz's theories of human resource development, etc., were therefore apparently rather influential in the expansionary postwar period. To be sure, there was a growing gap

TABLE 11.5 Social conditions

	HUMAN DEVELOPMENT INDEX	Trends in human development												
		Life expectancy (years)			Under-five mortality rate (per 1,000)		Pop. with access to safe water (%)		Daily calorie supply (as % of requirements)		Adult literacy (%)		GNP per capita (US$)	
		1960	1975	1987	1960	1988	1975	1985–87	1964–66	1984–86	1970	1985	1976	1987
HIGH HUMAN DEVELOPMENT (1)	0.993–0.800	68	71	73	67	27	—	—	121	123	—	—	4,350	9,250
MEDIUM HUMAN DEVELOPMENT (2)	0.796–0.510	48	61	67	209	72	33	59	88	113	57	71	540	690
Excluding China		48	56	63	214	94	—	—	92	115	—	73	740	1,250
LOW HUMAN DEVELOPMENT (3)	0.499–0.048	42	49	55	285	170	31	48	89	95	29	41	180	300
Excluding India		40	46	52	287	186	30	39	88	91	23	40	220	300

Countries ordered with respect to human development index:

(1) Japan, Canada, Iceland, Sweden, Switzerland, Norway, USA, Netherlands, Australia, France, UK, Denmark, Finland, Germany, New Zealand, Belgium, Austria, Italy, Luxembourg, Spain, Israel, Barbados, Ireland, Greece, Hong Kong, Cyprus, Czechoslovakia, Bahamas, Malta, Hungary, USSR, Uruguay, Bulgaria, Yugoslavia, Korea, Portugal, Singapore, Chile, Trinidad y Tobago, Costa Rica, Poland, Brunei, Argentina, Venezuela, Mexico, Antigua y Barbuda, Mauritius, Kuwait, Albania, Qatar, Bahrain, Malaysia, Dominica.

(2) Panama, Suriname, United Arab Emirates, South Africa, Romania, Jamaica, Brazil, Colombia, Cuba, Seychelles, Grenada, St. Kitts & Nev., Thailand, Belize, St. Lucia, Saudi Arabia, Turkey, Fiji, Syrian Arab R., Paraguay, R.Dem. Korea, Sri Lanka, Libya, Ecuador, Peru, St. Vincent, Dominican R., Samoa, China, Jordan, Philippines, Nicaragua, Oman, Mongolia, Lebanon, Guyana, Tunisia, Iraq, Iran, Maldives, El Salvador, Botswana, Solomon Islands, Gabon.

(3) Indonesia, Viet Nam, Honduras, Vanuatu, Algeria, Guatemala, Swaziland, Namibia, Myanmar, Lesotho, Morocco, Cape Verde, Bolivia, Zimbabwe, Sao Tome & Principe, Kenya, Egypt, Congo, Madagascar, Papua New Guinea, Zambia, Cameroon, Pakistan, Ghana, Cote d'Ivoire, India, Zaire, Haiti, Comoros, Tanzania, Laos, Nigeria, Yemen, Togo, Liberia, Rwanda, Uganda, Senegal, Bangladesh, Equitorial Guinea, Malawi, Burundi, Cambodia, Ethiopia, Central Africa Rep., Sudan, Bhutan, Nepal, Mozambique, Angola, Mauritania, Somalia, Benin, Guinea-Bissau, Chad, Djibouti, Burkina Faso, Niger, Mali, Afghanistan, Guinea, Gambia, Sierra Leone.

Source: *Human Development Report*, United Nations Development Programme-UNDD, 1990 (New York and Oxford: Oxford University Press).

between expectations and reality, because in spite of the successes there were also great disappointments: social, sectoral, and regional progress was very uneven; inequality, underemployment, and poverty, although diminished, remained widespread; and a new and by then unrecognized scourge—environmental degradation—increased exponentially.

Therefore, I believe that the prevailing wholesale condemnation of earlier development theories, strategies, and policies—and of the consequent government intervention—is based on a lack of adequate historical information and interpretation as well as extreme ideologization; it is thus mostly unwarranted, vastly exaggerated, and in need of serious and unbiased reconsideration. Fortunately this has begun to be recognized, even in U.S. academic circles. "This paper argues that in the light of new developments in industrial organization, international economics, and growth theory, the old development economics now looks much more sensible than it seemed during the 'counter-revolution' against interventionist development models . . . Thus this paper calls for a 'counter-counter-revolution' that restores some of the distinctive focus that characterized development economics before 1960" (Krugman 1992).

The Special Case of the Asian NICs

The extraordinary growth, industrialization, and export performance of the Asian NICs, coupled with a relatively less unequal income distribution than in other developing countries—all miraculously sustained during the late 1970s debacle, when the rest of the world was reeling from the oil shocks and Reaganomics, crumbling under the debt crisis, or suffocating under centralized planning—boosted the neoliberal development paradigm. By neoliberal I mean here the "Chicago School" subset of neoclassical economists who think that neoclassical prescriptions for short-run optimal resource allocation are also the core recipe for maximizing long-term growth rates; that is, that letting prices find their relative values in freely operating domestic and international markets is a necessary and "almost" sufficient condition for development ("almost" because they accept that the state ought to do something about extreme poverty). They also believe that most cases of market failure result from government policies, and that the welfare costs of remedial government intervention are greater than the welfare gains. In the neoliberal view, growth is an inherent property of capitalist economies. Governments have an important role in providing "public goods," but beyond that they should not go. It must be acknowledged that this is not the view of other neoclassicists, who by contrast draw more of a distinction between short-term equilibrium and long-term development, introducing a more complex array of variables into growth issues than they use for the optimal allocation of resources.

Finding empirical support for such neoliberal views in the experience of the Asian NICs seems highly questionable, for all these countries have gone well beyond the strict limits to government intervention set by neoliberalism generally and also by more conventional neoclassicism (Amsden 1989; Bradford forthcoming; Wade 1990). Even neoliberals admit that governments have been "deeply involved" in the economies of all the East Asian countries (Wade 1992a). I believe that most of the confusion arises from the largely false dichotomy that has been posited to exist between import-substitution and export-led policies. The extraordinary growth performance of the Asian NICs has been rightly associated with their industrial export drive, but this came after a first phase of import substitution (Gereffi and Wyman 1990), and has been wrongly attributed to a "hands-off" neoliberal or even neoclassical policy stand regarding state action.

One of the many interesting questions that have not been sufficiently analyzed in this regard is why the Asian NICs continued growing during and after the stagnation period inaugurated with the first oil shock, while the Latin American economies, which had initiated economic reform program in the mid-1960s and grew substantially throughout the 1970s, collapsed with the debt crisis of 1982 (see again table 11.4).

Some of the main reasons seem to me to be the following. The Asians enjoyed the advantages of being late starters in the industrialization and development game; although the Asian NICs started in the mid-1950s, industrialization in some Latin American countries goes back almost a century earlier, and deliberate industrialization policies date to the 1930s. Moreover, they lacked a strong comparatively advantaged natural resource sector on which to build a significant commodity export activity. Therefore they did not develop an internal market derived over the years from an important export activity, which would allow much import substitution, nor could they capture and redistribute export sector surpluses to finance industrialization, modernization, and social policies, while avoiding the creation of a reasonably effective taxation system, as was the case in Latin America. After U.S. aid declined, they had no choice but to embark as soon as possible on an all-out savings, investment, industrialization, and export effort, while the Latins could continue to rely for foreign exchange and fiscal receipts (albeit increasingly precariously) on the relatively diminishing returns of commodity exports, and since the mid-1970s, on heavy external borrowing.

Geopolitics undoubtedly also played a crucial role, particularly in the cases of South Korea and Taiwan, threatened by communist neighbors. Another important element helping the initiation and continuation of their Asian export boom is the fact that the NICs are located in the midst of by far the most buoyant trade, investment, and growth region of the world, the area least affected by the deceleration of the world economy and the catastrophic decline in the terms of trade that affected other Third World regions in the last decade. Furthermore, as far as long-term development strategies and policies are concerned, they have followed the Japanese, not the neoliberal, model.

On the other hand, lacking the shortcut of being able to rely on access to commodity export surpluses, macroeconomic management in these countries has historically been much more prudent than in Latin America, and heavily concentrated on increasing domestic savings and investment. When foreign borrowing became abundant, it was used to increase domestic investment, growth, and exports, and then rapidly replaced by domestic savings. Furthermore, a much higher proportion was borrowed from governments and international institutions on concessional or fixed terms rather than from commercial banks at floating terms. Fiscal and monetary policy has been more conservative and also more effective, favored by downward price and wage flexibility given negligible social security commitments, trade union activity, and farm income support schemes.

It is impossible here to delve further into the many relevant aspects of this vast subject; I have only referred to some questions that are not normally covered in the economic controversy. In any case, I believe that the one-sided neoliberal reading of the Asian success story is at least in doubt, if not considerably discredited.

A New Role for the State in Development?

As mentioned, one of the consequences of the crisis of capitalism in the interwar period was the emergence of the state as the most powerful institutional economic actor, which had rather positive effects on development from the postwar period until the mid-1970s. Therefore there is urgent need for a less ideological view of the role of the state in that period than the prevailing view. A more objective critical revision is required, both to acknowledge the positive role of the state during that historical phase and to examine the reasons for its decline in the last decade or so, and the ensuing consequences. The role of the state seems to have gone through a cycle of increasing and then declining returns. In the earlier phase, the state was seen as a solution in times of crises. More recently it has been regarded as the very problem causing the crisis. This is an interesting reversal of opinion that requires some comment.

Several arguments from different perspectives contribute to explaining such a complex phenomenon. In the economic sphere, the increasing state intervention in the functioning of markets hindered their indispensable complementary function in the allocation of productive resources, with increasingly negative effects on resource utilization, efficiency, productivity, competitiveness, and growth. The state's insatiable thirst for fiscal revenues derived from its increasing role, combined with growing difficulties in raising further taxes, led to growing deficits, inflationary pressures, demand for wage increases, and declining profitability and investment in the private sector.

In the case of developing countries specializing in commodity exports, the formerly abundant tax and foreign exchange revenues from that source shrank in relative (and sometimes absolute) terms over time as the public sector and import needs grew much faster than proceeds. The ruling elites were thus confronted with the very difficult political task of establishing an effective tax system and promoting exports; this could be postponed during the 1970s as cheap and abundant foreign borrowing became available, but it had to be faced inevitably after the debt crisis (Griffith-Jones and Sunkel 1986).

From an institutional point of view, there was excessive bureaucratization, increasing administrative abuse, interference and control of private life and economic activities, with growing arbitrariness, rigidity, incompetence, and corruption. At the socioeconomic level, conflict heightened between the increasingly overbearing state apparatus and the strengthening of citizens' aspirations to more participation, decentralization, and greater freedom for the individual and social organizations. Furthermore, there appeared a growing mismatch between the trasnationalization processes of the economic and financial systems and of social and cultural life, and the attempts of the national state to regulate them. All of these processes contributed to questioning the political legitimacy of the state.

It seems important to set the historical record straight on the role of the state and on the development experience more generally. In this age of a rather naive belief in laissez-faire it is crucial to distinguish the rights from the wrongs in that experience, instead of condemning them wholesale under the prevailing ideological mantle. More unbiased research is urgently needed on comparative development experiences, not only for theoretical but also for very practical policy reasons. Several recent neoliberal experiments seem to have had seriously negative consequences for the concentration of wealth and income, inequality, poverty, unemployment and underemployment, the decay of inner cities, the abuse of the environment, and the threat posed to democratic institutions, without having produced the spectacular growth records of the postwar period. If this is so, there is dire need for an alternative—or at least for strong qualifications—to the simplistic current menu of privatization, deregulation, and liberalization as the cure-all for statism. To rely entirely on private sector dynamism under an impartial regulatory institutional framework without any guiding development strategy and principles does not seem advisable.

The "neoliberal myth" derived from the Asian experience and then contrasted to the "failure of past development myth" of other regions has been based on a false, historically misplaced diagnosis. A confusion exists between the rather positive record of the postwar period until the mid-1970s and the dismal showing of the 1980s, which was strongly influenced by dramatically changed international conditions. Furthermore, economists have given into the special geopolitical circumstances and considerable state intervention that prevailed in several Asian countries. Lack of an adequate historical perspective obscures the fact that the development collapse of the recent past in all regions except Asia is not a problem of the whole postwar period, but only of the last decade or so. Certainly, there were serious development problems since the late 1960s in these regions, but they were a far cry from what followed after the first and second oil shocks, the debt crisis of 1982 and its devastating sequels, and the adjustment and restructuring policies of the 1980s.

The first two of these momentous events contributed decisively to the process of transnationalization of the financial system, and this in turn encouraged the predominance of speculative overproductive capital. It also helped to strengthen neoconservatism and monetarism and set the stage for heavy external indebtedness through deregulation and liberalization policies. This also led eventually to policies that generated recession, exceptionally high interest rates, and extremely low commodity prices, and thereby to the debt crisis, with the exception of the much more prudent Asians. The enforcement of the adjustment/restructuring menu and continuous debt servicing dramatically reversed highly positive into strongly negative net external financial flows. This led to recession, unemployment, low wages, poverty, and the collapse of investment and public finance, followed by runaway inflation.

Is this dramatic socioeconomic reality of most Third World countries today only or predominantly the consequence of the internal development policies of the 1950s and 1960s? Or is it, at least to some important extent, even in the socialist countries, the result of the severe external shocks of the 1970s, the profound transformations in the structure and dynamics of the globalized world economy, and the overwhelming financial and institutional power of neoliberal economic doctrines? Or is it a combination?

I submit that these latter shocks and changes compounded the defects of the earlier phase. Moreover, the handling of the external shocks and new conditions by the elites of most developing countries (excepting again Asia) has been abysmally inept, both when they were riding the debt boom and when they were collapsing under the debt burden. The overall historical picture looks like an interruption of vigorous but flawed development processes that could have been corrected, and in some instances were being reoriented by the end of the 1960s, and then pursued with great success in Asia.

Most countries abandoned their efforts at reorienting their development strategies, influenced by financial permissiveness and short-sightedness fostered nationally and internationally by neoliberal policies of liberalization and deregulation. U.S. and international financial liberalization and the lack of international experience and the irresponsibility of U.S. banks that recklessly expanded their lending to developing countries, coupled with the vested interests of highly protected and increasingly transnationalized recipient-country elites, led to the waste of abundant resources that could have been used to redress the accumulating economic and social development problems of the late 1960s. In this sense the so-called lost development decade was not that of the 1980s but rather of the 1970s, when both the need for adjustment and restructuring and the resources to carry them out were abundant. And the opportunity was also there, as shown by the growth of the Asian NICs, to target investment and trade expansion on the microelectronics and semiconductor revolution. This opportunity was understood and acted on by several Asian countries but missed by Latin America, the socialist countries of the Soviet bloc, and Africa.

Understanding this historical process and the new internal circumstances as well as the changed international context, and the relations between them today and in the future, is of the utmost importance. This is particularly true because of the implications of the highly transnationalized world economy and society, the profound changes taking place in technology, the reorganization of institutional structures and international arrangements of the emerging geopolitical and economic areas, and the radically new conditions for world development posed by the environment, all of which will have to be faced explicitly or implicitly by economic reform.

The long-term success stories are in those countries that have been able to organize cooperative or corporative managerial capitalism, such as Germany, Austria, Japan, Korea, and Taiwan (Chandler 1990; Ostry 1990). "The new interventionism seeks to guide, not replace, the market. It uses price and nonprice methods to channel investment away from unproductive uses, expand technological capacity, strengthen links with foreign firms and give a directional thrust to selected industries. These interventions need to be based on a plan for the pattern of trade and industry over time, and this plan must be open to feedback from the market . . . That is . . . assistance . . . must be made conditional on performance" (Wade 1992b). An interactive government–business–finance interface seems crucial to producing national strategies of market penetration. This is quite different from the individualistic neoliberal model pursued by the United States or United Kingdom, which is the model that prevails in the economics profession and the one that inspires economic reform programs everywhere.

Economic Reform, Democracy, and the State

Another rather formidable subject has to be incorporated as a central concern in discussions about economic reform in this age of democracy. I have already referred to social participation, decentralization, social movements, and the strengthening of civil society and nongovernmental organizations as challenges to the old state. But this rise in civil society and organization also poses a challenge for the new state. An ample and complex field, this challenge seems to concern what I would call the "widening and deepening" of democracy, an area in which the economically successful Asian economies have not been similarly effective. One way of interpreting the present transitional historical period would be to recognize that development has been sacrificed to growth, and to contrast "the irrationality of capitalism with the nonviability of socialism" (Przeworski 1990).

How to impregnate capitalism with the public concerns of socialism without frightening the animal spirits of the capitalist entrepreneur, while avoiding militarized authoritarianism of the right or the left and striving for more individual and social freedom? How to achieve a synthesis of the capitalist engine of growth with the socialist concern for the improvement of the oppressed, exploited, and marginalized majorities and minorities? How to keep the trend toward transnational integration and the pressure for increased competitiveness from leading to further national economic, social, and cultural disintegration (Sunkel 1973). How to protect public goods from private, bureaucratic, and technocratic assault, as in the case of the environment, human rights, justice, etc.?

Perhaps the common thread of the concern and proposals surrounding these issues could be summed up by the search for a more radical conception of democracy: stronger and wider structured participation through a strengthened civil society; less big state as well as less big business; and closer democratic social control of both by a strengthened web of private citizens' organizations to fulfill public functions and represent in particular the weaker groups of society. One implication is more support for social and political institution building and reform, by and for civil society, leading directly to improved governance. Another is that developed countries should support developing countries committed to democracy with increased market access, decreased debt service, easier terms for technology transfer, etc., rather than imposing neoliberal conditionality.

Another implication is the need to explicitly reconsider the role of the state. To frame the debate in terms of more or less state, or the state as the solution or the problem, is to miss the real issues. It is clear that the state has to fulfill certain basic functions to make the working of the market at all possible; the point here is to clarify what works and what does not. Furthermore, it is also accepted by neoclassical theory that the state has certain functions to perform in cases of recognized market failure; the point is to find ways to perform those functions efficiently, avoiding government failure. Third, most economists recognize that developing countries have special characteristics, over which several assumptions of neoclassical economics do not obtain or apply only very imperfectly, there being therefore a case for government interventions to foster development, provided they have a minimum capability. Obviously these cannot be the same as those that took place earlier, if only because conditions have changed considerably. But still the state must perform regulatory and strategic coordination and guidance functions, in interaction with the private sector. Sometimes it may have to enter into the production sphere, provided these interventions are temporary and made conditional on performance, so that when effective private groups eventually emerge, they can successfully take over and let the state move on to other strategic areas. A dialectical, mutually reinforcing process between the state and the private sector must be worked out, its nature highly dependent on the concrete circumstances of each country.

The same strategy could be followed with transnational corporations, so that national producers could enter into some form of association with them, gradually seeking greater independence as the national learning and growth processes give them sufficient strength.

These and other forms of public and state evolutionary action are required for practical rather than ideological reasons, to face up to the prevailing conditions: the critical importance of knowledge and education; the changed and rapidly evolving nature of technology; the reorganization of the work process, business organization, and labor relations; the heightened environmental awareness and restrictions; the increasing competitiveness in the world economy; the advanced degree of transnationalization and global interconnectedness; the growing inequality within and among countries; and the universal aspiration for democratic societies, which requires the state to promote greater and more equal opportunities for its citizens.

The neoliberal stand will tend to be that "government failure" is generally so bad that even if such market failures and development requirements should exist, it would be preferable to live with them rather than bring the government in, because the results of the cure will inevitably be worse than the consequence of the ills. And anyway, from this point of view, government intervention is not required for development.

This position does not seem reasonable. Recent history belies it on at least two accounts. First, the record of countries that have taken this stance until recently—the United States, the United Kingdom, New Zealand, and Chile are perhaps the more extreme examples—is rather poor in terms of growth and abysmal in social equity and environmental terms. Second, there are many cases of government activism—several European countries, Japan, Korea, Taiwan and others in Asia, and Costa Rica and Chile (since returning to democracy) in Latin American—that have obtained positive results.

The question then seems to be how to get the right kind of institutions able to adopt the right kind of policies at the right moment and for a limited period, rather than accepting the comfortable position of reducing government intervention to the bare minimum on the assumption that this is the best that can be done, once macroeconomic equilibrium is established. Only the democratic state, controlled by civil society, can promote the long-term national interest, which requires stabilization, the recovery of economic growth, the alleviation of poverty and the reduction of inequality, the preservation of the environment, and a dynamic integration into the world economy. All of these requirements involve the need for determined public strategies, policies, and actions.

The processes of economic reform under way all over the world are creating a whole new institutional setup, national as well as international, which is providing de facto answers to these questions. Are they right or wrong? We had better find out.

Note

I am grateful to R. Devlin, A. Hofman, and M. Mortimore for useful comments.

References

Agosin, M., and D. Tussie. 1992. "Globalization, Regionalization and New Dilemmas in Trade Policy for Development." *World Competition*. Geneva, June.

Amsden, A. 1989. *Asia's Next Giant: South Korea and Late Industrialization*. New York and Oxford: Oxford University Press.

Armstrong, P., A. Glyn, and J. Harrison. 1991. *Capitalism since 1945*. Oxford and Cambridge, MA: Basil Blackwell.

Bouin, O., and Ch. Michalet. 1991. *Rebalancing the Public and Private Sectors*. Paris: OECD.

Bradford, C. Forthcoming. "The East Asian Development Experience." In Grilli, E., and Salvatore, D., eds., *Handbook of Economic Development*.

Castells, M. 1989. *The Informational City; Information Technology, Economic Restructuring, and the Urban-Regional Process*. Oxford: Basil Blackwell.

Chandler, Alfred D., Jr. 1990. *Scale and Scope: The Dynamics of Industrial Capitalism*. Cambridge, MA: The Belknap Press of Harvard University Press.

Colclough, Ch., and J. Manor, eds. 1991. *State or Markets? Neoliberalism and the Development Policy Debate*. Oxford: Clarendon Press.

Drucker, P. 1986. "The Changed World Economy." *Foreign Affairs* (Spring).

Dunning , J. 1991. "Governments–Markets–Firms; Toward a New Balance?" *CTC Reporter* UN, New York, Spring.

ECLAC. 1990. "Changing Production Patterns with Social Equity," Santiago.

ECLAC. 1992. "Social Equity and Changing Production Patterns: An Integrated Approach," Santiago.

Freeman, C., J. Clark, and L. Soete. 1982. *Unemployment and Technical Innovation*. London: Frances Pinter.

Gereffi, G., and D. Wyman, eds. 1990. *Manufacturing Miracles: Paths of Industrialization in Latin America and East Asia.* Princeton: Princeton University Press.

Gilpin, R. 1987. *The Political Economy of International Relations.* Princeton: Princeton University Press.

Griffith-Jones, S., and O. Sunkel. 1986. *The Latin American Debt and Development Crises: The End of an Illusion.* Oxford: Clarendon Press.

Hoffman, K., and R. Kaplinsky. 1988. *Driving Force: The Global Restructuring of Technology, Labour and Investment in the Automobile Components Industries.* Boulder, CO and London: Westview Press.

Journal of Commerce. December 11, 1991, p. 1A.

Keane, J., ed. 1988. *Civil Society and the State.* London: Verso.

Krugman, P. 1992. "Toward a Counter-Counter Revolution in Development Theory." World Bank Annual Conference on Development Economics, Washington, Abstract.

Lal, S. 1983. *The Poverty of "Development Economics."* London: Institute of Economic Affairs.

Lipietz, A. 1987. *Mirages and Miracles: The Crisis of Global Fordism.* London: Verso.

Maddison, A. 1982. *Phases of Capitalist Development.* Oxford and New York: Oxford University Press.

Maddison, A. 1989. *The World Economy in the 20th Century.* Paris: OECD.

Maddison, A. 1991. *Dynamic Forces in Capitalist Development. A Long-Run Comparative View.* Oxford: Oxford University Press.

Mortimore, M. 1992. "A New International Industrial Order: Increased International Competition in a TNC-Centric World." *CEPAL Review* 48 (August), Santiago.

Ostry, S. 1990. *Government and Corporations in a Shrinking World: Trade and Innovation Policies in the United States, Europe and Japan.* New York: Council on Foreign Relations, Inc.

Piore, M., and C. F. Sabel. 1984. *The Second Industrial Divide: Possibilities for Prosperity.* New York: Basic Books.

Prebisch, R. 1950. *The Economic Development of Latin America and Its Principal Problems.* New York: United Nations.

Przeworski, A. 1990. "La irracionalidad del capitalismo y la inviabilidad del Socialismo." *Pensamiento Iberoamericano. Revista de Economía Política*, Madrid, 18, Julio–Diciembre 1990.

Reich, Robert B. 1991. *The Work of Nations. Preparing Ourselves for 21st Century Capitalism.* New York: Knopf.

Rodríguez, F. 1991. "La endogeneización del cambio tecnológico: Un desafío para el desarrollo." In O. Sunkel, ed., *El subdesarrollo latinoamericano.*

Salazar, J. M. 1991. "El papel del Estado y del Mercado en el desarrollo económico." In O. Sunkel, ed., *El subdesarrollo latinoamericano.*

Shonfield, A. 1965. *Modern Capitalism.* Oxford: Oxford University Press.

Sunkel, O. 1973. "Transnational Capitalism and National Disintegration in Latin America." *Social and Economic Studies* 22, no. 1. (March).

Sunkel, O., ed. 1993. *Development from Within; Toward a Neo-structuralist Approach for Latin America.* Boulder, CO: Lynne Rienner.

Sunkel, O., and P. Paz. 1970, *El subdesarrollo latinoamericano y la teoría del desarrollo*. México, D.F.: Siglo XIX Editores.

Sunkel, O., and G. Zuleta. 1990. "Neo-structuralism versus Neo-liberalism in the 1990s." *CEPAL Review* 42 (December): 35–53.

Thurow, L. C. 1992. *Head to Head; The Coming Economic Battle among Japan, Europe and America*. New York: William Morrow and Co., Inc.

Tokman, V. 1991. "Pobreza y Homogeneización Social: Tareas para los 90." *Pensamiento Iberoamericano. Revista de Economía Política*. Madrid, Enero.

Tomassini, L. 1992. *Estado, Gobernabilidad y Desarrollo*, Santiago, CINDE-FORO 90.

United Nations Development Programme (UNDP). 1990. *Human Development Report 1990*. New York and Oxford: Oxford University Press.

United Nations Center on Transnational Corporations (UNCTC). 1991. *World Investment Report, 1991: The Trial in Foreign Direct Investment*. New York: United Nations.

United Nations Center on Transnational Corporations (UNCTC) (1992), *World Investment Report, Transnational Corporations as Engines of Growth*. New York: United Nations.

Wade, R. 1990. *Governing the Market; Economic Theory and the Role of Government in East Asian Industrialization*. Princeton: Princeton University Press.

Wade, R. 1992a. "East Asia's Economic Success: Conflicting Evidence, Perspectives, Partial Insight, Shaky Evidence." *World Politics*. 44, 2: 273.

Wade, R. 1992b. "State and Market Revisited. How Interventionist Should Third-World Governments Be?" *The Economist*, April 4, p. 77.

CHAPTER 12

After Socialism and Dirigisme: Which Way Now?

Andrés Solimano

Economic reform is becoming a household word, used to describe the current attempts at transforming the structure and institutions of whole economic systems, in a wide variety of countries and contexts. Economic reform programs have been or are currently being undertaken in Latin America by countries like Chile, Mexico, Bolivia, and very recently, Argentina. Post-socialist Eastern Europe and the former Soviet Union are also embarking on radical programs of economic reform that combine macroeconomic stabilization with liberalization policies. In the context of industrialized countries, the drive toward free-market economic reform gained impetus in the 1980s with the Thatcherist experiment in England and Reaganomics in the United States.

Clearly some common currents in policy formulation are permeating many countries that not so long ago followed very dissimilar economic strategies; the most obvious case being the economies of the former socialist bloc. The new economic reform orthodoxy places strong emphasis on the role of free markets in resource allocation and growth, smaller government, trade liberalization, business deregulation, and privatization. In addition, macroeconomic austerity is seen as a prerequisite for the implementation of these more structural reforms.

Evidently the new paradigm represents a sharp departure from previous development strategies in nonsocialist developing countries based on state dirigisme, controlled trade regimes, and regulated markets for goods and factors of production. The departure is even more striking in the former socialist bloc where the institutions of capitalism are absent, key markets work poorly or simply do not exist, and the state is the main owner of physical productive wealth in the country.

The Emergence of a New Paradigm
of Economic Reform: Origins

The 1990s is producing a remarkable sight, as both capitalist and formerly socialist economies are embracing economic policies conducive to reshaping their economic landscapes along free-market lines. State-led development is clearly out of fashion, largely because of the Latin American crises of the 1980s and in spite of the East Asian record. Furthermore, Stalinist socialism is definitely dead.

Explaining the emergence and widespread acceptance of a new economic policy paradigm is a hard task that involves grasping a complex interaction between events and ideas. Major shocks to the world economy in the 1970s affected economic performance and led to a reassessment of priorities and the content of economic policies. The first oil shock in 1973 gave rise to the worsening of macroeconomic conditions in industrialized countries, as inflation accelerated, and simultaneously an increase in unemployment, a slowdown in output growth, and a trend of slower productivity growth (particularly in the United States and Great Britain). In the realm of economic policy ideas, the traditional post–World War II consensus combining demand management at the macroeconomic level with a welfare state came under strong challenge. Reflecting these trends, England under Prime Minister Margaret Thatcher applied stiff anti-inflationary measures along with policies aiming at reducing the role of the state in the economy through the privatization of public enterprises, tax cuts, and economic deregulation. A similar shift in emphasis and policy priorities took place in the United States after the election of President Ronald Reagan in 1980. The new U.S. policies centered on tax reduction, business deregulation, and financial liberalization, in the context of increased fiscal deficits. Both in the United States and Britain, excessive government involvement in economic activity and its outlets of taxes and regulation (and also the outgrowth of public enterprises in England) were identified as the main causes of sluggish capital formation, reduced entrepreneurial effort, and meager productivity growth.

These changes in two main industrialized countries in the 1980s certainly shaped, albeit gradually, a new climate in economic policy thinking and formulation that eventually reached the developing world and the socialist bloc.[1]

In the developing-country context, particularly in Latin America, the strategy of import-substitution industrialization (ISI) pursued since the 1930s was already the subject of ample criticism because of its lack of dynamism, its anti-export bias, and its failure to correct endemic concentration in income distribution. The role of the state as a supporter of the ISI strategy and the deteriorating record in terms of fiscal imbalances and inflation led to a questioning of its role in the economy. The experience with radical market-oriented reform in Latin America can be traced to the early to mid-1970s. Following the collapse of populist-socialist experiments, newly installed military regimes implemented sharp programs of macroeconomic restraint and liberalization in Chile, Argentina, and Uruguay.[2]

Beyond the Southern Cone, the single most important shock that catalyzed the drive toward economic reform in Latin America was the debt crises of the 1980s. The debt shock triggered a protracted period of stagnation, high inflation, fragile balance-of-payments positions, and increased economic instability in the region. Increasingly the economic dislocation of the 1980s led to the perception that overcoming the economic crisis would require the restoration of macroeconomic equilibrium, a comprehensive change in the structure of the economy, fiscal reform, privatization, and an opening of the domestic economy to foreign competition. In the 1980s, comprehensive programs along these lines were implemented in Mexico and Bolivia (Chile, as mentioned above, started its reforms in the mid-1970s), followed by Argentina, Venezuela, and Peru in the early 1990s.

In East Asia, the impressive performance of the NICs (Korea, Taiwan, Singapore, Hong Kong) in terms of high growth, rapid technical progress, enhanced international competitiveness, and aggressive export penetration provided a case for outward orientation and stable macro policies as an engine for growth and development. Certainly the experience of the NICs backed the new drive for economic reform in the developing world, although these experiences, as we shall see later, represent a more eclectic model of reform regarding the role of the state and the relative importance given to liberalization vis-à-vis macro consolidation in the process of economic transformation.

The coup de grace, perhaps, in favor of market-based reform was the collapse of the socialist experiment in Eastern Europe in the late 1980s, followed by the economic and political disintegration of the Soviet Union in late 1991. The sudden collapse of the socialist regimes gave rise to more radical programs, particularly in their liberalization component, in Eastern Europe compared to their Latin American counterparts in the 1970s and 1980s.

Program Design and Performance

The standard package of market-based economic reform in an economy starting from pervasive imbalances includes measures of both macroeconomic stabilization and liberalization. Macro restraint involves tight demand policies (oriented to cut domestic absorption) coupled with real depreciation of the exchange rate (to gain external competitiveness).

Liberalization policies include reform of the trade regime, deregulation of controlled interest rates and other quantitative allocative mechanisms for credit, elimination of regulation preventing domestic and foreign investment in certain activities, privatization of public enterprises, and changes in the tax system. Those policies are oriented to give markets a prominent role in the resource allocation and growth process, and to reshape existing institutions to make them more supportive of a market-based system.

The effects of changes in specific policy instruments on economic activity, inflation and real wages, and other indicators of economic performance have been the subject of debate for a long time. The controversy surrounding whether currency devaluations are contractionary or expansionary in the short term is one example; the rigidity of inflation in the face of cuts in money growth in chronic inflation countries, and the stagnationist effects of cuts in real wages, are others.[3] Recently, new evidence has emerged on the slow transition to medium-term growth in the aftermath of adjustment—in particular, the existence of a long investment lag and reduced capacity utilization in the aftermath of adjustment.[4]

Radical and Moderate Packages: Two Views

Two views can be distinguished regarding the intensity and priority given to macro adjustment and consolidation vis-à-vis liberalization in a reform program. One view emphasizes the fact that protracted austerity involves a contraction in both current and probably future output, through the adverse impact of sharp demand contraction on capital formation.[5] This view calls for gradualism—or at least moderation in the amount of demand contraction and currency depreciation—in an adjustment program to avoid large cuts in real wages and a protracted slump in economic activity and growth. In addition, this view highlights the potentially deleterious effects of rapid liberalization on macroeconomic stability. For example, a cut in tariffs may involve a reduction in fiscal revenues, hampering an already flimsy fiscal budget; moreover, overly costly programs from a social point of view may give rise to future reversals because of the erosion of sociopolitical support for reforms associated with a protracted squeeze of living standards. Furthermore, an important distinction (see chapter 1) is made between shock treatment for stabilization purposes and gradualism in structural reforms that involve the restructuring of enterprises, banks, tax systems, and the building of new institutions.[6]

The other (more radical) view downplays the adverse effects of macro restraint on capital formation and growth and emphasizes the positive effects of liberalization on the productivity of investment and the alleged efficiency of growth in a liberalized policy regime. Moreover, this view favors shock therapy and rapid liberalization as a way to alter *dramatically* the expectations of the private sector, thus boosting capital accumulation and growth. This view rests on the notion that a change in policy regimes, as distinguished from specific changes in policy instruments, is the fundamental force driving private sector response to the new set of policies put in place by a program of economic reform.[7]

In the context of postsocialist transformation, an important area of controversy between "gradualists" and "big bangers" is over the pace of privatization. The gradualist approach assumes that privatization is a problem of social transformation, therefore an inherently slow, evolutionary process.[8] The gradualist approach emphasizes the privatization of small to medium-sized enterprises to create a critical mass of "genuine Schumpeterian entrepreneurs" with strong incentives for innovation and creation of new business. The privatization of large-scale public enterprises would be a slow process whose progress will depend upon advances in the creation of other market institutions such as a commercial banking system, regulatory agencies, etc.

The radical approach to privatization of large-scale public enterprises of postsocialist countries[9] emphasizes the need for the state to quickly get rid of the large number of big state-owned enterprises. Because these enterprises are often loss-making units, they put a burden on public finances that will ultimately be destabilizing; in addition, rapid privatization will reduce the capacity of patronage by the state.

Performance Criteria

To assess the performance of economic reform, we will focus on three criteria: (1) the results of stabilization efforts, in particular the speed of disinflation; (2) the response of investment and growth to adjustment policies; and (3) the distributive impact of the reforms. Of course, other criteria could be added for a more detailed evaluation of the programs.

Macroeconomic Stabilization
An important component of the programs of economic reform is macroeconomic stabilization. The accumulated experience on stabilization in developing countries shows that reducing inflation, on a more or less permanent basis, is not an easy task, particularly in economies with a long history of inflation. Inertia, indexation, and credibility problems are pervasive in these economies, making the task of stabilization more complicated. For example, the stabilization of high-inflation in countries like Mexico, Chile, and Israel shows that it may easily take half a decade or more for high inflation to converge to annual rates of the order of 20%–25%. In socialist economies that start with repressed inflation, the process of stabilization is proving to be complicated, too. The magnitude of the initial inflationary outburst after price reform is large, and the persistence of inflation after the initial price shock is not trivial.

Investment and Growth Response
Macroeconomic restraint often leads to drastic cuts in public and private investment rates, at least during the initial phases of the adjustment process.

When the contraction in investment rates becomes protracted, as has been the case in most Latin American economies during the 1980s, this endangers the rate of expansion of productive capacities in the medium term. In addition, it has been detected that the resumption of private investment after the initial contraction in adjusting economies may take several years.[10] Moreover, the recovery of public investment may take even longer, negatively affecting the creation of complementary infrastructure needed to support private investment and export and output growth. There are several reasons for the pattern of initial investment contraction followed by a delay in the response of private investment during an adjustment program: initial demand contraction and the creation of excess capacity, an increased value of waiting in a context of unconsolidated economic reform, the lack of supportive systems (public physical infrastructure, credit, legal system, etc.). Again, these problems are bound to be particularly critical for reforming socialist systems.

Distributive Impact
Macroeconomic adjustment often brings about a cut in real wages, both in the private and public sectors, to support real currency depreciation and reduce current fiscal expenditures. In addition, the slashing of government subsidies to credit and basic consumption goods also produces changes in real incomes of various groups (not necessarily a regressive move). Liberalization and privatization policies also have (largely unexplored) effects on the distribution of wealth.

The evidence gathered in two recent studies[11] conducted under the auspices of WIDER and the OECD show that macro restraint and external shocks that entail massive cuts in real wages and/or increases in unemployment hurt the poor disproportionately. Moreover, major regressive redistributions of wealth have taken place during financial crises following experiments with unregulated financial liberalization.[12] On the other hand, efforts aimed at targeting social spending in health and education during the course of adjustment have helped reduce the social impact of these policies on the very poor, in spite of a trend of declining real social spending per capita detected in Latin America.[13]

Radical Economic Reform in Latin America:
Chile, Mexico, and Bolivia

Comprehensive market-oriented programs of economic reform in Latin America started to be implemented in the mid-1970s in Chile, and in the mid-1980s in Mexico and Bolivia; see table 12.1 and figures 12.1 and 12.2. (Argentina and Peru are currently following similar policies, though these are still new and unconsolidated).

TABLE 12.1 Economic indicators of reforming economies in Latin America: Chile, Mexico, Bolivia (annual averages, percent)

			Growth rate of			Inflation Rate (CPI)	Investment (Ratio of GDP)	Terms of trade (1980 = 100)
			GDP	Exports	Real wages			
Chile	Prereform period	1960–70	4.3	3.0	6.0	25.7	20.6	165.1
		1971–73	0.7	–3.8	–8.7	296.0	14.7	175.3
	Reform period	1974–81	3.9	14.4	10.0	163.9	17.2	121.5
		1982–85	–1.5	4.8	–4.4	19.0	10.5	82.4
		1986–91	6.0	11.9[a]	2.9	19.2	16.7[a]	86.8
		1974–91	3.4	11.4	3.7	84.1	15.6	101.3
Mexico	Prereform period	1970–81	6.8	7.7	0.9	16.8	22.1	105.9
	Reform period	1982–85	0.4	9.2	–7.0	71.0	16.8	99.4
		1986–91	1.7	5.1[a]	1.6	67.0	16.8[a]	69.5
		1982–91	1.2	6.9[a]	–2.6	69.7	16.8[a]	81.5
Bolivia	Prereform period	1970–81	3.5	–0.9	1.0	19.6	14.4	76.2
		1982–85	–2.5	2.2	–3.3	3,358.3	7.2	87.9
	Reform period	1986–87	0.0	1.3	–7.3	38.4	5.1	56.0
		1988–91	2.9	16.8[a]	9.5[c]	15.7	6.1[a]	55.0
		1986–91	1.9	10.6[a]	—	24.8	6.4[a]	55.3

Source: World Bank, ECLAC (1990, 1991).
Note: a. Exports and real investment figures are available only up to 1990.
b. Stabilization-cum-structural adjustment program was launched in August 1985.
c. Figures refer to 1988–1990 period and are not directly comparable to previous years.

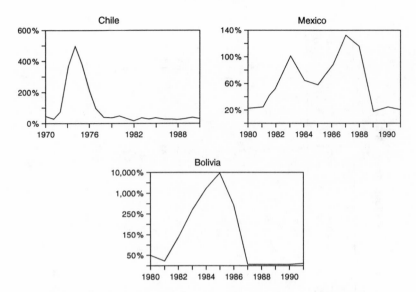

Figure 12.1   Monthly inflation rates in Chile, Mexico, and Bolivia

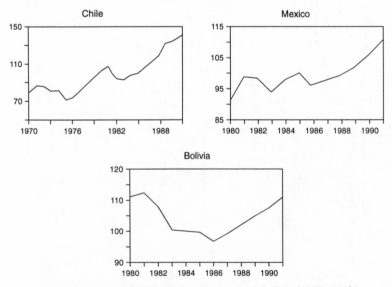

Figure 12.2   Real GDP in Chile, Mexico, and Bolivia (1985=100)

Chile

The military regime that toppled Allende in 1973 initiated a very ambitious program of free-market economic reform, at least given the economic climate prevalent at the time in Latin America. The program, implemented under tight authoritarian conditions, involved comprehensive macroeconomic stabilization and liberalization. At the time the reforms were first applied, the Chilean economy exhibited large macroeconomic imbalances in the form of high inflation rates and a large fiscal deficit.[14] Inflation was slow to decline in spite of tough austerity measures—the fiscal deficit was reduced from 25% of GDP in 1973 to near 3% in 1975. In October 1973 most of the system of controlled prices was dissolved, and the exchange rate sharply devalued. Subsidies on credit and consumption goods were eliminated and all controls on interest rates lifted. In addition, a gradual program (over a four-year period) of tariff reduction was enacted to bring down tariff rates from three-digit levels to an uniform import duty of 10% (by mid-1979). Public sector reform included large cuts in public sector employment, privatization of public enterprises (many of them nationalized under Allende), and the imposition of a value-added tax to improve tax collection. In the second half of the 1970s, the Chilean economy experienced rapid growth in a context of declining inflation and consolidating fiscal adjustment. Nevertheless, during most of that period unemployment remained very high. Financial deregulation and currency overvaluation led to an overexpansion of financial intermediation and the accumulation of a large stock of internal and external debt. In 1982–83 the Chilean economy suffered a deep recession and a severe financial crisis as a consequence of adverse external shocks and previous policy mistakes. The post-1984 recovery was strong, with GDP growing at more than 6% per year (1984–89) in a context of relative macroeconomic stability, lower real interest rates, and favorable copper prices (since 1987). In addition, a depreciated real exchange rate—coupled with depressed real wages and a considerable pool of unemployed labor—favored the rapid expansion of nontraditional exports, therefore helping to consolidate the improvement in external accounts (see table 12.1 and figures 12.1 and 12.2).

The political economy of reform in Chile is an important element to be considered. The intensity of the reform effort as well as its large social costs were possible, to a considerable extent, because the reforms were applied under the particular conditions of a military regime that governed for many years without open political opposition: political parties were banned, the main labor organizations were declared illegal, and there was no parliament in operation. The situation started to be relaxed toward the late 1980s following a preannounced transition to democracy that included a plebiscite in 1988 and a national election of a president and a parliament in late 1989. The democratic administration that took office in early 1990 maintained most of the economic policies implemented under the military regime. The bulk of the market-oriented system was preserved, although changes were introduced in the labor legislation to rebalance the bargaining power of labor vis-à-vis capital, taxes were increased modestly, and a program of social spending to alleviate poverty and improve income distribution patterns was initiated. The performance of the economy has been very strong since 1990.

Mexico

The Mexican economy for decades followed a strategy of import substitution, growing state involvement in the economy, and corporatist politics. In the second half of the 1970s, following the discovery of oil, Mexico engaged in a cycle of fiscal expansion, currency appreciation, and large foreign debt accumulation that came to a sudden halt in 1982. In that year the country embarked in a drastic program of macroeconomic adjustment comprising demand restraint, real depreciation of the exchange rate, and large cuts in real wages. Those policies were further deepened since 1985 with trade reform, deregulation, and market liberalization. Quotas were reduced from covering 100% of (non-oil) tradable goods production to less than 17% at present, with a similar trend in tariffs.[15] The tax system was reformed, regulations on domestic and foreign investments were phased out, and the financial system was revamped. Moreover, a severe program of disinflation was launched in late 1987 that combined additional fiscal adjustment with incomes policies to abate a stubbornly high rate of inflation.[16]

After a long period of sluggish growth and slow disinflation, the Mexican economy started to show signs of recovery in 1988. Disinflation and the gradual recovery were boosted by a debt-reduction deal struck in the context of the Brady initiative in 1989, the hastening of the privatization and deregulatory process, and the initiative for a free trade agreement with the United States. During 1990–91, GDP grew at an average rate of 4% per year, though that growth slowed thereafter.

The political economy of the reforms in Mexico is interesting. They have been generated from within the ruling political system by a generation of young, highly qualified economists within the PRI (Partido Revolucionario Institucional), a party that for many decades had backed a radically different development model based on state dirigisme and import substitution.

Bolivia

This is a case of free-market reform in a small, poor economy (its level of income per capita is below $600),[17] strongly dependent on the export of a few mineral commodities—natural gas and tin—and with a small base of human capital and physical infrastructure.

Bolivia suffered mounting economic instability and negative GDP growth in the first half of the 1980s. This process culminated in the hyper-inflation of the first eight months of 1985. In August 1985 a drastic and successful anti-inflationary program was launched; as a result inflation declined from more than 25,000% in 1985 to an average annual rate of 16.5% in 1987–1990. In addition, the anti-inflationary program was followed by a series of policies of structural adjustment including trade liberalization (tariffs rates were rapidly reduced after 1985 to a range between 5% and 10%). Most of the system of price controls, state subsidies, and guaranteed prices were eliminated. Public sector prices were adjusted to reflect opportunity costs, interest rates ceilings were removed, and domestic and foreign commercial banks were allowed to receive deposits denominated in dollars.

The Bolivian program of economic reform provides an example of rapid elimination of a hyperinflation. On the real side, the program of disinflation and liberalization was followed by a protracted period of depressed private investment and slow, albeit positive, GDP growth.

In spite of the success on the stabilization front, the Bolivian program still shows signs of incomplete adjustment. The fiscal deficit averaged 5.4% of GDP in the period 1986–90, pushing real interest rates up and crowding out private investment.[18] In addition, the financial system is highly dollarized, as near 80% of the liabilities of the banking system are denominated in foreign currency, reflecting a lack of confidence in domestic assets.

The Bolivian economic reform program was launched by a civilian government led by President Paz Estenssoro, elected in 1985, after two decades of alternation of civilian and military government implementing a wide range of economic policies ranging from populism to orthodox austerity programs. The post-1985 reforms were implemented in a democracy, though in a country with a large peasant population with little experience with formal politics.

A Look at Performance in the Three Countries

A full evaluation of the reform policies in the three countries, considering counterfactuals and alternative policies, is beyond the scope of this chapter. Nevertheless, let us look at our performance criteria in the three countries.

Stabilization Performance
The experience with stabilization in Chile and Mexico, and to a lesser extent in Bolivia, shows that reducing and stabilizing inflation is a costly and often lengthy process. In Mexico and Chile, it took between six and seven years to reduce three-digit inflation to levels around 20%–25% per annum (see table

TABLE 12.2   Indicators of speed of adjustment, Latin America

	Number of years for inflation to reach the threshold of 15%–20% per year[a]	Number of years for private investment to recover to sustained levels (more than three years of consecutive expansion)
Chile[a]		
1974–89	7	5
Mexico		
1982–91	7	6
Bolivia		
1985–91	2	—

a. Counting from the stabilization plan of 1975.

12.2). In Chile the rate of inflation was over 600% in 1974, converging to levels below 20%–25% per year just after 1981, in spite of stiff stabilization measures. In Mexico the rate of inflation was near 100% in 1982, reaching the critical range of 20%–25% per year just in 1989. In contrast, stabilization in Bolivia was faster than in Chile and Mexico. The Bolivian case fits well with the international evidence showing that the stabilization of a hyperinflation is often more rapid than the stabilization of chronic inflation.[19]

Impact on Investment and Growth of Reform
The stabilization and adjustment programs in the three countries came along with an initial output contraction, although the degree of the output decline varied in each case: GDP fell by around 12–15 percentage points in the recessions of 1975 and 1982–83 in Chile; output contracted (cumulatively) by nearly 5% in Mexico in 1982–83, and in Bolivia it fell by 2.5% in 1986. In all episodes, these economies also suffered from negative external shocks.

Regarding investment, the experience of Chile in the 1970s and Mexico in the 1980s is that public investment tends to suffer in the initial phases of an adjustment program. In Chile between 1976 and 1984, public investment was maintained at around 3 to 4 percentage points of GDP below its level of the 1960s. In Mexico, public investment declined by nearly 5% of GDP in the period 1982–89 as compared to 1978–81. In contrast, public investment started to recover in Bolivia after the program of 1985.

The response of private investment to the reform process in the three countries was mixed.[20] In Chile, private investment increased strongly in the second half of the 1970s, to drop sharply during the recession of 1982–83 and recover a few years later. In Mexico, private investment declined from 1981 to 1983, then remained virtually stagnant until 1987, recovering afterward. In

Bolivia, private investment was declining in the first half of the 1980s, before the reform program. That decline stopped with the launching of the adjustment program in 1985; however, investment levels remained quite depressed afterward (see table 12.2).

Distributive Impact

An important and contentious issue is the impact of the adjustment programs on poverty and income distribution. Table 12.1 shows that in Chile (1971–73) and Bolivia (1982–85), real wages were falling before the adoption of the stabilization programs. In general, the rapid escalation of inflation before reform in these two countries was the main cause of the decline in real wages. Thus, stopping high inflation becomes a sine qua non condition for reversing a negative trend in real wages. However, real wages remained depressed for a long time in Chile; in fact, the average real wage was still lower in 1989 than in 1970. During most of the Pinochet regime the rate of unemployment was more than two times higher, on average, than the rate of previous decades. This suggests that low-income groups bore a large share of the costs of adjustment in Chile.

Several indicators portrayed in tables 12.3 and 12.4 convey useful information on the distributive consequences of the policies applied in Chile after 1974. The Gini coefficient increased (greater inequality) by around 4 points (a non-negligible amount) between the late 1960s and the early 1980s. In addition, the share in consumption for the lowest 40% income group declined steadily both in 1978 and 1988 compared with 1969 (Meller 1991). These effects were ameliorated in part with an improvement in some social indicators. There was a decline in the rate of infant mortality (now one of the lowest in Latin America) and in different indicators of malnutrition, as a consequence of an increased targeting of some social programs to more vulnerable groups living in extreme poverty.

In Mexico, the adjustment policies implemented after 1982 had a nega-

TABLE 12.3   Trends in income distribution in Chile for selected years, 1969–84

		Share of income					
	Gini coefficient of family income	Lowest 40%	Middle 40%	Highest 20%	SEN indicator	Real wage indicator	Unemployment rate (%)
Period	(1)	(2)	(3)	(4)	(5)	(6)	(7)
1969–71	0.493	11.5	32.7	55.8	19.0	100.0	5.5
1979–81	0.523	11.1	31.4	57.6	17.6	89.6	16.5
1982–84	0.543	10.0	30.6	59.5	28.3	90.5	27.4

Source: Meller (1991).

TABLE 12.4   Household consumption by income group in Santiago, Chile (1969, 1978, and 1988, percentage)

Income group	1969	1978	1988
Lowest 40%	19.4	14.5	12.6
Middle 40%	36.1	34.5	32.8
Highest 20%	44.5	51.0	54.6
Total	100.0	100.0	100.0
Average monthly household consumption (1988 pesos)	75,535.0	76,260.0	76,094.0

Source: Meller (1991).

tive impact on total labor incomes and particularly on real wages (Lustig 1992). Real wages in manufacturing declined by a cumulative 38.5% in the period 1983–88, with an even larger decline of real wages in the public sector (table 12.5). Nevertheless, real per capita consumption declined by 11.5% over the same period, suggesting that nonwage incomes (of poor and rich) must have declined by less than wage incomes.[21] Regarding the evolution of social expenditure in Mexico, spending on education per capita between 1981 and 1989 declined by around 1.0% of GDP; expenditure on health care over the same period decreased by 1.6% of GDP (Lustig 1992).

To sum up, the review of three Latin American experience with market-based economic reform in the 1970s and 1980s shows that reforming distressed economies is a long process. Putting the house in order in macroeconomic terms is not easy. In the cases reviewed, stabilizing inflation took longer than anticipated and involved considerable costs in terms of real eco-

TABLE 12.5   Mexico—Distributive indicators

		Cumulative change in: Real wages		Private consumption per capita (percent)
	Total wage income (percent)	Industrial sector (percent)	Government sector (percent)	
1983–88	−39.7	−38.5	−46.1	−11.5

	Share of non-wage income in national income[a] (percent)
1980	61.4
1989	72.7

Source: Lustig (1992).
a. Includes urban informal sector and agricultural self-employed income.

nomic activity and real wages. Moreover, the transition to sustainable growth in the aftermath of stabilization is cumbersome. Public and private investment tend to suffer in the initial phases of an adjustment program. Moreover, a sustained recovery of private investment after a large initial contraction may take several years.

Regarding the distributive impact of adjustment programs, the available evidence shows that adjustment policies (compounded by negative external shocks) involved cuts in real wages and/or increases in unemployment rates in Chile, Bolivia, and Mexico, with low-income groups bearing a large share of the adjustment burden. On the positive side, the expansion of nontraditional exports and the discipline of enhanced foreign competition on the domestic economy are valuable effects of the reforms.

Radical Economic Reform in Eastern Europe after 1989

The current attempts in Eastern Europe to transform socialist economies based on state ownership and central planning into market economies is perhaps one of the most ambitious attempts at economic reform in modern times. Far worse, there is practically no previous experience with economic transformation of this magnitude.[22]

Free-market experiments of economic reform started in 1990, following the political collapse of the socialist regimes. This process is very complex given that the initial conditions of these economies are particularly poor in terms of initial macro imbalances, pervasive micro distortions, and oversized public sectors. In addition, the reforms are taking place in emergent democracies with a considerable degree of political fragmentation.

Country Programs

Poland launched the first comprehensive program to establish a market system in Eastern Europe in January 1990.[23] The Polish program combined fiscal austerity with price deregulation, trade liberalization, and privatization. The Polish economy started its program of economic reform with large macroeconomic imbalances, shortages in consumer goods markets, and a large stock of external debt. Inflation was 640% in 1989, following large devaluations coupled with wage increases in 1988–89. GDP growth slowed during 1980–88 (see table 12.6) and turned negative (-1.4%) in 1989. The current account deficit in convertible currency was 2.5% of GDP in 1989, and debt servicing represented nearly 56% of merchandise exports in 1990.

The program entailed the dismantling of most price controls and sharp increases in energy prices and public tariffs. The exchange rate was fixed at a substantially depreciated level, and the zloty was made convertible for current

TABLE 12.6 East-Central Europe: Economic indicators

Countries	GDP $Bil 1990	Growth rates (percent)[a] NMP 1970–80	NMP 1980–88	GDP 1989	GDP 1990	GDP 1991	Inflation (percent year end) 1989	1990	1991[a]	Current acct./GDP (conv. curr.) (percent) 1989	1990	1991[b]	Ext. debt/GDP (conv. curr.) (percent) 1990
Bulgaria	22.4	7.0	4.4	−1.4	−10.2	−26.0	6.3	64.0	430.0	−6.4	−2.7	0.0	40.2
Czechoslovakia	46.5	4.7	2.0	1.3	−3.5	−16.4	1.3	13.9	49.0	0.9	−1.0	−5.1	16.5
Hungary	32.1	4.5	1.3	−0.9	−6.5	−7.8	18.0	30.0	32.0	−4.9	−0.2	1.0	62.2
Poland	62.3	5.4	1.0	−0.5	−14.0	−9.0	640.0	249.0	60.4	−2.7	−2.5	−1.2	74.3
Romania	35.5	9.3	4.7	−5.8	−10.2	−10.0	2.5	27.0	184.0	5.4	−3.9	−4.8	5.6

Source: World Bank.
a. January–November.
b. Cash basis. The current account on an accrual basis was −7.5% in Bulgaria (due to arrears on foreign debt servicing).

account transactions. Tariffs and other quantitative restrictions to international trade were rapidly eliminated.

On the fiscal side, a reduction of the fiscal deficit on the order of 7% of GDP was planned, although much less was actually attained. Monetary and credit policy was tightened and a tax on wages was instituted to prevent wage increases granted by enterprises to exceed government guidelines. Privatization was initiated by selling restaurants, shops in the trade sector, and small enterprises. However, little progress has been made in the privatization of large state-owned public enterprises, in spite of the proliferation of sophisticated schemes devised for that purpose.

Czechoslovakia started its program of economic reform in 1990 with apparently small macro imbalances, no monetary overhang (Bruno 1992), and a low level of external debt (the ratio of foreign debt to GDP was 19% in 1990).[24] In the 1980s, Czechoslovakia decelerated growth sharply, though maintaining low open inflation. The program in Czechoslovakia involved a stepwise deregulation of controlled prices in 1990, followed by a complete elimination of most price subsidies and controls in early 1991. In addition, fiscal policy was restrictive, as was credit and wage policy. After a substantial initial devaluations of the crown, Czechoslovakia pegged the exchange rate as a nominal anchor. As in Poland, privatization took place at a fast pace at the level of retail trade and services. A massive plan for auctioning shares, through a voucher system, of 1,200 state-owned enterprises to more than 8.5 million citizens was launched in 1992.

Hungary started its reforms as early as 1968, although they were partial and experienced setbacks. By 1982 nearly half of the prices for consumer goods were free, a proportion that went up to 80% in 1990. Private property in housing and small-scale enterprises were allowed in the 1980s, accompanied by new tax and banking laws. Hungary was caught in late 1980 with almost no monetary overhang; however, its level of external debt was high (65% of GDP in 1990). In early 1991, the exchange rate was devalued by 15% and additional consumer goods prices were freed in the context of fiscal, monetary, and wage restraint. The exchange rate regime followed a fixed peg.

Bulgaria, an agrarian economy before socialism, industrialized and become strongly dependent in its foreign trade with the Soviet Union under a highly orthodox socialist regime. Bulgaria started its reform program in 1990 with a large monetary overhang, repressed inflation, and a high level of external debt, mostly accumulated during the second half of the 1980s.[25]

Price reform started piecemeal in 1990, although it accelerated in February 1991 when most price controls were abolished, subsidies phased out, and the exchange rate left floating (due to the lack of international reserves to support a fixed parity). The ensuing exchange rate depreciation was huge (500%), and it produced a price hike of vast proportions. Current account convertibility was introduced and trade taxes sharply reduced. In addition, wage and credit policy turned very tight. Plans for privatization are under way and some progress has already been made in retail trade and services.

Romania entered the process of economic reform after the violent overthrown of Nicolae Ceausescu in late 1989. In spite of some independent foreign policy stances from those of the USSR, the economic policies followed by the Ceausescu regime were extremely orthodox (in a socialist sense). The trend toward some decentralization and reform of the other socialist countries in the 1980s and before never reached Romania.[26] On the contrary, the tendency was toward further centralization and deepened central planning. In the 1980s, the Ceausescu regime followed a deliberate policy of paying—even prepaying—its external debts at almost any cost. For that purpose the country was running increasing trade surpluses by compressing consumption, investment, and imports. Moreover, fiscal surpluses were increased through the curtailment of social spending, further squeezing living standards. At the end of the regime the external debt of Romania was almost nil, although the economy was in shambles.

Price liberalization took place in three rounds: November 1990, and April and July 1991.[27] As of 1992, nearly 80% of prices are determined in the market. The exchange rate was devalued in each of these rounds, jumping from 20 leu per dollar before November 1990 to 60 leu after the last adjustment, thus accumulating a nominal devaluation of 300% in nearly eight months. The exchange rate was left floating, to be determined in an interbank market, with the exception of some basic imports. The trade regime has been reformed by abolishing the state monopoly on international trade and eliminating quantitative restrictions and reducing the average level of tariffs to the range of 10% to 30%. On the fiscal side, the forced profit remittance system was replaced by a corporate income tax. A new privatization law was enacted in 1991, though with little progress so far in encouraging actual privatization.

Initial Results and Performance

Some common features from the experience in Eastern Europe are starting to emerge. Price reform produced an immediate and often sharp increase in the price level. In most of these countries, the price hike in general exceeded what was expected.[28] Poland and Bulgaria experienced the sharpest increases in prices following the lifting of price controls and the elimination of subsidies. The CPI in January 1990 increased by 77% in Poland. In Bulgaria inflation was 110.1% in February and 46.7% in March. Hungary avoided a major price jump, and in Czechoslovakia the CPI increased by nearly 26% in January 1991 following price adjustments. In Romania, prices increased by near 25% in the first month after price liberalization (table 12.7).

TABLE 12.7   East-Central Europe: CPI monthly inflation rates (percent)

	Bulgaria	Czechoslovakia	Hungary	Poland	Romania
1990					
January	0.8		15.4	77.3	—
February	0.8	2.4	2.9	15.8	—
March	0.7		1.2	4.7	—
April	0.8		1.9	6.6	—
May	0.8	0.8	0.2	4.5	—
June	3.5		−0.1	3.8	—
July	3.4		2.2	4.9	—
August	16.6	10.0	3.2	1.8	—
September	4.5		1.3	4.6	—
October	4.2		1.0	5.7	—
November	5.4	4.3	1.0	4.9	23.4
December	10.2		−0.1	5.9	11.6
1991					
January	14.4	25.8	7.5	12.7	14.8
February	110.1	7.0	4.9	6.7	7.0
March	46.7	4.7	3.7	4.5	6.6
April	3.6	2.0	2.4	2.7	26.5
May	2.5	1.9	2.1	2.7	5.1
June	7.4	1.8	2.1	4.9	2.0
July	9.8	−0.1	0.9	0.1	9.5
August	5.0	0.0	0.2	0.6	11.2
September	4.2	0.3	1.5	4.3	7.3
October	3.8	−0.1	1.3	3.2	10.4
November	5.1	1.6	1.4	3.2	10.9

Sources: IMF staff estimates.

Another important issue is the degree of inflationary persistence after the initial outburst of inflation. Table 12.7 shows that persistence has been relatively important in Poland, Bulgaria, and Romania and less so in Czechoslovakia and Hungary.

Apparently there is considerable cross-country variation in the extent of inflation acceleration following price decontrol, and adjustment in the exchange rate and public tariffs (see figures 12.3a–b). These differences seem to reflect different initial macro imbalances and the size of the monetary overhang existing before price reform. Regarding monetary accommodation and wage indexation, a common feature of the Eastern European stabilization programs implemented since 1990 has been a stance of restrictive monetary and credit policies supplemented with wage repression (or deindexation). An important medium-term issue relates to the rate of inflation at which these postsocialist economies will converge after the stabilization period (assuming it succeeds); in particular, whether the inflation rates in Eastern Europe will

358   Andrés Solimano

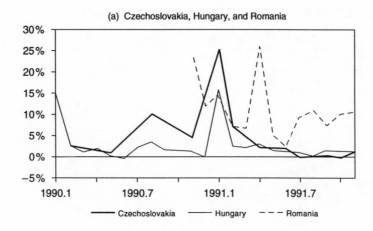

(a) Czechoslovakia, Hungary, and Romania

━━━ Czechoslovakia   ───── Hungary   ─ ─ ─ Romania

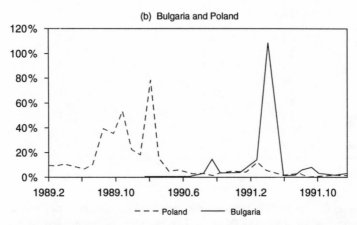

(b) Bulgaria and Poland

─ ─ ─ Poland   ━━━ Bulgaria

Figure 12.3   (a) Monthly inflation rates in Czechoslovakia, Hungary, and Romania (1990.1–1991.11); (b) Monthly inflation rates in Bulgaria and Poland (1989.2–1991.12)

converge to OECD levels (single-digit rates) or approach the inflation rates of successful non-OECD stabilizers like Mexico, Chile, and Israel (namely, to annual rates around 10%–15%).

On the real side, the adjustment programs in Eastern Europe have been accompanied by unprecedented output contraction (see figures 12.4a–e). In Poland GDP fell by 12.5% in 1990, and by an additional 9.0% in 1991, completing a cumulative decline on the order of 20% in two years. The magnitude of the output losses has been even larger in Bulgaria, where GDP fell by 10.2% in 1990 and by an extra 26% in 1991—a cumulative drop of

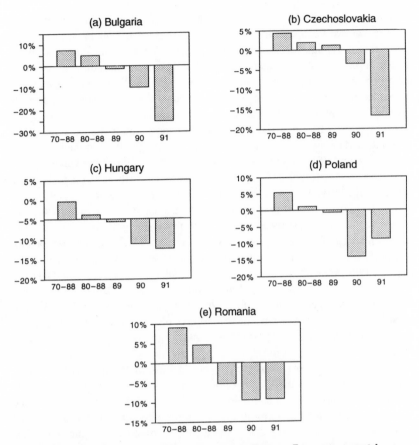

Figure 12.4(a)–(e)   GDP growth rates in Eastern European countries

output of over 35% in two years. In Czechoslovakia GDP fell by 3.5% in 1990 and by 16.4% in 1991. In Hungary GDP dropped 6.5% in 1990 and 7.8% in 1991.

From an international perspective, the extent of the contraction in measured economic activity in Eastern Europe since 1990 is much greater than the corresponding declines in output initially observed in Chile, Mexico, and Bolivia after the implementation of their stabilization programs. The extent of output contraction in Eastern Europe has to be qualified somewhat, however, because it mostly reflects the decline in economic activity in the socialized sector. Casual and anecdotal evidence suggests that a burgeoning private sector is emerging in the services and retail sectors. But because the state sector is still dominant (and it is bound to be for many years), the decline in GDP is worrisome. Moreover, there is a slow but persistent increase in unemployment in Eastern Europe, which already exceeds 11% in Poland and Bulgaria.

Several hypotheses are being put forward to explain the current drop in output in the region: (1) demand contraction as part of the stabilization effort; the combination of tight credit and fiscal policies as well as large drops in real wages led to a decline of effective demand and a drop in output in Keynesian fashion[29]; (2) adverse supply and organizational shocks; the dismantling of central planning has involved a disruption of the traditional supply networks of inputs and capital to enterprises, thus contributing to the decline in production. A context of high uncertainty about the future rules of the game regarding the property structure also has a discouraging effect on worker effort and managerial motivation. At a macro level, another adverse supply-side effect comes from a crunch in the supply of working capital (Calvo and Coricelli 1992); (3) external shocks associated with the disintegration of the CMEA; the elimination of the subsidies in Soviet exports to CMEA countries-typically oil, coal, and other forms of energy—amounted to a terms of trade shock for Eastern Europe, with the ensuing adverse real income effect[30]; and (4) too rapid trade liberalization; a rapid switching in domestic demand toward foreign goods has recessionary results in the short term because a sizable shift to exports to Western markets is unlikely to take place in a short period of time, in spite of highly competitive exchange rates (quality problems, particularly in manufacturing, are serious).[31]

Regarding the social costs of reform in Eastern Europe, recent experience shows that adjustment is involving large cuts in real wages and a slow but steady upward trend in unemployment. The medium-term outlook may be gloomy, as a rapid turnaround in the decline in aggregate output in the state sector is not in sight, and the restructuring of state-owned enterprises has barely started. The current rise in economic insecurity and "adjustment distress" is greatly complicating the politics of transition, making the threat of a slide back to authoritarianism and/or populism quite real.

Gradual Economic Reform I: Korea

The East Asian experience of the last three decades, particularly the case of Korea, provides an extremely interesting example of highly dynamic development based in export growth and high levels of capital formation (table 12.8). Korean policies were pursued in a context of active but competent state intervention and a stable macro environment.[32] Korea embarked after 1962 on an aggressive strategy of investment-cum-export-led growth. The new program of economic transformation reform combined orthodox policies of exchange-rate management to increase exports with liberalized imports. Poli-

TABLE 12.8   Korea—Economic indicators

	1963/73	1974/80	1981/86	1987/90
Inflation	17.1	22.9	6.6	5.9
Real GDP growth	9.5	7.3	9.2	10.3
Manufact. production	19.7	14.1	10.0	10.8
Share in GNP	35.2	21.5	14.0	10.7
Agriculture	15.7	28.1	31.4	32.1
Manufacturing	49.1	50.4	54.6	57.2
Other				
Exports as share of GNP	13.2	30.6	37.3	37.3
Investment as share of GNP	20.0	29.2	29.5	31.9
Foreign saving share of GNP	8.3	7.4	3.9	−3.4
Domestic saving of GNP	11.7	21.8	25.6	35.3

Source: IFS, IMF, *World Tables*. World Bank.

cies relied on a series of five-year plans oriented to boost industrialization, with active support from credit and exchange-rate policies. Foreign aid was substituted by increased domestic savings and foreign borrowing. The results were remarkable, as GDP grew at an annual rate of 10% per year between 1965 and 1973, while exports were expanding at an annual rate of 40%–50% between 1960 and 1973 (Collins and Park 1989). In 1973, the Korean government launched a "Big Push" aimed at increasing investment in heavy and chemical industries, while introducing additional import restrictions and new credit controls. These policies allowed rapid growth, although the excessive investment drive and government subsidies led to increasing inflationary pressures and a loss of external competitiveness.

The problems with heavy industrialization and accelerated inflation, compounded by the second oil shock, forced the adoption of adjustment measures in 1980–81. Monetary policy become tighter, the fiscal budget deficit was reduced from 4.7% of GDP in 1981 to 1% in 1985, imports were liberalized in a selective way, and regulations over the financial system and foreign direct investment gradually were lifted. A new period of rapid growth, low inflation, and current account surplus has taken place since the mid-1980s.

Regarding macroeconomic stability, Korea managed to keep inflation in the range of 15%–20% per year during the 1960s and 1970s. After the stabilization of 1980–81, inflation was reduced to below 10%. In general, Korea avoided the kind of macroeconomic crises so common in Latin America, even though during 1980–81 inflation accelerated and GDP growth slowed sharply. Korea ran large current account deficits—of the order of 8%–9% of GDP—in the late 1960s, in 1974, and in 1980–81, although it managed to correct them without compromising GDP growth in a major way. Fiscal imbalances never reached large proportions and the budget was kept, in general, under control. Besides the episode of currency overvaluation of the late 1970s, the exchange rate policy, along with active credit policies, were directed to enhance external competitiveness and boost export growth. In short, the process of economic development in Korea has unfolded without large shocks and destabilizing macroeconomic crises.

In relation to the investment and growth performance, what is striking about the Korean experience is its ability to sustain very high growth rates, on the order of 8% per year, for nearly three decades. Behind that strong growth performance we find an impressive investment drive, with rates of capital formation of 30% of GDP in the 1970s and 1980s. In addition, the Korean economy was able to mobilize domestic savings effectively to support the effort at capital formation by raising the domestic saving rate from nearly 6% of GDP in 1963 to 30% in 1985 (Collins and Park 1989). This growth performance did not take place in a laissez-faire regime. Governments encouraged export growth and investment using trade restrictions, directed credit intervention, and increased taxation in a context of close cooperation with business conglomerates; though government intervention avoided the anti-export bias of most Latin American cases. Finally, another factor behind the strong growth performance of Korea is the country's ability to maintain high rates of productivity growth. Like other "late industrializers," Korea pursued a deliberate policy of borrowing advanced foreign technologies to enhance competitiveness and growth (see Amsden 1989). An interesting feature of the Korean model is that income distribution was kept relatively equitable during the transformation process, unless compared to the standards of other developing countries, particularly those in Latin America. In fact, the share in national income of the bottom 40% of the population in Korea is higher than the corresponding ratio in countries like Brazil, Mexico, Thailand, and Hong Kong. Moreover, the income share of the top 20% is lower in Korea than the corresponding share in Brazil, Mexico, Thailand, and Hong Kong.

The agrarian reform undertaken in the late 1940s has been identified as one of the most important factors in Korea's relatively egalitarian income distribution (Collins and Park 1989). Another major factor has been a sustained effort to improve the educational levels of the population since the 1960s.[33]

As for the political economy of the Korean model, the program of economic transformation started in the early 1960s was launched by a military regime, led by General Park Chung Hee, that took power in a coup in 1961; he remained president until 1979. In the 1980s the military still ran the country, although the system started to implement measures of political liberalization toward the mid-to-late 1980s.

Gradual Economic Reform II: China

China's experience with economic reform following the death of Mao Zedong and the abandonment of the policies of the Cultural Revolution of the period 1966–76 represent quite a different pattern of economic reform to that followed in Eastern Europe in the last two years. First, in China the process of economic reform was sparked from within the socialist regime. The leadership of the Communist Party became convinced that moving away from central planning was needed to accelerate economic growth and improve the standard of living of the population. Unlike Eastern Europe, economic reform in China was not the natural corollary of a political crisis of the whole socialist system. Second, the economic reform process in China was not openly envisaged as the replacement of the socialist economic model by a market economy based on private property. Socialism was never officially dismissed in China and public property has not been officially challenged. Third, economic reform was perceived as a gradual process of increasing coexistence between markets and the state, with greater concern for maintaining price stability and macroeconomic balances than rapidly achieving liberalization policies. Fourth, the structural characteristics of the Chinese economy at the start of the reform process makes it very different from the economies of Eastern Europe. China is a large economy with a population above 1 billion, with a large agricultural sector, and with a level of per capita income now estimated between U.S. $1,500 and $2,000 per year. Unlike Poland, Bulgaria, or Romania, China started its program of reform in the late 1970s with low open inflation and no clear monetary overhang (see chapter 7, this volume).

The program of economic reform started in 1978 with the deregulation of the agricultural sector (the "household responsibility system").[34] This implied an increase in agricultural procurement prices paid by the state, allowing farmers to sell their production surpluses in free markets after delivering a predetermined quota to the state. Moreover, they were allowed to retain profits. This led to flourishing agricultural activity and the growth of small-scale enterprises in rural markets and townships. Starting in 1984, an "enterprise responsibility system" was established for state enterprises in the industrial sector. The system comprised a dual or two-tier price scheme. As in agriculture, state-owned enterprises were allowed to sell the excess of output over the quota delivered to the state agency at market-determined prices.[35] In 1986, the system of compulsory remittance of profits to the central government was abolished and a corporate income tax of 55% was instituted. The rationale was to accept the profit motive in the behavior of public enterprises in order to promote efficiency and decentralization. As of 1991, around 50% of prices were determined in unregulated markets (Schmidt-Hebbel and Xu 1991). On other fronts, "special economic zones" were created, mostly in the south of the country near other East Asian markets. In these zones (particularly in the Guangdong and Fujian province), direct foreign investment, oriented to export processing, receives special treatment for profit remittances and tax obligations. The basic aim of those special zones is to attract foreign investment, expose segments of the economy to foreign competition, and get access to new technologies and markets.[36]

In contrast to other experiences of economic reform, the Chinese process has evolved in a context of relative macroeconomic stability, albeit punctuated by periods of inflationary acceleration following price reforms. In particular, inflationary outbursts took place in 1980–81, 1985–87, and 1988–1989. The most serious acceleration of inflation was in 1988–89, when the retail price index rose to near 20% on an annual basis (see figure 12.5b). Inflationary pressures were, in part, compressed: subsidies for consumer agricultural goods increased from 0.3% of GDP in 1978 to around 4.0% in 1984. As of 1991 the price subsidies on consumer goods still represent around 1.5% of GNP (Schmidt-Hebbel and Xu 1991). At the macro level, the policy response to outbursts of inflation observed after the periods of price reform has been one of tightening credit policy and restraining wage increases in state-owned enterprises. In general the Chinese government seems to have a genuine distaste for inflation.[37] Table 12.9 shows that the fiscal deficit (central government) has been maintained at a relatively modest level throughout the reform period, at around 2.0% of GDP during 1978–1991.[38] Moreover, it is interesting to note that fiscal deficits tended to widen during the periods of price reform. In particular, the share of subsidies on operating losses of state-owned enterprises increased after 1986, as the enterprise sector moved toward greater decentralization and away from forced profit remittances; in fact, the share of subsidies to state-owned enterprises went up from 1.3% of GNP in 1978–85 to 3.5% of GNP, on average, in the period 1986–91 (Schmidt-Hebbel and Xu 1991). Finally, on the external sector China enjoyed a relatively comfortable position during the reform process, with considerable levels of international reserves (as share of imports) and moderate, though increasing, levels of external debt (table 12.9).

The response of the Chinese economy to the reforms begun in the late 1970s was impressive, in terms of output growth (see table 12.9 and figure 12.5a). Average GDP was growing at 8.7% per year in the period 1978–1991. In contrast, the rate of growth of national income in the period 1970–77 was 4.6% (Hussain and Stern 1991). In the period 1978–1991, GDP per capita grew 7.3% per year with a similar trend in per capita consumption; clearly the standard of living of the population increased drastically during the reform period; although it is still at a low level, as proxied by the level of income per capita.

To summarize, the Chinese reform process has been gradual and conser-

TABLE 12.9   China—Main economic indicators

	(1) Growth rate, GDP		(2) Agriculture output (growth rate percent)	(3) Inflation rate		(4) Budget deficit (percent of GDP)	(5) International reserves (months of imports)	(6) External debt (percent of GDP)
	(a) Total	(b) Per capita		(a) GDP deflator (percent)	(b) Retail price index (percent)			
1971–77	4.6[a]		1.6		0.4			
1978	12.3		3.4		0.7	−0.3	4.9	0.3
1979	7.2	5.8	6.4	3.6	2.0	5.2	6.7	0.9
1980	7.9	6.6	−1.8	4.0	6.0	3.3	6.1	1.5
1981	4.5	3.2	7.1	2.2	2.4	1.3	5.5	2.1
1982	8.7	7.1	11.7	0.1	1.9	1.4	10.7	3.1
1983	10.1	8.7	8.5	1.4	1.5	1.7	11.1	3.3
1984	14.5	13.2	13.0	4.6	2.8	1.6	9.3	4.0
1985	13.0	11.7	1.7	9.1	8.8	0.5	4.8	5.7
1986	8.4	7.1	3.7	4.6	6.0	1.9	4.6	8.5
1987	11.2	9.9	4.8	5.0	7.3	2.0	6.2	11.6
1988	10.8	9.5	3.2	11.5	18.5	2.6	5.2	11.3
1989	3.9	2.6	3.3	9.0	17.8	1.8	5.1	10.0
1990	4.9	3.6	6.9	4.9	2.1	1.5	7.7	14.4
1991	5.0	3.8	3.5	—	3.0	—	7.5	15.3
Average: 1978–1991	8.7	7.3[b]	5.4	5.0[c]	5.8	1.9	6.8	6.6

Source: World Bank. Schmidt-Hebbel and Xu (1991).
Notes: a. Net national income. Hussain and Stern (1991).
          b. 1979–1991.
          c. 1979–1990.

vative in macroeconomic terms, and apparently it has preserved the gains in social welfare and distribution achieved in the prereform period (see Perkins 1988). In contrast with the recent experience of Eastern Europe, the economic reforms in China have taken place without serious macroeconomic dislocation. Nevertheless, the reforms are still partial: nearly half of the economy still operates under controlled prices, and national wealth is almost completely in the hands of the state.

Summing Up

Before summing up the main findings of this chapter, a caveat is in order. It is apparent from this review of reform experiences that a blueprint of universal validity on "how to reform an economy" simply does not exist given the enormous country diversity in initial conditions, structural features of the

366   Andrés Solimano

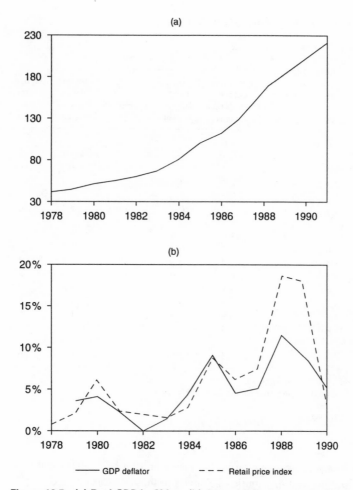

Figure 12.5   (a) Real GDP in China; (b) Annual inflation rate in China

economy, and political conditions (see table 12.10 on page 368). Broad generalizations on preferred policies have necessarily to be complemented with a
knowledge of the specific economic conditions and political realities of the
country beginning a process of reform. Nevertheless, some valid generalizations are apparent, as described below.

Reform Strategy: Shock versus Gradualism
It is clear that the choice between these two alternatives will be greatly
influenced by at least two elements (see also chapter 1): the initial conditions
(disequilibria) at the beginning of reform and the political feasibility of carry-

ing forward a certain program, besides an analysis of the costs and benefits of each course of action. If the economy is in a macroeconomic crises with accelerating inflation and severe balance-of-payments problems, comprehensive macro restraint might be almost inescapable. Several economies of Eastern Europe after 1989 and Russia in 1992 are apt examples, as well as the Latin American cases reviewed in here. On the contrary, if reforms start from relatively balanced macroeconomic conditions, there is much more room for gradualism, as the cases of China and Hungary eloquently show.

Regarding the political preconditions behind a program, shock treatment requires a strong government with broad social support, because the costs of the policies are paid up front and the benefits may take time to accrue. However, if the program brings protracted social hardship (due to cuts in real wages, unemployment, and slow recovery of growth), the initial political support may start evaporating, and pressure will build for an eventual reversal of the reforms.

Macroeconomic Consolidation
versus Rapid Liberalization

The issue refers to the sequence of macroeconomic adjustment and stabilization, and structural reforms. There are areas in which both set of policies reinforce each other; conversely, there are other areas in which stabilization and liberalization may conflict. On the one hand, implementing a tax reform and the conversion of quotas to tariffs are structural policies that improve the fiscal budget, thus they contribute to macroeconomic stabilization. Conversely, premature financial liberalization, before the budget is balanced and real interest rates are at a reasonable level, may lead to a financial crisis whose solution is fiscally costly and destabilizing (e.g., the Southern Cone of Latin America in the late 1970s and early 1980s).

Massive privatization of large-scale firms can have either stabilizing or destabilizing macroeconomic effects. It may save the government scarce resources if it implies getting rid of loss-making public enterprises; in this case public finances improve, with the ensuing contribution to macro stabilization. But if privatization involve massive liquidation of existing enterprises, the output and unemployment costs may become socially unsustainable, and pressure will mount for the government to rescue those enterprises. In this latter case the process of macroeconomic stabilization will be hindered.

Price Reform and Inflation

The shift from an economy with a vast array of controlled prices to a system in which most prices are market determined in general involves an (often large) initial hike in the price level. Recent examples of this are the outbursts of inflation observed in most economies of Eastern Europe during 1990–1991

TABLE 12.10 Scorecard on economic reform

(1) Initial conditions before reform

Macroeconomic crises	Extensive price controls trade barriers financial repression but moderate open macro imbalances
Chile	Czechoslovakia
Mexico	China
Solivia	Bulgaria
Poland	Romania

(2) Structural features

Income levels per capita				Share of state sector	
Large economy	Small economy	Low	Medium	High	Intermediate
China	Bolivia		Chile	Eastern European	Chile
			Mexico	China	Mexico
			Poland		Bolivia
			Czechoslovakia		
			Hungary		
			Bulgaria		
			Romania		

Program design

Price reform		Current account convertibility and trade liberalization		Fiscal adjustment		Capital account convertibility	
Shock	Gradual	Shock	Gradual	Deep	Moderate	Shock	Gradual
Chile	China	Bolivia	Chile	Chile	Bolivia		Chile
Bolivia	Hungary	Poland	Mexico	Mexico			Eastern Europe
Poland		Czechoslovakia	China				
Bulgaria		Bulgaria	Hungary				
Romania							
Czechoslovakia							

Policy performance

Inflation

Initial acceleration		Speed of disinflation	
Sharp (more than 50% per year)	Moderate (less than 50% per year)	Rapid	Slow
Bulgaria	Czechoslovakia	Bolivia	Chile
Romania	Hungary	Czechoslovakia	Mexico
Chile	China	Hungary	Poland
Poland		China	Romania
Mexico			Bulgaria

GDP Response

Initial contraction	Initial expansion	Speed of resumption of growth	
		Rapid	Slow
Chile	China	Chile	Bolivia
Mexico			Mexico
Bolivia			Eastern Europe
All Eastern Europe			

Political economy

Reforms conducted by

Authoritarian regimes	Non-authoritarian regimes
Chile	Mexico
Korea	Bolivia
China	Post-1989 East-Central European regimes

and in Russia in early 1992, following price decontrol, currency devaluation, and adjustment in the prices of public utilities and energy. Moreover, the initial price shock has been followed by considerable inflationary persistence in Poland, Bulgaria, and Romania. In nonsocialist countries, inflationary persistence because of monetary accommodation, indexation, and credibility problems is a well-known phenomenon, particularly in the chronic inflation economies of Latin America.

Patterns of Output, Investment, and Export
Response to Adjustment
A contraction in aggregate economic activity of considerable magnitude was observed after the implementation of shock programs, compounded by negative external shocks, in several Latin American and Eastern European economies in the 1980s and early 1990s.

Comparatively, the degree of economic contraction in the postsocialist transitions of Eastern Europe is far deeper than in the adjusting Latin American economies reviewed here. In contrast, socialist China avoided that pattern of initial contraction as GDP growth accelerated sharply in the aftermath of gradual reform.

The recovery of capital formation and the resumption of sustainable growth is often a stalled process. In Chile and Mexico it took half a decade or so to get a sustained response of private investment following reform. The response of private capital formation in Eastern Europe might take even longer.

In the Latin American context, Chile (and to a lesser extent Mexico and Bolivia) experienced a strong expansion of nontraditional exports (though with a still modest intensity of value added) following the establishment of competitive real exchange rates and lower import duties. In Eastern Europe, an initial expansion in exports to the West also took place in Poland and other countries in response to large currency depreciations and declines in domestic absorption. Thus, in the aftermath of adjustment, exports are bound to be the main engine of growth given the often timid initial investment response to the reforms.

Distributive Effects and the Costs of Adjustment
The available evidence for Chile and Mexico suggests a worsening in income distribution in the initial years of reform as a consequence of cuts in real wages and/or increases in unemployment. Those effects were ameliorated for very low income groups receiving targeted social spending. In Eastern Europe after 1989, real wages declined substantially (30% or so on average) and unemployment is growing (over 10%) following the implementation of adjustment programs. The scope of social safety nets to protect vulnerable

groups during adjustment is bound to be limited both by a lack of fiscal resources and by the organizational and institutional complications of reshaping social policies to the new setting of a market economy.

Political Economy Considerations

The sample of countries reviewed here can be partitioned into two groups as to the political conditions under which economic reform is undertaken. One group is formed by countries that launched economic reform under authoritarian conditions. This is the case of Pinochet's Chile, China, and Korea. In these cases, economic reforms were carried out by authoritarian governments that postponed political reform to gain political legitimacy from the fruits of consolidated economic reform. A second group is formed by countries where economic reform is conducted in (emergent) democracies. This is the case of Eastern Europe and Russia, where reforms are pursued simultaneously on the political and economic fronts. As could be anticipated, fragile democracies with a fragmented party system and weak social institutions and governments do not provide the most favorable political environment for implementing and consolidating complex and painful economic reforms. Under these conditions, governments are bound to face the difficult dilemma of either postponing economic reform to avert a political crisis or backsliding on the democratization process to apply painful economic policies. Certainly both are unsavory choices. Russia provides an eloquent case of this in 1993–94.

Notes

I appreciate the comments made by Stanley Fischer and other participants at the El Escorial conference. I also acknowledge suggestions and comments offered by Alice Amsden, Nancy Birdsall, Michael Bruno, Max Corden, Cheryl Gray, Peter Knight, Martha de Melo, Klaus Schmidt-Hebbel, Luis Servén, and Raimundo Soto to a first draft of this paper. Efficient assistance from Raimundo Soto is appreciated.

1. It is interesting that the reform policies in China freeing agriculture and giving a new impetus to private sector activity started in the late 1970s, before the experiments in the United States and the United Kingdom. The dominant influence in the Chinese process probably came from the remarkable dynamism of the neighboring newly industrialized countries (Korea, Taiwan, Hong Kong, Singapore).
2. See Ramos (1986), Solimano (1990a), Cardoso and Helwege (1992), and Dornbusch and Edwards (1991) for analysis of that period.
3. See Kiguel and Liviatan (1992), Solimano (1990a), Taylor (1991a and 1991b).
4. See Dornbusch (1991), Solimano (1992), Servén and Solimano (1993).
5. See Servén and Solimano (1992a and 1992b).
6. See Bruno (1992).
7. An influential paper along these lines, in the context of stabilization programs, is Sargent (1982).
8. See Kornai (1990a) and (1990b).
9. See Lipton and Sachs (1990).

10. See Solimano (1992).
11. The results of the WIDER project is reported in Taylor (1991a), and the conclusions of the OECD project are presented by Bourgignon, de Melo, and Morrison (1992).
12. For example, massive subsidies to commercial banks and major debtors placed an enormous burden on public finances and forced cuts in social and infrastructure spending in Chile after 1982.
13. See Lustig (1992) for Mexico, and Meller (1991) for Chile.
14. See Corbo (1985), Meller (1991), and Corbo and Solimano (1991) for a discussion of the reforms adopted in the Chilean economy in the last two decades.
15. See Van Wijnbergen (1991).
16. An analysis of the stabilization program of late 1987 appears in Ortiz (1991).
17. World Bank, 1991.
18. Incidentally, real interest rates in Bolivian pesos and also in dollars have remained well above international rates. See Calvo and Guidotti (1991).
19. See Sargent (1982), Dornbusch and Fischer (1988), and Solimano (1990a).
20. A detailed analysis of the cycle of private investment in adjustment programs appears in Solimano (1992).
21. Nonwage income recipients include low-income groups in the rural and the urban informal sectors (self-employed workers, small enterprises, workers employed in the service sector).
22. Attempts at partial economic reform are much older in Eastern Europe. Hungary started a program of economic decentralization and gradual "marketization" in 1968. Poland and Yugoslavia also tried reforms in the early 1980s, though those programs were seen as existing within the current economic system rather than designed to replace the socialist regime with a market economy.
23. A growing literature on the Polish case now exists. See Lipton and Sachs (1990), Berg and Sachs (1992), and Calvo and Coricelli (1992).
24. Historically, Czechoslovakia was characterized by prudent macro management. Czechoslovakia avoided hyperinflation (unlike Austria, Germany, and Poland) in the early 1920s and also suffered only mildly from the depression of the early 1930s, as it had accumulated little external debt in previous years; see Solimano (1991b).
25. See Solimano (1991b).
26. See Demekas and Khan (1991).
27. See Demekas and Khan (1991).
28. See Bruno (1992).
29. Berg and Sachs (1992) argue that demand contraction, in the context of the stabilization program, has been the main cause behind the drop in GDP in Poland in 1990–91.
30. The response to the terms of trade shock has been a mix of adjustment and financing; the latter is from multilateral and bilateral official sources, besides some private capital inflows.
31. See McKinnon (1991) for an argument in favor of gradualism in trade reform in postsocialist transitions.
32. Excellent analyses of the Korean experiences are found in Collins and Park (1989), Dornbusch and Park (1987), and Amsden (1989).
33. Secondary enrollment, as a percentage of age group, increased from 35% in 1965 to 89% in 1988. In addition, the percentage of higher education with respect to age group went up from 6% in 1965 to 37% in 1988. See World Bank (1991).
34. Good references on the Chinese experience with economic reform are: Perkins (1988 and chapter 7, this volume), Blejer, Burton, Dunaway, and Szapary (1991), Hussain and Stern (1991), and Schmidt-Hebbel and Xu (1991).
35. See Schmidt-Hebbel and Xu (1991).
36. See Perkins (1992).

37. This may have historical roots, as China experienced a virulent hyperinflation in the late 1940s.
38. Unfortunately data on the quasi-fiscal deficit of the central bank is not yet available for China.

References

Amsden, A. 1989. *Asia's Next Giant. South Korea and Late Industrialization.* New York: Oxford University Press.

Berg, A., and J. Sachs. 1992. "Structural Adjustment and International Trade in Eastern Europe: The Case of Poland." *Economic Policy* 14 (April).

Blejer, M., D. Burton, S. Dunaway, and G. Szapary. 1991. "China Economic Reform and Macroeconomic Management." *Occasional Paper* 76, IMF, January.

Bruno, M. 1992. "Stabilization and Reform in Eastern Europe: A Preliminary Evaluation." Mimeo. IMF.

Bourguignon, F., J. de Melo, and C. Morrison. 1992. "Poverty and Income Distribution during Adjustment: Issues and Evidence from the OECD Project." In *Adjustment with Growth and Equity.* Special Issue, *World Development* 19, 11 (November).

Calvo, G., and P. Guidotti. 1991. "Interest Rates, Financial Structure and Growth. Bolivia in Comparative Perspective." Paper presented at the Conference on Structural Adjustment and Growth. La Paz, Bolivia, June.

Calvo, G., and F. Coricelli. 1992. "Stabilizing a Previously Centrally Planned Economy: Poland 1990." *Economic Policy* 14 (April).

Cardoso, E., and A. Helwege. 1992. *Latin America's Economy. Diversity, Trends and Conflicts.* Cambridge, MA: MIT Press.

Collins, S., and W. Park. 1989. "External Debt and Macroeconomic Performance in South Korea." In J. Sachs, ed., *Developing Country Debt and the World Economy.* Chicago: University of Chicago Press.

Corbo, V. 1985 "Reform and Macroeconomic Adjustment in Chile during 1974–1985." *World Development* 13, 8.

Corbo, V., and A. Solimano. 1991. "Chile's Experience with Stabilization Revisited." In M. Bruno et al., eds., *Lessons of Economic Stabilization and Its Aftermath.* Cambridge, MA: MIT Press.

Demekas, D. G., and M. S. Khan. 1991. "The Romanian Economic Reform Program." *IMF Occasional Paper*, November 1989.

Dornbusch, R. 1991. "Policies to Move from Stabilization to Growth." *Annual Conference on Development* 1990. The World Bank.

Dornbusch, R., and Y. C. Park. 1987. "Korea's Growth Policy." *Brookings Paper on Economic Activity* 2.

Dornbusch, R., and S. Edwards. 1991. *The Macroeconomies of Populism in Latin America.* Chicago: University of Chicago Press and NBER.

ECLAC. 1990, 1991. *Preliminary Outlook for Latin America and the Caribbean.* United Nations, Santiago, Chile.

Hussain, A., and N. Stern. 1991. "Economic Reform in China." *Economic Policy.* A European Forum. Vol. 12.

374   Andrés Solimano

Kiguel, M., and N. Liviatan. 1992. "When Do Heterodox Stabilization Programs Work? Lessons from Experience." *The World Bank Research Observer* 7, 1 (January).

Kornai, J. 1990a. *The Road to a Free Economy*. New York and London: W.W. Norton and Company.

Kornai, J. 1990b. Comments on Lipton and Sachs (1990), "Creating a Market Economy in Eastern Europe: The Case of Poland." *Brookings Papers on Economic Activity* 1.

Lipton, M., and J. Sachs. 1990. "Creating a Market Economy in Eastern Europe: The Case of Poland." *Brookings Papers on Economic Activity* 1.

Lustig, N. 1993. *Mexico. The Remaking of an Economy*. Washington, D.C.: Brookings Institution.

McKinnon, R. 1991. *The Order of Economic Liberalization*. Baltimore: Johns Hopkins University Press.

Meller, P. 1991. "Adjustment and Social Costs in Chile during the 1980s." In *Adjustment with Growth and Equity*. *World Development* 19, 11 (November).

Ortiz, G. 1991. "Mexico Beyond the Debt Crisis: Towards Sustainable Growth." In M. Bruno, et al., eds., *Lessons of Economic Stabilization and Its Aftermath*. Cambridge, MA: MIT Press.

Perkins, D. 1988. "Reforming China's Economic System." *Journal of Economic Literature* 26 (June).

Perkins, D. 1992. "China's 'Gradual' Approach to Market Reforms." Paper prepared for the El Escorial Conference on "Economic Reform: Recent Experiences in Market and Socialist Economies," July 6–9, 1992. (Chapter 7, this volume.)

Ramos, J. 1986. *Neo-conservative Economies in the Southern Cone of Latin America*. Baltimore: Johns Hopkins University Press.

Rodrik, D. 1990. "How Structural Adjustment Programs Should Be Designed." *World Development* 8.

Sargent, T. 1982. "The End of Four Big Inflations." In R. Hall, ed., *Inflation: Causes and Effects*. Chicago: University of Chicago Press.

Schmidt-Hebbel, K., and L. Xu. 1991. "Price Reform and Inflation in China." Mimeo. The World Bank.

Servén, L., and A. Solimano. 1992a. "Private Investment and Macroeconomic Adjustment. A Survey." *The World Bank Research Observer* 7, 1 (January).

Servén, L., and A. Solimano. 1992b. "Economic Adjustment and Investment Performance in Developing Countries: The Experience of the 1980s." In V. Corbo et al., eds., *Revisiting Adjustment Lending: Policies to Promote Growth*. A World Bank Symposium.

Servén, L., and A. Solimano. 1993. *Striving for Growth After Adjustment. The Role of Capital Formation*. The World Bank.

Solimano, A. 1990a. "Inflation and the Costs of Stabilization: Historical and Recent Experiences and Policy Lessons." *The World Bank Research Observer* 5, 2.

Solimano, A. 1990b. "Macroeconomic Adjustment, Stabilization and Growth in Reforming Socialist Economies. Analytical and Policy Issues." WPS 399. The World Bank.

Solimano, A. 1991a. "Inflation and Growth in the Transition from Socialism. The Case of Bulgaria," WPS 659. The World Bank.

Solimano, A. 1991b. "The Economies of East-Central Europe: An Historical Background." In V. Corbo et al., eds., *Reforming Central and Eastern European Economies. Initial Results and Challenges.* A World Bank Symposium.

Solimano, A. 1992. "Understanding the Investment Cycle in Adjustment Programs. Evidence from Reforming Economies." Mimeo. The World Bank.

Taylor, L. 1991a. *Varieties of Stabilization Experiences. Towards Sensible Macroeconomics in the Third World.* Oxford: Clarendon Press.

Taylor, L. 1991b. *Income Distribution, Inflation and Growth. Lectures on Structuralist Macroeconomic Theory.* Cambridge, MA: MIT Press.

Van Wijnbergen, S. 1991. "Mexico and the Brady Plan." In *Economic Policy* 12 (April). Cambridge: Cambridge University Press.

World Bank. 1991. *World Development Report* 1991. Oxford: Oxford University Press.

Rebuilding Capitalism:
The Lessons

Panel Presentations

Yilmaz Akyuz

Much of the debate in this volume concerns state intervention; I will concentrate my remarks on this subject. In developing countries, the ultimate objective of the state is to raise the rate of capital accumulation and growth above the level that would be attained by market forces alone, and to alter income and/or wealth distribution to alleviate poverty. The dominant view is that the state has not generally been successful in promoting these goals. I am not, however, convinced that this is so.

Clearly, to reach a verdict one needs to assess what kind of growth and welfare market forces alone can generate, a question that has occupied the minds of many distinguished economists including Malthus, Ricardo, Marx, and Schumpeter. This is not easy, but historical experience can shed some light. As Sunkel has reminded us, the Western industrial countries have grown at an average rate of 3% over the last two centuries. The postwar "Golden Age," characterized by a much greater state presence in the economy, has produced much faster growth; until the oil shocks of the 1970s, the average growth rate of major OECD countries was close to 5%, surpassing virtually all historical records. Growth since 1973 has been slower, but still above the historical average. Moreover, perhaps the most spectacular case of industrial development has taken place in a country, Japan, where state intervention was much more pervasive than in any other successful industrialization.

The average historical growth rate of Western industrial countries falls far too short of the aspirations of many developing countries, which have indeed sought and attained much faster growth rates in the postwar period. They include not only Korea and Taiwan, but also a number of "less successful" countries, such as Brazil, India, Mexico, Turkey, and many others with growth rates ranging from 6% to 9% per annum.

Neither growth theory nor the historical record of capitalist development convinces me that such growth rates are built into the market mechanism. There is no example from history of industrialization at such a pace based on market forces alone (except in a couple of city-states). It thus appears that the state has not done as badly as many people assume. However, I also concur that governments are capable of doing much worse than markets; many poor countries could have at least maintained their per capita incomes over the last few decades if not for misplaced government intervention. But this does not alter my conclusion that it is not easy to attain growth rates that match the aspirations of many developing countries today without government machinery capable of improving considerably on what market forces can deliver.

This brings me to the question of government failure. This concept has two different meanings. First, governments fail for the same reason markets do. Here reference is often made to problems arising from incomplete markets and information. Second, governments fail where markets do, or they fail more. This is the case of rent seeking, political patronage, and corruption. Thus, although efficient market allocation may not be attained without government intervention, there is no guarantee that intervention will represent an improvement over market outcomes.

The first notion of government failure is often invoked to argue against "picking winners." For instance, it is said that there is little scope for government intervention when there are capital market failures. This is a very important issue, because in developing countries credits are one of the principal instruments of industrial policy. I find this proposition somewhat overstated. In developing countries, markets tend to discount the future heavily because of great uncertainties inherent in economies undergoing drastic structural changes. For this reason capital markets are not always willing to take a long view to finance investment and production during the learning process that is essential for industrialization. Granted, governments may make wrong choices in directing credit allocation because of imperfect information. However, relations between the state and business can function like internal capital markets that large firms organize in developed countries as a way of dealing with capital market failures. For instance, government intervention in credit allocation in Korea, through its close relations with *chaebols*, can be seen in this light. Such an internal capital market can increase the predictability of the cost and availability of finance, thereby reducing investors' risk and allowing them to take a long view.

Besides, the issue is not really about picking winners, but rather one of creating winners. Some countries are more successful than others in almost everything they support, even though they operate under similar conditions regarding incomplete and costly information, missing markets, and incentive problems. Differences in the design of policies are part of the explanation. However, differences of politics, or government failure arising from clientelism and corruption, often account for a greater part; besides, political differences often underlie policy differences. It is through politics, not economic policy, that one deals with such government failures. Liberalization does not deal with it. Unleashing market forces and introducing new incentives often create new forms of corruption. Recent scandals and irregularities in privat-ization, securities, and banking industries have been unprecedented. There are also serious allegations that the corruption and political patronage now observed in some of the newly liberalized economies of Latin America and elsewhere is of a kind and a degree not hitherto experienced in these countries.

These considerations are no less true for former socialist countries. In these countries, too, there has been too much emphasis on policy and too little on politics. But markets can replace a command economy, not the state. It may be very difficult for them to make a successful transition and create a market economy without a major political reform, transforming the state machinery into one that is capable of promoting capitalism. This has, indeed, been an important role of the state in many developing countries. In those countries, it has taken decades to create capitalists by giving them protection, cheap credits, tax breaks, investment privileges, subsidies, etc., and allowing them both to accumulate capital and to acquire know-how, and hence emerge as the driving force of the society. Such a class cannot simply and readily be created by transferring property rights to the citizen in the street. Until it emerges as the principal force, the state will have to be the main actor. Continued widespread state ownership in industry appears unavoidable.

There is yet another reason why the state may have to play a much more important role than is typically envisaged. The only class of people with primitive capital accumulation and some capitalistic know-how belong to the old ruling elite. This class is politically discredited; in the eyes of the people it represents the past rather than the future. This conflict between economic and political realities is likely to shape events in the coming years, and determine the type of state than can emerge.

Nancy Birdsall

This volume presents two major lessons about the process of adjustment, in particular in Eastern Europe and the former Soviet Union. One is that there needs to be more emphasis not just on reform, but on reform with growth. This in turn leads to the second lesson: that there needs to be more emphasis placed on managing the transition to growth, that is, on what government can do to manage as rapid and smooth a transition to growth as possible.

On the conditions conducive to reform with growth, consider this simple matrix (see figure P.1). On one axis is the initial macroeconomic state of the reforming country, either relatively strong or relatively weak. On the second axis is the initial situation with respect to the structure of the economy, or let us say the business environment: the size of the private sector, the competitiveness of industry, the institutional and regulatory regime—again, either relatively strong or weak. I have put several countries—in a very stylized way—into the resulting four cells.

Korea and Malaysia, typical of the East Asian economies, adjusted in the 1980s starting from a relatively healthy fiscal, monetary, and exchange rate situation, and with large and competitive private sectors. China, with virtually no business sector and no competition, began a process of structural change in the 1980s (e.g., decollectivization of agriculture), generally in the context of a reasonably healthy macroeconomic situation. Latin American economies such as Mexico, Brazil, and Chile entered the 1980s with large distortions on the macro side, but reasonably dynamic and competitive private sectors. In Africa, and more recently in Eastern Europe and the republics of the former Soviet Union, adjustment reforms began with great weaknesses on both fronts.

What has been the growth experience in these various settings, as adjustment reform (macro and structural) took hold? Korea and Malaysia, with relatively minor adjustments to make (primarily on the macro side), made them successfully and have grown throughout the 1980s. Growth continued throughout the 1980s in China as well, where the government actively managed the introduction of structural changes—price liberalization, agricultural

		Macro	
		Strong	Weak
	Strong	Korea Malaysia	Mexico Brazil Chile
Structure of economy/business environment			
	Weak	China	Ghana Tanzania Eastern Europe Former Soviet Republics

[Government capacity]

Figure P.1   Conditions before reform

reform, and so forth—at times slowing the pace of structural change to minimize macroeconomic disruptions. In Latin America growth slowed greatly as both categories of reforms were implemented. In particular, the recovery of private investment has come slowly. It took almost a decade for Chile to reverse the decline in private investment; in Mexico it took seven to ten years; in Bolivia, we are not yet sure whether and when private investment will recover. In Africa, even in countries that undertook extensive reforms in both categories, growth is still slow and private investment is still low. At growth rates of just 1% or 2% per capita per year, growth is not sufficient for development or the escape from poverty. Finally, of course, in Eastern Europe and the former Soviet republics, we have seen an output collapse, at least some of which is the natural response to macro policy reforms—and no sign yet that growth will recover.

So the lesson on achieving growth with reform seems to be: where you start from and how quickly you can fix the macro fundamentals matters; where you start from and the pace of structural reforms matters less, if at all. If you compare Latin America's and East Asia's starting points on the macro fundamentals, what you see is that East Asia didn't have very far to go, and growth recovered quickly and vigorously. In Latin America, despite the existence of a dynamic private sector, it took time before macro reforms restored private sector confidence. China and Cuba further illustrate the point. In Cuba growth recovered for a while in response to limited structural reforms in the early 1980s. In fact, as is the case with China, apparently you can have major structural and institutional deficiencies and under at least some circumstances maintain growth as reforms are undertaken.

So it is easier to resume growth if you have not got too far off the macro track in the first place, and if you get back on track as quickly as possible. In contrast, at least in some circumstances, you can pursue structural reforms rather more slowly. (In fact, if you have gotten off the macro track, you have little choice but to get back on. This seems to be less a normative than a positive issue. When there is a crisis, something has to be done, and even reluctant governments are driven to do something. There seems to be a consensus that once you have to do the macro adjustment, the quicker it is undertaken, the better.)

Revisiting the matrix, note, however, that we have a kind of identification problem. On the horizontal axis, we can substitute some measure of initial government capacity for the initial macroeconomic situation. Most East Asian economies, including China, have been characterized by strong and relatively autonomous states, whereas most countries of Latin America, Eastern Europe, and Africa are characterized by weak states (at least in the recent past). It is actually difficult to disentangle the extent to which the relatively rapid return to growth in East Asia and China in the 1980s was due to the fact that they had fewer distortions on the macro fundamentals or that they had strong states—which may, of course have ensured that they did not get into deep trouble in the first place on those fundamentals.

So—and this is oversimplifying—on the macro reforms, at some critical point change cannot be avoided, and the quicker it is effected the better. The deeper the crisis, the longer it will take to resume growth—apparently independent of whether and how much structural change occurs. In contrast, structural changes can be undertaken slowly, without sacrificing growth, if they can be managed.

What is the lesson for Eastern Europe? In terms of initial conditions, there are similarities to East Asia: relatively high levels and equal distribution of human capital; relatively equal distribution of income and potentially of assets; and good potential for strength in terms of government capacity, given legitimacy (because of the changes in regimes) and the development of a good civil service. So there is the potential to build a consensus around a competent state that could manage strategy-led growth and possibly even a strategy-led industrial policy. (When I say industrial policy, I do not mean picking firms; I mean that there might be potential for picking industries, for example, those that have export potential and are high tech, and will exploit the relative abundance of human capital, especially engineering skills. The example of a state-owned enterprise producing software in Armenia was raised as deserving of state support. But why pick a particular enterprise, SOE or private? There is also in Armenia a profitable private sector firm producing software. It would be unfortunate if the government subsidized the SOE and crowded out this private firm. A policy to provide public support for the marketing and export of software products could benefit both firms.)

The need to focus on managing the transition—especially in Eastern Europe and the former Soviet republics—is brought out clearly once we consider the social costs of adjustment. The problem of social costs is not the same as in Latin America and Africa; it is an issue less of poverty than of income shock due to unemployment, and of the trade-off between incurring the fiscal burden of unemployment compensation versus the allocative efficiency costs of immobile labor. Another way to put it: it is a problem of managing the downsizing of state-owned enterprises in a manner that would minimize the combination of fiscal and allocative costs.

To go back to where I started, I think we are still pretty weak in terms of our know-how on managing the process of transition to minimize the costs—and to ensure to the greatest extent possible that growth quickly follows reform.

Colin I. Bradford, Jr.

It is crucial to keep in mind a number of conceptual issues when thinking about the relevance of economic policy reform experiences in dynamic developing countries for the challenges being faced by the former socialist economies.

First, the East European and CIS countries are dealing with an unusual circumstance of democratization occurring at the same time as systematic economic transformation. In providing economic policy advice, economists looking in from the outside need to be clear about the interaction between these two processes. We may have to think hard about whether economic reform is more important than democracy or vice versa, and condition economic advice accordingly. The East Asian NICs, unfortunately, provide an example of how extraordinarily dynamic development and structural change was achieved prior to democratization. The NICs had twenty to thirty years of very dynamic development before it became necessary to democratize and address the issues of social balance more directly. Therefore the degree to which they can serve as models for economies in systemic transition is open to question.

There is a contrast between this problematic as manifested in China, where an authoritarian regime is still in place, and Russia, where democratic reform is preceding structural reform. The political process can facilitate the transformation process, but the economic discipline that is so necessary for the process of economic reform can in fact abort the democratic process if it is not managed correctly.

Second, there is a difference between a strategy for systemic transformation and macroeconomic policy reform. One of the reasons that the East Asian NICs succeeded in their dynamic development path is because they were very successful on the real side of the economy, namely investment, output, and employment. These are some of the objectives that are now high-priority goals in the transformation process in Eastern Europe. And these real-side objectives condition the financial system to support the transformation process. The priority given to macroeconomic policy reform needs to be assessed in relation to these other objectives. It is not for outside economists to establish these priorities, but for the people in the countries themselves, especially the elected political leadership, to set them.

Third, a clear distinction needs to be made between strategy-led growth and "picking winners." There are some bad labels in economic jargon; "picking winners" gives a wrong representation of the strategy-formulation process, and even "industrial policy" does not capture the nature of the process. In the successful East Asian cases, a strategy emerged out of a complicated process that involved the business sector, the industrial sector, the financial sector, the commercial sector, and government officials. It involved choices around a variety of industries. In Korea, for example, the priority given to the steel industry, the automobile sector, and shipbuilding was clearly beneficial because of the self-reinforcing interaction among these three sectors. That in turn affected roads, ports, transportation, communications, and the like and involved the public and the private sectors.

A strategy-formulation process comes from the assets in society, including business leadership, educational leadership, and government leadership, and combining them to generate a strategic direction. All the different elements in the system are brought together in a highly synergistic and dynamic fashion in a strategy-formulation process. It is not a matter of government bureaucrats "picking winners." It is, rather, having a process in which democracy can make a positive contribution, because the democratic process elicits collaboration, cooperation, coalition building, and the building of alliances and linkages. This has very positive potential for the former socialist economies.

Fourth, rather than conceptualize this as an issue of the strong state versus the weak state, I would propose that we think of the state as a catalyst. And the problem with strong versus weak state is that it seems to be tied up with how much actual intervention there is by the state in the economy, how much public ownership of the economy, and the state's role in the economy. But the more important aspect of the process for the state is its political role and its policy-formation role, which are fundamentally different from the economic roles. In the end it matters who is the state, whether they can be trusted, whether they are going to govern on behalf of the society as a whole or on behalf of particular interests. In the East Asian cases the dynamism of the economy as a whole was sufficient so that most of the society benefited, but these benefits derived from the dynamism rather than from policy design or a representative political process. Therefore it is necessary to be clearer about what is meant by the state and not identify it either with "picking winners" or with a strong role in the economy, but to understand it as a catalyst that can bring dynamism to development through a broader process of participation in national economic decisions.

Fifth, a catalytic state must define clear limits on supportive policies. Ernest Hemingway wrote a book called *The Sun Also Rises*. The principle that policymakers in former socialist economies should apply is, "The sun always sets." In the United States, sunset legislation means that any government program has a termination date. Every policy or law that contains a preferential benefit should have a maximum of three, five, or at most seven years of life. The end should be clear from the moment it is offered. This assures that rent seeking is not built into the system. It must be possible to have government play a positive role, but that the support role will end. Over time the market mechanism is going to play a determining role, and firms will have to become efficient by looking to the outside world to gauge what is efficient and what is not.

Sixth, economists should be very humble about giving recommendations to the former socialist economies trying to launch a process of systematic change. Offering policy advice to economies in transition is qualitatively different from giving macroeconomic advice to developing countries, or to advanced countries for that matter. Economists need to go and look and listen and learn and watch to understand how this process appears from within the system that is trying to transform itself. Programs in universities, sponsored by the World Bank and other institutions, need to get the next generation of international economists to live in these countries as they go through the process and see how the different threads are woven together; they will then be able to appreciate the politics as well as the economics, the institutions as well as the market forces, that operate there. Then they will better able to come up with ideas about the transformation process that can be useful in those contexts.

Seventh, economists should be cautious about making claims for the universalism and scientism of economics. Economists make value judgments, too; they are embedded in our analytic apparatus—if we are honest with ourselves—and we must be clear about those biases. Nobody has elected outside economists to make value judgments or set priorities in the former socialist economies that now have democratic regimes. The task for elected leaders is to figure out how to use the advice of outside economists to implement their own policy priorities. The task for economists is to avoid making the mistake of confusing the role of consulting economists with that of elected leadership.

Lance Taylor

This workshop raised interesting questions about the process of economic reform; the discussion showed that they have no simple answers. In my remarks, I would like to concentrate on three such queries: interactions between the market and state, the role of binding macroeconomic constraints, and (at a more micro level) the relative costs and benefits of price- versus quantity-based interventions.

The Market and the State

A variant on the ideas presented by Nancy Birdsall can be constructed using figure P.2, in which horizontally the state is "weak" toward the left and "strong" toward the right. In the vertical direction, the market is fully liberalized toward the top and highly distorted toward the bottom. Where are real countries placed in such a picture, and does their position (or movement between positions) influence their economic performance?

The Bretton Woods institutions or (BWIs) follow recent neoclassical approaches to the state in not addressing such questions directly. Rather, they start from the diagram's extreme positions with regard to both the market (highly distorted or fully competitive) and the state (pluralistic and reacting passively to pressures or monolithic and proactive) and reason about the implications. Although oblique, this approach does help our understanding of blocked attempts at economic reform.

For example, toward the northwest in the figure, the "public choice" school led by Buchanan (1980) elevates "rent seeking" induced by government interventions—lobbying for state favors, paying a bribe to get an import quota or Pentagon contract, fixing a ticket for a traffic violation—to a deadly social ill. If real resources are devoted to pursuing rents or "directly unproductive profit-seeking" (DUP) activities in the jargon, the outcome can be pessimal for the society as a whole: deep wells of postulated corruption allow the BWIs in some country studies to arrive at satisfyingly large estimates of welfare losses imposed by meddling bureaucrats and their distortions.

391

392   Lance Taylor

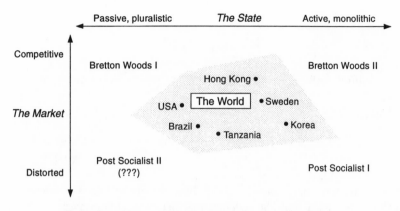

Figure P.2   The neoclassical political economic vision

Contrariwise, the saving social grace becomes a thoroughly hands-off state supervising a competitive market—the latter condition to be guaranteed by internal liberalization and international free trade. Under these conditions, DUP activity supposedly becomes unrewarding, and the invisible hand will guide society toward the position labeled "Bretton Woods I" where publications such as the World Bank's 1991 *World Development Report* want developing countries to be. Unpleasant externalities such as transnational corporations taking advantage of a country's unregulated trade or external capital markets that impose binding foreign exchange restrictions are banished from the scene.

A second form of bliss takes a more authoritarian cast. For Buchanan, the ideal state mimics the Cheshire Cat by vanishing to avoid being taken over by the interests. Alternatively, the state can force the interests to vanish, or in Lal's (1983) words, "A courageous, ruthless, and perhaps undemocratic government is required to ride roughshod over these newly-created special interest groups"—the current Mexican leadership may share such dreams. In the diagram we move toward Bretton Woods II, although it is not clear why its ruthless, etc., generals and bureaucrats will abstain from taking over the market also. The record of Third World authoritarian states in avoiding corruption and distortions is not encouraging in this regard.

A market distorted by the state for its own ends is a third extreme possibility in the diagram, which can be associated with North's (1981) theories of economic history. In a typical North example, a state may choose to raise revenue by creating monopolies and then marshall political arguments in their support. The fate of Leninist centrally planned systems suggests that economic damnation may lie well toward the southeast at the end of such a path; such a position marks the initial condition from which postsocialist economies began their transitions a few years ago.

If the states in these countries prove to be pathologically weak, they may not move northwest toward the middle of the figure, but rather to a Postsocialist II position as described by Olson (1982). He argues that because of bargaining costs and the presence of free riders, coalitions within the society form to protect their own interests. They seek to redistribute income toward themselves, instead of increasing efficiency in the national interest. A weak state cannot intervene, so the system tends toward a highly distorted market structure with the coalitions distributing the spoils.

Developing countries that have helped coalitions form themselves around import-substituting industrialization or other strategic interventions may drift toward such situations as the subsidized groups take over decisionmaking: Argentina comes to mind for this pathology (along with numerous others). With the members of the ex-*nomenklatura* forming warring factions against each other, Olson's form of anarchy is certainly a possibility in some parts of the former USSR.

The message that neoclassical scholars and the BWIs read from the diagram is that the state and market in principle can arrive at extreme configurations that are easy to characterize: theorems can be proved about social pathologies like DUP and conflicts among coalitions. However, the BWI I combination of a purely night-watchman state and a completely undistorted market has never been observed in practice (certainly not in eighteenth-century Britain and contemporary Hong Kong—the two most widely cited putative examples). If it were ever created, the BWI II equilibrium would probably not be stable. Toward the bottom, recent events show that centralized authoritarian control cannot endure forever, and the same may well be true for the anarchic societies in the southwest corner.

Indeed, as the central section of the picture illustrates, all existing nations combine mixtures of state activism with market distortions—the placement examples are arbitrary but meant to illustrate stylized facts. Moreover, if it were possible to attach numerical coordinates to nations' points in the diagram, statistical analysis would almost certainly detect scant association between their positions or movements and indicators of economic performance such as GDP growth rates, except for the likelihood of poor growth in countries with extremely distorted markets.

Beyond this hypothetical regression, a much more fundamental point is that the BWI's view of the state is ahistorical and timeless—although it may shed light on tendencies, it elides the messy dynamics of transitions. A typical neoclassical story would please Dr. Pangloss: all of its "agents" successfully optimize all possible choices so that the system inevitably arrives at the best (and only, presuming uniqueness) possible world. There is not much hope for "development," in Schumpeter's sense of jumping from one pattern of circular flow to another, in such models.

Abba Lerner caught the flavor when he remarked that "Economics has gained the title of queen of the social sciences by choosing solved political problems as its domain." Under postsocialism, both the economic and political problems are far from resolution. Complex, real-time interactions between state and market have characterized economic development since it began three centuries ago. In postsocialist economies, they certainly will go far beyond the simple liberalization and debureaucratization recipes of some of the chapters in this volume.

Binding Restrictions

The next question is how to judge the macroeconomic possibilities. One illuminating way follows from two thirty-year models—the two-gap framework originally presented by Chenery and Bruno (1962) and the financial programming exercises of the IMF that stem from Polak (1957). It can be summarized by the observation that in developing countries, policy analysis is almost always set up "in terms of four sets of accounts—the balance of payments accounts, the fiscal accounts, the consolidated accounts of the banking system, and the national income and product accounts which usually offer only a pale reflection of what is going on in the real economy, out there. Now fairly simple models can be constructed using the . . . identities represented by the four sets of accounts just mentioned" (Sobhan 1990).

Different analysts view the economy in terms of subsets of the identities. For example, financial programming boils down to asking how the fiscal position should adjust to satisfy inflation and balance-of-payments targets in terms of the fiscal, monetary, and external accounts. The IMF pays scant heed to national income and product (or saving-investment) balance. Similarly, in its medium-term projections, the World Bank typically solves a "one-gap" model in which capital formation is assumed to be trade constrained. Both BWIs typically postulate full utilization of available resources whereas by contrast, recent structuralist "three-gap" models focus on how external obligations impose recessions via binding fiscal restrictions in severely indebted developing economies (Taylor 1992).

Without going into great detail, the implication is that different postsocialist economies may be constrained in different ways. If import capacity is strictly limited by available foreign exchange (Russia when the $24 billion Western package turns out to be smaller than meets the eye?), then inflation and supply-induced recession are likely to result. Heavy external debt obligations (Poland, Hungary?) can force cutbacks in state expenditures including public investment. If the latter "crowds in" private capital formation, then slow growth may result from low accumulation. At the other extreme, ample capital inflows relative to the size of the economy may be hard to absorb in macro terms (the Baltics?).

Deciding which one or two of a few key balances—fiscal, monetary, external, saving-investment, and inflation pressure from the side of costs— are "more" constraining in given national circumstances is an essential aspect of macro policy analysis. Standard recipes of the sort often applied by ortho- dox analysts and the BWIs rarely apply.

Prices and Quantities

A central question under postsocialism is how much the state should rely on the market in guiding the economy. In the first flush of reform, of course, enthusiasm for the price system reigned. But is reliance on price-mediated as opposed to command and control (CAC) interventions economically wise?

Two decades ago, Weitzman (1974) took up this question, in response to theoretical suggestions that decentralized planning via price signals might well converge to a social optimum but only after many confusing revisions. As is often the case with good neoclassical economics, Weitzman's answer embodies common sense: In an uncertain situation, quantity regulation is appropriate when its marginal benefits in reducing damages rise sharply but its marginal costs do not. In environmental regulation, for example, the inade- quate ability of emission charges to control the spread of toxic substances can create high social costs; hence one should opt for quantitative regulation. Contrariwise, excessive burdens may be imposed on both polluters and soci- ety as a whole if marginal benefits from excessively stringent controls are constant but their marginal costs rise at a rapid rate—price-based instruments make more sense under such conditions.

In the environment as well as other areas, the "distortions" that exist in postsocialist economies are extreme—pollution sources and unviable produc- tion operations abound. The implication is that "marginal abatement cost" curves for welfare-reducing activities are low and fairly flat, which conforms to economic intuition. Economic reconstruction is in its early days in the postsocialist world. In terms of Weitzman's model, relatively blunt CAC interventions may be more cost-effective than sophisticated market manipula- tion, at least until decreasing returns to regulation by fiat begin to kick in. This observation may be paradoxical, but reflects the fact that fine tuning the market is impossible if a market system doesn't exist. As Polanyi observed in the epigraph to my chapter in this volume, an enormous amount of prior public intervention underlies any system of laissez-faire.

References

Buchanan, James. 1980. "Rent Seeking and Profit Seeking." In J. M. Buchanan, R. D. Tollison, and G. Tullock, eds., *Toward a Theory of Rent-Seeking Society.* College Station, TX: Texas A & M University Press.

Chenery, Hollis B., and Michael Bruno. 1962. "Development Alternatives in an Open Economy: The Case of Israel." *Economic Journal* 72: 79–103.

Lal, Deepak. 1983. *The Poverty of "Development Economics."* London: Institute of Economic Affairs, Hobart Paperback No. 16.

North, Douglass C. 1981. *Structure and Change in Economic History.* New York: W. W. Norton.

Olson, Mancur. 1982. *The Rise and Decline of Nations.* New Haven, CT: Yale University Press.

Polak, J. J. 1957. "Monetary Analysis of Income Formation and Payments Problems." *International Monetary Fund Staff Papers* 6: 1–50.

Sobhan, Rehman. 1990. "Introduction." In R. Sobhan, et al., *Structural Adjustment in Third World Countries.* Dhaka: Bangladesh Institute of Development Studies.

Taylor, Lance. 1992. "Gap Models." Cambridge, MA: Department of Economics, Massachusetts Institute of Technology.

Weitzman, Martin L. 1974. "Prices vs. Quantities." *Review of Economic Studies* 41: 477–491.

Index

172, 228, 313, 340, 342. *See also*
Hyperinflation; Stagflation
in China, 179–180, 182, 198, 200, 364
chronic, 3, 17
controlling, 64–65, 116–117, 347
and demand, 26–27
in Eastern Europe, 357–358, 370
enterprises and, 27–28
in Latin America, 242, 250–251, 272,
273, 346(fig.), 348
price reform and, 369–370
and rural markets, 184–185
in Spain, 279, 283, 287, 292, 298,
306nn33, 34
stabilization and, 168n1, 255, 343,
349–350, 352–353
and wages, 25, 116
Inflation tax, 22, 24
Informal sector, 269–270
Infrastructure, 167, 189, 305n29, 315
Initiative for the Americas, 258
Institutionalized Revolutionary Party. *See*
Partido Revolucionario Institutional
Institutions, 12, 5, 67–68, 69, 335–336
Insurance. *See* Unemployment insurance
Interest rates, 28, 29, 84, 287, 288(fig.),
299, 323
International Bank of Reconstruction and
Development (IBRD), 315
International Development Bank (IDB),
274
International Monetary Fund (IMF), 25,
73, 190, 245, 274, 319, 392
and former Soviet Union, 162, 163
in Latin America, 248, 251, 273
and Russia, 141, 165, 166, 168n6, 172–
173, 174
Inter-republican Payments Mechanism
(IRPM), 162–163
Inti Plan, 251
Investment, 22, 44, 94, 210, 329, 330,
333, 343–344, 353, 362, 385. *See
also* Direct foreign investment
in Cuba, 230–231, 234
demand for, 31, 219
and economic reform, 350–351
in equipment, 100–101
financial system and, 45–46
in industry, 91–92

in infrastructure, 167, 305n29
in Latin America, 264–268, 274, 370
public, 47, 275n18
in Spain, 280, 291(fig.), 297, 299,
305n29, 306n31
IRPM. *See* Inter-republican Payments
Mechanism
ISI. *See* Import substitution industrialization
Israel, 27, 343
Italy, 35, 314

Jamaica, 38
Japan, 35, 45, 83, 164, 230, 274, 314,
319, 333
and China, 181, 188
economic growth in, 48, 324, 326
government intervention in, 82, 335
industrial development in, 97, 377
JUCEPLAN. *See* Central Planning Board

Kazakhstan, 143, 173
Kenya, 43
Korea. *See* South Korea
Kreditanstalt, 315
Kuwait, 31, 51n13

Labor, 102, 205–206n39, 304n2
in Cuba, 213–215
productivity of, 47, 131, 230
Labor market, 6, 11, 122, 253, 269
Spanish, 281–282, 287, 295, 300, 301,
306nn32, 42, 44
Land. *See* Property rights
Laos, 50n2, 51n18, 127, 131, 135n3,
137n47
Latin America, 3, 13, 14, 16, 151,
275n19, 335, 382. *See also various
countries*
disequilibrium in, 243–247
economic reform in, 7, 11, 17–18, 270–
272, 329, 339, 341, 344–353, 369
economy in, 241–242, 249(table), 324
exchange rate policies in, 260–262
fiscal reform in, 248, 250
inflation in, 22, 27, 370
investment and savings in, 264–268
privatization in, 262–264
social costs of reform in, 268–270